ENOUGH TO MAKE YOU SICK...

Tainted and Counterfeit Imports!

*

'Made in China'
– Is It Time for this Label to Leave America?
– Is Capitalism, as we know it, Failing?

A true account of why imports are
dangerous to our health
and are being recalled by our government...
while the list of problems continue to grow.
This book is based on actual correspondence
from writers of various publications,
doctors, scientists and economists
who have been there and
know from experience,
why panic has been spreading over foreign imports
and how the FDA failed to stop these products
from coming into our country...
and finally, what we can do to help ourselves!

JERRY A. GRUNOR

iUniverse, Inc.
New York   Bloomington

Enough to Make You Sick...
Tainted and Counterfeit Imports!

Copyright © 2009 Jerry A. Grunor

All rights reserved. No part of this book may be used or reproduced by any means, graphic, electronic, or mechanical, including photocopying, recording, taping or by any information storage retrieval system without the written permission of the publisher except in the case of brief quotations embodied in critical articles and reviews.

iUniverse books may be ordered through booksellers or by contacting:

iUniverse
1663 Liberty Drive
Bloomington, IN 47403
www.iuniverse.com
1-800-Authors (1-800-288-4677)

Because of the dynamic nature of the Internet, any Web addresses or links contained in this book may have changed since publication and may no longer be valid. The views expressed in this work are solely those of the author and do not necessarily reflect the views of the publisher, and the publisher hereby disclaims any responsibility for them.

ISBN: 978-1-4401-4740-1 (pbk)
ISBN: 978-1-4401-4742-5 (cloth)
ISBN: 978-1-4401-4741-8 (ebook)

Printed in the United States of America

iUniverse rev. date: 6/09/09

— CONTENTS —

— 1 —

To Understand What Went Wrong...
We Start by Looking at Ourselves

I am constantly doing research and keep finding more information on what is happening to our way of life and how we are allowing our one-time enemy, the Chinese government, take control of the way we live and what we are buying. I must also state emphatically that I fault our government, the distributors who purchase the items that are bad, and the retail establishments who keep recirculating the bad items under other labels or selling them on E-Bay. Then I fault the consumer who sits back and does not report the illnesses, the changes in their lives, the dangers they now face with their children and pets, and the ignorance they have or the fact that they are in denial. This is an important issue that must be talked about and we have to approach this problem carefully and immediately.

Although it is impossible to know for sure, industry experts estimate counterfeiting costs at about $100 billion to $200 about billion annually...or nearly 10% of all electronic equipment sold worldwide. Not all of this comes from China, but most industry experts claim that the problem is escalating and note that, although the federal government and several industry associations have taken measures to limit counterfeiting, it continues to plague the components industry.

If you total up all the industries including the electronics, clothing, appliances, auto-after market, drugs, food, furniture, electrics and more, we could be talking about trillions. In the past couple of years, counterfeiters have found a new market in hard-to-get parts and obsolete parts.

1

Before we can even attempt to fix these problems of tainted and counterfeit imports, we first must understand why they are occurring in the first place. Is it China's will to try to destroy the people in America by putting lead in toys or poison in toothpaste, or polluting the fish? Are they not aware of these acts of treason that they are doing, or is it stupidity on the part of the workers in their facilities who either don't know what they are doing or will not open up their mouths for fear of their lives and the lives of their families?

I suppose it starts with a very simple thing like shopping in a retail store for an item that you like and its label is well-known throughout the industry as the in-fashion to wear. As much as I do not like to wear 'logos' on my clothes, I just happen to like this type of fashion.

For that reason, I like Tommy Bahama clothes and have a wardrobe of shirts and sweaters with the Tommy Bahama label. I remember going to Macy's two days before Christmas in 2007 and picked up a nice sweater with a Tommy Bahama label and then noticed that the collars were frayed and discolored. I reached for others in the pile and noticed the same thing. The sweater had a price tag of $85.00 and upon looking at the other label, it said, "Made in China."

I felt deceived, cheated and turned away from the rack and walked away. How could one of my favorite designers do this to me? Why did he have to go to China to make his clothing? Didn't he have enough people in Hawaii or in California, or even in the garment center of New York to handle all of his apparel manufacturing? Then I thought of the cost of producing a sweater in China...perhaps $3.00 each? And the price he sold it wholesale to Macy's at maybe, $15.00 each? And we are about to pay the retail establishment $85.00 for a sweater that is frayed and discolored and was made in China? No more would I buy anything with a Chinese label on it. I would rather pay more for an item and expect it to be perfect...to last for at least a year...and to feel proud that I had bought a product that was made in the United States of America.

I would like to say that I have all of the answers and I am able to find solutions to many of the problems that I face everyday. But the more I get involved with what is usually troubling me, I find myself getting deeper into a maze of controversy and false hopes that even I have problems understanding why these things are happening. At one time I thought I had it made, being the middle man between offshore manufacturers and American companies seeking to get the best products available for the most competitive costs known to man. And I found the answer. Only the answer was making me crazy and I was losing faith in what I was doing.

The latter part of 2007 brought many candidates into the fold to campaign for the highest office in the land, if not the world. The Democrats and Republicans had different agendas as to how they would run the Executive Branch of the government, and one of the key issues was how to bring jobs back to the United States from China. After all, because of NAFTA, we opened up the doors to Asia whereby we were teaching them how to become capitalists while at the same time, we were losing jobs in our country, and not only were we in debt to China for billions of dollars, but our economy was so bad that people were losing, not only their jobs, but their homes.

If only a candidate would have had some smarts and stood before the people and stated that the only way we can level the playing field was to change the way we were doing business with the Chinese. They were manufacturing tires that exploded. They built toys that had lead in them. They made toothpaste that had chemicals that are found in Ante-freeze in them for flavor. They became the largest exporter of fish that made people sick and many others died in the Philippines, and Indonesia and other countries. Why had we not placed stricter rules on the way the products were coming into our country, how they were packaged at the docks and not checked thoroughly enough to catch the flaws. And why did these politicians who were campaigning for the job as president not bring out the fact that this was becoming one of the main issues in our country that need attention and no one was even making an attempt to fix this problem.

Yet, the Democratic candidates were only too eager to bring out the fact that the Iraqi war was a waste and we never should have gotten into the war and defeated Saddam Hussein. With a later surge, we pushed the insurgents back so the Iraqi people could finally have a somewhat decent lifestyle instead of being killed by bombers who thought that by killing themselves as well would put them in a better place. We never should have gotten into a war with Iraq. Not only did it divide our country, but it gave Iran an opportunity to build up its nuclear capabilities.

In retrospect, we flittered with the notion that by buying electronic equipment, toys, household items, fish, tires and other products from China, it would truly save us a lot of money...both in business and consumer related. We went along with NAFTA and GAT and before we knew it, China was becoming a major exporter of so many goods that no one wanted to buy from our own manufacturers. Jobs were lost and we started to owe China tons of money because we kept borrowing from them...to the tune of nearly a trillion dollars. And then the shit hit the fan...the products all had problems and people started to rebel against the Chinese made toys, the fish, the toothpaste, the tires, the printed circuit boards, and many other items that were being made by a country that was once considered our biggest enemy in the east.

So we were in a mid-eastern nation fighting against insurgents who never caused any harm to this country. The terrorists fled to another country and because of the failings of the intelligence of our state department, we were fighting a battle that never should have taken place.

At the same time, we were in bed with a communist nation who was building everything from soup to nuts for us because we did not have the competitive edge to do it ourselves. We basically lost our "Yankee Ingenuity" and it was going to be a long time before we would ever got it back.

One of the largest industries China got involved in during the mid nineties was the printed circuit board industry. There are approximately 2,311 products alone shown on listings, from Google to other mailing lists, in the category of 'Circuit Boards' which includes PCB (printed circuit board) manufacturing and assembly, suppliers, quick-turn prototypes, small quantity and mass production, PCBA, PCB assembly, multilayer, rigid, flex and flexible PCB, immersion gold, integrated circuits, professional supplier and Chinese manufacturer of printed circuit board and on and on and on.

Many of the Chinese manufacturers in China, as well as in Taiwan, Hong Kong and now India, South Korea, Indonesia and the Philippines, promote themselves as a reliable business partner for electronics outsourcing to overseas customers. As a PCB and FPC supplier, they offer a technology menu of boards that can be tailored for any product line.

Others indicate that they have won fame nationwide as professional manufacturers of all kinds of high density printed circuit board's (PCB's) as well as having a processing factory to do SMT (surface mount technology) weld installment, and testing by enjoying a good reputation home and abroad because of powerful technical forces, strict process controls and advanced inspection manners, all with top-grade product quality.

Still others claim their superiority by being able to perform SMT PCB assembly (PCBA) lines in purified workshops, handle gold immersion with ENIG surface finish qualities used for mobile phones and are able to make unleaded boards that will not be harmful to the health and welfare of the end-users. But things had occurred in the past 15 to 20 years. There was a health problem brewing and no one saw it coming until people got sick and many had died.

Being in the printed circuit board business for nearly 15 years, having Chinese manufacturers as my offshore partners, I realized the many problems that were occurring like producing bad products that would fail during assembly and not being able to change from leaded boards to unleaded boards. By taking the lead out of the boards and flushing them into the rivers only tainted and polluted the newly grown fish farms that produced shrimp, salmon, tilapia and other fish that were shipped all over the world… millions of tons of farm-raised fish…now tainted because of the waste from the manufacturers up the river.

Every time the fish farmers moved further south, the manufacturers also moved further south, and there was no escaping the pollution that was getting into the rivers. Did they know about this? Of course they did…and they kept selling tainted fish to countries all over the world.

— 2 —

My Own Personal Experience Was the Eye Opener

Picture this if you will...a marketing person who stumbles into a situation where a manufacturing company in Guangzhou, China sets up an office in Santa Ana, California and wants to sell...of all things...printed circuit boards...to assembly houses and contract assembly users and these boards, from single sided to multilayer boards, in all shapes and sizes, were now available for sale in China, Hong Kong and Taiwan. And the same boards could be bought for one twentieth of the price, if only the boards were certified and approved. That was the key.

I helped a new trading company that opened its doors in Santa Ana, California called Printec to find customers in the United States while they represented Printronics, a manufacturing company in Guangzhou, Guangdong China. The major hurdle that was apparent was that they hardly spoke English, and I could not speak or understand Chinese, and we needed to learn from each other. The first thing I did was to teach the president of the company how to play golf.

The computer and the internet afforded everyone to do their own development of marketing and advertising programs and they did not need the services of an advertising firm. The more advanced typists became IT specialists and that was more important than an artist or a writer who spent their entire careers developing marketing programs that would move companies into a good prospective for a takeover by an investment firm in the future. That was everyone's dream. After all, who truly wanted to work if not for the large buy-outs that were given to top management?

I needed to find something else to do aside from handling the marketing and advertising for companies, which I had done for many, many years. Then the Printec matter came up and I was hired to find customers in America for this firm that was stationed in Guangzhou. There were two people working at this small office in Orange County and it was up to me to move this company and China into a position of authority, large gross sales, and lots of continued growth.

Realizing the ever-changing business cycles that are continually shortened by internet time, many companies were discovering that a knowledge framework can provide a critical backbone to give shape to the amorphous yet immediate world of e-business. Building up such a roaring head of steam, e-business was being touted as the solution for every industry's problems, including industries and problems that haven't even been invented.

Many companies that previously offered enterprise products and services have been quick to re-label their expertise as something like "e-business provider." This internet integration into the way we started to do business that continues to expand today started to shift the winds of success from one company to another with just a mouse click. This new way of doing business was quickly becoming essential to enterprises not only looking to sell, but to supply, to market, to inform, to track, and to link all parties that had been involved in these activities.

I had realized that the key was to give your clients what they want, and give it to them with speed and accuracy. To be in the game, you must learn to e-power your business by getting information into the hands of your customers at the right time, efficiently and competitively. No more, no less. This, I had realized, was the path to e-business success.

What I had learned in my 30 plus years of marketing was that creating a business on the fly is a necessity in this changing world. Who could have correctly forecast even in 1995 or before, the impact the internet would have on the success or failure of business even today? Internet strategy was about balancing the value of strategic certainty versus time-to-market and that it can eventually be an effective part of over 80 percent of the success of a growing business. I therefore used my knowledge in public relations, advertising, direct mail, web site design, development and programming, and basic marketing to build a company that in two years went from ground zero to one that exceeded $50 million in sales.

It was in 1996, that I found myself with this new client from Guangzhou, China who opened up a small office in Santa Ana, California. They represented their office in China, a printed circuit board manufacturer that wanted to make an entry into the North American marketing. I knew nothing about printed circuit boards, how they were made, what they were used for and who would buy them.

I was basically a dummy about these useful products and my curiosity and the fact that I liked my two Asian friends, kept me in the game to find out what this was all about. Not only did my own New York background and experience in advertising and public relations help me to establish a marketing plan for this Chinese company but most of the work that I would have used was passé because companies were able to use their own computers and do the work themselves. I was paid a monthly retainer fee to find them customers in the U.S. Little did I realize that in time it would be a real money making proposition for me because of circumstances that had arisen out of the control of my two Chinese golfing partners.

Working with Global Communications (my marketing company), the new board company Printronix made inroads; and within one year, its southern California sales office Printec had reached nearly $5 million in sales. One of the main reasons was that we were able to produce these custom-made bare boards with the same quality as American companies, at one third the price of its American competitors. The customers had to make sure that the company had an ISO certification and UL approvals (policies set up by the government and IPC standards) or they could not do business with them. I went so far as to attend trade shows and found the best equipment to do the boards including solder machines, pick and place and other equipment that would give the Chinese company an edge over other companies in China, Taiwan and Hong Kong who were just waking up to find out that they too can take a piece of the American market if they knew how. I realized that I was one of the first marketing individuals to put offshore manufacturing on the map.

The following year, however, the company closed its manufacturing facilities in Guangzhou because of some legal problems with the Chinese government, and called on its personnel in the California office to return to China. Seeing the potential of producing products at a discounted rate in China, compared to the same products being manufactured in this country, I hired the Chinese engineer of the two, traveled to China, Taiwan and Hong Kong, and signed exclusive agreements with ten major printed circuit board manufacturers. Using my experience that I had learned back in New York as a director of advertising of a major company and being on the board of the company at 30 years of age, I knew how to market this new venture by working with the engineer and began to promote this newly organized printed circuit board company under the banner of Global Communications and ultimately took over the customers of the defunct Chinese supplier.

I realized that there was a need for printed circuit boards that would have the same excellent quality as those made in the U.S., that were competitively priced, and built by offshore PCB manufacturers that became certified with ISO 9001:2000 and QS 9000 certifications for the automotive industry, plus UL approvals. There was also a need for quick turnaround as potential customers asked about lead time and that became a necessity. Both from a need to integrate and assemble products efficiently and profitably, contract manufacturing had become the new establishment within the industry. Global Communications saw that need, and within a short period of time, was servicing over 75 contract manufacturers and OEMs (end users).

Within two years, we already set projections of nearly $40 to $50 million by the end of five years, with new customers throughout the United States, Canada and Europe. All of the data was transferred by e-mail, some hard copy drawings by fax, and quotation forms were submitted via the internet. All correspondence eventually went over the internet and thus, no long distance phone calls or mail. A system was set up whereby we received payment net 30 days, and we sent wire transfers to our suppliers net 40 days. The process worked well throughout the years that followed. We were working day and night, and we had enough customers to keep us busy.

The Internet was playing an ever increasing part in the business. More than 80 percent of the sales were done over the Internet, either through Internet e-mail or through the Web site. Since Global Communications dealt with companies all over the world, including New Zealand, Germany, the Philippines, England and France, plus the manufacturing in China, many hours were spent between the project engineers, sales and marketing personnel, quality and analysis and operational people over the Internet.

At first, the printed circuit board customers would mail schematics but they were later condensed into Gerber data files and sent over the Internet e-mail. It was then that they were sent directly to the manufacturers overseas that would review them and get back to us with pricing based on quantity per shipment, within 24 hours. We then sent quotes to the customers which covered the cost of freight forwarding from China, Taiwan or Hong Kong, directly to the customer's warehouse, by air and then by truck. This fast service allowed our customers, the CEMs (contract manufacturers) to bid on their projects much faster. Often large Gerber data files with fab drawings that were received by our customers, would take over an hour to transmit overseas. I made sure that our operation was set up in an area that had cable modem service from the very beginning which enabled the large files to take no more than 15 seconds to transmit.

The bottom line was that the business would not have grown as well and as fast as it did if it were not for the Internet. Today, the use of the Internet brings millions of products from thousands of sources to any desktop, anywhere in the world. Quick as a 'mouse!' The e-mail feature gave our customers as well as our PCB manufacturers immediate one-on-one communication capability, quoting prices, setting lead times, changing panelization drawings, silk screen dimensions, and making revisions as fast as the customer could say "how soon." Quick service had attracted new customers and this provided the growth of many new business relationships as well as solidifying the trust of present ones.

We were able to build to IPC, IEC and military standards and therefore we were able to meet qualifications of most any type of customer. This also gave us recognition as a top supplier of printed circuit boards, and we were known at trade shows, seminars and throughout the industry. The only problem that we encountered were many phone calls from companies in southern California and elsewhere who complained to us that we were taking away their customers and that they were losing business. But there was a need for PCBs that had the same quality as those made in the U.S. and that were competitively priced, as well as built by PCB manufacturers with all of the same ISO standards and UL approvals. If we didn't do it, someone else would have.

As production started to grow, contract manufacturers approached Global Communications with their needs for wire harness and cable assemblies, labels for all types of packaging, static control products, adapters, transformers and power switching supplies and other types of products. Global Communications started to partner with more companies within Taiwan and Hong Kong, as well as throughout China, meeting the needs of the ever-increasing industry. We increased our sales force and those who did well survived quite well just on sales commissions.

We found that the solution was experience, knowledge, quality, price, and on time delivery. We also found the right formula to serve the electronics community to its fullest. Within the marketplace, there is a solution to very problem, once you have that formula.

In June of 2004, I saw a downturn occurring. I then decided to write a book on the "Collaboration with Offshore Companies in a Rising Economy" and talked about what would happen if the economy decided to go south. The book was well recognized by many in the industry and I was asked to speak at seminars and offer my own views on scaling back if the situation warranted it, or to cope with other challenges that were coming on to the scene.

Here are some abbreviated concepts from the June, 2000 text:
"When you are a small PCB supplier or a small contract manufacturer, how do you solve the problem of a down turn in the economy and stay

afloat until business resumes? You look at the marketplace and analyze what is happening and cure those terminal ills by giving what the OEMs want. Global positioning requires viable technology platforms from which to build an effective business by understanding what has happened in the past and plan your approach wisely. If it means buying more equipment, or finding more suppliers, then do it.

"Global Communications, a supplier of printed circuit boards, power supplies and other electronic products, for the past twelve years, has had a successful run working with OEMs and CEMs, supplying medium to large quantities of PCBs from China, Taiwan and Hong Kong. The company has now taken on the task of manufacturing power transformers for the banking industry, wire harness and cable assemblies and other electronic products that are made in China, Taiwan and Hong Kong for all industries throughout the United States, Canada, Mexico and Europe. The products are ISO, QS or LPS certified and UL approved, and most of all, cost about one third of the identical products, made in the United States. For OEMs and CEMs to pay less for the same products produced offshore, has given them more product for the buck, thus enabling them to be more competitive in the business of design and development, while being able to stay in business. This meant that suppliers, such as Global Communications, have come to be a huge source of value potential, by creating partnerships with offshore companies as well as those OEMs and CEMs in the United States.

"During the down time, when there were periods of less than adequate business, and customers filing Chapter 11, as President of Global Communications, I visited China, Hong Kong, Taiwan and Korea. I assisted a group of newly formed PCB manufacturers to get new equipment and to be ISO 9001:2000 and QS 9000 certified, plus UL94V-O approved. I had thought by helping these companies become certified to do business in the U.S. that they would follow the rules and regulations set up IPC standards. Acting as a catalyst, our company had increased its stable of PCB facilities to 24, that were able to build boards, as small as single sided and two layers, plus small quantities of prototypes, and multilayer boards, up to 64 layers. Global Communications had even produced large size boards and arrays within a delivery time of 7 to 12 days. Price was most competitive, and the quality at the time was excellent. Already, this had paid off during the downtime, as many orders from new customers had been processed leading into the year, 2004.

"But I was sadly mistaken. When the offshore companies learned how to meet the standards of IPC and UL approval, they also found ways to try to beat the system by cutting corners, building thinner layers on the inside and trying to fool the customer until the boards failed during assembly. Many manufacturers told us that all boards were produced in house, when in fact, many of the processes to manufacture the boards were out-sourced to other facilities.

"The same companies that came to Global Communications with small orders, looking to the future for large, annual shipments to help them keep their own costs down to a minimum, began requesting such items as 120v and 230v power transformers that were used in check scanning machines for banks. We were able to find shops in Taiwan that manufactured such items and if they did not, were willing to following the designs and create the items from scratch.

"Other items that were difficult and expensive to get in the U.S. were cable assemblies that we were successful in building in Taiwan that met all UL approvals, and at a much lower price. These same companies had asked Global Communications if they would handle the assembly offshore by getting the component parts and doing all of the assembly work. This type of turn-key operation had paid off for many companies that would have had to pay a lot more for their products and assembly if the same work was done in the United States. Outsourcing became a way of life in the United States and started to generate a direct impact on a company's bottom line.

"The 'Return on Investment' started to pay off as we started to see a recovery in the marketplace. Global Communications went after the small business from the companies that were trying to develop new products in the market. These new customers needed to keep their costs to a minimum and any one of our manufacturing facilities whom we partnered with was able to accomplish this. The trick was to keep after them to make sure the jobs were done properly as there were always blame thrown back and forth…from the customer who claimed that the manufacturer did not follow the design…or the manufacturer who kept saying that the design was wrong and it had to be altered. In any case, there was much blame placed by both sides.

"By working with companies that needed good, competitively priced products, combined with excellent quality and on time delivery, Global Communications had contributed to their focusing on growth through cost-reduction. This also eliminated waste in the company's internal process by utilizing our connections with our newly found partners in Asia.

"Global Communications realized that its ability to supply many products and services offshore would create a huge source of value potential, by developing partnerships. By becoming a procurement company, that in itself has changed the way companies started doing business, not only in the U.S., but in other countries, including Asia. Suppliers with the right connections overseas were able to truly become a source of market intelligence and save on wasteful time, effort and money for companies of all sizes. Whether the market was short term, it was now possible to find the exact products you wanted, at the least expensive price, and still have money left over at the end of the month for new innovations and design ideas."

Let's look at the history of how all of this happened...

The promise of low labor rates and an access to a potential huge market had lured scores of original manufacturers (OEMs) and electrical manufacturing services (EMS) to China, Taiwan and Hong Kong, then on to India, South Korea and other Third World countries where the labor was extremely cheap as was the cost of doing business. Engineers were abundant but not as efficient as those in the U.S. Yet, the low costs attracted one company after another until nearly every company in the various industries in this country was dealing with an offshore manufacturer in one way or another.

Seeing this opportunity back in 1994, Global Communications had increased its partnerships with Asian companies that were diversified in building all types of electronic components, products, supplies and services. By most accounts, companies in the United States were satisfied with the cost savings they had achieved by working with suppliers who had the knowledge and contacts with offshore manufacturers. Although India came into the fold in later years, they still had taken a back seat to China due to fact that many of their facilities needed to be certified and UL approved and the fact that they had more of an English speaking problem than the Chinese.

As reported in trade journals, the first five years of the 21st century would be a key period in China. Asia-Pacific was expected to become the largest electronics component market, which in turn would create opportunities for component companies in China. Since China's entry into WTO (World Trade Org.), the outside government had changed. Imports and exports had grown, bringing further incentive to supporting industries. Digitalization and networking were pushing the rapid development of the information industry. Eventually, China was to become one of the world's foremost IT manufacturing bases, the source of production and export of thousands of different products.

Growing demand for (and standardization of) electronics would start to raise the requirements of production volume, efficiency and profit. It also meant that competition would become more complex. With China's entry into WTO, the domestic market started to open up to foreign enterprises. Tariffs were coming down and the service industry had opened, giving foreign corporations the chance to compete with domestic firms. The "globalization" of the domestic market did raise general concerns but at the time, no one took the time to truly delve into the oncoming problems.

Companies were too much in awe about making lots of money and the heck with the downturn of our economy or the quality of the products produced offshore. Prices for almost all consumer electronics and other consumer products were decided by the market, which meant, first and foremost, price competition, but also meant technology content, quality, service and motivation. In essence, all enterprises in mainland China, whether state-owned, privately owned, joint ventures or foreign-funded, were considered Chinese enterprises.

By 2004, printed circuit output grew by 20%. Too many new enterprises and domestic expansion were the main reasons for oversupply and price erosion. By the end of 2004, China had become the second-largest source for PCB production, after Japan. By 2005, China would become the leading source, going neck and neck with Japan. Globalization had become a domestic challenge, yet the Chinese economy rested its hopes on it. Due to the downturn of the U.S. economy in the early years of the 21st century, global PCB output suffered. Many PCB manufacturers in North America were seeking long-term development via a global strategy, especially by promoting American standards across Asia.

China's trade reforms and stable society were attracting overseas investors, making this a great opportunity for Chinese enterprises. Global Communications invested in this new venture by assisting many of the Chinese manufacturers in securing the proper equipment to make high quality printed circuit boards, and thus, getting ISO and QS certifications plus the UL approvals. But problems arose as Chinese companies were still not used to working with American companies. They lacked the understanding of deadlines, of competitive pricing, of the importance of communication, and the fact that quality was still the number one ingredient to keep its customers happy. It took a lot of teaching by those intermediary companies who saw this as an important window to continue the business of importing products from anywhere in Asia.

Based on experience, Global Communications had found that newly formed printed circuit board manufacturing companies in Asia were limited to four layer boards, and that it was important to work with many manufacturing facilities that specialized in all layers, from single sided boards, up to 64 or more layers. The facilities that specialized in larger layers would be more competitive. These companies that offered lower per piece pricing, may have had a higher set up, tooling and electrical testing fixture cost. It was with negotiations, that Global Communications guided the offshore facilities to lower their set up and tooling costs, while still offering more competitive per piece pricing, and guided the manufacturers to what the going rate structure was in the U.S. Everyone would win, as the manufacturer got the business, and the CEM got a good quality product at a lower price.

Another major concern was the way goods were packaged from offshore companies, whether they were shipped by air or by ocean. Most air shipments consisted of cartons of products, compared to the pallets that were used when the products were shipped by boat. Normally, a shipment by ocean from Hong Kong to the Long Beach terminal in Los Angeles would take about 14 days, plus a day to clear customs, prior to trucking them directly to the customer. Freight weighing about 9000 pounds by air would probably cost about $5,000. at the time around 2004, whereby if the same freight went by boat, the cost would have been around $500.

We had to train the offshore facilities how to package the products in cartons using one and one half inch foam to protect the boards instead of thin cardboard that did not do the job during the long distance shipment and by lining up each board in the same direction so the corners would not get damaged during shipment. Packing lists were essential with each carton marked and the amount of boards and weight in kilos were indicated on the packing list.

All shipments going by air that weighed over 40 pounds would be more suitable for freight forwarding shipment than express mail, due to costs. It was most important to make sure that all specifications of jobs were clearly written on packing lists, and what the job consisted of, so that everyone would have an understanding of the product to be received. The performance of both the supplier and the customer would be measured by this understanding.

Another criterion in freight forwarding that had come to light was that shippers had to deal with a new world when it came to security especially after 9/11. They would have to pay attention to an information-fueled business evolution whose pace was as inexorable as it was rapid. The last thing we wanted was to see the cargo stalled and delayed, or pay financial penalties due to the new security environment. Companies that formerly focused on shaving dollars from their transportation costs now needed to concentrate on functionality and to follow the rules more than ever before. From a general standpoint, there was a greater reliance and greater demands being placed on the forwarding industry as never before. Forwarders and customs brokers were immersed in the complexities of global transportation transactions.

Irrespective of the mode of transport, the security of the supply chain from origin to ultimate user was of prime concern to all parties to the supply chain...not only to the government, but to the private sector. Shippers certainly needed to increase their collaboration with their forwarders and third-party logistics providers. The key was that shippers had to recognize that adapting to the new regulations meant not just dealing with shipments, but providing a one-stop shop for international trade. Logistics providers and transportation intermediaries were now asked to follow whole new ways of business, not only in the printed circuit board and electronics industry, but in all industries, including food, clothing, toys, gifts, sporting goods and more. Forwarders were becoming the international trade industry's technology providers of choice, providing shipment information so that customers' freight would move seamlessly and without service failures.

But complexities of freight forwarding and understanding the same old problems of first building, and then shipping the products didn't stop here. Companies still had to employ the best practices under supply management that included customer service, loyalty and cost advantage, so that the customer would have the trust and confidence in the supplier.

Yet, with all of the precautions, things never truly went along without a hitch. The Chinese manufactures always changed personnel, tried to go back to bad habits, felt that the American requests were too rigid and ignored them when they chose to, and felt that all of these new rules were costing them money and they tried to avoid following all of the regulations put forth by the middle man, the supplier, who was hoping that his manufacturing facilities would follow protocol. No matter how many times they screwed up and were told not to go back to the old ways of shipping, they inevitably did which caused bad relations between the supplier and the customer. And it wasn't just one or two manufacturers; it was most of them who worked out of China, Hong Kong, Taiwan, India and all of the other countries in Asia. It was either lack of respect they had for the American companies or they just did not care. Sooner or later it was going to affect the way we would be doing business with China and the other countries.

Imagine when a distributor tells his customer that the power transformers that he is getting from Taiwan is LPS certified and he starts to order thousands per shipment, every month. When the transformers arrive, there is a document that says that that similar transformer had been certified, but does not actually indicate that the transformer ordered by the customer was. The customer had to pay $5,000. to his distributor to get this certification because that was what the distributor told the customer. To add to the problem of working with a dishonest distributor, the labels on the transformers had shown UL approval, when in essence, they were not approved. In order for a transformer to get its UL approval, it must be LPS certified. The distributor obviously lied to get the business, and now the customer was out of the $5,000. and he was left sitting with thousands of transformers that were not certified. This kind of abusive outsourcing has been happening time and time again.

As president of Global Communications, I stepped in and corrected the problem by going to the manufacturer in Taiwan and requested that they redesign the transformers for LPS certifications and send new samples to Global's headquarters in Dana Point, California. I had told them that if the new transformers were acceptable, I would resume doing business with them instead of the other distributor and give them orders of over 150,000 transformers for the first year. Upon receiving the new sample transformers, I presented them to the customer for their approval. Not only were the transformers LPS certified and UL approved, but the cost of each transformer was about $3.00 less than what the customer originally paid to the former distributor.

The best part was that the manufacturer agreed to get the certifications without charging any money. Basically, the certifications and approvals did not cost $5,000. to begin with so that too was a scam. In this case, the distributor, who was from California, had lied to the customer and the manufacturer had no idea what was going on. In this case, the Taiwanese manufacturer did its best to accommodate the customer by supplying the proper transformers based on the designs made by the engineering department.

Eventually, when the transformers did not work, we found out that the customer's engineer kept making changes that were not in the best interest of the production of the transformer, and the manufacturer kept indicating this to us. But the engineer tried to cover his mistakes and did not adhere to these allocations. The manufacturer was honest and did a good job. The customer was looking for excuses and finally, all relationships ended. That happens in business as well.

Another challenge that had been working, both collaboratively and supportively, was the partnering of small, contract manufacturers located in southern California. Once again we stepped in and developed a good working relationship with these few, small contract assembly manufacturing companies all located in Orange County that were eager to offer quick turn assembly at a most competitive price, compared to the larger contract assembly manufacturers located around the nation. By getting components competitively priced offshore, including bare boards, these small contract manufacturers were able to offer quick turn service and lower pricing than before. When the quantities got larger, the customer was offered the opportunity to have their boards assembled offshore at a tremendous savings in cost.

For the last fifteen years, more complex boards for telecommunications and the like were developed. Much of the PCB manufacturing moved to Asia, but we invented new electronic products that required more complex circuitry, and the PCB industry as such prospered, despite the fact that many consumer electronics' plants closed in the United States. We started to lose production when everything started to move to Asia. Then, in the beginning of 2000, it started to happen very fast. In the next few years, experts predicted that China would provide 50% of the world's EMS with product, but the domestic market was likely to grow as quickly as well because of the opportunity to design and create new products by having more cash on hand due to the lower cost of buying components. How they were so wrong! The "Fit hit the sham!"

What started as a move East of low-tech PCBs and other components, had accelerated to a full-scale exodus of component and system design, as well as the production of finished goods, benefiting the Western consumer… unfortunately, hurting the Western manufacturer.

Around that time, one of the largest contract manufacturers, Siemens indicated that they were moving most of the 15,000 software programming jobs from its offices in the United States and Western Europe to India, China and Eastern Europe. They had recognized that a huge amount of software development activity needed to be moved from high-cost countries to low-cost countries and about 3,000 of the 30,000 software programmers that Siemens employed worldwide were already in India.

Dell Computer set up a service department in India so that when their customers had problems with their computers, they were speaking to people in India who had a difficult time understanding each other. Eventually, Dell lost its edge in the hardware marketplace and Michael Dell eventually came back to the company after having left it to enjoy the fruits of its labor. Now that fruit was rotting and in order to find its way back to the core of the industry, they had to bring back some of the service from India to this country. But their customers did not forget what had happened and they went to MAC and Hewlett Packard for their next computers.

Scores of Western firms had farmed out software development and back-office work to India and other countries, where wages were significantly lower. India was expected to earn $13 billion from such services during 2004 and 2005 alone. The job shift had led to a backlash from unions and politicians in Western nations. It was calculated that programmers worldwide would lose their jobs once the planned shifts were implemented as the Indian subsidiary would fight hard to get a portion of the pie, and China too would get a chunk of the pie. But it was not going that way as companies started to see the downside of outsourcing. There were just so many pieces of the pie to give away and the big losers were the companies in the United States.

Lower labor costs had been the major factor in losing jobs to Asian manufacturers. But on the other hand, Asian PCB companies had access to cheap and plentiful financing from the stock exchanges and they used this opportunity. There was no question about the dramatic growth rate that had occurred in China, as well as Taiwan and Hong Kong. On the other hand, there had been a dramatic effect on companies in the U.S. that had been manufacturers of PCBs and other electronic products for years. This change was only building as the Chinese became more knowledgeable and financially secure. We used to have "YANKEE INGENUITY" but we had given in to the sleeping giant who was sitting at our back door.

The electronics industry was not the first to utilize offshore manufacturing. This type of manufacturing started back in the 40's and 50's by wholesalers and American manufacturers in the retail industry. By the 1970's, many large retail giants went offshore to get many of their apparel, housewares and other goods manufactured including toys, lawn and garden, lighting, plastics, and so many items that it became a household name..."Made in China."

Wal-Mart, who was not just the world's largest retailer, but the world's largest company...larger than ExxonMobil, General Motors, and General Electric...had sold $244.5 billion worth of goods in 2006. It sold in three months what the number two retailer at that time, Home Depot, had sold in a year. Wal-Mart no longer had any real rivals.

Like many OEMs in the electronics industry, Wal-Mart wielded its power for just one purpose: to bring the lowest possible prices to its customers. Wal-Mart had the power to squeeze profit-killing concessions from vendors. To survive in the face of its pricing demands, makers of everything from bras to bicycles to blue jeans had to lay off employees and close U.S. plants to favor outsourcing products from overseas. This was part of the similarity in most industries.

Of course, U.S. companies had been moving jobs offshore for decades, long before Wal-Mart was a retailing power...long before the electronics industry started to see this trend around 1994. Long before the small manufacturers of printed circuit boards and contract manufacturers and other hardware companies started to lose their customers because of the importers who started to manufacture and assemble goods and services in China, Taiwan and Hong Kong. This process of elimination of jobs and companies did not only start in the electronics industry in the late 1990s, but was slowly creeping into our market for decades. The die was cast many years ago, even before NAFTA, WTO and GAT, when China was opened up to our country. The electronics industry only advanced the stages of offshore outsourcing. Not all the blame for lost jobs in the electronics industry was because of the import of electronics from Asia.

But there is no question that a company like Wal-Mart was helping to accelerate the loss of American jobs to low-wage countries such as China. Wal-Mart, which, in the late 1980s and early 1990s trumpeted its claim to

"Buy American," yet had doubled its imports from China in the past ten years alone, buying some $12 billion in merchandise in 2002. That's nearly 10% of all Chinese exports to the United States.

Think of it this way! One way to think of Wal-Mart is as a vast pipeline that gives non-U.S. companies direct access to the American market. "One of the things that limits or slows the growth of imports is the cost of establishing connections and networks," said Paul Krugman, the Princeton University economist and NY Times editor. "Wal-Mart is so big and so centralized that it can all at once, hook Chinese and other suppliers into its digital system. So-wham! You have a large switch to overseas sourcing in a period quicker than under the old rules of retailing."

As outsourcing continues, the future OEM is no longer a manufacturer, but more of an IP provider with marketing capabilities. How we do business had changed, and unless we find that we are in the throes of another industrial revolution, we have to keep up with the demands of our customers, not by choice, but by demand. This transition has given companies a strategic advantage by knowing the best outsourcing facilities, enabling them to provide more manufacturing services than ever before. The key is to diversify your product range and be able to provide quantities, both small and large, as well as excellent quality, competitively priced, and of course, on time delivery.

But even knowing the best outsourcing facilities, they too had to keep up with the changes that the OEMs needed, such as unleaded products and keeping humidity from the products before they were packaged and shipped to the U.S. If you kept products in a warm, humid place such as the warehouses of Hong Kong and China, many of the products would be deteriorated before they reached the United States and thus, they were no good for any OEM. It started to occur in 2006 but only a few industries noted the difficulties that had taken place, while the others just covered up the deficiencies and never alerted anyone. Thus, many illnesses and deaths occurred in countries where the checkpoints were not as rigid as they should have been. It was all about money and the distributors were repackaging the goods once they arrived in the U.S. so that they would not appear as if they were made in China. The consumer did not know until 2007.

But we did expect to see price hikes in China as well as tightened supply conditions as problems started to arise. China has been one region that was seeing more aggressive price increases because they had been so far below the curve. This was not favoring the buyer's market as demands started to increase and supplies tighten which began to cause lead times to stretch. It was starting back then in 2004 and we did not think that it would get worse but it did. Starting in April, 2004 the Chinese facilities started to raise the cost of raw materials, and the manufacturers were requesting longer lead times to build the products. The manufacturers were also asking for an increase of 8% to 10% to cover the cost of materials.

In 2004, due to strong end-equipment demands from the computer, cell phone and consumer electronics, equipment manufacturers had shown tremendous growth of over 10%. IT spending was on the move, therefore companies were upgrading their obsolete computer systems for the first time since 1999. Growing demand for wireless devices helped drive the building of more wireless infrastructure which would further boost electronic components demand.

The small manufacturer would honor lower pricing to get new business. Once they had a few large customers to book most inventory levels, they did not take on any new business, thus leaving less competitive pricing for buyers. Pricing kept increasing about 2% per quarter compared to the price drops of 12 to 15% in 2003, especially for some part that had been selling below margin, such as those raw materials. Many suppliers, to stay in the game, were just about breaking even, while others were losing money. Therefore, an increase in pricing was evident.

Due to the downturn in the past couple of years, 2005 ~2007, buyers had gotten used to quarterly price declines and the availability to buy parts whenever they wanted, at prices they wanted to pay. People in purchasing thought that they would always get price reductions. However, even without price increases, suppliers could not increase capacity anytime soon and that started to pose problems when demand started to skyrocket. The key was to build a backlog to remain high for some time. But that too caused problems. When manufacturers of printed circuit boards built an inventory and kept the products in their warehouse, the heat and humidity caused delaminating, as too much moisture was found on the bare boards and the extra moisture prevented the assembly house to place components on the boards. Even though re-baking was needed, this caused delays in assembly, cost of components and labor, and loss of money.

In essence, scarcely two years after China joined the World Trade Organization, more and more of the global economy seemed to be falling into orbit around the world's most populous country. Yet, the transportation and communications were still unreliable in China, so it was important for the U.S. Company's operation to have good freight forwarding in Hong Kong where it was less expensive to ship out goods than using express mail from China. It was also essential to have people who were able to communicate well in English and Chinese by getting to know the habits, the culture, and the fundamentals of the way Chinese people react to Americans.

In China, many rules were fixed, but people were able to be somewhat flexible…if they truly wanted to work with Americans. Personal networks on a daily basis were most important between American suppliers and their counterparts in China. The greatest partnerships between American companies and those in Asia were the ones that were made by daily communications over the internet, and sharing the same problems, the same grievances, and the same social worries and family ties.

After years of dealing with companies in China, Taiwan, Hong Kong and Korea, such relationships had materialized between the employees of Global Communications and the many facilities it had partnered with overseas. That was the first step in a good partnership.

We also had differences with many facilities as they too had their own rules. One of the major criteria was to get T/Ts or advanced payment prior to their shipping the goods to us. If we already established a net 30 payment schedule with out own customers, why would we then have to pay the Chinese companies in advance of getting paid by our own customers? We tried it once or twice with new vendors from China only to find out that their products were so bad that they refused to redo them and we were out of the tooling costs and cost of the prototypes.

When other companies refused to adhere to our payment by wire transfers in 40 days, they would try to negotiate with us telling us that they were the best thing since white rice. But we knew better. Their management refused to build boards for us unless we paid them money in advance, and we refused to take them on as suppliers. In the long run, they lost out as we realized that they could not build to the standards set up by IPC and UL approvals. It was best that we stayed away from them to begin with as they would never make a mark in the United States.

Then there were some companies in the U.S. who would ask us to build small quantities over seas for them, such as a company in Chicago, Illinois. The order was under 100 boards but they were large boards that cost around $50.00 each. We accomplished this and had the boards shipped directly to them from our vendor in Hong Kong. They also paid for the expensive tooling and set up which was still way less than if they had the boards done in the United States.

We never received another order from them again until three years later when they contacted us and wanted us to build 50 boards for them. By that time the manufacturer in Hong Kong had gone by the wayside and there was no way we could use them to build just 50 pieces as that was not profitable for any company to do anyway. The customer from Chicago got pissed off at us and wanted the tooling from the Chinese facility that had probably gone out of business.

I refused to give it to them as I had claimed that it was a one time shot and we don't own tooling. Even if the customer had the tooling, it would not work on the equipment of another manufacturer. They wanted to sue us but they could not even go that far as the original purchase order did not state that this was an ongoing project and that all sales are final. No one owns the tooling in this case. The manufacturers usually discard the tooling after a year if they do not receive any more orders as the tooling usually become obsolete or worn out.

At the time we were producing so many products for so many customers, we could not foresee the future nor were we able to be certain what would lie ahead on the horizon. All we knew was that we had gone through some rough times before, as the years we were in business with offshore companies, had its highs and lows as in any other type of business. We knew that many hard working people in this country had lost their jobs and that there may not be any jobs for them in the near future.

I also felt that unless we started to see growth and a potentiality of new business in our country, where the interest rates would climb and people would feel more comfortable in investing in new products, we would be bound and tied with our Chinese adversaries who wished to take over the industrial world by investing heavily in their manufacturing. Losing jobs to competitors may have been a blessing in disguise if the jobs were not profitable as each job had to have a profit margin for the company to stay in business.

The recession started to have an adverse effect on many electronic manufacturing services, both large and small. But the small electronic manufacturing service (EMS) company battling the same woes as the larger suppliers did have an edge. The steps they had taken, although less challenging but just as painful, enabled them to ride this recession out and they became the leaders in the manufacturing picture in the long run.

By trying to dialogue the problems and work out solutions, each company was able to reap the benefits that enabled them to become most successful businesses. But that only lasted for another couple of years. Then the worst nightmare happened. The rules had changed. Products had to be built differently and the Asian manufacturers were not ready for change. They fudged on the products, the products failed, and the cycle of working with the Chinese facilities started to look dim once again.

One of the fallouts of globalization is the squeezing of a skilled yet aging workforce. When nearly half of the workforce would have a feeling of accomplishment, the other half had felt that their jobs were in jeopardy because their own companies let them down. Basically in the coming years, manufacturing industries will be faced with a very real skills shortage. The three million plus jobs lost in the manufacturing industries since the year 2000 has tended to push or keep younger managers out of manufacturing, while retaining highly qualified and experienced managers. This poses serious human-capital management challenges in these industries in the coming years. When asked about the base salaries in the next few years, respondents see the same picture, that being of a no-change, or a raise of not more than 5 percent forthcoming.

Despite strong productivity growth in manufacturing industries… given profit-margin pressures caused by global competition and production overcapacity…efficiencies gained are being used to keep customers happy rather than increase managers' compensation. Although there may be a feeling of accomplishment and job satisfaction, there is still that pressure to keep cutting costs and lead-time and cycle-time reduction.

But the overall worry to those who are employed by manufacturing industries and those owners of American companies is "globalization" itself. Having offshore manufacturing taking over much of the way systems are operating on today, either you have to be more flexible and have more agility with the way our Chinese friends conduct business or learn how to take back the business and bring it home.

Manufacturers' Web sites have become the primary source for research and purchasing. Consumers used to come to a manufacturing site to address a specific problem or file a complaint, but that's no longer the case. Who are you going to file a complaint with…a company that operates out of China or India and your consumer rep cannot speak English well enough to understand what you are talking about? Look what happened to Dell when it started to use young college students in India to take complaints from Dell customers.

There were enough complaints from Dell users that Michael Dell had to come back to the company after their stocks started to take a landslide. They were no longer the top hardware manufacturer any longer. Hewlett Packard started to get the idea and sold their computers at computer outlets and the stores became service people. That was more convenient as it took hours to first find a consumer rep in India, and another few hours to try to resolve the problem until the customer finally said, "The Hell with it."

What had occurred with consumer recalls from China may very turn out to be 'the straw that broke the Camel's back.' People became very skeptical of products that were being made in China. It started with the electronic equipment that kept failing; then it moved to eatables, toys, tires, pet food, and other various products that started to get mentioned in the dailies and periodicals. The media started to do stories on products made in China and people started to take notice of what was going on by reading labels of products that they were buying and staying away from products that had said, "Made in China."

In October, 2006 it was reported in many publications that Indonesia's textile and apparel producers were confronted with a surge in illegal imports from China. Corruption was the main reason behind the rising share in foreign products on Indonesia's domestic market. And there was no improvement in sight during this time, as our own envoy to Jakarta had reported. Basically, the export-Oriented companies were quite happy about the current state of affairs, while the domestic-oriented manufacturers complained that they suffered heavily from illegal imports.

It was determined that Chinese imports, most of them consisting of allegedly smuggled goods, have in a brief time conquered the Indonesian domestic market. According to the national Textile association API, the share of the domestic production in Indonesian consumption of textile goods (mainly garments) plummeted from 72% in 2002 to around 25% in 2005. Although the government had taken some measures to stem the influx of smuggled imports, the domestic market reportedly continued to be flooded by unbelievably cheap Chinese goods.

A big success in the struggle against smuggling would have come as a surprise, as Chinese exporters are notoriously inventive and Indonesian customs are notoriously corrupt. According to the annual survey by the Berlin-based organization Transparency International, Indonesia is perceived as one of the most corrupt countries in the world.

In May, 2007 the Washington Post reported that tainted Chinese imports was common in this country which included dried apples preserved with a cancer-causing chemical; frozen catfish laden with banned antibiotics; scallops and sardines coated with putrefying bacteria; and mushrooms laced with illegal pesticides.

These were among the 107 food imports from China that the Food and Drug Administration detained at U.S. ports in April of 2007 alone, agency documents had revealed, along with more than 1,000 shipments of tainted Chinese dietary supplements, toxic Chinese cosmetics and counterfeit Chinese medicines.

For years, U.S. inspection records have shown that China had flooded the United States with foods unfit for human consumption. And for years, FDA inspectors have simply returned to Chinese importers the small portion of those products they caught-many of which turned up at U.S. borders again, making a second or third attempt at entry.

Now the confluence of two events-the highly publicized contamination of U.S. chicken, pork and fish with tainted Chinese pet food ingredients and the resumption of high-level economic and trade talks with China-had activists and members of Congress demanding that the United States tell China it was finally fed up.

Dead pets and melamine-tainted food notwithstanding, change will prove difficult, policy experts said, in large part because U.S. companies have become so dependent on the Chinese economy that tighter rules on imports stand to harm the U.S. economy, too.

"So many U.S. companies are directly or indirectly involved in China now, the commercial interest of the United States these days has become to allow imports to come in as quickly and smoothly as possible," said Robert B. Cassidy, a former assistant U.S. trade representative for China and now director of international trade and services for Kelley Drye Collier Shannon, a Washington law firm.

As a result, the United States finds itself "kowtowing to China," Cassidy said, even as that country keeps sending American consumers adulterated and mislabeled foods. It's not just about cheap imports, added Carol Tucker Foreman, a former assistant secretary of agriculture now, at the Consumer Federation of America. "Our farmers and food processors have drooled for years to be able to sell their food to that massive market," Forman said. "The Chinese counterfeit. They have a serious piracy problem. But we put up with it because we want to sell to them."

U.S. agricultural exports to China have grown to more than $5 billion a year-a fraction of 2007's $232 billion U.S. trade deficit with China but a number that has enormous growth potential, given the Chinese economy's 10 percent growth rate and its billion-plus consumers.

Trading with the largely unregulated Chinese marketplace has its risks, of course, as evidenced by the many lawsuits that U.S. pet food companies now face from angry consumers who say their pets were poisoned by tainted Chinese ingredients. Until recently, however, many companies and even the federal government reckoned that, on average, those risks were worth taking. And for some products that have had little choice, as China has driven competitors out of business with its rock-bottom prices. But after the pet food scandal, some are recalculating.

"This isn't the first time we've had an incident from a Chinese supplier," said Pat Verduin, a senior vice president at Grocery Manufacturers Association, a trade group in Washington. "Food safety is integral to brands and to companies. This is not an issue the industry is taking lightly."

— 3 —

New Focus on the Problem...The Recalls Begin

China's less-than-stellar behavior as a food exporter is revealed in stomach-turning detail in FDA "refusal reports" filed by U.S. inspectors; Juices and fruits rejected as "Filthy." Prunes tainted with chemical dyes not approved for human consumption. Frozen breaded shrimp preserved with nitrofuran, an antibacterial that can cause cancer. Swordfish rejected as "poisonous."

In the first four months of 2007, FDA inspectors-who were able to check out less than 1 percent of regulated imports-refused 298 food shipments from China. By contrast, 56 shipments from Canada were rejected, even though Canada exports about $10 billion in FDA-regulated food and agricultural products to the United States-compared to about $2 billion from China. Although China is subject to more inspections because of its poor record, those figures mean that the rejection rate for foods imported from China, on a dollar-for-dollar basis, is more than 25 times that for Canada.

Miao Changxia, of the Chinese Embassy in Washington, said China "attaches great importance" to the pet food debacle. "Investigations were immediately carried out...and a host of emergency measures have been taken to ensure the hygiene and safety of exported plant-origin protein products," she said in an e-mail to the Washington Post.

But deception by Chinese exporters is not limited to plant products, and some of their most egregiously unfit exports are smuggled into the United States.

Under Agriculture Department rules, countries cannot export meat and poultry products to the United States unless the USDA certifies that the slaughterhouses and processing plants have food-safety systems equivalent to those in this country. Much to its frustration, China is not certified to sell any meat to the United States because it has not met that requirement.

But that has not stopped Chinese meat exporters. In 2006, USDA teams had seized hundreds of thousands of pounds of prohibited poultry products from China and other Asian countries. Agriculture Secretary Mike Johnson announced in March, 2007. Some were shipped in crates labeled "dried lily flower," "prune slices," and "vegetables," according to news reports. It is unclear how much of the illegal meat slipped in undetected.

Despite those violations, the Chinese government is on track to get permission to legally export its chickens to the United States-a prospect that has raised concern not only because of fears of bacteria such as salmonella but also because Chinese chickens, if not properly processed, could be a source of avian flu, which public-health authorities fear may be poised to trigger a human pandemic.

In 2006, however, under high-level pressure from China, the USDA passed a rule allowing China to export to the United States chickens that were grown and slaughtered in North America and then processed in China-a rule that quickly passed through multiple levels of review and was approved the day before Chinese President Hu Jintao arrived in Washington in April, 2007.

Now the rule that China really wants, allowing it to export its own birds to the United States, is in the works, said Richard Raymond, USDA's undersecretary for food safety. Reports in China have repeatedly hinted that only if China gets its way on chicken exports to the United States will Beijing lift its four-your-old ban on importing U.S. beef. Raymond denies any link.

"It's not being facilitated or accelerated through the system at all," Raymond said of the chicken rule, adding that permission for China to sell poultry to the United States is moving ahead because recent USDA audits found China's poultry slaughterhouses to be equivalent to those in the United States.

Tony Corbo, a lobbyist for Food and Water Watch, a Washington advocacy group, said that finding...which is not subject to outside reviews... is unbelievable, given repeated findings of unsanitary conditions at China's chicken slaughterhouses. Corbo said he has seen some of those audits. "Everyone who has seen them was grossed out," he said.

An Official Response

The Cabinet-level "strategic economic dialogue" with China, which began in September, 2006 and was scheduled many times thereafter, had been described early on as a chance for the United States and China to break a long-standing stalemate on trade issues. When it comes to the safety of imported foods, though, they may highlight the limited leverage that the United States has.

It is not just that food from China is cheap, said William Hubbard, a former associate director of the FDA. For a growing number of important food products, China has become virtually the only source in the world. For example, China controls 80 percent of the world's production of ascorbic acid, a valuable preservative that is ubiquitous in processed and other foods. Only one producer remains in the United States, Hubbard said.

"That's true of a lot of ingredients," he said, including the wheat gluten that was initially thought to be the cause of the pet food deaths. Virtually none of it is made in the United States, because the Chinese sell it for less than it would cost U.S. manufacturers to make it. So pervasive is the U.S. hunger for cheap imports, experts said, that the executive branch itself has repeatedly rebuffed proposals by agency scientists to impose even modest new safety rules for foreign foods.

"Sometimes guidances can get through, but not regulations," said Caroline Smith DeWaal, food safety director at the Center for Science in the Public Interest, and advocacy group. Guidances, which the FDA defines as "current thinking on a particular subject," are not binding.

Under the Bush administration in particular, DeWaal said, if a proposed regulation does get past agency or department heads, it hits the wall at the White House Office of Management and Budget. Andrea Wuebker, an OMB spokeswoman, said that the office reviewed 600 proposed rules in 2006 and that it is up to agencies to finalize rules after they are reviewed. She did not tally how many reviews sent agencies' rule-writers back to the drawing board. She noted that some food safety rules had been finalized, including some related to mad cow disease and bioterrorism. Critics pointed out that the bioterrorism-related regulations were required by an act of Congress.

John C. Bailar III, a University of Chicago professor emeritus who chaired a 2003 National Academies committee that recommended major changes in the U.S. food safety system...which have gone largely unheeded...said he had become increasingly concerned that corporation and the federal government seemed willing to put the interests of business "above the public welfare."

"This nation has...and has had for decades...a pressing need for a wholly dedicated food safety agency, one that is independent and not concerned with other matters...to bring together and extend the bits of food safety activities now scattered over more than a dozen agencies," he said. Legislation to create such an agency was recently introduced, though many suspect that is too big a challenge politically.

But in the aftermath of the recent food scandals, a growing number of companies and trade groups, including Grocery Manufacturers of America, are speaking in favor of at least a little more protection, starting with a doubling of the FDA's food safety budget. China is talking tough too. "Violations of the rules on the use and addition of chemicals or other banned substances will be dealt with severely," said Miao, of the Chinese Embassy. It is a threat some doubt will be enforced with great vigor, but nonetheless it reveals that China recognizes that the latest scandal has shortened Americans' fuses.

Chinese Products Choke, Burn, Drown, Drop, Trap Americans

The *WorldNetDaily* reported in June, 2007 that it's not just Chinese food and drug imports that can kill you. Many of those bargain-priced products you pick up at Wal-Mart, Target or Sam's Club could do you in, too.

Imports from China were recalled by the U.S. Consumer Product Safety Commission twice as often as products made everywhere else in the world, including the U.S., a WND study of government 2007 reports show. Of the 152 product recalls announced by the commission since the beginning of 2007, 104 have been for products made in China. They include:

- Portable baby swings that entrap youngsters, resulting in 60 reports of cuts, bruises and abrasions
- Swimming pool ladders that break, resulting in 127 reports of injuries, including leg lacerations requiring up to 21 stitches, five reports of bone fractures, two back injuries, two reports of torn ligaments and eight sprained ankles
- Faulty baby carriers that result in babies falling out and getting bruised, getting skulls cracked and hospitalizations
- Easy-Bake Ovens that trap children's fingers in openings, resulting in burns
- Oscillating tower fans whose faulty wiring results in fires, burns and smoke inhalation injuries
- Exploding air pumps that have resulted in 13 lacerations including six facial injuries and one to the eye
- Bargain-priced oil-filled electric heaters, selling for less than $50. that burn down homes

- Notebook computer batteries that burn up computers, cause other property damage and burn users
- Circular saws with faulty blade guards that result in cutting users, not wood

It's the latest blow to Chinese imports, which have been hit in the past for poisoning America's pets, risking America's human food supply and reintroducing lead poisoning to American's children. Electrical products made in China represent a significant percentage of the recalls. During "National Electrical Safety Month" in March 0f 2007, the commission noted the proliferation of "dangerous counterfeit electrical products, many of which come from China, that pose serious risk to life and limb.

The CPSC noted the market is saturated with counterfeit circuit-breakers, power strips, extension cords, batteries and holiday lights that are causing fires, explosions, shocks and electrocutions. "Many counterfeit products are made in China and CPSC is actively working with the Chinese government to reduce the number of unsafe products that are exposed to the United States," said the alert issued in May, 2007. The agency suggested that if the price of such an item seems to be too good to be true, it could be because the product is an inferior or unsafe counterfeit.

Imagine, if you will, an attractive, normal-looking table lamp that should be safe. But 1,500 manufactured in China had to be recalled because of faulty light sockets that posed the risk of electrical shocks and fire hazards.

Or, how about emergency lights that look just like other emergency lights but whose circuit board malfunctions, preventing illumination during emergencies? The CPSC recalled 3,200 of those in 2007 alone.

And be careful which heated massaging recliners you relax in. If you chose any of the 1,700 manufactured in China and recalled by the commission, you might have found yourself medium rare because of an overheating and burn hazard discovered.

Even the simplest, most inexpensive items from China seem to pose massive risks. About 2,700 $12 pine cone candles had to be recalled when it was determined the exterior coating, not just the wick, caught fire.

The problem is Americans see a cheap electrical power strip with a circuit breaker and assume it does what it is supposed to do. That is not the case with many Chinese counterfeits. They are not only counterfeits in the sense of improperly using brand names, they are actually counterfeits in the sense of pretending to do something they were never intended to do. But big problems occur when an over-taxed power strip doesn't trip a circuit. Fires can occur. Property can be damaged. People can be killed.

Likewise, when Americans buy attractive-looking glassware at a bargain price, they might ask themselves: "How can I go wrong?"

Pier 1 Imports found out when 180,000 pieces of glassware were ordered recalled by the CPSC because the items broke for no apparent reason, sometimes cutting the hands of those holding them.

How could one go wrong purchasing an attractive kitchen stool engraved with a rooster on the seat? After all, it was only $30. Well, several people found out when the stools collapsed, even under the weight of small children.

You might want to think twice before entrusting your child to something as simple as a crib made in China. For years, American manufacturers scrupulously lived up to the exacting safety standards imposed by agencies like the CPSC. Not so with Chinese manufacturers. Some 40,000 cribs had to be recalled when it was discovered directions instructing consumers to assemble them in ways that would result in the baby falling out and becoming entrapped. Additionally, locking pins on the side of the crib could pop off and cause a choking hazard.

About 450,000 infant car seat carriers manufactured in China had to be recalled when it was determined that infants were falling out because of a faulty design. The Evenflo Co., which imported the carriers from China, received 679 reports of the handle on the car seat releasing for no reason, resulting in 160 injuries to children, including a skull fracture, two concussions and cuts and bruises.

American manufacturers also adapted years ago to requirements that products designed for young children avoid small parts that could result in choking accidents. But, again, based on a survey of recalls in the first six months of 2007, this seemed to be a foreign concept among Chinese companies.

Even books for the young children have been found to contain plastic squeaker toys that have become lodged in babies' throats and metal clips that break off, potentially injuring children. Graco received 137 reports of infants mouthing, chewing and sometimes choking on tiny pieces of its soft blocks tower toys imported from China. At least 32 infants were found gagging on the pieces and 49 choked on the plastic covering. In all, 40,000 had to be recalled.

A slew of Chinese exports recently have been banned or turned away by U.S. inspectors, including wheat gluten tainted with the chemical melamine that has been blamed for dog and cat deaths in North America, monkfish that turned out to be toxic pufferfish, drug-laced frozen eel and juice made with unsafe color additives.

China, the leading exporter of seafood to the U.S., has been found to be raising most of its fish products in water contaminated with raw sewage and compensating by using dangerous drugs and chemicals, many of which are banned by the FDA. The stunning news followed WND's report that FDA inspectors reported on the tainted food imports from China that are being rejected with increasing frequency because they are filthy, are contaminated with pesticides and tainted with carcinogens, bacteria and banned drugs.

China has consistently topped the list of countries whose products were refused by the FDA, and that list includes many countries, including Mexico and Canada, who export far more food products to the U.S. than China. While less than half of Asia has access to sewage treatment plants, aquaculture-the raising of seafood products-has become big business on the continent, especially in China.

In China, No. 1 in aquaculture in the world, 3.7 billion tons of sewage is discharged into rivers, lakes and coastal waters-some of which are used by the industry. Only 45 percent of China has any sewage-treatment facilities, putting the country behind the rest of Asia.

China not Sole Source of Dubious Food

In July of 2007, *The New York Times* reported the following: Black pepper with salmonella from India! Crabmeat from Denmark that is mislabeled!

At a time when Chinese imports are under fire for being contaminated or defective, federal records suggest that China is not the only country that has problems with its exports. In fact, federal inspectors have stopped more food shipments from India and Mexico in 2006 than they have from China, an analysis of data maintained by the Food and Drug Administration had shown. China has had much-publicized problems with contaminated seafood-including a temporary ban in June of 2007 on imports of five species of farm-raised seafood from China-but federal inspectors refused produce from the Dominican Republic and candy from Denmark more often.

For instance, produce from the Dominican Republic was stopped 813 times in 2006 alone, usually for containing traces of illegal pesticides. Candy from Denmark was impounded 82 times. By comparison, Chinese seafood was stopped at the border 331 times during 2006.

"The reality is, this is not a single-country issue at all," said Carl R. Nielsen, who resigned from the Food and Drug Administration in 2005, after 28 years. His last job was director of the division of import operations and policy in the agency's Office of Regulatory Affairs. "What we are experiencing is massive globalization," he said.

The F.D.A. database does not necessarily capture a full and accurate picture of product quality from other countries. For one thing, only one year of data is available on the agency's Web site, and F.D.A. officials declined to provide more data without a formal Freedom of Information request, a process that can take months, if not years.

In addition, the F.D.A. inspects only about 1 percent of the imports that fall under its jurisdiction. So the agency may miss many of the products that are contaminated or defective. The F.D.A. database also fails to disclose the quantity of products that are refused, so it is impossible to know whether just a box of cucumbers was refused or a shipload.

In cases of recurrent problems, the F.D.A. may issue an import alert, which leads to additional scrutiny at the border. In June of 2007, for instance, the F.D.A. issued not only the import alert for the Chinese fish, but also import alerts for Mexican cantaloupes and basmati rice from India, among others.

Rafael Laveaga, a spokesman for the Mexican Embassy in Washington, said the number of food safety problems from Mexican imports was minuscule given the huge volume of trade. He said that Mexican food products were scrutinized more thoroughly since they arrived by road transit, rather than by ship or airplane. "The proactive and professional relationship that exists between Mexican authorities and the F.D.A. has always helped to expeditiously mitigate and control any potential risks," he had said.

Banarshi Harrison, minister of commerce at the embassy of India, said India had recently strengthened its food safety laws. He said that contamination of spices and pickles might occur on occasion because they were processed by many small manufacturers. "There is really no evidence of a systematic problem for any particular product," he said.

Food safety officials from the Dominican Republic and Denmark could not be located for comment. Yet, despite the shortcomings with the F.D.A. database of import refusals, the available information makes clear that quality problems extend well beyond China, where officials recently admitted that nearly 20 percent of the country's products are substandard or tainted.

Critics say the F.D.A. has not changed to deal with the flood of imports in the last decade, as trade agreements have opened up borders to products from across the globe. The United States imported $1.86 trillion in merchandise in 2006, compared with $1.14 trillion in 2001, a 63 percent increase, according to Commerce Department records.

An F.D.A. plant to revamp the way it inspects imports, called the Import Strategic Plan, was completed in 2003, but shelved because of budgetary constraints, several former F.D.A. officials said. The plan would have focused more on finding potential risks in the food supply using vast quantities of information-from inspectors and manufacturers to foreign governments and consumers-to aim at problem imports.

William Hubbard, a former F.D.A. associate commissioner who resigned in 2005 and is now a part of a coalition that is advocating for more financing for the agency had stated, "It basically got deep-sixed. There was no capacity to cover as imports went up."

Noting that the number of import shipments had vastly increased in the last 15 years, he said, "That's a huge, huge increase and they've lost people. These guys are going to war without enough troops. They don't even have guns."

Nancy M. Childs, a professor of food marketing at St. Joseph University in Philadelphia, said the quality problems were an inevitable result of companies pursing the cheapest possible products. "As long as we are pushing for the lowest price all the time, driving our supply chain, you get more efficient," she said. "But at a certain point, there is no more efficiency and you sacrifice quality."

Ms. Childs added that countries that produce the cheapest products often have little regulation and lackluster enforcement.

Dr. David Acheson, the F.D.A.'s assistant commissioner for food protection, agreed that the agency's system for reviewing imports was antiquated and needed to be changed. He said that the F.D.A. should revise its domestic food safety strategy to focus more on prevention rather than simply reacting to crises. The agency, he said, was currently working on a plan to revise how it monitored food safety, both for domestic food and imported, which was scheduled to be released in the fall of 2007. The plan would depend on the F.D.A. working with foreign governments and American companies to identify potential risks to the food supply before they reach ports in the United States. "Fundamentally, starting at the border is not where we need to be," he said.

The F.D.A. inspects foreign shipments of food, drugs, cosmetics, medical devices, animal drugs and some electronic devices. From July 2006 through June of 2007, agency inspectors stopped 1,901 shipments of all such items from China, followed closely by India, 1,782; Mexico, 1,560; and the Dominican Republic, 862.

But China sends more products into the United States than any of those countries, at least in terms of the dollar value. In 2006, for instance, China shipped $288 billion in merchandise to the United States, compared with $198 billion from Mexico; $22 billion from India; and $5.3 billion from the Dominican Republic, records show.

Salmonella was the top reason that food was rejected from India, and it was found in products like black pepper, coriander powder and shrimp. "Filthy" was the primary reason food was stopped from Mexico, and the rejections included lollipops, crabmeat and dried chili. Products from the Dominican Republic were mostly stopped because of pesticides.

— 4 —

China Warns U.S. Against "Smear Attacks" on Imports

On July 19th, 2007 *Reuters* reported that China warned the United States against "groundless smear attacks" against Chinese products and said it was working responsibly to address concerns over a spate of recent food safety scares.

"The Chinese Government has not turned a blind eye or tried to cover up. We have taken this matter very seriously, acted responsibly and immediately adopted forceful measures," said a statement by China's embassy in Washington.

"Blowing up, complicating or politicizing a problem are irresponsible actions and do not help in its solution," the Chinese mission said in a rare policy pronouncement. "It is even more unacceptable for some to launch groundless smear attacks on China at the excuse of food and drug safety problems," it said.

Echoing the Beijing government's complaints about U.S. media reports, the embassy said food safety concerns were not unique to China while 99.2 percent of food exports to the United States in 2006 met quality standards.

Problematic U.S. imports from China-including toxic ingredients mixed into pet food and recalls of toy trains and toothpaste-were isolated cases and "hardly avoidable" amid huge and rapidly growing bilateral trade, the statement said. "It is unfair and irresponsible for the U.S. media to single China out, play up China's food safety problems and mislead the U.S. consumer," it added.

Appealing for strengthened cooperation between Chinese and U.S. food inspection authorities, the statement urged Americans to "respect science and treat China's food and drug exports fairly." In the case of China, they are not the sole source of tainted imports.

The publication, More Health News also reported in July of 2007 that the U.S. rejected more than 3,000 shipments from Mexico and India in 2006. The Mexican cantaloupe irrigated with water from sewage-tainted rivers. Candy laced with lead. Chinese toothpaste is not the only concern for U.S. consumers wary of the health risks posed by imported goods.

Producers in other developing nations are big violators of basic food safety standards, even as they woo consumers with a growing appetite for foods like pickled mangoes from India and winter-season fruits and vegetables from Mexico. In July of 2007, President Bush established a high-level government panel to recommend steps to guarantee the safety of food shipped into the U.S. and to improve policing of those imports.

China, already under suspicion as the source of tainted toothpaste, contaminated fish and toxic medicine, had the largest number of violations in the last six months of 2006 and the first six months of 2007, with the U.S. Food and Drug Administration rejecting 1,901 shipments of food or cosmetics. But India and Mexico weren't far behind, with inspectors rejecting 1,787 and 1,560 shipments, respectively.

The biggest reasons? Foods that were unapproved or contained poisons and pesticides were unfit to eat! Some were simply dirty, with inspectors finding that the shipment "appeared to consist in whole or in part of a filthy, putrid, or decomposed substance or be otherwise unit for food…period!"

And those were just the problems that were caught. F.D.A. inspectors only have the money and resources to check about 1 percent of the 8.9 million imported food shipments a year. Many of those inspections target problem products from problem nations, like Indian relishes or Mexican cantaloupe. The F.D.A. banned all cantaloupes from Mexico in 2002 after four salmonella outbreaks traced to the fruit killed two people in the United States and hospitalized at least 18 others.

While some Mexican cantaloupe exporters have regained the F.D.A.'s trust by adopting cleaner irrigation methods, Mexican melons are often contaminated by sewage-laced water. In June, 2007 alone, the FDA rejected six shipments of Mexican cantaloupes, 4 percent of the 139 total shipments from Mexico, because of salmonella.

Mexican green onions were blamed for a 2003 outbreak of hepatitis A in Pennsylvania that was traced to the Chi-Chi's restaurant chain. Four people died and more than 600 people were sickened. And three Mexican candy manufacturers, including two subsidiaries of Mars, Inc. and Hershey Co., agreed last year to lead testing and annual audits after The Orange County Register found that California state and federal regulators knew spicy Mexican candies could cause lead poisoning in children, but did nothing.

Candy makers are still major violators, making up at least 15 percent of the FDA's June 2007 rejections for Mexico after inspectors determined that shipments were filthy, unsafe or contained pesticides. In the same month, FDA inspectors determined that four shipments of oral electrolyte solution-used to treat dehydration in children with acute diarrhea or vomiting-contained unsafe coloring and false labeling.

While the products carried the name of Abbot Laboratories of Mexico, a spokeswoman for the Chicago-based company, Tracey Noe, said it had not been notified of any product rejection and noted that products are sometimes counterfeited or diverted for sale to the wrong country. Still, food safety issues are relatively small amid the $10.3 billion in food Mexico exported to the U.S. in 2006 and higher in 2007.

Suzanne Heinen, a U.S. Department of Agriculture official in Mexico City, said Mexico has come a long way in protecting its food exports, with close government oversight of the industry and large-scale producers who employ U.S. agriculture practices. "They don't want to have a problem and lost that market," she said.

Developing nations also aren't the only food safety violators. The U.S. spinach and green onion supply was called into question in 2006 after two E. coli outbreaks, both linked to the U.S.-based Ready Pac Company. And U.S.-based ConAgra Foods, Inc. launched a massive recall of Peter Pan peanut butter in February, 2007 after more than 600 people reported salmonella poisoning. Yet, developing countries still have their own food safety concerns.

Mexico questions the widespread U.S. use of genetically modified crops, and has banned them because of concerns they could be harmful. President Felipe Calderon, however, has said he will ease those restrictions. Many other nations, including South Korea, have rejected U.S. beef because of fears of mad cow disease.

Fears over Chinese products began in 2006 after dozens of deaths in Panama blamed on medicine contaminated with diethylene glycol, a chemical used in anti-freeze that can cause kidney failure, paralysis and death. The same chemical has been found in Chinese toothpaste, although there have been no reports of resulting health problems.

China is instituting a daily food safety reporting system to try to win back consumer confidence, and it executed the head of the State Food and Drug Administration, Zheng Xiaoyu, for taking bribes and gifts in exchange for approval of untested, substandard and fake products.

Two Sources: July 19th, 2007 , Reuters' and July 2007, More Health News

— 5 —

List of Problem Imports Grow

In July, 2007 the *NPR* reported that the number of unsafe products imported to the United States from China-ranging from seafood and pet food to toys and toothpaste-has grown steadily. China-made products have accounted for more than 60 percent of recalls in 2007, said Scott Wolfson, spokesman for the U.S. Consumer Product and Safety Commission. So far they had recalled 338 products overall in the first half of 2007 and they expected more than that before the year was up, Wolfson stated. For the most part, the businesses responsible for the faulty products and bad food had denied the problems, saying their products were safe.

After initially guaranteeing the safety of the country's products, Chinese officials admitted during the month of July, 2007, after much international pressure, that "as a developing country, China's current food and drug safety situation is not very satisfactory." They had hoped to downplay the safety and health problems before the 2008 summer Olympics, to be held in Beijing. At the same time, officials in Beijing had been attempting to clean up the problems. In early July, inspectors announced that they had closed 180 food factories in China in the first half of 2007, and that they seized tons of candy, pickles, crackers and seafood **tainted with formaldehyde, illegal dyes and industrial wax.**

Here is a rundown of the items that had been found hazardous since the massive recall of pet foods in early March, 2007:

Fish.

The U.S. Food and Drug Administration had placed a hold on five types of farmed fish and seafood containing traces of antifungal and antibiotic drugs that are potentially harmful to humans. Federal officials said that repeated tests on shrimp, catfish, eel, bass and dace imported from China revealed that presence of drugs not approved in the United States for use in farmed seafood. The hold means the FDA is not allowing the import of these types of Chinese farmed seafood until the exporters can prove the seafood is free from harmful contaminants. The FDA stopped short of ordering an outright ban because there is no immediate risk.

The FDA said that between October 2006 and May 2007, tests on some imported Chinese fish repeatedly found traces of the antibiotics nitrofuran and fluoroquinolones, as well as antifungals malachite green and gentian violet, that the FDA forbids in seafoods, in part to prevent bacteria from developing resistance to the drugs. The best known example is ciprofloxacin, an antibiotic sold under the name of Cipro that is used to treat a variety of infections. The drug made headlines as a treatment option during the 2001 anthrax attacks.

China is one of the top exporters of seafood to the United States. More than half of its global seafood exports are farmed, yet the FDA only inspects about 5 percent of farmed Chinese fish imports.

Toothpaste.

The FDA increased inspection of toothpaste made in China after reports that some of the products may contain an ingredient used in antifreeze. The ingredient, diethylene glycol, is a thickening agent not normally used in toothpaste. The chemical has been used as a low-cost, but sometimes deadly substitute for glycerin-a sweetener commonly used in drugs.

Diethylene glycol was found in three products manufactured by Goldcredit International Trading in China: Cooldent Fluoride, Cooldent Spearmint and Cooldent ICE. The FDA also found the chemical in Shir Fresh Mint Fluoride Paste, which is manufactured by Suzhou City Jinmao Daily Chemical Co.

The FDA is not aware of any poisonings from toothpaste, but has found that the toothpaste was distributed in some U.S. bargain retail stores, including a Dollar Plus in Miami and a Todo A Peso in Puerto Rico. The toothpaste also was shipped to prisons in North Carolina and Georgia and hospitals in Florida and Georgia.

The same chemical found in the toothpaste was blamed for the deaths of 51 people in Panama after they ingested tainted cough medicine. China has said that it was the source of the deadly diethylene glycol, but also stated that it was originally labeled "for industrial use only."

Drugs.
In Beijing, local officials banned the use of 10 types of drugs as a result of their makers' exaggerated and false claims. It is unclear whether the drugs have been exported.

The drugs were genuine, but the results they claimed to produce in fighting high blood pressure, diabetes and other ailments could not be supported in clinical testing. Beijing stores have been ordered to stop selling them, and media outlets that carried their advertising were told to print retractions.

Ceramic Heaters and Toy Grills.
In June of 2007, some 1.2 million ceramic heaters made in China and distributed by Lasko Products, Inc., of West Chester, Pa., were recalled because of safety concerns. The heaters were a possible fire hazard, due to faulty power cords that overheated where they entered the base of the units. Lasko received 28 reports of failed power cords, including six instances of minor property damage. No injuries had been reported.

The recall only affected models manufactured in 2005. The heaters were sold at major retailers, home centers and discount department stores nationwide from September 2005 to April 2006 and cost $20. to $50.

The Play Wonder Toy Grill, also recalled due to safety concerns, is made in China and distributed by Schylling Associates Incorporated, of Rowley, Mass. The 2,300 products recalled posed a danger of laceration.

The circular ash tray attached to the stainless steel legs of the grill could contain sharp edges. No injuries had been reported. The toys were sold in Target Stores nationwide from December 2006 to February 2007 for about $20.

Toy Trains.
The popular Thomas and Friends Wooden Railway toys were voluntary recalled in early June, 2007 due to the presence of lead in some of the surface paints. The recall was particularly troubling for parents whose children had been playing…and chewing…on the toys for years. The recall affected two dozen items, which amounts to about 1.5 million toys. Imported from China, the toys were distributed in the United States by RC2 Corp. of Oak Brook, Ill. The contaminated toys were sold nationwide at toy stores and various retailers from January 2005 to June 2007 and ranged in price from $10 to $70.

Yellow and red paint on the recalled products contain lead. If ingested by young children, lead is toxic and can cause adverse health and development effects, including long-term neurological problems affecting learning and behavior. No incidents of lead poisoning connected to the trains have been reported yet.

Parents can have a simple blood test performed to check the level of lead in their child's body. The company has not yet said whether they will reimburse parents for the costs associated with the blood tests and any further treatment needed. The company had stated that it will pay for the shipping of recalled products and for a free replacement.

Tires.

U.S. regulators have ordered tire importer Foreign Tire Sales, based in Union, N.J. to recall as many as 450,000 tires. The company reported that the treads on light-truck radials manufactured by Hangzhou Zhongce Rubber Co. in Hangzhou, China, might separate. Foreign Tires Sales said that many of the tires were missing a safety feature called a gum strip, which helps bind the belts of the tire to each other. The gum strip prevents tread separation, which can cause a tire to blow, possibly making a driver lose control of the vehicle and crash.

The Chinese-made tires were sold under at least four brand names: Westlake, Compass, Telluride and YKS. The tires, which were sold for use on vans, sport utility vehicles and pickups, had been linked to at least two deaths in accidents involving tread separation. Since the Chinese manufacturer does not have an office in the United States, the importer is responsible for any damages. But Foreign Tire Sales had stated that it does not have enough money to fund a recall. The small, family-owned importer is suing the Chinese manufacturer-the second-largest tire maker in China-saying that it should pay for the recall.

Foreign Tire Sales would have to pay for advertisements announcing the recall, hundreds of thousands of replacement tires, and the environmentally safe recycling of all recalled tires. The recall could cost as much as $60 million.

Pet Food.

Wheat gluten imported from China was linked to the deaths of pets nationwide earlier in 2007. The FDA blocked the import of wheat gluten from Xuzhou Anying Biologic Technology Development Company in China, saying it suspected the gluten was contaminated with melamine, a chemical used to make plastic products.

The tainted food caused kidney failure in dogs and cats across North America. Distributors of the contaminated food recalled several varieties, following the deaths. Menu Foods of Canada recalled nearly 95 brands of "Cuts and Gravy" pet food. Other companies including Nestle Purina Pet Care, Del Monte Pet Products and Hill's Pet Nutrition also recalled some varieties of their food products in the United States. Many pet owners resorted to cooking homemade meals for their pets because of uncertainty surrounding which products were contaminated.

More Unsafe Imports From China – Where's Our Import Control?

On August 1ˢᵗ, 2007 the *Lamplighter News Edition* reported another Chinese import scandal, this one involving "967,000 plastic preschool toys made by a Chinese vendor and sold in the United States between May and August 2007 that contained excessive lead in the paint."

If this were the first, or second or maybe even the third large scale problem with Chinese imports then we would just chalk it up to normal problems. However, just in 2007 alone we had heard of potentially dangerous imports from China on a massive scale including shipments of food, cosmetics, pet food, drugs, toothpaste, ceramic heaters, and toys.

In April 2007 alone, 1,000 shipments of tainted Chinese dietary supplements, toxic cosmetics and counterfeit medicine were intercepted. That is a huge number considering that only 1 percent of Chinese imports are inspected. Remember, these are only the ones that we have heard about… how many more shipments of dangerous, or potentially dangerous items from China were in the 99 percent of imports that are not checked and have gotten into the U.S.? Simply put, China has a systematic problem with ignoring our laws and exporting dangerous food and other goods to the U.S. Our government has a systematic problem with ensuring that the food and other goods that are imported into this country are safe. It is time for Congress to forget partisan politics and put effective measures in place that will ensure imports meet U. S. Standards. Until that time, I for one am going to avoid Chinese products.

By the way, the discovery that 967,000 toys for pre-school aged children had excessive amounts of lead in them was detected by Mattel-the company that imported the toys-not the government. Another major blunder by the feds one might say! The lack of border control includes lack of import control as well.

Next, we look at another new threat from China: Shoddy Steel Imports

As reported in the *Kiplinger Business Resource Center* in September of 2007, steel imports from China that fall apart easily are making U.S. manufacturers and constructions firms more than a little nervous. Reports of failures during initial fabrication and questions about certification documents have meant closer scrutiny now and in the future. The American and Canadian institutes of steel construction have already advised member companies to be vigilant and report any problems.

The biggest concern is hollow structural sections widely used in construction of skyscrapers, bridges, pipelines, office, commercial and school buildings. This high-strength steel is also commonly used in power lifts, cranes, farm equipment, furniture and car-trailer hitches.

Chinese high-strength steel tubes and pipes are also a potential problem. They're used extensively in power plants and in large industrial boilers, and must withstand enormous pressures and hellish heat around the clock for weeks or months on end. This kind of steel also is used extensively in scaffolding that's erected on building exteriors during construction or renovation, as well as for interior work.

Inferior high-strength steel could cause catastrophic failures of buildings, pipelines, or in power plants' boiler tubing. This is a large worry for structural engineers who will be working overtime as states embark on what amounts to a crash program to shore up bridges, following the collapse of the Minnesota span over the Mississippi River. China is already seeing problems. A Chinese power plant exploded recently when high-strength steel tubing blew out, said Roger Schagrin, general counsel for the Committee on Pipe and Tube Imports, which represents U.S. manufacturers of these products.

Dan Malone, construction manager for Garneau Manufacturing, based in Morinville, Alberta, Canada, an energy service company that works with many imports, said that tests on a lot of 80 tons of Chinese steel tube products found "the welds failed horribly." Malone said there was no question that if the steel had been fabricated into a finished product and installed, it would have failed and "would have killed somebody."

It's possible that existing buildings or bridges are in imminent danger of collapse. U.S. metals fabricators periodically test imported steels to assure they meet specs for strength, hardiness and durability. Construction firms generally do likewise. It is also possible that some of the substandard Chinese high-strength steel did slip through, so we should expect construction companies to recheck with their suppliers to determine whether any of the steel they used was purchased from Chinese mills. If so, U.S. contractors, building owners and power plant operators will bring in structural engineers to test the steel. If any structurally deficient steel is found, companies will shore up pillars, girders and trusses or replace boiler pipes entirely.

Imports of specialized structural pipe and tubing steel from China are soaring, up from almost nothing in 2005 to 102,000 metric tons in the first six months of 2007, according to American Iron and Steel Institute data. China now provides about 25% of U.S. supplies of this high-strength steel, making it the second largest source behind Canada. U.S. steel mills supply about 16%.

U.S. and Canadian manufacturers and steel wholesaler service centers started testing hollow structural steel and other high-strength Chinese steel in the beginning of 2007 when suspicions arose over mass-produced documents certifying that the tubular products met strength standards of the ASTM International, a private group that sets standards for industrial and consumer goods. This reflected on the nature of Chinese companies hell-bent on jumping on the country's industrial boom bandwagon. "Most of China's 800-plus steelmakers are small fabricators that have no idea what quality is all about, so there is risk that some guy with a welding torch buys some hot-rolled coil steel and just welds it together," said Charles Bradford, president of Bradford Research, a metals consulting firm.

Imports of high-strength steel products from China are likely to plummet as result of concerns. This will benefit Canadian suppliers and some U.S. Steel specialty firms such as Atlas Tube, Columbia Structural Tubing, Ex-L-Tube, Ipsco, Longhorn Tube, Novamerican Steel and others.

Still more tainted imports hit the American shores: Meat, Fish, Toys, Flip-Flops, Clothing, Pet Products, Peanut Butter, Drywall and Spiked Diet Pills,

Meat and all types of beef.

On December 6, 2007 The *New York Times* reported that meat processors were looking for ways to keep ground beef safe. In the last decade, Tyson Fresh Meats had transformed its slaughterhouse in Lexington, Nebraska to combat a potentially deadly type of food poisoning, adding huge chambers to scald carcasses and wash them in acid, steam vacuums to suck away microbes and elaborate gear to test hundreds of meat samples a day. In all, the beef industry says it spends upward of $350 million a year to keep harmful pathogens out of the meat it sells to the public. But even as expenditures keep rising, the industry appears to be losing ground.

In November, 2007 the Agricultural Department announced its 20th recall of beef in one year because of contamination with a toxic strain of the bacterium E. coli. That was only one recall shy of a record set in 2000 and matched in 2002. No one knew for sure what was causing the jump in recalls, though theories abound, from the cyclical nature of pathogens to changes in cattle-feeding practices caused by the popularity of ethanol.

This much is clear: Fifteen years after an outbreak at Jack in the Box restaurants made people aware that hamburgers could kill them, the American beef industry is still searching for a practical method to prevent the toxic E. coli strain from contaminating ground beef.

"If you gave me a million, zillion dollars and said give me a plant that doesn't have E. coli, I couldn't do it," said Michael T. Osterholm, director of the Center for Infectious Disease Research and Policy at the University of Minnesota. "It's not about the will. It's about the ability."

What makes all of the spate of recalls of 2007 so surprising is that it comes after several years in which the number of recalls dropped sharply, to eight in 2006 and five in 2005. And it includes not just small and midsize firms with less rigorous food-safety protocols-like Topps Meat of New Jersey, which recalled 21.7 million pounds of frozen hamburger because of potential E. coli contamination-but also large companies that have spent tens of millions of dollars to prevent E. coli contamination. Topps closed its doors and had declared bankruptcy on October 5 of 2007,

Tyson Fresh Meats, for one, had had two relatively minor recalls in 2007; there were no reported illnesses. Cargill Meat Solutions, which has won plaudits for its efforts to combat E. coli, has had two recalls, including one in October, 2007 affecting about 845,000 pounds of ground beef that had made more than a dozen people sick.

The Agriculture Department issued new guidelines in October of 2007 urging the meat industry to adopt the latest technology to combat harmful forms of E. coli-essentially the measures that Tyson already had in place. But department officials acknowledge that short of irradiating the meat, there is no magic bullet to prevent E. coli contamination.

"The big challenge for them is you are dealing with people and biological systems," said Kenneth E. Paterson, assistant administer for field operations for the Agriculture Department's Food Safety and Inspection Service, "To execute the program consistently every hour of every day they operate, that's the challenge. They do a pretty good job at it. You can't take your eye off the ball for any period of time or you get into trouble."

The federal government said that it believes that exposing meat to radiation is a safe and effective way to kill E. coli and other pathogens. But meat companies have been hesitant to use irradiation because of fears that it would make meat more expensive, change the taste and color, and provoke consumer opposition.

Escherichia coli bacteria are commonly found in the lower digestive tract of humans and animals, and they are usually harmless. But one strain, E. coli 0157:H7, produces a toxin that can make people sick, typically after eating ground beef or produce that has been contaminated by cattle feces.

It is difficult to say whether the amount of E. coli in ground beef has increased in 2007 over 2006, or shall increase even more so in 2008, since the number of recalls is an imperfect measure. Limited sampling by the Agriculture Department has found a slight increase in the level of E. coli 0157:H7 in 2007 over recent years, though it remains lower than it was five or six years ago.

But some meat industry officials say that they are sure that more E. coli is turning up in cattle than in previous years. That impression is shared by William Marler, a lawyer in Seattle who specializes in food-borne illness and who has seen a marked increase in clients who say they became sick from eating E. coli-contaminated meat.

"This is real stuff," he said. "It is a fundamentally different year than in the past five years and growing."

As part of its efforts to eradicate E. coli, the meat industry is experimenting with vaccines, antibiotics and feed additives that may reduce the level of E. coli 0157:H7 in cattle intestines. But so far, those are not commercially available. To date, nearly all of the efforts to curb E. coli have focused on interventions at slaughterhouses and at grinding plants that produce ground beef.

Hamburger meat poses an elevated risk of illness because grinding can mix live E. coli bacteria throughout the meat, and consumers often undercook their hamburgers. Steaks pose less of a risk because any E. coli on the surface are likely to be killed during cooking.

Mohammad Koohmaraie, director of the Agriculture Department's U.S. Meat Animal Research Center in Nebraska, said his research had determined that most E. coli contamination came from the hides of cattle, which became matted with mud and manure in feed lots. As a result, his research had focused on ways to reduce the likelihood that manure from the hides comes in contact with a carcass during slaughter and subsequent handling.

"If you don't do a good job of removing the hide, a whole bunch of it gets on the carcass," Mr. Koohmaraie said, "If you do a good job, just a little bit to none gets on the carcass,"

His research, for instance, found that spraying the hides of cattle with a chemical wash immediately after they are killed drastically reduces the incidence of E. coli 0157:H7. JBS Swift & Company and Cargill are now using hide-washing procedures, which can cost several million dollars to install.

Dean A. Danilson, Tyson's vice president for food safety and quality assurance, said that his company might install hide-washing equipment as it built new plants or retrofitted old ones. In the meantime, in the rear of the Lexington plant, a former combine factory converted to a slaughterhouse, an employee in rain gear hoses down cattle in a pen before they are slaughtered to rinse away manure and limit the amount of dust when the hide is removed.

"Keeping the dust down, knocking some of the cake-on mud and things off, any little bit helps," Mr. Danilson said.

It is the first of many steps that Tyson employs to reduce the chances that pathogens like E. coli survive processing. Once the animal is killed, the hide is removed, first by knives and then by machines, in a manner intended to keep it away from the exposed carcass, starting near the anus and hind legs.

After each cut is made to remove the hide, a worker follows behind with a steam vacuum to kill and suck away microbes. The carcass, pulled along on an overhead rail, is then sent into a cabinet with pivoting nozzles that soak it with water at about 185 degrees.

After the head is removed and before the animal is gutted, the carcass is sprayed with a mild acid wash, again to reduce the level of microbes. Besides removing the hide, one of the most critical steps to prevent E. coli 0157:H7 comes when the animal is eviscerated and its internal organs are removed.

The workers who remove the organs are careful not to cut the bowel, which could spread manure, and a worker looks over the internal organs to make sure the intestines are intact. The carcasses are then sawed in half, and the cut line is steam vacuumed.

In one of the most important interventions, the split carcasses are sent into a 30-foot-long, hissing stainless steel cabinet, where rows of nozzles spray them with steam for at least 13 seconds before they enter a second chamber that douses them with a disinfectant for at least 15 seconds.

The last step comes after the carcasses have been cut into steaks and roasts and leftover scraps, with the latter tossed into 2,000-pound bins for grinding into hamburger meat. Workers are assigned to cut at least 60 four-inch by one-half-inch strips from each lot of trimmings; a lot if five 2,000-pound bins.

Those samples are then ferried to a laboratory, where they are mixed with solution that encourages E. coli 0157:H7 to grow. After incubating for eight hours, the samples are tested, and if positive for the germ, that lot is diverted from being used as ground beef. Instead, it is used in cooked products or otherwise processed to kill the microbes.

"I wish I had a silver bullet. We have done a lot, and it's a continuing ongoing process to look for more," Mr. Danilson said. But he acknowledged that it was impossible to create a perfect system for stopping E. coli 0157:H7. "Taking a dirty animal and turning it into food-from the time of the cave men, that has not been an easy process."

Switching back to offshore methods of how they handle their food factories, the New York Times on December 12, 2007 reported that China agreed to post U.S. safety officials in its food factories. In Xianghe, China, both China and the United States, seeking to ease the furor over the safety of food exports, signed an agreement calling for a greater American role in certifying and inspecting Chinese food products, including an increased presence of American officials at Chinese production plants.

The agreement came as Chinese and American representatives exchanged tough words over recent trade and economic disputes in Beijing on Tuesday of that week, and later on Wednesday at the opening of high-level talks in this suburb of the capital.

The safety accord, part of the several aimed at easing economic tensions with China on a number of divisive subjects, would impose new registration of inspection requirements by Chinese food exporters for 10 specific products, with the United States government maintaining a public list of the exporters' records.

Michael O. Leavitt, secretary of health and human services, said he expected that Food and Drug Administration officials would eventually be embedded in China's food safety bureaucracy to help train Chinese officials and keep records on their inspections.

"The Chinese recognize, as do we, that having F.D.A. personnel here would expedite the process of capacity building and increase cooperation and communication," Mr. Leavitt said. "I am optimistic that it will occur."

American officials said that the agreement did not cover all the food products sought for tighter inspections, but that it could be expanded. It is to cover some preserved foods, pet food ingredients and farm-raised fish, all products that the United States has said were tainted.

Andrew C. von Eschenbach, F.D.A. commissioner, said that agency officials were already allowed to inspect Chinese facilities under limited conditions, but that the agreement that was signed would expand that role and possibly set a model for similar agreements in other parts of the world.

"This agreement will provide an opportunity to have our people here on a continuous basis with expertise so that we can work with our Chinese colleagues in helping to develop good practices," Dr. von Eschenbach said.

Despite the accords, the economic talks in Beijing and at the Grand Epoch conference in Xianghe were filled with tough talk, including angry complaints by China over the Bush administration's challenge to Chinese practices before the World Trade Organization and its imposition of duties on Chinese goods.

Opening the "strategic economic dialogue" during that conference in the latter part of 2007, Vice Premier Wu Yi warned the American delegation not to engage in "confrontation and finger pointing" or in "politicizing trade issues," and suggested that American leaders were blaming China for their country's own economic shortcomings.

In his opening comments, Treasury Secretary Henry M. Paulson Jr. declared that "economic nationalism and protectionist sentiments" were rising in China as well as in the United States. If China is unhappy with anti-Chinese sentiment in Congress, he said, it must respond by doing more to open its own economy to American investments and goods.

According to American officials, the piracy of videos, music and other intellectual property was a source of heated discussion behind the scenes between Susan C. Schwab, the top American trade envoy, and Ms. Wu.

At the opening of the talks, Ms. Wu defended China's record of fighting piracy and counterfeiting and suggested that the United States' action at the W.T.O. was unfriendly. She also charged that the American news media had "hyped" the issue of food safety, "causing serious damage to China's national image."

After reporters were ushered out, Ms. Schwab was reported by American officials to have said that despite American concerns, the Bush administration would continue to go to the W.T.O. to get satisfaction and "we will win" in that forum.

The exchange over the issue was so heated that the meeting concluded more than an hour late, American officials said. The food and feed accord that was signed during that week was the centerpiece of a flurry of 14 separate agreements worked on over the last several months and completed in the last couple of days of that conference. Most of them came under the heading of a joint commission on trade and economic issues that met most of the day at China's official guest house.

Most of these agreements involved familiar commitments by the Chinese to take stronger action against piracy and counterfeiting of trademarks and of software, movies and other intellectual property. The deals are also meant to ease some restrictions in Chinese regulations that have made it difficult for American companies to export to China. Carlos M. Gutierrez, the Commerce secretary, hailed the accords as helpful in improving the atmosphere leading up to the bigger set of meetings set up for the days that followed.

In addition to agreements to impose registration and certification requirements on imported Chinese drugs, medical devices and active ingredients in pharmaceuticals, there were accords on promoting American tourism for Chinese, on joint development of biofuels and on expanding science and technology exchanges.

Mr. Gutierrez said that China agreed not to impose, at least for now, an inspection requirement on imported medical devices like heart monitors, stents and surgical implants, which had been the focus of complaints by big producers like Medtronic, Johnson & Johnson and Boston Scientific. That restriction was to be directed at imported medical devices, not ones made in China, which American officials saw as evidence that China was beginning a new policy of "economic nationalism" aimed at discouraging American investments and imports in favor of its own industries.

American officials have recently stepped up complaints that China was using sophisticated regulations to make it more difficult for American products and investments to enter its markets. The complaints had focused on financial services, cell phones, motorcycles and other goods. After Ms. Wu spoke, Mr. Gutierrez repeated concerns about "economic nationalism" just as reporters were ushered out. At a news conference the next morning, he said that he was somewhat reassured by what he had heard.

"I felt that the assurance was quite strong," he said. But other American officials said they were not so sure.

The biggest breakthrough was accomplished not by the administration's economic team of Ms. Schwab, Mr. Gutierrez and Mr. Paulson, but by Mr. Leavitt on the food safety issue. American officials said that this was an essential agreement to defuse American anxieties. But Mr. Leavitt acknowledged that much remained to be done to put it into effect.

Fish.
One of the major complaints was the farming of fish in toxic waters in China. The *New York Times* reported on December 15th that in Fuqing, China, beneath the looming mountains of Fujian Province, lie dozens of enormous ponds filled with murky brown water and teeming with eels, shrimp and tilapia, much of it destined for markets in Japan and the West.

Fuqing is one of the centers of a booming industry that over two decades has transformed this country into the biggest producer and exporter of seafood in the world, and the fastest-growing supplier to the United States. But that growth is threatened by the two most glaring environmental weaknesses in China: acute water shortages and water supplies contaminated by sewage, industrial waste and agricultural runoff that includes pesticides. The fish farms, in turn, are discharging wastewater that further pollutes the water supply.

"Our waters here are filthy," said Ye Chao, an eel and shrimp farmer who has 20 giant ponds in western Fuqing. "There are simply too many aquaculture farms in this area. They're all discharging water here, fouling up other farms."

Farmers have coped with the toxic waters by mixing illegal veterinary drugs and pesticides into fish feed, which helps keep their stock alive yet leaves poisonous and carcinogenic residues in seafood, posing health threats to consumers. Environmental degradation, in other words, has become a food safety problem, and scientists say the long-term risks of consuming contaminated seafood could lead to higher rates of cancer and liver disease and other afflictions.

No one is more vulnerable to these health risks than the Chinese, because most of the seafood in China stays at home. But foreign importers are also worried. In recent years, the European Union and Japan have imposed temporary bans on Chinese seafood because of illegal drug residues. The United States blocked imports of several types of fish in 2007 after inspectors detected traces of illegal drugs linked to cancer.

Officials from the United States and China signed an agreement in Beijing to improve oversight of Chinese fish farms as part of a larger deal on food and drug safety. Yet regulators in both countries are struggling to keep contaminated seafood out of the market. China has shut down seafood companies accused of violating the law and blacklisted others, while the United States regulators have been concentrating on Chinese seafood for special inspections. Fuqing (pronounced foo-CHING) had been at the top of the list in 2007 for refused shipments of seafood from China, with 43 rejections though November, 2007 according to records kept by the United States Food and Drug Administration. All of those rejections involved the use of illegal veterinary drugs. By comparison, Thailand, also a major exporter of seafood to the United States, had only two refusals up to that time, related to illegal veterinary drugs. China as a whole had 210 refusals for illegal drugs, just through November of 2007.

"For 50 years," said Wang Wu, a professor at Shanghai Fisheries University, "we've blindly emphasized economic growth. The only pursuit has been G.D.P., and now we can see that the water turns dirty and the seafood gets dangerous. Every year, there are food safety and environmental pollution accidents."

Environmental problems plaguing seafood would appear to be a bad omen for the industry. But with fish stocks in the oceans steadily declining and global demand for seafood soaring, farmed seafood, or aquaculture, is the future. And no country does more of it than China, which produced about 115 billion pounds of seafood in 2007.

China produces about 70 percent of the farmed fish in the world, harvested at thousands of giant factory-style farms that extend along the entire eastern seaboard of the country. Farmers mass-produce seafood just offshore, but mostly on land, and in lakes, ponds, rivers and reservoirs, or in huge rectangular fish ponds dug into the earth.

"They'll be a major supplier not just to the U.S., but to the world," said Richard Stavis, the chairman of Stavis Seafoods, an American company that imports Chinese catfish, tilapia and frog legs.

China began emerging as a seafood power in the 1990s as rapid economic growth became the top priority in the country. But environmental experts say that headlong pursuit of higher gross domestic product has devastated Chinese water quality and endangered the country's food supply. In Guangdong Province in southern China, fish contaminated with toxic chemicals like DDT are already creating health problems.

"There are heavy metals, mercury and flame retardants in fish samples we've tested," said Ming Hung Wong, a professor of biology at Hong Kong Baptist University. "We've got to stop the pollutants entering the food system."

More than half of the rivers in China are too polluted to serve as a source of drinking water. The biggest lakes in the country regularly succumb to harmful algal blooms. Seafood producers are part of the problem, environmental experts say. Enormous aquaculture farms concentrate fish waste, pesticides and veterinary drugs in their ponds and discharge the contaminated water into rivers, streams and coastal areas, often with no treatment.

"Water is the biggest problem in China," said Peter Leedham, the business manager at Sino Analytica, an independent food safety testing firm that works with companies that buy from China. "But my feeling is China will deal with it, because it has to. It just won't be a quick process."

Fuqing is called qiaoxing, or home, for those who go overseas, because for decades this port city on the East China Sea is where thousands of people fled as stowaways.

In the 1980s, some emigrants began sending home money and ideas at just about the time that investors were arriving from Japan and Taiwan, promising to help the country build fish farms.

"Aquaculture was popular in Japan, so I saw the future," said Wang Weifu, a longtime eel producer.

Thousands of peasants who had struggled to earn a living harvesting rice and potatoes began carving up huge plots, digging rectangular pits and filling them with water to create fish ponds. Other parts of the country followed, creating fish farms alongside roads, near rivers and streams and in big lakes, ponds and reservoirs.

Today, the mighty Yangtze River is lined with fish farms. Historic Lake Tai is stocked with crab pens. Near Ningde, 90 miles north of here, thousands of people live in a huge bay area, where they float on large wooden rafts, feeding and harvesting caged fish, like the yellow croaker. The government hoped the building boom would life millions out of poverty. And it did. There are now more than 4.5 million fish farmers in China, according to the Fishery Bureau.

Lin Bingui, 50, is one of them, a former bricklayer with an easy smile who now manages 20 enormous shrimp and eel ponds in western Fuqing, on reclaimed land with access to a narrow strait of seawater.

"This doesn't take a lot of technology," he said while walking into an outdoor pond, where he raises baby eels. "You just learn it as you go along."

The boom did more than create jobs. It made China the only country that produced more seafood from fish farms than from the sea. It also helped feed an increasingly prosperous population, a longstanding challenge in China. Many growers here struck it rich as well, people like Lin Sunbao, whose 25-year-old son is now studying at Cambridge University in England. "My best years were 1992, '93, '94," he said. "I only had one aqua farm, and I earned over $500,000 a year."

As early as the mid-1990s, though, serious environmental problems began to emerge after electronics and textile manufacturing plants moved into central Fuqing. Water shortages appeared in the southeastern part of the city, and some fish farmers said that their water turned black. Government records document the environmental ills in the region. The nearby Dongxiang Reservoir, a water source for agriculture and more than 700,000 people, was recently rated level 5, near the bottom of the government scale, unfit for fish farming, swimming or even contact with the human body.

The Long River, the major waterway in Fuqing, has been degraded by waste dumped by paper factories and slaughterhouses. The government, in 2007 had rated large sections of the river below level 5, or so highly polluted that it is unfit for any use. And nearby coastal waters which are also heavily fish farmed are polluted with oil, lead, mercury and copper, according to the State Environmental Protection Administration in China. As water quality in Fuqing declined, farmers who often filled their ponds with too much seafood tried to fight off disease and calm stressed fish with an array of powerful, and often illegal, antibiotics and pesticides.

Eel producers, for example, often used nitrofuran to kill bacteria. But that antibiotic has been banned for use in animal husbandry in the United

States, Europe, Japan, and even China, because it caused cancer in laboratory rats.

Importers of Chinese seafood quickly caught on. In recent years, eel shipments to Europe, Japan and the United States have been turned back or destroyed because of residues of banned veterinary drugs. Eel shipments to Japan have dropped 50 percent through August of 2007, dealing a heavy blow in Fuqing. And the future of these farms only seems to be getting worse. Chinese farmers say they have stopped using the banned medicines, and have suffered a 30 percent decline in survival rates of their fish and other seafood.

"Before 2005, we did use drugs blindly. They were very effective in fighting disease," said Wang Weifu, chairman of a local eel association, noting that drug residues might still be in the water. "But now we don't dare because of the regulations."

Some growers have lashed out at Japan, arguing that it keeps raising the drug residue standard simply to protect its own eel farms against competition. But growers here say buyers from Japan will eventually be forced to purchase eels from China.

"Our market will expand in Russia and Southeast Asia, and the E.U.," Mr. Wang said. "Also, we see big prospects in the Chinese market. In five or six years, as we transfer our export destinations, Japan will be begging us."

The drive about 175 miles west of Fuqing leads into the lush subtropical mountains of Fujian Province, where some of China's richest bamboo and timber reserves can be found. There, near the city of Sanming, Fuqing eel producers have built a collection of aquaculture farms, huge cement tubs wedged into the mountainside, covered by black tarps and stocked with millions of eels.

"This costs a lot more up here, but we had to do it," said Zheng Qiuzhen, a longtime Fuqing eel producer who now operates near Sanming. "We had to do something about the water problems."

In much of the country, seafood growers are leaving crowded coastal areas for less developed regions, where the land is cheaper and there is cleaner water. But they say the overall cost of doing business so far from the coast is higher, given the expense of shipping the fish in oxygenated trucks to the processing plant in Fuqing and their forswearing illegal drugs, which lowers survival rates and increases the growth period of most fish to five years from three years.

"You can't find many places as beautiful as this, covered by trees and bamboo," said Lin Sunbao, who moved from Fuqing to Sanming. "We use water from mountain streams. And because our water is better, it's harder to get disease."

This is one of the solutions to the water crisis in China: to seek out virgin territory and essentially start the cycle all over again. And that worries scientists, who say that aquaculture in China is not just a victim of water pollution but a culprit with a severe environmental legacy.

Industrial fish farming has destroyed mangrove forests in Thailand, Vietnam and China, heavily polluted waterways and radically altered the ecological balance of coastal areas, mostly through the discharge of wastewater. Aquaculture waste contains fish feces, rotting fish feed and residues of pesticides and veterinary drugs as well as other pollutants that were already mixed into the poor quality water supplied to farmers. Besides algal blooms, some of the biggest lakes in China, like Lake Tai, are suffering from eutrophication nutrient bombs, brought on partly by aquaculture, that can kill fish by depleting the water's oxygen. The government is forcing aquaculture out of these lakes, and also away from the Long River in Fuqing.

Places like Sanming may not be pristine for long. Heavy industry is moving in, lured by mineral riches and incentives from local governments, which are pushing for development. And Sanming already has 72 giant eel farms, producing 5,000 tons of seafood a year. Those farms together use about 280 million gallons of water a day and then discharge the wastewater the following day, back into the Sanming environs.

There are efforts to operate aquaculture in a sustainable way. In Norway, for instance, salmon producers use sophisticated technology, including underwater cameras, to monitor water quality and how much fish food is actually consumed. But nothing like this is being done in China, and specialists like Li Sifa of Shanghai Fisheries University insist that Chinese regulations are too lax and that enforcement efforts are often feeble or nonexistent.

The government has stepped up its inspections of fish farms and seafood processing plants here, alerting workers of the dangers and consequences of using illegal drugs. But the drugs have remained a problem, partly because of poor water quality. A possible solution to the water woes is to move aquaculture well out to sea, specialists, say, with new technology that allows for deepwater fish cages served by automatic feeding machines.

The United States is already considering such a plan, partly as a way to make it less dependent on imports, which now fill 80 percent of its seafood needs. China is also considering adopting what is now being called "open ocean" aquaculture.

Currently, China's coastal fish farms face many of the same challenges as those on land. Waters there are heavily polluted by oil, lead, mercury, copper and other harsh substances. Veterinary drugs dropped in shoreline waters may easily spread to neighboring aquaculture farms and affect species outside the cages, and while coastal waters are less polluted than those on land, aquaculture farms, with their intensive production cycles, are prone to polluters.

Still, said An Taicheng of the Chinese Academy of Sciences: "China has to go to the sea because it's getting harder and harder to find clean water. Every year there are seafood safety problems. One day, no one will dare to eat fish from dirty water, and what will farmers do?"

In mid-December, 2007 it was reported in the New York Times, that during the three days of talks in Beijing on economic issues, a half-dozen Bush administration cabinet members and their aides sat in rows of tables facing their Chinese counterparts in an ornate conference room. The talk was polite, the atmosphere convivial and the pledges of cooperation profuse.

But it was also obvious to the American side that relations with China were going through a difficult phase, with discord sometimes crowding out the areas of agreement. The Chinese frequently threatened retaliation over actions that displeased them, in the political and military spheres as well as in the economic.

Now, however, even the industry had recognized that everybody needs a Food and Drug Administration that really works. Food industry lobbyists and the most fervent public health advocates-normally bitter rivals-have joined forces in Washington to help push the White House and Congress to grant more power and funds for the F.D.A. The consumer-industry coalition wants food-related spending to increase more than $100 million over 2008's budget.

Michael Leavitt, secretary of the Department of Health Services, which includes the F.D.A., told a Senate committee recently that he had asked the White House to go for "substantial additional resources" in the 2009 budget. It is not known whether the White House will back those "substantial" increases for the F.D.A.

What extra funds the agency squeezes out of this year's budget should be spent as soon as possible on inspectors and up-to-date computer technology. The agency still uses handwritten reports of food problems, and the data collection system runs at horse-and-buggy speed.

As for imports, everyone recognized that the government cannot inspect every crate of raspberries that comes into the country. What makes sense is to find a workable way to refuse goods from the worst actors. As part of such a system, the F.D.A. needs more inspectors at the nation's ports and more laboratories certified by international standards. It seems the least President Bush could have done to protect the nation's food supply.

Wondering what happened to all of the lead-tainted products that have been recalled recently?

One company that recalled 350,000 lead-tainted journals and bookmarks-that's correct...*lead-tainted journals and bookmarks*-plans to burn them in an incinerator. In the meantime, it is storing the hazardous parts in 55-gallon drums near its headquarters.

Toys.

Toy makers are investigating whether they need to treat their tainted products with stabilization chemicals or if they must seal the toys in giant polyethylene bags. Mattel has decided to recycle some of its recalled toys into items like park benches-after it fights pending litigation. In China, meanwhile, several of Mattel's recalled toys can still be found on store shelves. A few toys have even shown up on eBay and on Web sites that sell products in bulk. And some children's jewelry, heavy laden with lead, may be legally shipped to other countries for resale. But that's only counting what is actually returned. Most of the unsafe toys and other products, it turns out, may still be in the hands of consumers.

"The first step is to recall the product," said Rachel Weintraub, director of product safety at the Consumer Federation of American. "The second step is the manufacturer and how it gets some of the product back. And the third step is: what happens next?"

American companies face strict federal regulations for the disposing of recalled toys, but they are only responsible for the toys that show up. The other products left out there-and in many cases, that is more than 80 percent-fall out of their purview, a crack in the recall system that consumer advocates say leaves a giant question mark over the trail of recalled toys.

Consumers are never told precisely how many products are returned, whether some are shipped abroad to be resold, or even which factory supplied the toys and whether companies are continuing to use that factory. Executives at companies involved in recent recalls answered questions about their returned toys, but they were not eager to discuss the whereabouts of the toys that have not come back.

"If they're out of their control but they don't know where they are, I don't think the companies care," said Pamela Gilbert, a partner at the law firm of Cuneo Gilbert & LaDuca, and the former executive director of the Consumer Product Safety Commission.

Mattel and RC2, the maker of Thomas & Friends toys, are both holding onto the returned toys while they fight off lawsuits accusing them of harming children with those products. After the cases are resolved, Mattel said that it would recycle parts, like pieces of the Polly Pocket magnetic toys, safely into items like park benches. Companies like Jo-Ann Stores, Tween Brands, and

Toys "R" Us said that they are holding the returned toys in warehouses until they come up with a disposal plan.

"It's not like it's a real threat, just sitting in our warehouse," said Robert Atkinson, a spokesman for Tween Brands. "It's not going to leach into the soil or anything like that."

The Environmental Protection Agency requires companies to test their returned products for an aggregate level of lead to determine a disposal plan. If the tests come in at higher than 5 parts per million, companies must take extra steps to make sure the lead will not contaminate the environment. If the average is under that level, the toys can go in normal landfills.

Mattel, for example, recently received test results back from Waste Management, which found that Mattel's mass of toys could be sent to regular landfills or recycled, rather than stored in toxic waste sites. With the exception of Rc2, which says it had received 60 percent of its Thomas toys back, most companies have not received many products back.

As of latter part of November, 2007 buyers had returned just over 1,100 of the roughly 100,000 children's gardening tools Jo-Ann Stores sold and recalled in October, 2007. And Kahoot Products, which recalled 1.6 million Cub Scout badges in early October, 2007, said that it had not received any back nearly two months later-though some may be with Cub Scout leaders.

It has long been the case that product recalls generally dismiss results. In the past, recalls have brought back 18 percent of products, on average, but low-prices toys and trinkets are returned at even lower rates-often less than 5 percent. Research firms found that some toys recalled during the summer of 2007 had appeared in the fall on auction Web sites like eBay and other sites that sell products in bulk to businesses, including Made-in-China.com Aubrey Liu, who works in Made-in-China's Web operations department, said in an e-mail message that it was difficult for her department to pick out recalled products on her site because the Consumer Product Safety Commission does not include the names of manufacturers in recall notices.

Instead, the commission lists the importer or United Stated-based company that is distributing the product. The Web site has asked the commission for a list of the Chinese manufacturers behind the recalls, though it has not received it yet, Ms. Liu said. There is no federal law or regulation against reselling recalled toys-a loophole that some legislatures are trying to close. Still, eBay, among others, has agreed to try to keep recalled products off the market.

Companies are also allowed to export products they recalled to resell in other countries, if the recall was based on a voluntary standard. Companies cannot export toys with lead paint, since it is banned on toys in the United States. But they can export lead jewelry and some of the metal trinkets that have been part of recent recalls. Companies must notify the product commission if they want to export such products.

Outside the United States, recalled products will show up in some stores but it is difficult to know how they got there. It was stated in the New York Times that one of its reporters in China bought three Mattel items that were supposed to be recalled from stores in Shanghai and at a Beijing shopping mall. The items-along with one other toy not purchased but on the shelves-all carried labels with product identification numbers that matched those on the recall list. The purchased toys included the Barbie Kitchen Gift Set and the Barbie and Tanner magnetic set.

Store clerks in China seem to be largely unaware of toy recalls and in one instance, a manager at the Shanghai ship, which carries a Fisher-Price label, insisted that the company's warehouse contained many of the recalled items and that they could still be purchased. When the reporter presented questions to Mattel's Shanghai representative about the recalled items, the store manager said the items were not available and repeatedly requested the return of another recalled item that was bought from the store.

A clerk at another store selling Fisher-Price toys said that she would alter the date of manufacture on toys for customers to whatever dates they requested. These products could have been on sale in China before the recall, or they might have come from factories there that did not want to destroy tainted products after the recall.

A spokeswoman for Mattel in the United States said that the toys appeared to be part of the recalls and must have come from a toy store's old inventory. Mattel, she said, was no longer distributing recalled toys anywhere in the world.

Adding to the confusion, some recalled toys are still on shelves in the United States. A Times reporter in Chicago found a Polly Pocket LimoScene toy on the shelves of a Wal-Mart there, but when she tried to buy it, the cash register blocked the purchase. She found the toy still on the shelves in three later visits. Wal-Mart said the cash register is a backup to make sure recalled toys are not sold.

After Mattel recalled toys this fall, retailers shipped all of the affected lines back to the toy maker, Mattel said. Then, Mattel determined which toys were manufactured during the dates covered in the recall and isolated them. Mattel put stickers with new bar codes and product numbers on the other toys and sent them back to stores. Shoppers today can buy Mattel products and peel stickers off them to see the product code of recalled toys. Mattel indicated that the toys with stickers are safe.

Companies are also trying to get their suppliers in China to shoulder some of the recall costs. Toy World Group/Chun Tat Toys, for example, had agreed to pay the costs incurred by Toys "R" Us in the Elite Operations recall in October of 2007. But other American importers say they will come out of the process at a loss.

The Antioch Company in Ohio found the lead problem on parts of its bookmarks and journals when it ordered tests after seeing Mattel's recalls in August of 2007. Tom Rogers, the president of Antioch Publishing, a unit of the company, said that he wondered how many other companies ordered tests, found problems but then hid them rather than issuing a recall. Antioch will be burning the charms and clips on its products that contain excess lead.

"It's a painful process," Mr. Rogers said. "Nobody wants to produce a product that is unsafe. But nobody wants to see their business brought to its knees."

Flip-Flops and Clothing.
Another major catastrophe out of China was called the "Flip-Flop-Flap."

Basically it was Wal-Mart who halted sales of Chinese-made flip-flops after some purchasers reported suffering skin rashes or chemicals. As many products that are coming out of China are being recalled due to unsafe materials to make the products and keep the budget at a low cost, it is the material LEAD that is mixed in the paint for toys as well as what happened when customers bought pairs of flip flops from Wal-Mart that produced CHEMICAL BURNS.

Rest of article at http://www.lamanaphotography.com/walmart2.htm

In June 2007, Kerry Stiles of Ocklawaha, Florida, purchased a pair of "Sand-N-Sun" flip flops at Wal-Mart. Soon after wearing the sandals, (which she donned only a few times), she developed a painful skin rash or chemical burn on her feet that corresponded with the thong portion of her flip-flops. Her experiences with the fearsome footwear were recounted in full on her web page where she chronicled the development of the injury in a series of photographs spanning the period between 22 June and 8 September, 2007.

The flip-flops had been manufactured in China. Others who had bought the same brand of sandals reported experiencing similar problems. In September, 2007, Wal-Mart instructed its stores to stop selling the product until it could conduct its own investigation.

The definitive cause of Stiles' reaction to the flip flops is not known-while there might have been a noxious chemical incorporated into the footwear, the unfortunate woman could also have experienced an unusual allergic reaction to some otherwise innocuous chemical used in the manufacturing process. Nevertheless, Wal-Mart asserted that it received only ten complaints about skin irritation related to these flip flops out of seven million pairs sold.

The company stated in a press release reported on by Dallas station *KDFW* in September, 2007 that "Product safety is a top priority at Wal-Mart and we are taking this report very seriously. Of several million of this product sold, we have had only a few similar claims. Nevertheless, we are removing the product from our shelves for testing and are preventing our registers from selling them."

I would think that if there were a few reports on finding a chemical reaction from these shoes, then the retailer should be apologetic and not say that 'only a few similar claims were made out of several million products sold.' One claim should be enough. Obviously, again, it is only about money and who cares about the welfare of the user?

However, on September 13, 2007 a reporter of Tulsa told of finding a pair of the recalled flip-flops at a Wal-Mart in Broken Arrow, Oklahoma. Said the reporter, "When we went to the check-out, the computer couldn't scan the price, but the cashier, just trying to be helpful, over-rode the machine and sold them to us."

Stiles challenged Wal-Mart's claim of receiving only ten complaints about the brand of flip-flops that injured her, providing accounts and photographs on her web site of hundreds of others similarly harmed. Obviously, like with toys and food products, the retailer hates to give up any products, even poorly made products that are dangerous to the buyer, all because of profit.

Too itemize all of the products made in China that may be harmful to the user, we would probably have to list just about every product made in the world, from Agriculture and food, to apparel and accessories, arts and crafts, auto parts and accessories, bags, cases and boxes, chemicals, computer products, construction and decoration, consumer electronics, electrical and electronics, furniture and furnishing, health and medicine, light industry and daily use, lights and lighting, machinery, metallurgy, mineral and energy, office supplies, security and protection, service, sporting goods and recreation, textile, tools and hardware, toys and transportation to name a few.

To connect with buyers and China suppliers: www.made-in-china.com

Pet Food and Pet Toys.
The latter part of 2007 also found problems for pet owners as well, from toys to food, for dogs and cats to other pets. When Lane Nemeth, who founded Discovery Toys in 1978 and sold the company to Avon two decades later, decided to start a pet products company a few years ago, one of the first things she did was to look for regulations about how to manufacture pet toys safely.

She could not find any.

"It was totally shocking," said Ms. Nemeth, whose company, Petlane, sells items like doggie tiaras and squirrel-shaped chew toys. "I was stunned because I had come from such a highly regulated industry to one that has no regulations."

After the pet food contamination in 2007, which is believed to have caused the deaths of at least 300 dogs and cats, and a spate of children's toy recalls, which highlighted the problem of lead in products from China, the New York Times reported that pet owners started to step forward to ask: "How safe are pet toys?"

"We get e-mails literally every day from people across the country saying, "Hey, we note your product is made in China-is it still safe for my dog or cat?" said Gerry Brostek, chief executive of Penn-Plax Plastics, which manufactures toys under brands like Rruff Stuff and Purr-Pet. In 2006, he said, pet owners rarely inquired about safety.

Although the concerns were different when it comes to pets-if a golden retriever loses a few I.Q. points, will anyone notice?-the inquiries had continued to pour in during the Christmas season of 2007, when people were most likely to buy pet toys. According to the American Pet Products Association, 56% of dog owners and 42 percent of cat owners buy their pets toys or other treats for Christmas, in an industry with $40 billion in annual sales.

Some companies, like PetSmart, do test their products for lead, and some individual dog lovers have taken matters into their own hands (call them the helicopter parents of the pet set), but nobody has stepped forward to report egregious problems.

Is there a risk to pet owners and their children who come into contact with these toys that these dogs have been slobbering on?" asked James R. Hood, who runs a Web site, ConsumerAffairs.com that recently sent dog toys purchased from Wal-Mart to a lab that found trace levels of lead and other toxins. (Wal-Mart responded in a statement that the levels the lab found were "barely traceable" and that its own testing found the toys safe.)

"A lot more lead will come off something when it's wet and it has been partially digested in a pet's mouth," Mr. Hood said. "There should be standards to protect humans first, and we need to find out what level is safe in this application. Somebody needs to look into this issue."

Such initiative is unlikely to come from the Consumer Products Safety Commission, whose lack of resources was an issue during the recent toy recalls. In its 34-year history, the commission has never recalled a pet toy because it was deemed hazardous.

"We do not have jurisdiction over pet toys or pet products," said Scott Wolfson, a commission spokesman. "Our jurisdiction would only come into play if we found that a pet toy or pet product was causing physical harm to the owner."

Lead is dangerous to animals as well as people. According to the Merck/Merial Manual for Pet Health, many species are susceptible to lead poisoning, but it is most common among birds and dogs, who, like children, face higher risks in older homes with lead paint. Symptoms of lead poisoning in dogs include "hysterical barking," vomiting, diarrhea, convulsions and blindness.

And many pet owners do worry about their animal's mental faculties. One product sold by Petlane is described this way: "The Hide-A-Squirrel will not only keep dogs occupied and eliminate boredom, but it also develops a dog's intelligence and puzzle-solving skills."

Nancy Rogers, who has had three dogs that died in the last four years-one from kidney problems, one from liver problems, and one from cancer-said she thinks twice about what she gives her dogs today. Ms. Rogers, 57, a registered nurse from Orland Park, Ill., said she recently checked and found all of her dog toys had "Made in China" labels.

After going to a Petco and searching in vain for toys made elsewhere, Ms. Rogers purchased 24 toys from Petco and PetSmart and had them tested for lead at a lab at the Illinois Department of Agriculture. All were found to fall below the federally regulated children's toy lead-content limit of 600 parts per million. (The American Academy of Pediatrics wants the limit reduced to 40 parts per million.)

"I'm concerned that we don't have any standards, but the levels were well below the lead point limit for children, and I thought that was good," said Ms. Rogers, who paid $192 for the tests.

The lab found the most lead in a PetSmart-brand tennis ball, which had 336 parts per million of lead. Jennifer Ericsson, a PetSmart spokeswoman, said that even before safety concerns were raised, the company happened to be in the process of switching tennis ball manufacturers and had been vigilant after the children's toy recalls.

"There's no cause for concern," Ms. Ericsson said. "We proactively test representative samplings of all our products and have even heightened our testing with all the new reports."

Toys often carry warnings that they should not be left with unsupervised pets and should be discarded at first signs of damage. Dogs tend to "eat first and think later," said Bernadine Cruz, a veterinarian from Laguna Hills, California. "I always tell new pet parents that if you thought it was difficult to childproof your house, it's even more difficult to pet-proof your house because it's more likely your dog will chew on electrical cords and toxic plants."

Parents have nothing on pet owners when it comes to fretting: the term "pet food recall" was searched on the internet more than twice as frequently as "toy recall" during those respective commotions, according to Hitwise, which tracks Web use.

The lack of lead-paint restrictions for pet toys was the subject of television news reports and discussions on pet blogs like Pet Connection, Itchmo and Dogster. Web sites for home lead-testing kits started recommending their products for pet toys.

"When the pet food issue hit, you started getting a little bit of noise, but once the toy recalls kicked in, it really ramped up," said Mr. Brostek of Penn-Plax Plastics.

Robert I. Vetere, president of the Pet Products Manufacturing Association, said that manufacturers were "ramping up on quality control," and reviewing their lists of factories, many of them also makers of children's toys.

The pet industry is unlikely to seek mandatory federal guidelines. "You never invite yourself to be handcuffed and regulated," Mr. Vetere said.

But Ms. Nemeth, the children's industry veteran who now owns Petlane, said she would welcome such oversight. "If lead paint is dangerous for children," she said, "it's more dangerous for animals because they're absolutely going to put it in their mouth."

Peanut Butter Products.

After years of FDA and Congressional Investigations, testimony and posturing...we are not any safer. Basically, the government has failed to improve the safety of products and of our lives. Like MSG, found in Chinese restaurants, there is a slow poisoning of America today!

When Chinese products are mislabeled or deemed poisonous, the end results have caused salmonella, avian flu and kidney problems. Chinese exporters have been smuggling unfit exports illegally into the United States and we were caught sleeping at the wheel.

These cheap products have been mislabeled and tainted. And it's not just Chinese food and drug exports that can kill you. Many of these bargain-priced products can be picked up at Wal-Mart, Target or Sam's Club or any store near you.

Just in the beginning of 2009 alone, a combination of epidemiological analysis and laboratory testing by state officials in Minnesota and Connecticut, the Food and Drug Administration (FDA), and the Centers of Disease Control and Prevention (CDC) had enabled FDA to confirm that the sources of the outbreak of illnesses caused by Salmonella Typhimurium are peanut butter and peanut paste produced by the Peanut Corporation of America (PCA) at its Bakely, Georgia processing plant.

The U.S. Food and Drug Administration reported that peanut butter that is sold by PCA in bulk containers ranging in size from five (5) to 1,700 pounds, are not sold directly to consumers. Neither is the peanut paste that is sold in sizes ranging from 35-pound containers to product sold by the tanker container.

However, through its investigation, FDA had determined that PCA distributed potentially contaminated product to more than 70 consignee firms, for use as an ingredient in hundreds of different products, such as cookies, crackers, cereal, candy and ice cream.

Identification of products subject to recall is continuing and this list is updated frequently and the product recalls now include some pet food products that contain peanut paste that was made by PCA. While the risk of animals contracting salmonellosis is minimal, there is risk to humans from handling these products. It is important for people to wash their hands and to make sure children wash their hands before and, especially, after feeding treats to pets.

An epidemiological investigation by the Minnesota Department of Health isolated and tested sub-samples from an open five-pound container of King Nut peanut butter obtained at a nursing home where three patients were sickened by the outbreak strain of Salmonella Typhimurium. The Minnesota Health officials found the peanut butter contained the same strain of Salmonella Typhimurium associated with the illnesses linked to the outbreak.

Because it is always possible that the open container was contaminated by someone or something else in the environment, the FDA and the states began testing unopened containers of the same brand of peanut butter. King Nut distributes peanut butter manufactured by the PCA to institutional facilities, food service industries, and private label food companies in several states.

The FDA and food manufacturers had been working to identify products that may be affected, and to track the ingredient supply chain of those products to facilitate their removal from the marketplace. Many of the company recalls include such products as Jenny Craig's Jenny's Cuisine Anytime Peanut Butter Flavor Nutritional Bars, Trade Joe's Sliced Green Apples with all Natural Peanut Butter, ShopRite's Peanut Butter on Toasty Crackers and Peanut Butter and Cheese Cracker Snacks; Amway's Global Nutrilite Energy Bars, Kroger's select Ice Cream Product, PetSmart's Grreat Choice Dog Biscuits, Country Maid's nationwide Classic Breaks Peanut Butter Cookie Dough, Kellogg's Austin and Keebler Branded Peanut Butter Sandwich Crackers and so many more products.

More than 180 peanut butter-containing products produced by a variety of companies may have been made with the ingredients recalled by PCA. The list of currently recalled products can be found on the FDA website: (www. cde.gov/salmonella/typhimurium/)

For the recalls of brownie products, cake products, candy products, cookie products, cracker products, fruit and vegetable products, ice cream products, peanut butter products, peanut paste products, pet food products, pet food peanut paste products, pre-packaged meals products, snack bar products, snack mix products, and all recalled peanut butter products, you can go to the following website: www.accessdata.fda.gov/scripts/peanutbutterrecall/index.cfm.

The conditions at the PCA Blakely plant, more circa 1955 than 2009, would have been enough to cause alarm in an industry where sanitation can be a matter of life and death, food experts had stated. But they were only one element in the salmonella outbreak and subsequent food safety train wreck that started here and swept through the country...claiming eight lives, sickening an estimated 19,000 people in 43 states and spurring an array of recalls, including TV dinners, snack bars and labeled organic and ready-made meals for disaster relief.

An examination of the Blakely case reveals a badly frayed food safety net. Interviews and government records show that state and federal inspectors do not require the peanut industry to inform the public...or even the government...of salmonella contamination in its plants. And industry giants like Kellogg used processed peanuts in a variety of products but relied on the factory to perform safety testing and divulge any problems. The government finally demanded the records and verified a whistleblower's claims, after hundreds of people were sickened by salmonella-tainted peanut butter produced at the plant in 2007.

The Peanut Corporation of America, a family-run business based in Lynchburg, VA., now under criminal investigation, declined to discuss events leading to the outbreak, saying in a statement: "We are sorry our process fell short of not only our goals, but more importantly, your expectations."

Kellogg said it was looking for ways to improve its procedures for buying ingredients. ConAgra, which makes Peter Pan peanut butter, which acknowledged its past mistakes as well, shut its plant down for months, studied the problem and spent $33 million to eliminate water leaks, air flows that might carry contaminates, and numerous other threats. Employees now have 80 rules to follow before beginning work, starting with uniforms that they can't take home.

Drywall Problems.
At least 550 pounds of Chinese drywall had come into the United States since 2006 so stated Aaron Kessler of the Herald Tribune of February 1, 2009 in his report on drywall problems. In its hold, the Great Immensity had more than

16 million pounds of Chinese drywall manufactured by Knauf Tianjin... enough to potentially make more than 1,700 homes.

Builders who used the material, like Miami-based Lennar Corporation acknowledged that the gases being emitted from some of the Chinese drywall were the cause of the corrosion eating away at the guts of homes. The gases had blackened metal components such as coils and wiring. Homeowners had reported televisions, computers and other electronics failing, and even silver jewelry turning black.

Many pallets of Chinese drywall had been in a Port Manatee warehouse since 2006. The owner said he believed it was safe and had sold some of it. Lennar, other builders and at least one of the manufacturers pointed to scientific tests they commissioned that showed that the amount of sulfur compounds being emitted was below the amount that federal guidelines say could endanger human health.

Residents, some with small children and some who had moved from their homes, remain unconvinced. Many had told the Herald-Tribune of similar health problems, including chronic respiratory ailments, sinus and eye pain, headaches and nosebleeds. In many of those cases, the symptoms diminished when residents moved out.

Dan Tibbetts, one of the 23 affected homeowners on Montauk Point Crossing in Manatee County's Heritage Harbour neighborhood, said that he had no doubt that he, his wife and even his dog got sick because of the material. Since moving out, their health had begun to improve. "It's still lingering a little bit with my sinuses, but overall, we're dong much better now; the dog is getting back to normal, too." Tibbetts said.

To date, Florida health officials had logged more than 50 complaints. Lennar had confirmed 80 of its homes in Sarasota, Manatee, Lee and Collier counties had the Chinese product and another 40 may have it as well. Two more homes had been identified in Miami-Dade. Taylor Morrison Homes also used Chinese drywall in the Greenbrook neighborhood of Lakewood Ranch and in Crystal Lakes in Palmetto. Given how much of the material came to the U.S. as the tail end of the housing boom, the list could lengthen.

The analysis covered shipments entering the country beginning in January 2006. More Chinese drywall is also believed to have been imported during 2004 and 2005, but full records for those years have not yet been obtained. The shipments were unloaded at more than two dozen ports throughout the United States...seven in Florida...and carried cargo exported by more than 100 companies. Drywall sitting in a warehouse may not emit a foul odor realizing how many foul odors are in a huge warehouse and the fact that drywall is packaged pretty well so that the odor may be hidden. Unless you have this drywall in your home, you may never know.

Nearly 60 percent of the drywall-also known as wallboard, gypsum board or plasterboard-came in through Florida ports. Miami was the largest, with more than 100 million pounds of Chinese drywall unloaded, followed by Port Everglades with at least 80 million pounds and Tampa with at least 50 million. Other destinations included Port Manatee in northern Manatee County, Pensacola, Port Canaveral and Jacksonville. While Florida has so far been the primary focus of public officials and builders, the shipping records show more than a dozen other states got the Chinese product, from New York to Texas to California. At least 60 million pounds of Chinese drywall went into New Orleans in 2006 and another 27 million into Pascagoula, Miss., two areas with post-Hurricane Katrina rebuilding.

Knauf's operation in Tianjin, Knauf Plasterboard Tianjin Ltd. had been found to be defective throughout Southwest Florida and was sued in the middle of January, 2009 in a class-action complaint filed in Sarasota County circuit court. Their officials had acknowledge they received complaints from builders and contractors about the smell of their product in 2006, and that a 2008 investigation showed copper corrosion was potentially connected to sulfur gases coming from the material. But like Lennar, the company claimed the sulfur compounds were not hazardous to humans.

By 2007, it was well known in the industry that there was already a stigma associated with any board from China, no matter who made it. Several drywall contractors were so sure that the York Building Supply, an affiliate of Georgia-based A1 Construction who got their drywall from Shandong, China, would not be able to sell the material, they offered to take it for free.

The Chinese drywall is especially problematic because the smell can permeate into the wood studs and continue to cause problems after it is removed. While some homebuilders are voluntarily assisting homeowners whose homes were constructed with the drywall, others are not. If you or a loved one has suffered from health problems, or has suffered property damage that you believe is a result of Chinese drywall, please contact a health provider for medial attention and an attorney to preserve your rights.

F.D.A. Finds 'Natural' Diet Pills Spiked with Drugs.

On February 10th, 2009, the *NY Times*, in an article written by Natasha Singer, stated that Grady Jackson, a defensive tackle with the Atlanta Falcons, said he used the weight-loss capsules called StarCaps. Kathie Lee Gifford was enthusiastic about them on the "Today" show. Retailer like GNC and the Vitamin Shoppe sold them, no prescription required.

But the Food and Drug Administration said that those weight-loss capsules, promoted as natural dietary supplements using papaya, could be hazardous to your health. In violation of the law, the agency had found, the capsules also contained a potent pharmaceutical drug called bumetanide which can have serious side effects. Yet, StarCaps are not the only culprits. In a continuing investigation that has prompted consumer warnings and recalls by some distributors, the F.D.A. had determined that dozens of weight-loss supplements, most of them imported from China, contain hidden and potentially harmful drugs. The agency planned to issue a longer list of brands to avoid that are spiked with drugs, and F.D.A. spokeswoman said.

The agency's warning list included more obscure pills sold under the name of Sliminate, Superslim and Slim Up, among many others. So far, the F.D.A. had cited 69 tainted weight-loss supplements. "A large percentage of these products either contain dangerous undeclared ingredients or they might be outright fraudulent on the ingredients and have no effect at all," said Michael Levy, the director of the F.D.A.'s division of New Drugs and Labeling Compliance. "We don't think consumers should be using these products."

As the F.D.A. continues to investigate, many questions remain to be answered, including who put the drugs in the pills and who knew about it. But some doctors and other experts say the F.D.A. inquiry raises a larger issue: Whether the regulations governing dietary supplements leave consumers who take so-called natural weight-loss supplements to unknowingly play Russian roulette with their health.

Web sites like www.911healthshop.com and www.fastdietusa.com continue to sell a variety of the other brands, including 3X Slimming Power and Imelda Perfect Slim. A full list of the tainted pills and other details are available on the F.D.A.'s Web site, www.fda.gov.

StarCaps, the best known of the brands cited, gained a large following through celebrity endorsement and articles in glossy magazines like People. A billboard featuring the company's founder and proprietor, Nikki Haskell, stood for years above Sunset Boulevard in Hollywood.

Last fall of 2008, Mr. Jackson and several other National Football League players who said they had taken StarCaps failed a drug test when they tested positive for bumetanide. The drug, which can mask steroid use, is on the list of substances banned by the league. Now Mr. Jackson has filed a class-action law suit against Ms. Haskell and the stores where he said he purchased StarCaps, including the Vitamin Shoppe and GNC.

Ms. Haskell said that she was shocked to learn from the news that her product contained the diuretic having sold this product over the last 25 years. She voluntarily recalled the products saying that she was completely devastated.

— 6 —

Tainted Drugs Tied to Maker of Abortion Pills

In the latter part of January, 2008 the *New York Times* reported that in Beijing, a huge state-owned Chinese pharmaceutical company that exports to dozens of countries, including the United States, has been at the center of a nationwide drug scandal after nearly 200 Chinese cancer patients were paralyzed or otherwise harmed in the summer of 2007 by contaminated leukemia drugs. Chinese drug regulators have accused the manufacturer of the tainted drugs of a cover-up and have closed the factory that produced them. In December, 2007 China's Food and Drug Administration said that the Shanghai police had begun a criminal investigation and that two officials, including the head of the plant, had been detained.

The drug maker, Shanghai Hualian, is the sole supplier to the United States of the abortion pill, mifepristone, known as RU-486. It is made at a factory different from the one that produced the tainted cancer drugs, about an hour's drive away.

The United States Food and Drug Administration declined to answer questions about Shanghai Hualian, because of security concerns stemming from the sometimes violent opposition to abortion. But in a statement, the agency said the RU-486 plant had passed an F.D.A. inspection in May of 2007. "F.D.A. is not aware of any evidence to suggest the issue that occurred at the leukemia drug facility in linked in any way with the facility that manufactures the mifepristone," the statement said.

When told of Shanghai Hualian's troubles, Dr. Sidney M. Wolfe, a leading consumer advocate and frequent F.D.A. critic, said that American regulators ought to be concerned because of accusations that serious health risks had been covered up there. "Every one of these plants should be immediately inspected," he said.

The director of the Chinese F.D.A.'s drug safety control unit in Shanghai, Zhou Qun, said that her agency had inspected the factory that produced mifepristone three times in recent months and found it in compliance. "It is natural to worry," Ms. Zhou said, "but these two plants are in two different places and have different quality-assurance people."

The investigation of the contaminated cancer drugs comes as China is trying to restore confidence in its tattered regulatory system. In the last two years, scores of people around the world have died after ingesting contaminated drugs and drug ingredients produced in China. Last year, China executed its top drug safety official for accepting bribes to approve drugs. Shanghai Hualian is a division of one of China's largest pharmaceutical companies, the Shanghai Pharmaceutical Group, which owns dozens of factories. Neither Shanghai Hualian nor its parent company would comment on the tainted medicine.

At this time in January of 2008, the New York Times asked the F.D.A. whether the Shanghai Pharmaceutical Group exported to the United States any drugs or pharmaceutical ingredients other than the abortion pill. But after repeated requests, the agency declined to provide that information; it did not cite a reason.

On at least two occasions in 2002, Shanghai Hualian had shipments of drugs stopped at the United States border, F.D.A. records show. One shipment was an unapproved antibiotic and the other a diuretic that had "false or misleading labeling." Records also show that another unit of Shanghai Pharmaceutical Group had filed papers declaring its intention to sell at least five active pharmaceutical ingredients to manufacturers for sale in the United States.

One major pharmaceutical company, Pfizer, declined to buy drug ingredients from Shanghai Pharmaceutical Group because of quality-related issues, said Christopher Loder, a Pfizer spokesman. In 2006, Pfizer agreed to evaluate Shanghai Pharmaceutical Group's "capabilities" as an ingredient supplier, but so far the company "has not met the standards required by Pfizer," Mr. Loder said in a statement.

Because of opposition from the anti-abortion movement, the F.D.A. has never publicly identified the maker of the abortion pill for the American market. The pill was first manufactured in France, and since its approval by the F.D.A. in 2000 it has been distributed in the United States by Danco Laboratories. Danco, which does not list a street address on its Web site, did not return two telephone calls seeking comment.

Problems with the cancer drugs first surfaced in the summer of 2007 after leukemia patients received injections of one cancer drug, methotrexate. Afterward, patients experienced leg pain and, in some cases, paralysis. At the People's Liberation Army No. 307 Hospital in Beijing, a 26-year-old patient, Miao Yuguang, was unable to stand up five days after being injected in the spine with the drug. "We were already unlucky to have this illness," her father, Miao Futian, said of the leukemia. "Then we ran into this fake drug."

The authorities recalled two batches of the drug, but issued only mild warnings because the cause of the problem was unclear. Officials with Shanghai Pharmaceutical Group stood by their products, saying that drug regulators investigating the plant had found no problems. But when another cancer drug made in the same factory-cytarabin hydrochloride-also began causing adverse reactions, investigators suspected contamination.

In September of 2007, health and drug officials announced that they had found that the two drugs were contaminated with vincristine sulfate, a third cancer drug, during production. After issuing a nationwide alert, the government announced a wider recall, and Shanghai's drug agency sealed manufacturing units at the plant.

"Many people thought there was a problem with the hospitals," said Zheng Qiang, director of the Center for Pharmaceutical Information and Engineering Research at Peking University. "It wasn't until later that they discovered the problem was with the medicine."

Chinese media attention on the case has surged, after a terse statement by China's drug agency in December of 2007, accusing Hualian company officials of a systematic cover-up of violations of the facility that made the drugs. Family members at the No. 307 hospital have counted 53 victims in Beijing, and say that they were told that there were at least 193 victims nationwide. It is unclear, even today, how many were paralyzed, because the authorities have not released an official figure. Relatives have joined to share information and advocate for the victims. Based on interviews with several families in Beijing and Shanghai, it appears that about half of those injected still cannot walk.

Wu Jianhua said that his daughter, Wu Xi, 15, collapsed on her way to school after an injection in August of 2007. "We thought she was tired," Mr. Wu said. Doctors now say she may never walk without a cane, he said.

Last week, on a window near the gate of the closed plant was a notice from the Shanghai Food and Drug Administration, dated September 8, 2007, accusing the plant of "producing substandard medicine that poses major risks of causing serious harm to human health." It identified a company official, Gu Yaoming, as the "person responsible" for the plant.

Records show Mr. Gu also met with the United States F.D.A. inspectors in May of 2007 as part of the routine inspection of the plant that makes RU-496. Reached by telephone, Mr. Gu declined to describe his role at the two plants. "I cannot answer your questions," he said.

A spokeswoman for China's Food and Drug Administration, Yan Jiangying, said that Shanghai Hualian had been stripped of its license to produce antitumor drugs, but that this action did not affect RU-486.

Hualian is the latest in a string of tainted medicine cases that have been undermined confidence in the safety of drugs here. In 2006, at least 18 Chinese died after an intravenous drug used to treat liver disease, Armillarisin A, was laced with diethylene glycol, a toxic chemical used in some antifreeze. Also in 2006, at least 14 Chinese died after taking a Chinese antibiotic, Xinfu, which was not properly sterilized during production. And more than a hundred people died in Panama after taking cold medicine containing a mislabeled and toxic chemical from China.

In 2006 and 2007, people in South America, Asia and in the United States also got ill or died because toothpaste they had used also had diethylene glycol, the same toxic chemical used in some antifreeze, to give the product color and taste. In each of these cases, the manufacturer failed to follow good manufacturing practices to ensure that the final product was safe.

Describing the cover-up at the factory, Ms. Zhou, the regulator who led the investigation, said that the workers did not tell investigators that vincristine sulfate-a drug too toxic for use in spinal injections-had been stored in a refrigerator with materials for other drugs.

"At the time, we didn't think they had lied to us," Ms. Zhou said. The deception sent investigators on a two-month hunt for other possible causes of the adverse reactions. "If they had been open about the vincristine sulfate in the beginning, maybe fewer people would have been harmed," she added.

While regulators have accused factory employees of a systematic cover-up of violations in production, they have not said whether superiors at Shanghai Pharmaceutical were aware of it. "We'll have to wait until the police investigation is finished" to make more details public, said Ms. Yan, the drug agency spokeswoman.

Mr. Zheng at Peking University said that producing multiple drugs in a single workshop was risky, but that some Chinese companies saw it as a way to save money. "It was an accident," he said of the Hualian case. "But it was bound to happen."

China Didn't Check Drug Supplier, Files Show

According to the report in the *NY Times* in February, 2008, a Chinese factory that supplies much of the active ingredient for a brand of a blood thinner that has been linked to four deaths in the United States is not certified by China's drug regulators to make pharmaceutical products, according to records and interview. The case was described in an article by The Times' Jake Hooker and Walt Bogdanich that stated because the plant, Changzhou SPI, has no drug certification, China's drug agency did not inspect it. The United States Food and Drug Administration said that it has not inspected the plant either-a violation of its own policy-before allowing the company to become a major supplier of the blood thinner, heparin, to Baxter International in the United States.

Baxter announced in February that it was suspending sales of its multidose vials of heparin after four patients died and 350 suffered complications. Why the heparin caused the problems-and whether the active ingredient in the drug, derived from pig intestines, was responsible-has not been determined.

The plant in Changzhou, west of Shanghai, appeared to fall into the type of regulatory void that American and Chinese health officials are trying to close-in which chemical companies export pharmaceutical ingredients without a Chinese drug license.

China provides a growing proportion of the active pharmaceutical ingredients used in drugs sold in the United States. And Chinese drug regulators have said that all producers of those ingredients are required to obtain certification by the State Food and Drug Administration. However, some of the active ingredients that China exports are made by chemical companies, which do not fall under the Chinese drug agency's jurisdiction.

In December of 2007, American and Chinese regulators signed an agreement under which China promised to begin registering at least some of the thousands of chemical companies that sell drug ingredients. Some of these companies are the source of counterfeit or diluted drugs, including those used to treat malaria.

Discussions that led to the accord began after an unlicensed chemical plant in China made a tainted drug ingredient that poisoned more than 170 people in Panama, killing at least 115. The heparin plant in China has not been accused of providing a harmful product. The American majority owner of that plant, Scientific Protein Laboratories, also owns a plant in Wisconsin that produces the active ingredient in heparin for Baxter.

In response to questions, Scientific Protein issued a statement confirming that its Chinese plant had no license from the Chinese agency, but said that its raw ingredients come from a licensed supplier. The statement added that an "independent private U.S. validation company" had found the plant to be in compliance with good manufacturing practices. And a spokeswoman for Baxter, which buys heparin's active ingredient from Scientific Protein, said it had inspected the China plant less than six months ago.

A spokesman for China's State Food and Drug Administration, Shen Chen, said that "as far as we know, it is not a drug manufacturer-it is a producer of chemical ingredients."

Eric S. Langer, managing partner of BioPlan Associates, which prepares and publishes reports on the biopharmaceutical and biotechnology industry, said that he found it hard to believe that a company exporting the heparin ingredient would not be licensed by Chinese drug regulators.

"Being able to produce a pharmaceutical or a biologic in the U.S. or anywhere without having regulatory oversight really doesn't happen," Mr. Langer said, adding, "I find it surprising from a regulatory perspective, and I find it surprising from a business perspective."

Karen Riley, a spokeswoman for the United States Food and Drug Administration, said inspectors from that agency would be visiting the Changzhou plant soon. Ms. Riley said that she could not be more specific. Earlier, she had described her agency's failure to inspect the plant as a "glitch."

Congress has criticized the oversight by the Food and Drug Administration of bulk pharmaceutical ingredients made by foreign manufacturers and sold in the United States. A growing number of those ingredients now come from China. Of the 700 approved Chinese drug plants, the United States agency has inspected only 10 to 20 per year.

Baxter makes roughly half of the United States supply of heparin, which is used widely for surgical and dialysis patients. Problems with Baxter's heparin were first noticed late in 2007 when four children undergoing dialysis in Missouri had severe allergic reactions minutes after being injected with the drug.

The F.D.A. then allowed Baxter to deliver heparin that it was in the midst of shipping, for fear that a total recall would lead to a shortage of the drug, but cautioned doctors to use as little of it as possible and to administer it very slowly. The agency also suggested that doctors give steroids or antihistamines with the Baxter heparin to help prevent allergic reactions.

Erin Gardiner, a spokeswoman for Baxter, defended Scientific Protein, saying it had been making the heparin ingredient for more than 30 years. "They have been a good supplier," she said.

Although the cause of the adverse reactions has yet to be determined, she said that tests performed by her company had detected unspecified differences between some lots of the ingredient. She did not say whether the lots had come from China or from the Wisconsin plant, which Scientific Protein also owns.

Those differences had not turned up in routine testing that the company does on active ingredients, Ms. Gardiner said, but she said Baxter had used "advanced testing techniques" to find the differences. She added that it was unclear whether the finding was significant.

Two Congressional committees have asked the Food and Drug Administration for more information about inspections of plants making the active ingredient of heparin.

China, You Have a Problem!!!

As reported in the *Chicago Tribune* in February, 2008, ever since contaminated Chinese pet food killed or sickened thousands of animals in the U.S. in the spring of 2007, consumers here have been turning a critical eye to foodstuffs-for people as well as for animals-imported from China. A famous, national food chain added its voice, and its buying power, to that wary market reaction. As of April 1st, 2008, Trader Joe's indicated that it will stop selling single-ingredient Chinese imports in its stores…such items as frozen spinach, garlic, ginger and edamame. The move, said a Trader Joe's spokeswoman, was in response not to any specific problems with Chinese foods, but to consumer sentiment.

"We will continue to source products from other regions until our customers feel as confident as we do about the quality and safety of Chinese products," Alison Mochizuki said.

The partial ban is the latest signal to China that the greatest danger to its export machine isn't U.S. government action, but consumer action. In the last year, people have been bombarded with stories of toxic Chinese fish, tainted Chinese toothpaste and lead-laced Chinese toys. And those consumers are reacting with their pocketbooks. Those who can afford to do so are looking local for everything from baby building blocks to apple cider.

China hasn't been the only shipper of dangerous products. Individual food items from Indonesia, Latvia and Mexico have shown up on the Food and Drug Administration's recall rolls since the start of December, 2007. But China's name has popped up more than that of any other country. The danger from contaminated Chinese food imports remains small.

According to the U.S. Agriculture Department, less than 1 percent of America's food supply comes from China. Even Trader Joe's will continue to sell multi-ingredient products that include imports from China. But as Trader Joe's action shows, consumers don't want to take a risk, and they have choices. For China, the Herculean task of cleaning up its food supply chain may be the easy part of protecting its export business. Cleaning up its image as a safe source of food may prove more difficult.

Here are some things that you should watch out for when you import from China: Give electronics a big detour. The prices you may be seeing are low because the brands are in fact fakes. The problem with dealing with these fakes is that you are left with a worthless piece of equipment if something should go wrong. There is no company to return the merchandise to and the manufacturer that you believed made the product is really not the maker.

Designer clothing and accessories that you find from China are also almost always fake. You should never try to pass off these goods as originals or you will be facing a great many problems. A good rule of thumb to use is that if the prices are too good to be true, then they probably are not true.

— 7 —

More FDA Limits on Chinese Food Additive Imports

For the past year, as reported in *USA Today*, the FDA finally decided to enforce a new import alert that greatly expanded its curtailment of some food ingredients imported from China, authorizing border inspectors to detain ingredients used in everything from noodles to breakfast bars. The new restriction has caused and will continually cause delays in the delivery of raw ingredients for the production of many commonly used products.

The move reflects the FDA's growing unease with what the alert announcement called China's "manufacturing control issues" and that country's inability to ascertain what controls are in place to prevent food contamination. For example, the agency said that, after weeks of investigation, it still does not know what regions of China are affected or what firms there are major manufacturers of vegetable proteins.

Inspectors, as of April, 2007 were allowed to detain vegetable-protein imports from China because they may contain the chemical melamine. Melamine, used in the manufacture of plastics, was found in the wheat gluten and rice protein concentrate that has led to the recall of 5,300 pet food products. Melamine's affects on humans, if ingested, is unclear. In fact, the chemical has not been found in earlier tests to be highly toxic, a fact that has scientists looking for a second chemical agent that could be increasing its toxicity.

The agency for the first time also said it had received reports, which it has yet to confirm, that approximately 1,950 cats and 2,200 dogs died after eating contaminated food. The only number of pet deaths that the FDA had confirmed thus far is 14. An import alert of this breadth is rare. Before this new FDA action, only products from two Chinese companies that exported the melamine-tainted wheat gluten and rice protein concentrate had been detained.

Now for the products to reach U.S. food makers, the importers will have to prove to the FDA that they are safe. They ingredients restricted include wheat gluten, rice gluten, rice protein, rice protein concentrate, corn gluten, corn gluten meal, corn by-products, soy protein, soy gluten, mung-bean protein and amino acids.

The FDA had not reported finding melamine in food imports for humans from China, yet it launched sample testing (in April of 2007), "out of an abundance of caution," said chief medical officer, David Acheson. The new restriction may be what's needed to shore up consumer confidence that the FDA can protect the food supply, said Jean Kinsey, director of the Food Industry Center at the University of Minnesota. Without such action, the public's distrust will grow, she said.

According to the alert notice posted on the FDA Website, the agency had so far taken 750 samples of wheat gluten and products made with wheat gluten and found 330 positive for melamine or melamine combined with another substance. It also found 27 positives out of 85 samples of rice protein concentrate and products made with rice protein concentrate. All of the samples that tested positive were imported from China.

Speaking for the Chinese manufacturers, Wu Yongning, Deputy Director of the National Institute of Nutrition and Food Safety, part of China's Ministry of Health, has said in Beijing, "I don't believe it has reached such a serious state that human food is at risk. Problems occur in all countries."

"Generally speaking, American consumers should not worry too much," said Luo Yunbo, Head of the Food Science and Nutrition Engineering Institute at China's Agriculture University in Beijing. "We selected the best products for the international markets."

As writer of this report, you be the judge!!!

Quality Problems with Soybean

And the list goes on...as reported in the *International Herald Tribune* in the latter part of 2007 and the WDDTY Health Shop Web site at the beginning of 2008, before the U.S. could make an issue about certain products not considered as problems in the past, China started to report quality problems on imports from the U.S.

China, known as the world's biggest buyer of soybeans, had reported that it had found "substantial" quality-related problems with imports of the U.S. oilseed and urged Washington to investigate and improve its procedures.

Soybeans shipped from the United States often contained low-quality seeds, as well as weeds that could threaten local agriculture, the General Administration of Quality Supervision, Inspection and Quarantine said on its Web site. Some shipments had herbicide residue, it added.

China's comments, following U.S. reports of unsafe Chinese products, including contaminated fish and pesticide-laced vegetables, may intensify trade fiction between the two countries. U.S. lawmakers have been trying to pass a bill that may cut off the American market for Chinese poultry, the official China Daily had reported.

"It's a knee-jerk reaction," Phil Laney, country director for the U.S. Soybean Export Council, said in Beijing. "They are saying the United States is no better than anyone else," at managing its exported products.

The problems with the soybeans indicate that there are "holes" in the U.S. production, transportation, export inspection and quarantine processes, the Beijing statement said, adding that China would step up monitoring of imported soybeans. It did not list specific shipments or companies. The statement by China may not significantly affect U.S. soybean exports, Laney said. In the past, the practice was to destroy the problematic shipments on arrival under the supervision of inspectors, he said.

Chinese soybean imports, mostly from the United States and Brazil, have almost doubled since 2003-04. Imports from January to July 2007 rose 2.6 percent to 16.9 million tons, with 7.8 million tons coming from America, according to customs data. The United States is the world's largest producer.

Dermatitis Sofa Imports Create Allergies

With regards to dermatitis from Chinese sofa imports that have been causing a rash of problems...better watch out...you could suddenly develop severe dermatitis. Doctors in the UK have reported a sudden rash (pun intended) of sufferers who'd recently treated themselves to a leather sofa...made in China.

At last count...at least through January, 2008, doctors have treated more than 130 people who suddenly developed the skin disorder. On further investigation, it seems that all of the sofas came from the same manufacturer in China. Dermatologists fear the sofas may contain an allergen that they've never seen before.

MSG...the Slow Poisoning of America Today

The Chinese may have a good point here! In essence, we are also trying to kill ourselves with certain ingredients that are put in our foods by our own people that are approved by our own government. One such ingredient is the food additive MSG (Mono-Sodium Glutamate), a well- known slow poison to those who have been affected by this additive.

MSG hides behind 25 or more names, such as 'Natural Flavoring,' MSG is even in your favorite coffee from Tim Horton's and other brand-name coffee shops. I personally have wondered if there could be an actual chemical causing the massive obesity epidemic and so did John Erb, a former research assistant at the University of Waterloo in Ontario, Canada, who had spent years working for the government. He made an amazing discovery while going through scientific journals for a book he was writing called the Slow Poisoning of America.

In hundreds of studies around the world, scientists were creating obese mice and rats to use in diet or diabetes test studies. No strain of rat or mice is naturally obese, so scientists had to create them. They make these creatures morbidly obese by injecting them with MSG when they are first born. The MSG triples the amount of insulin the pancreas creates, causing rats (and perhaps humans) to become obese. They even have a name for the fat rodents they create: 'MSG-Treated Rats.'

Why not be like me and rush into your kitchen...check the cupboards and the refrigerator. You will find that MSG may just be in everything...the Campbell's soups, the Hostess Doritos, the Lays flavored potato chips, Top Ramen, Betty Crocker Hamburger Helper, Heinz canned gravy, Swanson frozen prepared meals, and Kraft salad dressings, especially the 'healthy low-fat' ones.

The items that didn't have MSG marked on the product label had something called 'Hydrolyzed Vegetable Protein,' which is just another name for Monosodium Glutamate. It was shocking to see just how many of the foods we feed our children everyday are filled with this stuff. MSG is hidden under many different names in order to fool those who read the ingredient list, so that they don't catch on.

(Other names for MSG are 'Accent,' 'Aginomoto,' 'Natural Meat Tenderizer,' etc.) But it does not stop there. If your family goes out to eat...start asking at the restaurants what menu items contain MSG. Many employees, even the managers, would swear to you that they don't use MSG. But when you ask to see the ingredient list, which they will grudgingly provide to you with a bit of persuasion on your part, you will find what you are seeking, sure enough...MSG and Hydrolyzed Vegetable Protein are everywhere.

Burger King, McDonald's, Wendy's, Taco Bell, every restaurant…even the sit-down eateries like TGIF, Chili's, Applebee's, and Denny's…use MSG in abundance.

Kentucky Fried Chicken seemed to be the worst offender: MSG is in every chicken dish, salad dressing, and gravy. No wonder people love to eat that coating on the skin…their secret spice is none other than MSG!

So why is MSG in so many of the foods we eat? Is it a preservative, or a vitamin? Not according to Mr. John Erb. In his book, 'The Slow Poisoning of America', he indicated that MSG is added to food for the addictive effect it has on the human body. Even the propaganda web site sponsored by the food manufacturers lobby group supporting MSG explains the reason they add it to food is to make people eat more.

A study of the elderly showed that older people eat more of the foods that it is added to. The Glutamate Association lobbying group says that eating more is a benefit to the elderly, but what does it do to the rest of us? *'Betcha can't eat just one,'* takes on a whole new meaning where MSG is concerned!

And then we wonder why the nation is overweight! MSG manufacturers themselves admit that it addicts people to their products. It makes people choose their product over others, and makes people eat more of it than they would if MSG wasn't added. Not only is MSG scientifically proven to cause obesity, it is an addictive substance. Since its introduction into the American food supply fifty years ago, MSG has been added in larger and larger doses to the pre-packaged meals, soups, snacks, and fast foods we are tempted to eat everyday.

The FDA has set no limits on how much of it can be added to food. The date of many tests regarding MSG with respect to the development of obesity were published in 1978 and still, nothing is being done to stop this as of 2008. Both the medical research community and food manufacturers have known about the side effects of MSG for decades and its link to diabetes, migraines, and headaches, autism, DHD, and even Alzheimer's.

So you ask, what can we do to stop the food manufacturers from dumping this fattening and addictive MSG into our food supply and causing the obesity epidemic we now see?

In the latter part of 2007, John Erb took his book and his concerns to one of the highest government health officials in Canada. While he was sitting in the government office, the official told him, "Sure, I know how bad MSG is. I wouldn't touch the stuff."

But this top-level government official refused to tell the public what he knew. The big media doesn't want to tell the public either, fearing issues with their advertisers. It seems that the fallout on the fast food industry may hurt their profit margin. The food producers and restaurants have been addicting us to their products for years, and now we are paying the price for it. Our children should not be cursed with obesity caused by an addictive food additive.

It takes more than one person whose one voice will not stop the poisoning of our children, while our governments are insuring financial protection for the industry that is poisoning us. It is important that this message goes out to everyone in an attempt to tell the truth that the corporate-owned politicians and media won't tell you. It is time to stop the politicians from passing legislation that protects those who are poisoning us.

China is one part of the problem, yet our own country is just as much at fault. The food industry learned a lot from the tobacco industry yet will not protect the lives of people who are at risk because of the MSG in the food. More of this data can be found on the National Library of Medicine web site at www.pubmed.com. Type in the words 'MSG Obese' and read a few of the 115 medical studies that appear.

The Coming China Wars...

In his book entitled *"The Coming China Wars"* Peter Navarro hit the nail on the head when describing China's thirst for oil and how it is driving nuclear proliferation in Iran, genocide in the Sudan, even Japan's remilitarization. This book describes China's shocking role in the drug trade and how its reborn flesh trade may help trigger tomorrow's worst AID's crisis. Navarro also reveals how China has become the world's most ruthless imperialist...how it is promoting global environmental disaster...and, perhaps most terrifying of all, how this nuclear superpower and pirate nation may be spiraling toward internal chaos.

As I had mentioned previously, China's breakneck industrialization is placing it on a collision course with the entire world. In my opinion as well as Mr. Navarro's, Tomorrow's China Wars will be fought over everything from decent jobs, livable wages, and leading-edge technologies to strategic resources such as oil, copper and steel...even food, water, and air.

Mr. Navarro described in his book of the myriad dangers from the Coming China Wars that are real...and increasingly personal. Consider these scenarios based on actual events:

- Your bank balance drops precipitously as rising interest rates drive your adjustable rate monthly mortgage payment off the charts at the same time you shell out more than you ever dreamed to fill your gas tank. Your mortgage payments are being held hostage to China's currency-manipulation policies. You pay dearly at the pump because of the price-shocking effects of China's rapidly thirst for oil.

- You walk out of a Wal-Mart with a big smile and a large basket laden with cheap Chinese goods ranging from a fancy new laser printer and plasma TV to shirts, socks, and running shoes. Your smile quickly turns to a frown as your eyes begin to sting and lungs burn from the Asian "brown cloud"-a particularly toxic atmospheric smog that has hitchhiked on the jet stream all the way from China's industrial heartland where everything in your basket was first manufactured.

- Your father almost dies from a massive heart attack because the "Lipitor" prescription he filled on the Internet was laced with Chinese fakes. Your mother breaks her hip because the phony "Evista" medication she took for osteoporosis was nothing more than molded Chinese chalk. Your house gets robbed by a drug addict high on methamphetamines made from ephedra grass grown on Chinese state-run farms and transported to New York via Panama by Triad gangs.

Let's examine some of these cholesterol drugs that are supposedly made in the United States...

Over-Promoted Cholesterol Drugs... An American Problem

The news keeps getting worse for two heavily promoted cholesterol drugs, Vytorin and Zetia. As reported in the April 2nd, 2008 edition of the NY Times.com editorial, these drugs were supposed to offer a valuable alternative to the older cholesterol-lowering agents known as statins, a class that includes Lipitor, Zocor and other drugs that not only reduce cholesterol but also reduce the risk of heart attacks. In clinical trial results released during the first week of April, the new drugs failed to reach their main goal: slowing the growth of artery-clogging plaques-a suggestion that they might not help ward off heart attacks.

It is distressingly late to be learning that these drugs may provide little or no benefit. They were approved on the basis of evidence that they reduce the level of so-called bad cholesterol in the blood. That data was taken as presumptive evidence that the drugs would reduce heart-attack risks. Despite this slim supporting data, vigorous promotion propelled them to combined sales of more than $5 billion last year, placing them among the world's top-selling drugs.

An analysis in the *New England Journal of Medicine* found that the drugs captured 15.2 percent of the cholesterol-lowering market in this country, driven by an advertising campaign aimed at consumers and aggressive marketing to doctors. But they claimed only 3.4 percent of the market in Canada, where advertising to consumers is prohibited, Vytrorin is unavailable and public programs restrict usage. These are drugs that became blockbusters thanks to marketing muscle, not scientific proof of effectiveness.

There are also justifiable concerns that Merck and Schering-Plough, the companies that make the drugs, may have sat on adverse data for more than a year lest their sales be undermined. In e-mail messages unearthed by Senate investigators, the lead scientist on the study warned that repeated delays in releasing the results made it look as if the company was trying to hide something.

In the clinical trial, 720 European patients with genes that cause abnormally high cholesterol levels were given either Vytorin, a combination pill that contains both Zetia and Zocor, or simply Zocor alone. As expected, the combination pill proved better than the statin alone in reducing the level of bad cholesterol. But to everyone's surprise, Vytorin failed to slow the growth of fatty plaques in the arteries, and it may have even allowed greater growth than the statin did.

Vytorin and Zetia are clearly down, but not necessarily out. It remains possible, for example, that the reason Vytorin had little effect in reducing plaque was that most of these patients had been taking statins for years and their plaque had already depleted to the point that Vytorin had little room to improve the situation. It is also possible, however, that Vytorin and Zetia are simply less effective than the statins. Other trials now under way may clarify Vytorin's value in coming years. Meanwhile, heart experts are surely right that Vytorin and Zetia should be a last resort for patients who can't get their cholesterol down any other way.

What are the reasons for all of this and why???

Guess what, folks...one of the major reasons for our capitalistic society as we once knew it, falling from grace is the "Blood for Oil" wars. "With its economy rocketing," as Navarro stated so eloquently in his book, "China has emerged as the world's second largest petroleum consumer behind only the United States. Astonishingly, China now accounts for almost half the growth in global oil demand and is the primary catalyst for an oil market hurtling toward...at this writing...over $120 a barrel.

"To lock down its petroleum supplies-and lock the rest of the world out-China has adopted a reprehensible foreign policy based on President Hu Jintao's amoral mantra of "just business, no political condition." It has shipped ballistic missiles and transferred nuclear weapons technologies to the radical Iranian regime, used it diplomatic veto in the United Nations to sanction genocide in the Sudan, and facilitated the looting of public treasuries by dictators in oil…and mineral-rich African countries from Angola to Zimbabwe.

"This unconscionable blood for oil diplomacy has resulted in the slaughter of millions, the impoverishment of millions more, and a rapid spike in nuclear proliferation in both the Middle East and Asia."

What this is, is the possible beginning of what may be called The China Wars…as China's economy continues to grow at unprecedented rates, the "strange bedfellow" combination of a totally unrestrained free market capitalism operating under a harshly repressive totalitarian umbrella is becoming more and more like a political and social Molotov cocktail rather than an exemplary economic model for the rest of the world. That is precisely why the greatest danger to the world community may be China's coming "wars from within." These wars from within may be triggered by any number of internal ticking economic and demographic time bombs that threaten to bring on that which the Chinese people fear most…"chaos"…or *luan*.

Of course, as Navarro puts it, much of this sound like it came from a fictional news release but it shows you one glimpse of a future that we all should urgently seek to avoid. Remember how this all started…"Cut your price at least 30% or lose your customers."

My business career started in the early 60's, the beginning of the discount revolution where the up-and-coming chains of stores consisted of Sears, K-Mart, Woolco, Ann & Hope, Interstate Department Stores and so many others. Many of these companies are long gone and some are soon to also join the fold. Wal-Mart stands tall as does Target, but they too will see loss of sales and so much more. Wal-Mart, although recognized as an American store, spends over $22 billion in imports from China. Yet, every manufacturer is vulnerable…from furniture to networking gear. The result: a massive shift in economic power is underway and growing fast.

In the 1990's and early 2000's, the United States lost millions of jobs because of the low-wage, high-quality work by a highly disciplined, educated and nonunion work force that included worker health and safety regulations; lax environmental regulations and enforcement; the supercharging, catalytic role of foreign direct investment (FDI); a highly efficient form of industrial organization known as "network clustering"; An elaborate, government-sanctioned system of counterfeiting and piracy; a chronically undervalued "beggar thy neighbor" currency; massive government subsidies to numerous targeted industries; and "Great Wall" protectionist trade barriers, particularly for "infant industries."

Let's go back as to why we are experiencing the problems of goods made in China. It stems from the fact that China has become counterfeit pirates and that its economy has staked a great deal on its counterfeiters. They provide people with affordable goods...as in the case of medicines, medical devices, foods, school textbooks, clothing, and anything they can copy and sell at a great deal less than the original products. And the consumer liked the idea of paying less for generic items that they thought would do the same thing... taste as good...provide the same kind of remedy in health related problems... and provide us with more for less. The Counterfeiters serve their country by usurping foreign technology China desperately needs to meet its industrial goals. The counterfeiters give China's growing number of globally competitive companies the means to compete with powerful foreign rivals who are forced to pay full fare for proprietary technology and similar goods.

But as we reported in the previous chapters, things began to happen that caused us to stop buying all of the products made in China...we were attacked and realized that not all of the products that China produced was worth, even their low prices Consider this:

- Your scalp develops a severe rash because your knock-off Head and Shoulders shampoo contains toxic chemical residue
- You complain to your optometrist about headaches and a recent deterioration in your vision, and he determines that the lenses in your counterfeit Oakley sunglasses are causing the problem
- The counterfeit power strip that you bought in the bargain bin of the local hardware store starts an electrical fire and your smoke detector does not work because your fake "Duracell" batteries leaked acid all over the alarm system
- The phony "Budweiser" you bought at the supermarket exploded in your hand as you were about to open it
- You order Viagra over the internet because you are too embarrassed to ask your doctor for a regular prescription. After a nice candlelight dinner with your spouse, you wind up in a hospital bed with a wild heartbeat
- A mental patient is administered a regimen of the antipsychotic drug Zyprexa and after several weeks of ingesting an unintentional placebo, he goes berserk in your local supermarket and injures one of your best friends

Oh, these are just but a few examples of what may very well tip the iceberg when it comes to importing so many products from China. The obvious question therefore arises: "Why does the Chinese government allow piracy and counterfeiting to flourish?"

This is a particularly interesting question because, at least at the federal level, the Chinese central government has made a big show of cracking down on counterfeiting and piracy. Yet, from an economic perspective, Chinese state-sanctioned piracy and counterfeiting is a vital *de facto* "policy tool" that allows all layers of the Chinese government to control inflation, create jobs, expand its tax base, and raise the standard of living for the Chinese people.

To be sure, there is a virulent form of "local protectionism" from government officials for counterfeiters and pirates. This same kind of local protectionism that one observes for both private and state-run businesses is obviously polluting the air or water or maims their workers but that provide an important source of employment and tax revenues for the local economy.

As one general manager of a security firm of China had put it, "Counterfeiting is now so huge in China that radical action would crash the economy overnight, ruining Deng Xiaoping's 27-year-old economic strategy. It would ruin local economies in the poor south of the country, and even destabilize a government where counterfeit factories and warehouses are often owned by local military and political grandees."

Let's look at a small sampling of China's counterfeit universe and how this pirate nation is affecting more and more people throughout the world:

- Baby food, soft drinks, and hard liquor
- Batteries and film
- Cigarettes and Zippo lighters
- Mobile phones and watches
- Makeup and perfume
- Shampoo and razors
- Air conditioners and refrigerators
- Automobiles and motorcycles
- Chemicals, including flame-retardant chemicals
- Elevators and toilet seats
- Power strips and extension cords
- Blank CDs and tapes
- Circuit boards and connectors
- DRAM modules
- Hard drives, network interface cards, and printer cartridges
- Resistors and potentiometers
- Servers, laptops, and monitors

Let's not stop here…one of the biggest and most lucrative sectors of China's knock-off economy is that of replacement auto parts. Chinese pirates account for 70% of all counterfeit auto parts in the world, and more than half of all Chinese vehicles contain counterfeit components that include brake pads, oil filters, fan belts to fenders, engine blocks, windshields and windshield wipers. In some cases, the quality and appearance of the fake auto parts is so good that it is difficult to distinguish between a fake and original product.

Ready for more? Many of China's cigarette pirates operate in a much more decentralized cottage industry structure. Many of the small production facilities are quite literally underground in basements or in subterranean rooms accessible only by tunnels.

In these hidden dens, "counterfeiters will hire workers for just a few days or even hours to produce a batch of counterfeit cigarettes using old machines and hand-rolling the finished product." In such clandestine environs, cigarettes, which already represent one of the most efficient ways of destroying human health, often become even more deadly.

Tests on counterfeit cigarettes at St. Andrews University in the UK found that they had on average five times as much cadmium as genuine cigarettes, and cadmium causes kidney disease and damages your lungs. There's six times as much lead in them too, which will damage your nervous system. And then there's the elevated level of arsenic, which could cause cancer.

There have been experiences of counterfeit goods such as the fake Louis Vuitton handbag or the refill of Lipitor, a popular cholesterol-lowering drug, contained of fake pills. Tie this in with cough syrup laced with antifreeze… meningitis vaccine and anemia drugs made from tap water…birth control pills that are nothing but compressed wheat flour…Viagra and Cialis with twice the recommended dose…flea medicine made of chalk…malaria pills without a trace of its critical ingredient, *artusenate*.

Now let's talk about how elderly people, living on Social Security, not being able to afford medical expense and drugs not covered by insurance or Medicare who try an online "Canadian" pharmacy that offers cheap drugs. Unfortunately, these drugs are really operating out of Heilongjiang Province in China.

Think of it this way…producers in the fake product industry are a diverse bunch, ranging from a large dedicated facility to the individual who concocts an imitation shampoo at home and outsources the packaging and labeling. Then there is the factory that is hired by a multinational to make 1000 units of a product per day. However, rather than just run two regular eight-hour shifts to produce the contracted-for amounts, the factory also runs a third "ghost shift" and then ships the extra 500 items out the back door.

Why does China not care about the rest of the world and what is it about this country that is so detrimental to being a part of society instead of trying to destroy it? Let's look at some facts:

- China is home to 16 of the 20 most polluted cities in the world
- China has almost 100 cities with more than a million people each, and fully two thirds of these large Chinese cities fail to meet World Health Organization air-quality standards
- China is the world leader in the sulfur-dioxide emissions-a key ingredient of photochemical smog. Smog not only reduces visibility; it also kills by attacking both the heart and lungs
- Carbon dioxide is a principal ingredient driving global warming. China produces the second highest CO_2 emissions in the world, and it will surpass the world-leading United States over the next several decades
- China releases 600 tons of mercury into the air annually, nearly a fourth of the world's non-natural emissions. Mercury is particularly harmful to the nervous system, and children exposed to mercury may be born with symptoms resembling cerebral palsy, spasticity… convulsions, visual problems, and abnormal reflexes
- China is the world leader in the generation of substances that deplete the world's ozone layer-a phenomenon that increases cancer risks, harms plant and marine life, and is leading to the melting of the polar ice caps and attendant rising sea levels and coastal flooding
- Acid rain, which severely damages forests, fisheries, and crops, affects one fourth of China's land and one third of its agricultural land. As much as 50% of the acid rain in Japan and Korea is of Chinese origin
- Dust storms associated with Chinese desertification regularly dump tens of thousands of tons of debris on cities from Beijing and Seoul to Tokyo, and their effects have spread as far as North America. These blizzard-like storms can cause destruction on the scale of a serious earthquake. The can kill people and livestock, destroy crops, and force whole communities to abandon their homes

Source: "The Coming China Wars" by Peter Navarro

— 8 —

The "Blood for Oil" and Accelerating the Global Arms Race

One of the most disturbing aspects of China's oil policy-and its far-ranging effects starts with the fact that Beijing has sold thousands of tanks, artillery pieces, and armored personnel carriers to Iran, more than 100 combat aircraft, and dozens of small warships. Beijing has also sold Iran an array of missile systems and technology, including air-to-air missiles, surface-to-air missiles, and antishipping cruise missiles. Most worrisome have been China's transfer of ballistic missile technology and its assistance with Iran's nuclear programs. China has sent entire factories to Iran for producing chemicals that, although they have legitimate purposes, can also be used to make poison gas, and tons of industrial chemicals that could be used in making nerve gas.

China's main purpose, forgetting the fact that these same weapons are being used against the American soldiers in Iraq and in Pakistan, and against Israelis by Hamas and Hezbollah, is to get the oil and gas its economy desperately needs while Iran would finally win the political support of a weighty friend. Eventually, a strong leader of the United States will understand the facts and realize that the Middle East is being used as a playing field for great power competition, and that more direct confrontation between China and the United States will eventually occur.

More broadly, Chinese gang syndicates use a variety of methods to smuggle illegally both precursor chemicals and finished products to world markets. These methods include mislabeling the shipment containers, forging documents, establishing front companies, using circuitous routing, hijacking shipments and bribing officials.

Although China's economy and its manufacturing facilities are first class, much of its banking system is still very much Third World, which has made China easy prey for drug syndicates seeking to launder money through the rickety Chinese banking system. As a result of the drug trade, China is now emerging not just as the "factory floor" for the world's hard-drug production but also as a major money-laundering center.

As Peter Navarro had so eloquently stated in his book, life in China is in catastrophic conditions. Of the 2000-plus villagers in Huang Meng Ying, nine are deaf, 14 mentally disabled, three blind and nine physically handicapped. The villagers also point to the surge in birth defects, lesions and gall bladder infections in recent years-a sure indication, they feel, that the water is contaminated...A glimpse of the river which once irrigated what was one of the most fertile regions of the country, reveals why the villagers have arrived at this conclusion. The once-clear waters are today a floating mass of garbage and chemical effluents, unfit for irrigation, let alone drinking.

Much of China's *fresh* water in its rivers, lakes, streams, and wells is simply too polluted to use in irrigation, much less for drinking, and this pollution contributes greatly to a rapidly growing water scarcity problem. The statistics are startling:

- 70% of China's seven major rivers are severely polluted
- 80% of China's rivers fail to meet standards for fishing
- 90% of China's cities and 75% of its lakes suffer from some degree of water pollution, and 700 million Chinese have access to drinking of a quality below World Health Organization standards
- Almost half of China's total population is exposed to water supplies that are contaminated by animal and human waste, and one in three countryside dwellers lack access to safe drinking water
- Liver and stomach cancers related to water pollution are among the leading causes of death in the countryside; for example, in Shangba, located in northern Guangdong, pollution in the local water supply is so bad that the small towns in the region are known as 'cancer villages' by locals
- 21 cities along the Yellow River are characterized by the highest measurable levels of pollution, which has resulted in mercury contamination of rice, increased incidence of intestinal cancer, and rivers devoid of aquatic life

- All of China's coastal waters are moderately too highly polluted, and the reddish discolorations of the coastal waters (known as "red tides") are dramatically increasing in both frequency and intensity

The pollution is caused not just by massive industrial dumping and indiscriminate industrial burning of toxic wastes. An avalanche of excess fertilizer and pesticide runoff and a mountain of animal and human waste stand equally tall as culprits.

At the beginning of this book, we spoke about how China's manufacturing industries are not only flooding the world with low-cost products, but also are flooding China's waterways with toxic ash and effluents. The worst-polluting industries include paper and pulp, food, chemicals, textiles, tanning and mining.

In some cases, small- to medium-size factories without adequate pollution-control technology wantonly dump a toxic stew of wastes and chemicals into rivers and streams. In other cases , large factories equipped with the latest and most sophisticated pollution-control technologies simply do not use the technologies for fear of driving up production costs-and without any fear of sanctions by lax regulators and often complicit local officials.

Although Chinese government officials and regulators are giving lip service to the problem, the flood of toxic industrial pollution is only likely to get worse. One big reason is that many of the polluting factories are small scale and locally owned. Even when such enterprises are highly unprofitable, they represent important job generators in rural areas plagued by high unemployment, making it difficult for a local environmental protection bureau to close down the polluters, fine them, or otherwise force them to comply with the pollution control standards.

What is the chain of command as to how food may get polluted and how does sewerage play a major role in this? Let's go to one province, Dongxing, which is just one example of how Guangdong's 80 million people live close to the animals, poultry and fish they eat. At any piggery, a farmer may keep young chickens next to his pigs. All the piggeries empty their waste into the ponds where shrimp and grass-carp are raised for the table.

In other places, battery chickens are kept above the pig pens, feeding their waste into the pigs' food troughs. The close proximity and cross pollution adds to the risk of animal viruses infecting humans, either directly or via pigs. Let's look at the extent as to how this affects us worldwide.

On the animal waste front, the United States is the world's red meat "beef king," and China has become the world's "emperor of pork." China's hog farmers produce 70% of all meat produced in China and 50% of all the pork produced in the world. The result is a mountain of piggery and other livestock wastes, much of which regularly is dumped, or seeps, into China's waterways. These wastes provide a rich source of fuel for the organic pollution process.

On the human waste front, China has the largest urban population in the world-and its cities generate more than a trillion tons of sewage each year. However, about 90% of these municipal wastes either go untreated or fail to receive proper secondary treatment. Adding significantly to the problem is the fact that the construction of sewer lines is failing to keep pace with rapid urban growth and many sewage treatment plants are run inefficiently.

A very different and even more deadly kind of pollution results from the overflow of animal and human wastes in China-one with the very broadest international reach. China has become the world's prime breeding ground for new and exotic strains of influenza and other viruses, including both the deadly SARS virus and avian flu.

And the New York Times reported, based on a report by Qui Baoxing, Deputy Minister of Construction, that more than 300 of China's 660 cities are facing water shortages while more than 100 of these cities are facing extreme water shortages. Affluent urban lifestyles also strain the water supply, as residents snap up Western-style toilets and washing machines, and consume more meat and alcohol, which requires more grain-and therefore more water-to feed livestock and to produce liquor.

The other problem is a lack of adequate infrastructure to manage water resources. Rampant rickety and aged plumbing and rusty pipelines result in prodigious leakages across the vastness of the country. There is also a general lack of any comprehensive water recycling facilities. Rather than directing substantial resources to more efficient water use, the Chinese government is rolling the dice on a high-risk gamble originally envisioned by Mao Zedong known as the South-to-North Diversion Project. This "mega-project is the largest of its kind ever planned." Its three canals will stretch across the eastern, middle and western parts of China, and eventually link four of the country's seven major rivers-Yangtze River, Yellow River, Huaihe River and Haihe River. If this ever comes about, it may not happen until the year 2050.

The goal is to bring more water into the cities by using the existing reservoirs and canals of China's ancient Beijing-Hanzhou Grand Canal. The program would require the forced relocation of as many as 400,000 people along the Han River alone and you would probably see the construction of the most massive web of dams ever attempted in any country/

Despite rapid economic growth, the unemployment rate remains stubbornly high in China. Some estimates peg it at upward of 25% and likely to rise rather then fall over the next several decades...one because of *privatization*, the other, *urbanization*. Over the next several decades, the goal of the central government is to move the equivalent of the entire population of the United States off the farm and into the industrial work force-300 million or more peasants.

Beyond the bodily carnage, there are diseases such as pneumoconiosis (from dusty working conditions), chemical poisoning, and leukemia that rank as the leading causes of early "retirement" in China. These problems are particularly acute in industries ranging from coal production and metallurgy to building materials, nonferrous metals, machinery and chemicals. Aside from corruption and the market in China being displaced into a plundering playground for the rich, at the root of China's all-pervasive corruption is a practice known as *quanxi.*

This word describes a process in which business gets done in China not on the basis of *what* you know, but *who* you know. *Quanxi* is all about connections and, as a practical matter, entrepreneurs must connect with Chinese government officials and party members because they have the power to seize lands and grant favors.

China is a nation rapidly graying. It is a nation that is getting increasingly sick,. Environmental pollution is proving to be an all too deadly catalyst for an explosion of a myriad of cancers and an epidemic of respiratory and heart diseases. This rapid rise in ill health is coming precisely when China's once-vaunted public health-care system has totally unraveled under the weight of China's ongoing privatization of social services and a host of other sweeping economic reforms. Basically, the other problem is that China is in danger of growing old before it gets rich.

But of all the challenges facing the PRC government, few are as important-or daunting-as fixing the national healthcare system. Not only do the health and welfare of the nation's 1.3 billion people depend on it, but in very real and direct ways, the rest of the world's health depends on it too. For instance, a 45-day hospital stay may exceed $1,400, nearly triple a worker's income whereby the doctors cast her out until she would have the money.

At this writing, the U.S. government reported that the United States recorded a $202 billion trade deficit with China in 2007. That's the highest recorded with a single country and up 25% percent (from the previous year). That deficit has brought renewed pressure from Congress for President Bush to be more forceful in cracking down on what China's critics see as blatant unfair trade practices in currency manipulation, theft of intellectual property and China's refusal to honor all the market-opening commitments it made when it became a World Trade Organization member in 2001. The obvious "hard line" policy here is for the United States, the counties of Europe, and other nations of the world to adopt a "zero-tolerance" policy toward intellectual property theft.

For the United States to run large budget deficits, there must be someone willing to buy U.S. government bonds. That's where China comes in. In less than a decade, China has vaulted to the top of the U.S. creditor heap and will soon surpass Japan as the single largest holder of U.S. debt. By buying so much of American debt, China is able to maintain a huge trade surplus with the United States-and thereby contribute mightily to chronic U.S. trade deficits. This result occurs because the recycling of U.S. dollars from China back into the U.S. financial markets artificially suppresses the value of China's currency, the *yuan*, relative to the dollar. That helps keep Chinese exports relatively cheap and U.S. exports to China relatively expensive.

Here, however, is the blackmail part and the increasing danger: As China acquires more and more U.S. securities, it has an increasing ability to destabilize U.S. financial markets and plunge the United States into recession. All China has to do to send U.S. interest rates and inflation soaring is to stop buying new U.S. government securities. If China wants to trigger a crash in the U.S. stock and bond markets-say, to back off the United States from protectionist tariffs or to lessen its political will toward protecting Taiwan-all China has to do is to start dumping large amounts of its current U.S. holdings.

Peter Navarro had written a great book that "will hit you between the eyes," stated Stuart L. Hart, of Cornell University. "A gargantuan wake-up call."

The Coming China Wars explains in part, what may occur in the future with China, where they will be fought, and how they can be won. But, in the meantime, there are conflicts of business, economics and strategic interests between China and the United States. The impact that China has on the world and the perils it creates is now surfacing as a horrific danger indeed.

China's Labor Pains

Let's start here...instead of independent and competing organizations, the labor union in China is the party-controlled All-China Federation of Trade Unions. Still, even great progress can start in tiny steps. But it's not news that China is the global workshop. It's also well known that this meteoric rise came on the back of the Chinese worker. These individuals toil for small wages, with little or no security, in the hopes of making a bit more than they could have on the farm.

Many arrive at a factory with the intention of staying a few years. They live in onsite dormitories supplied by their employer, separated from their families from months or longer. They typically save or send their earnings to their families. For those of us with regular day jobs, their living conditions and work experience are hard to identify with.

Things are about to change. In 2007, China ratified two statutes to help to protect workers' rights. The Labor Contract and Employment Promotion laws have emerged from the back rooms and went into effect January 1st, 2008. According to a report from Foreign Policy in Focus, the new laws came under strong opposition from companies like Wal-Mart, Google, UPS, Microsoft, Nike, AT&T and Intel (acting through the American Chamber of Commerce) to block passage. There were a number of revisions to the statute based on input from organizations like AmCham representing foreign corporations.

International companies lobbied forcefully against many of the proposals, claiming that they would fuel rising labor costs that have already crept steadily higher over the past five years. These companies were also concerned over the possibility that China would become a more difficult place to do business if they were forced to be more cognizant of employees' rights and consult with state unions before layoffs. Such issues weren't given much thought when companies dealt with workers individually, not collectively.

The thrust of this statute is the labor contract system. Under Chinese law, contracts have long been required to protect employees, but the government looked the other way while many companies ignored them. The new statute complicates noncompliance with standard contract provisions, even for migrant employees, and the government has indicated enforcement will occur. Certain reports state the new statutes will have the power to enable change in labor-management relations and improve Chinese workers' standing. Foxconn, for one, has already acknowledged them, issuing a statement in December of 2007, that it will extend contracts to workers.

There are a number of employee protections incorporated into the statutes, including new limits on probationary periods and reducing the time employers can pay employees (lower) probationary salaries. There are also a number of age discrimination protections, including the right to severance pay and protection from termination for aging workers.

What the new laws don't do is provide Chinese workers with what many would consider fundamental protections. Chinese workers still lack the right to form independent unions, or strike. In the past, the All-China Federation of Trade Union has played only a minor role in employee negotiations, rarely pressing for higher wages or enhanced benefits. It is hoped that it will be more pro-worker in future dealings because defusing worker unrest and improving social stability are certainly at the root of these labor law changes.

It is possible that these new labor laws will help with a number of related labor issues that technologies companies face when operating in China. The turnover rate for employees is among highest in the world. Large companies have entire departments whose sole purpose is new employee orientation and training. The more specialized the job, the more arduous the task. It is anticipated that employees with hard contracts and longer contractual tenure may ease the burden, a win-win for workers and their employers.

I picked up the following from the Internet whereby it truly hits home with regards to Chinese goods and what they are doing to our society...

"Are we Americans as dumb as we appear or is it that we just do not think? While the Chinese, knowingly and intentionally, export inferior products and dangerous toys and goods to be sold in American markets, the media buries its hands.

"Simply look on the bottom of every product you buy, and it says 'MADE IN CHINA' or 'PRC' (and that now includes Hong Kong); simply choose another product or none at all. You will be amazed at how dependent you are on Chinese products; however you will be equally amazed at what you can do without. Who needs plastic eggs to celebrate Easter? If you must have eggs, use real ones and benefit some American farmer. Easter is just an example. The point is...do not wait for the government to act. Just go ahead and assume control on your own.

"If 200 million Americans refuse to buy just $20 each of Chinese goods, that's a billion dollar trade imbalance resolved in our favor...fast!!! If you want to fix America's economy real fast, stop buying anything imported from wine to cars and watch what happens nearly overnight."

Source: "The Coming China Wars" by Peter Navarro

— 9 —

Recall News from the
U.S. Consumer Product Safety Commission

Starting in May, 2008, the *Office of Information and Public Affair from the U.S. Consumer Product Safety Commission* out of Washington, DC sent out immediate releases on hundreds of products that were manufactured, not only in China, but in the United States, South and Central America and parts of Europe. Voluntary recalls of the following products were publicized so that the consumers would stop using these recalled products immediately. Let's mention a few:

Sure Grip Paint Brushes Recalled by Early Childhood Resources Due to Violation of Lead Paint Standard...
The name of the product is Yellow Sure Grip Paint Brushes and the importer is Early Childhood Resources LLC, of Mt. Laurel, N.J. The hazard includes the surface paint on the handle of these yellow paint brushes contains excessive levels of lead, violating the federal lead paint standard. The description is that the paint brushes were sold in multi-color packages of four. Only the yellow brushes are included in the recall. The paint brushes have a rounded cylinder body with tan bristle tip brushes and measure about 4 inches in height. They were sold nationwide from May, 2007 through December, 2007 for about $4.00. They were manufactured in China.

American Scientific Recalls Magnets Due to Violation of Lead Paint Standard...

The name of the product is Magnets and the units produced total 87,000. The importer is American Scientific LLC, of Columbus, Ohio. The hazard includes the surface paint on the magnets that can contain levels of lead, violating the federal lead paint standard. The recall involves horseshoe, rectangular bar and U-shaped magnets sold primarily to schools for use in science classes. The magnets have red and blue paint on the surface of the magnet. They were sold nationwide from October, 2006 through February, 2008 for between $1.00 and $4.00. They were manufactured in India.

Floppy Friends Horse Toys Recalled by Toy Investments Due to Violation of Lead Paint Standard...

The name of the product is Floppy Friends Horse Toys and the units total 300. The importer is Toy Investments, Inc., d/b/a Toysmith of Auburn, Washington. The hazard includes surface paint on the toy horse that contains excessive levels of lead, violating the federal lead paint standard. The description is that the recalled horse toy has a push up base. When the base is pushed up, the toy horse is floppy. When released, the toy horse stands up straight. The horse is brown and white and the base is green with orange, red flowers and dark blue flowers. They have been sold at hobby stores, gas stations, gift shops and toy stores nationwide from February, 2008 through April, 2008. They were manufactured in China.

Additional Incidents Prompt Re-Announcement of Recall of Gel Candles Due to Fire Hazard...

The name of the product is Gel Candles and the units in question total 1,700. The manufacturer is M & A Global Technologies, Inc., doing business as Spa at Home, of Tallahassee, Florida. Incidents and Injuries include higher than normal flames and flames coming in contact with nearby combustibles resulting in minor fires, smoke and soot damage. The company has also received one additional report of burn injuries to a consumer's hand. The description includes the Everlasting Jelly Candles. They were sold at Spa at Home stores and Spaathorne.com nationwide from October, 2003 through December, 2003 and October, 2005 through December, 2005 for between $9.00 and $50.00. They were manufactured in the United States.

Batting Helmets Recalled by Rawlings Sporting Goods Due to Violation of Lead Paint Standard...

The name of the product is Rawlings Junior Batting Helmets and about 2,300 units are in question. The importer is Rawlings Sporting Goods Co., Inc., of

St. Louis, Missouri. The hazard includes surface paint on the helmets that contain excessive levels of lead, violating the federal lead paint standard. The description includes junior batting helmets with model number CFHLJR and they come in yellow and orange with black accents. The model number can be found on the rear of the helmet. They are sold by sporting goods retailers nationwide from July, 2007 through November, 2007 for about $40.00. They were manufactured in China.

Counterfeit Circuit Breakers Recalled by Specialty Lamp International Due to Fire Hazard...

The name of the product is Counterfeit Circuit Breakers labeled as "Square D" and about 371,000 units were manufactured. The distributor is Specialty Lamp International, Inc., of Deerfield Beach, Florida. The hazard is that these circuit breakers are labeled "Square D" and have been determined to be counterfeit and can fail to trip when they are overloaded, posing a fire hazard to consumers. The description includes the color black and are labeled as Square D QO-series and have the amp rating written on the handle in white paint on the front of the breaker. The authentic Square D circuit breakers manufactured prior to 2003 did not have white paint on the amperage numbers. They are also counterfeit if the Square D insignia is molded onto the breaker side and there is a yellow chromate mounting clip with half of the top of the clip visible. They are sold by Electrical product distributors nationwide from May, 2005 through June, 2006 for between $3.00 and $23.00. They are manufactured in China.

Fireplace Wall Controls Recalled by Hearth & Home Technologies; High Temperatures Can Result in Property Damage...

The name of the product is IntelliSwitch Fireplace Wall Controls and about 22,000 were manufactured. The manufacturer is Hearth & Home Technologies, Inc., of Lakeville, Minnesota and the manufacturer (wall controls) is Nortech Systems, Inc., of Wayzata, Minnesota. The hazard includes failure in the wall control system that can cause the fireplace to turn on by itself creating a risk of property damage. If the control fails and the consumer has left combustible objects directly in front of an unattended fireplace, there may also be a risk of fire. Incidents and injuries include 13 reports of a fireplace turning itself on and continuing to operate, plus two reports of minor property damage caused by high temperature. The description includes the WSK-300 IntelliSwitch Fireplace Wall Controls that were sold with Heat & Glo gas direct vent fireplaces. The recall also includes wall controls sold separately as well as attached to the fireplaces.

Kids Station Toys Recalls Little Tikes Toy Cell Phones Due to Choking Hazard...
The name of the product is Little Tikes Chit 'N Chat Toy Cell Phones and about 1 million were manufactured by Kids Station Toys International, Ltd., of Miami, Florida. The hazard includes the hinge cover on the toy cell phone that can detach from the phone, posing a choking hazard to young children. With regards to injuries, the Consumer Product Safety Commission (CPSC) and the firm have received three reports of the toy breaking, including one report of a child beginning to choke on a small part. The item has been sold in the juvenile department of retail and drug stores nationwide from June 2006 through March 2008 for about $8.00 (individually) or about $20.00 a set. They are manufactured in China.

Children's Hooded Sweatshirts Recalled by Adio Footwear Due to Strangulation Hazard...
The name of the product is Boy's Hooded Zip Fleece Sweatshirts and about 300 units were sold by Adio Footwear, of Carlsbad, California. The hazard includes a drawstring through the hood, which can pose a strangulation problem for children. In February, 1996, CPSC had issued guidelines to help prevent children from strangling or getting entangled on the neck and waist by drawstrings in upper garments, such as jackets and sweatshirts. The item has been sold at Tilly's and Bob's stores nationwide from October, 2007 through December, 2007 for about $40.00. And it was again manufactured in China.

QuinCrafts Children's Jewelry Recalled Due to Risk of Lead Exposure...
The name of the product is Makit & Bakit Jewelry Sets and Suncatcher Sets and about 70,000 units were sold by the importer, QuinCrafts, of Dexter, Michigan. The hazard includes the clasps that are on the jewelry that contain high levels of lead, which is toxic if ingested by young children and can cause adverse health effects. The children's jewelry was sold in a variety of sets that contained necklace, bracelet and earring or ring combinations and sold at AC Moore, CVS, LTD Commodities, Marshall's/TJ Maxx, Michaels Corp. and other toy and independent craft supply stores nationwide from August, 2007 through March, 2008 for about $2.00. The products were made in China.

Remote-Controlled Helicopter Toys Sold Exclusively in Walgreens Recalled Due to Fire and Burn Hazards by TWIE...
The name of the product is "Sky Champion" Wireless Indoor Helicopters and about 120,000 units were manufactured and distributed by importer TWIE, also known as Tradewinds International Enterprises, Inc., of San Francisco,

California. The hazard includes the rechargeable battery that is contained inside of the helicopter that can catch fire, igniting the helicopter and nearby combustible materials. This poses a burn or fire hazard to consumers. TWIE has received two reports of helicopters catching fire but no injuries as of this writing or property damage had been reported. The product has been sold at Walgreens stores nationwide from June, 2007 through November, 2007 for about $20.00 and was made in China.

Jo-Ann Fabric & Craft Stores Recall Outdoor Benches Due to Fall Harzard...

The name of the product is Best Value Park Benches and about 4,500 units were distributed by Jo-Ann Fabrics and Craft Stores, of Hudson, Ohio. The hazard includes the fact that the benches can become unstable and break, posing a fall hazard to consumers. They were sold nationwide from January, 2008 through March, 2008 for about $30.00 and again, were made in China.

Miele Recalls Gas Dryers Due to Risk of Gas Leak or Fire...

The name of the product is Residential Super-large Gas Dryers, model T 9820 and about 3,100 units were imported by Miele, Inc., of Princeton, New Jersey. The hazard of the dryer occurs if it is improperly installed. The dryer's internal gas fitting can loosen, posing a risk of gas leaking into the house. Any gas leak that is not detected can cause asphyxiation, a fire or an explosion. Also, one or both of the caps on the internal exhaust duct can become dislodged, which can cause lint to build up and be carried through the gas burner. This poses a risk of fire. Miele had received 11 reports worldwide in which consumers reported smelling gas after installation of their dryers. The firm has also received a report of a fire causing property damage. No injuries have been reported. Miele distributors had sold these gas dryers between March, 2007 and December, 2007 for about $1,300. They were manufactured in the Czech Republic.

Electric Candle Warmers Recalled by Provo Craft & Novelty Due to Fire Hazard...

The name of the product is Candisense Warmers and about 730,000 units were manufactured by Provo Craft & Novelty, Inc., of Spanish Fork, Utah. The hazard begins when the internal heating element of the candle warmer is detached at any time and will melt the bottom of its plastic casing, which can in turn, ignite or scorch the surface on which the candle warmer is placed, posing a fire hazard to consumers. Provo Craft had received 11 reports of incidents in which the heating elements detached, including two fires and nine incidents of property scorching. One consumer reported a blistered finger. The products have been sold at Wal-Mart and other retailers nationwide from August, 2006 through October, 2007 for between $5.00 and $10.00. Again, these products, like the many others, were manufactured in China.

Michelin Recalls Children's Car Seats after Poor Rating from Customer Magazine...

The name of the product is Michelin Cockpit Car Seats for children and was recalled as a precautionary measure following a poor safety rating from French consumer magazine Que Choisir. About 4,000 of the seats had been sold, mainly in France and Italy, since they were launched in certain European countries in March, 2007.

Source: Office of Information and Public Affair from the U.S. Consumer Product Safety Commission, Washington, DC

— 10 —

Recall News from the
U.S. Food and Drug Administration

As recently as April 25th through the end of May, 2008, the *U.S. Food and Drug Administration* had posted press releases and other notices of recalls and market withdrawals from the firms involved as a service to consumers, the media, and other interested parties. FDA does not endorse either the products or the companies, and these recalls are but a few that have been mentioned.

Actavis Totowa (formerly known as Amide Pharmaceutical, Inc.) recalls all lots of Bertek and UDL Laboratories Digitek (digoxin tablets, USP) as precaution...
On April 25th, 2008, Actavis Totowa LLC, a United States manufacturing division of the international generic pharmaceutical company Actavis Group, of Morristown, New Jersey initiated a Class I nationwide recall of Digitek under a "UDL" label. The voluntary all lot recall is due to the possibility that tablets with double the appropriate thickness may have been commercially released. These tablets may contain twice the approved level of active ingredient than is appropriate. Digitek is used to treat heart failure and abnormal heart rhythms. The existence of double strength tablets poses a risk of digitalis toxicity in patients with renal failure. Digitalis toxicity can cause nausea, vomiting, dizziness, low blood pressure, cardiac instability and bradycardia. Death can also result from excessive Digitalis intake. Several reports of illness and injuries have been received. Actavis manufactures the products for Mylan

and the products are distributed by Mylan and UDL under the Bertek and UDL labels. Bertek and UDL are affiliates of Mylan.

Lifetime Brands Voluntarily Recalls Certain Items Nationwide from its Pfaltzgraff Villa della Luna pattern and Nautica J Class pattern (Red Only) Stoneware Dinnerware Product Lines...

On April 28th, 2008, Lifetime Brands, Inc. of Garden City, New York, announced that, as a result of its internal compliance and independent product testing programs, it became aware that certain Pfaltzgraff Villa della Luna pattern and Nautica J Class pattern stoneware dinnerware products may exceed the Food and Drug Administration's guidance levels for lead and/or cadmium. No illness related to these products has been reported to date.

Little Bay Baking Company Recalls all Bags of Cornbread and Muffin Mix

On May 2nd, 2008 the Little Bay Baking Company of Newmarket, New Hampshire recalled all bags of corn bread and muffin mix sold before this date because it contains undeclared soy. People who have an allergy of severe sensitivity to soy run the risk of serious or life-threatening allergic reaction if they consume these products. These products were distributed throughout the United States through retail stores and internet orders.

Hydrox Labs Issued a Voluntary Recall of Alcohol-Free Mouthwash Nationwide Distributed by Cardinal Health...

On May 2nd, 2008 Hydrox Labs, Elgin, Illinois had issued a voluntary recall of the Cardinal Health labeled alcohol-free mouthwash and the FDA had been apprised of this action. The mouthwash had been tested and been found positive for *Burkholderia cepacia (B. cepacia)*. The CDC had confirmed hospital illnesses in one state associated with the use of the affected mouthwash as it was distributed to hospitals, medical centers, and long term care facilities nationwide. *B. Cepacia* poses little medical risk to healthy people. However, people who have certain health problems such as weakened immune systems or chronic lung diseases, particularly cystic fibrosis (CF), may be more susceptible to infections with *B. cepacia* which is a known cause of infections in hospitalized patients. *B. Cepacia* bacteria are often resistant to common antibiotics. The effects of *B. cepacia* on people vary widely, ranging from no symptoms at all to serious respiratory infections, especially in patients with CF.

Lezza Blue Raspberry Italian Ice Recalled...
On May 6th, 2008 Cedar Crest Specialties, Inc., Manitowoc, Wisconsin announced a recall on one lot code of Lezza Blue Raspberry Italian Ice because, it may contain milk allergen protein that is not listed in the product's ingredient statement. People who have an allergy or severe sensitivity to milk may experience a potentially serious or life-threatening allergic reaction if they consume this product, which was distributed to retail outlets in Illinois, Wisconsin, Oklahoma, Texas, Michigan, Louisiana, Kansas, Indiana, Georgia, Florida, Ohio, Missouri, Kentucky, Nebraska, Pennsylvania, Arkansas, and Minnesota during 2006 and 2007.

Blount Fine Foods Issued Allergy Alert on Undeclared Shrimp in All Natural New England Clam Chowder, 20 Oz. Cup...
On May 8th, 2008 Blount Fine Foods of Fall River, MA recalled Blount All Natural New England Clam Chowder because it contained undeclared shrimp. People who have an allergy or severe sensitivity to shrimp run the risk of serious or life-threatening allergic reaction if they consume these products. This clam chowder was distributed through supermarket chains including Shaw's in MA and CT; Omni in Weston, MA; and the Blount Factory Store in Warren, RI.

Medtronic Initiated Voluntary Field Actions for Selected Heparin-Coated Products Used During Cardiopulmonary Bypass...
On May 8th, 2008 Medtronic, Inc. announced that it was initiating a voluntary and precautionary recall of selected products featuring the Carmeda BioActive surface. The affected devices are disposable products used during cardiopulmonary bypass (CPB) for heart surgeries. Affected products include blood oxygenators, reservoirs, pumps, cannulae, and tubing packs.

This action was being taken subsequent to the U.S. Food and Drug Administration's April 8th, 2008 recommendation to device manufacturers that heparin supplies be checked with newly-developed tests, and that affected products be evaluated for possible field corrective action. Limited lots of Carmeda-coated products were manufactured with heparin found to have contaminated with over-sulfated chondroitin sulfate (OSCS). The patient risk associated with the presence of OSCS in heparin-coated medical devices is not known at this time.

Sweetwater Valley Farm, Inc. Recalled Tennessee Aged Black Pepper Cheese...
On May 15th, 2008 Sweetwater Valley Farm, Inc. of Philadelphia, TN recalled Tennessee Aged Black Pepper Cheese because it had the potential

to be contaminated with Listeria monocytogenes, an organism which can cause serious and sometimes fatal infections in young children, frail or elderly people, and others with weakened immune systems. Although healthy individuals may suffer only short-term symptoms such as high fever, severe headache, stiffness, nausea, abdominal pain and diarrhea, Listeria infection can cause miscarriages and stillbirths among pregnant women. The product was distributed between December 27, 2007 and May 12, 2008 and less than 100 pounds was distributed.

Atrium Initiates Voluntary Recall Action Regarding HYDRAGLIDE Brand Heparin-Coated Thoracic Drainage Catheters used for Autotransfusion during Cardiopulmonary Bypass Surgery…

On May 15th, 2008 Atrium Medical Corporation announced that it was initiating a voluntary and precautionary recall of selected lots of HYDRAGLIDE Brand Heparin-Coated Thoracic Drainage Catheters. Limited lots were manufactured with heparin found to have been contaminated with oversulfated chondroitin sulfate (OSCS). The patient risk associated with the presence of OSCS in heparin-coated medical devices is not known at this time. The U.S. FDA has received reports of serious injury and death in patients who have been administered injectable heparin products containing high levels of OSCS.

FDA Shuts Down Seafood Processing Company, Requires Products Be Recalled…

On May 16th, 2008 the U.S. Food and Drug Administration directed Hope Food Supply, Inc., a Pasadena, Texas food processing company, to shut down and immediately recall all products manufactured from its Texas facility since 2007. The company, under a different name, had manufactured dried smoked catfish steaks and other smoked seafood products and had been subject to a consent decree of permanent injunction requiring it to develop and implement and adequate Hazard Analysis and Critical Control Point (HACCP) plan for its fish and fishery products. The firm had not developed this plan. The company cannot restart manufacturing until they have implemented and FDA-approved HACCP plan.

The FDA's HACCP regulations require that all seafood processors develop and implement adequate HACCP plans that identify all food safety hazards that are likely to occur for each kind of seafood product that they process, and set forth preventative measures to control those hazards. The HACCP violations documented by the FDA pose a public health hazard because, without adequate controls, Hope Food Supply's seafood products could harbor pathogenic bacteria such as *Staphylococcus aureus* and *Listeria monocytogenes.* Food products with these kinds of pathogens can cause serious illnesses in people who eat them. The products were distributed nationwide and any consumer who has eaten these products should consult their health care professional if they have experienced adverse reactions.

Medicis Announced Voluntary Recall of Solodyn (minocycline HCL, USP) 90 Mg Tablets, Extended Release; Lot Numbers B080037 and B080038 Due to Product Mix-Up...

On May 16th, 2008 in Scottsdale, Arizona, Medicis announced that the Company voluntarily recalled the above lot numbers as Medicis received a report that one bottle had contained AZASAN (azathioprine tablets) 75 mg instead of SOLODYN Extended Release Tablets, 90 mg.

AZASAN is an immuno-suppressive agent used in transplant patients to prevent kidney rejection and for the treatment of rheumatoid arthritis. Taking AZASAN instead of SOLODYN presents a health hazard and safety risk to patients. Side effects associated with the use of AZASAN, particularly in the elderly, include mylosuppression (decrease in the number of red and white blood cells and platelets), infection, bleeding, chills, nausea, vomiting and diarrhea. Joint and muscle pain are also common side effects. Unanticipated interactions with other drugs may also lead to serious adverse events. SOLODYN is manufactured by AAIPharma, Inc. under contract to Medicis. The two lots were manufactured during February 2008. The recall is limited to these lots, and ample supplies of SOLODYN remain on the market.

Orval Kent Foods Recalled Single Limited Production Run of Amish Macaroni Salad Sold Under the Orval Kent and Yoder's Brand Names...

On May 26th, 2008, the Orval Kent Foods had voluntarily recalled approximately 23,000 pounds of Amish Macaroni Salad that may very well pose a health risk. This voluntary action took place by the Ohio Department of Agriculture and Consumer Services in response to the results of a test conducted on a single package of Amish Macaroni Salad. The products were shipped to customers who had distribution to retail and food service establishments in the following areas: Delaware, Illinois, Indiana, Maryland, Michigan, New Jersey, New York, Ohio and Pennsylvania. The Salad may cause E. coli plus a diarrhea illness often with bloody stools. Young children, the elderly and those with weak immune systems are most susceptible to foodborne illnesses.

Supreme Cuts Announced Voluntary Recall of Small Sample of *Off The Cob* Fresh Kernel Corn...

On May 27th, 2008, in Mahwah, New Jersey, as a precautionary measure, Supreme Cuts LLC had announced that it was voluntarily recalling 87 cases of *Off the Cob* Fresh Kernel Corn in 12 oz bags. The Product may be contaminated with *Listeria monocytogenes,* an organism which can cause serious and sometimes fatal infections in young children, frail and elderly people, and others with weakened immune systems. Although healthy individuals may experience only short-term symptoms such as high fever, severe headache, stiffness, nausea, abdominal pain, and diarrhea, listeria infection can cause miscarriages and stillbirths in pregnant women.

International Pharmaceuticals Announces Voluntary Recall of all Virility Products

On May 29th, 2008 in Bradford, MA, the International Pharmaceuticals, Ltd., announced that it was conducting a voluntary recall of all the company's supplement product sold under the brand name of Viril-ity-Power Tabs after being informed by representatives of the FDA that lab analysis of a sample form one lot of the product revealed that it contained a potentially harmful undeclared ingredient, hydroxyhomosildenafil.

FDA asserts that this ingredient is an analog of sildenafil, which is the active chemical ingredient of an FDA-approved drug used for Erectile Dysfunction (ED) in men to enhance sexual performance. The use of undeclared chemicals pose a threat to consumers because they may harmfully interact with nitrates found in some prescription drugs (such as nitroglycerin) and may lower blood pressure to dangerous levels. Consumers with diabetes, high blood pressure, high cholesterol, or heart disease often take such nitrates. VIP Tabs are sold in retail outlets nationwide and are packaged into 2-capsule blister packs and 8-capsule bottles. CB Distributors of Benoit, Wisconsin sold the products nationwide.

National Highway Traffic Safety Administration Recalls Cars / Tires / Infant Car Seats

Just in one day, May 30th, 2008 many manufacturers had voluntarily or forced to recall many items relating to traffic safety that involves automobiles, infants, and the health and welfare of all passengers on the road. The National Highway Traffic Safety Administration's Vehicle Safety Hotline is 1-888-327-4236 or go to HTTP://www.safercar.gov.

- **EVENFLOW** recalled 1,000,000 models 390, 391, 534, and 552 Discovery Car Seats or Associated Travel Systems manufactured from April 2005 through January 2008. In recent laboratory tests conducted by **EVENFLOW** and NHTSA to evaluate the performance of these seats in high impact side collisions, it was revealed that the car seat could potentially become separated from its base under these conditions.

- **RECARO** recalled 7,498 Signo and Como Convertible Child Restraint Systems with color model codes of 330.00 and 331.00, manufactured prior to December 18, 2007. The harness may become disconnected from the harness connector when a child is placed in or removed from the child seat.

- **COMBI** recalled 67,167 Centre, Centre ARB, and Shuttle Infant Child Restrain Systems, model numbers 8065, 8074, 8086, 8087, and 8520, and associated travel systems, model numbers 4400, 4515, and 4520, that contain Centre and Shuttle Car Seat Models. This recall includes the entire production of these models from October 2005 through December 2007. In the event of a frontal crash, the car seat could potentially become separated from its base.

- **GRACO** recalled 121,042 Cargo Booster Seats (Child Restraint Systems) manufactured between January 9th, 2007 and March 3rd, 2008. These seats were labeled with an incorrect telephone number for the national highway traffic safety administration (NHTSA) which fails to conform to the labeling requirements of federal motor vehicle safety standard #213, Child Restrain Systems.

- **EVENFLO** recalled 1,038 Discovery Infant Child Restraints, models 3021769Z and 3021854Z, manufactured on February 4, 2008. Due to a manufacturing variability, some units may have been produced without complete assembly of the release handle located on the back of the seat. Under certain conditions, the seat may become separated from the base, potentially resulting in serious injury to the child.

- **GENERAL MOTORS** recalled 5,862 MY 2000-2002 Chevrolet Blazer, MY 2000-2001 GMC Jimmy, and MY 2000 Oldsmobile Bravada sport utility vehicles. The multifunction switch could develop an open circuit condition that results in the stop lamps and the rear hazard lamps becoming inoperative. The center high mounted stop lamp and turn signal functions are not affected. The loss of stop lamps and rear hazard lamps could fail to warn a following driver that the vehicle is braking and/or is stopped and could result in a crash.

- **BENTLEY** recalled 13,420 MY 2004-2008 Continental GT, Continental GT Speed, Continental Flying Spur, and Continental GTC vehicles. There is the potential for road salt to corrode the outer surface of the fuel filter. This could lead to the filter housing becoming porous with a corresponding fuel leak. A fuel leak in the presence of an ignition source could result in a fire.

- **KAWASAKI** recalled 1,393 MY 2009 KLX250T9F and KLX250T9FL Motorcycles. The throttle grip and the handlebar grip may come loose and separate from the handlebar and throttle tube. This creates the potential for a crash resulting in injury or death.

- **DEL-NAT** recalled 968 Load Range E Tires, size LT265/75R16, produced between December 2 and December 30, 2007. These tires fail to conform to the requirements of federal motor vehicle safety standard #139, "New Pneumatic Radial Tires for Light Vehicles." After testing, a bulge can occur in the lower sidewall on the white sidewall side which indicates the existence of a separation between two lower sidewall components. This condition could result in a vehicle crash.

- **PIRELLI** recalled 8,273 tires, size LT 235/80 R 17 Load Range E, produced from July 11, 2005 to October 30, 2007. Tread chunking, tread chunkout, partial tread separation and/or belt edge separation can occur. Any of these conditions can result in a vehicle crash.

- **PRO COMP** recalled 1,206 Load Range E Tires, size LT 265/75R 16, produced between December 2, 2007 and January 12, 2008. These tires fail to conform to the requirements of federal motor vehicle safety standard number 139, "New Pneumatic Radial Tires for Light Vehicles." After testing, a bulge can occur in the lower sidewall on the white sidewall side which indicates the existence of a separation between two lower sidewall components. This condition could result in a vehicle crash.

- **HERCULES TIRE** recalled 2,005 Load Range E Tires, size LT 265/75R 16, produced between December 2, 2007 and January 12, 2008. These tires fail to conform to the requirements of federal motor vehicle safety standard number 139, "New Pneumatic Radial Tires for Light Vehicles." After testing, a bulge can occur in the lower sidewall on the white sidewall side which indicates the existence of a separation between two lower sidewall components. This condition could result in a vehicle crash.

- **NOKIAN TYRES** recalled 931 Load Range E Tires, size LT 265/75R 16, produced between December 2, 2007 and February 8, 2008. These tires fail to conform to the requirements of federal motor vehicle safety standard number 139, "New Pneumatic Radial Tires for Light Vehicles." After testing, a bulge can occur in the lower sidewall on the white sidewall side which indicates the existence of a separation between two lower sidewall components. This condition could result in a vehicle crash.

- **BFNT (BRIDGESTONE / V-STEEL G-TRACTION, BRIDGESTONE / FIRESTONE NORTH AMERICAN TIRE** recalled 143 Bridgestone V-Steel G-Traction 24R21 truck tires manufactured during the months of March and October 2007. These tires fail to conform to the endurance requirements of federal motor vehicle safety standard number 119, "New Pneumatic Tires for Vehicles other than Passenger Cars." The purpose of this standard is to provide safe operation performance levels of tires used on motor vehicles with a GVWR of more than 10,000 pounds.

- **ACCC / AMERICAN PROSPECTOR A/T** through its manufacturer American Car Care Centers, Inc. recalled 1,018 American Prospector A/T Load Range E Tires, size LT265/75R 16, produced between December 2, 2007 and February 2, 2008. These tires fail to conform to the requirements of federal motor vehicle safety standard number 139, "New Pneumatic Radial Tires for Light Vehicles." After testing, a bulge can occur in the lower sidewall on the white sidewall side which indicates the existence of a separation between two lower sidewall components. This condition could result in a vehicle crash.

- **TBC CORPORATION** recalled 17,014 various Load Range E Tires, size LT265/75R 16, produced between December 2, 2007 and February 2, 2008. These tires fail to conform to the requirements of federal motor vehicle safety standard number 139, "New Pneumatic Radial Tires for Light Vehicles." After testing, a bulge can occur in the lower sidewall on the white sidewall side which indicates the existence of a separation between two lower sidewall components. This condition could result in a vehicle crash.

- **SURE TURE / SUMMIT TRAIL CLIMBER AT** recalled 295 Load Range E Tires, size LT265/75R 16, produced between December 9, 2007 and December 15, 2007. These tires fail to conform to the requirements of federal motor vehicle safety standard number 139, "New Pneumatic Radial Tires for Light Vehicles." After testing, a bulge can occur in the lower sidewall on the white sidewall side which indicates the existence of a separation between two lower sidewall components. This condition could result in a vehicle crash.

- **COOPER / DISCOVER ATR** recalled 48,037 Load Range E Tires, sizes LT265/75R 16 and LT235/85R 16, produced between

December 2, 2007 and February 9, 2008. These tires fail to conform to the requirements of federal motor vehicle safety standard number 139, "New Pneumatic Radial Tires for Light Vehicles." A bulge can occur in the lower sidewall on the white sidewall side which indicates the existence of a separation between two lower sidewall components. This condition could result in a vehicle crash.

Note: Whoever made these tires for the companies above made the same mistake for all Load Range R Tires in the same sizes and models. They should be investigated.

United States EPA (Environmental Protection Agency Toxic Chemicals and Pesticide News

On May 29th, 2008, the *Con Edison Company of New York* had made a commitment to the U.S. Environmental Protection Agency (EPA) to replace underground cables containing lead with less hazardous alternatives. This commitment was made through EPA's National Partnership for Environmental Priorities Program (NPEP). EPA Regional Administrator Alan J. Steinberg and Deputy Director for the Office of Solid Waste Maria Vickers welcomed Con Edison into this voluntary program that promotes the reduction and elimination of priority chemicals in the operations of companies and organizations nationwide. The commitment by Con Edison is one of the largest in the national NPEP program to date, and is by far the largest in EPA Region 2, which covers New York, New Jersey, Puerto Rico and the U.S. Virgin Islands.

The NPEP program partners with private and public entities to eliminate or reduce their use of chemicals that, when released into the environment, can linger for decades. EPA has identified 31 priority chemicals, lead and PCBs included, on which NPEP partners focus. If improperly disposed of, these chemicals can repeatedly cycle through the land, water and air affecting the environment and human health. Probably, this is what China should be doing right now!

"By significantly reducing its use of lead, Con Edison is exhibiting environmental leadership and improving power service for New Yorkers," said Regional Administrator Alan Steinberg. "By taking the steps necessary to be a partner, Con Ed is embracing the NPEP motto: 'Better Environment, Better Neighbor, and Better Business.' "

Con Edison's plan is to remove 2,400 sections of underground paper insulated lead-clad electric feeder cables in 2008 and another 2,400 sections in 2009. Each section of lead-clad cable is estimated to contain approximately 1,000 pounds of encased lead sheathing, which will be recycled at a nearby local recycling facility. As a long-term goal, Con Edison plans to replace all of these cables by 2020. Con Edison estimates that by 2020, at the conclusion of this project, as much as 15,000 tons of reclaimed lead sheathing will be recycled as a result of these recycling efforts. Currently, paper insulated lead-clad cables make up 20 percent of Con Edison's underground electric network.

When these cables are removed, they will be replaced by solid dielectric cables, which are made of copper conductors surrounded by synthetic rubber. This alternative is considered superior to lead-clad cables in both environmental and electric distribution characteristics.

Beyond its commitment to lead reduction, over the past decade, Con Edison has also removed most of its equipment that contained high levels of polychlorinated biphenyls (PCBs). To date, all recovered equipment has been decontaminated and recycled.

Nationwide, EPA has close to 180 NPEP partnership facilities, including 32 in Region 2. It is encourages that all interested parties to look further into the NPEP program and apply on-line at http://www.epa.gov/npep.

EPA Requires Safety Measures for Rodent-Control Products To Protect Children and Wildlife

In Washington, D.C., on May 29th, 2008 it was announced by the *U.S. Environmental Protection Agency* that new safety measures will protect children from accidental exposure to rodent-control products. These measures will also reduce the risk of accidental poisonings of pets and wildlife. EPA is requiring that then rodenticides used in bait products marketed to consumers be enclosed in bait stations, making the pesticide inaccessible to children and pets, and is also prohibiting the sale of loose bait, such as pellets, for use in homes.

"The new restrictions will better protect our children, pets and wildlife from thousands of accidental exposures that occur every year," said EPA Assistant Administrator Jim Gulliford. "These practical and low cost measures provide protection while ensuring rodent control products will continue to be effective and affordable for all consumers."

Rodenticide products containing brodifacoum, bromadiolone, difethialone and difenacoum are known to pose the greatest risk to wildlife and will no longer be allowed to be sold or distributed in the consumer market. Bait stations will be required for all outdoor, above-ground uses for products containing these ingredients. EPA believes that these steps will significantly reduce the amount of product in the environment, providing additional protection for wildlife from poisonings by these more toxic and persistent products.

EPA had required that companies manufacturing these products respond to EPA within 90 days of this notice regarding their intention to comply with the new requirements. Over the past ten years, EPA has used a public process and rigorous scientific information to evaluate and address the risks associated with use of the standards. For additional information, visit:

www.epa.gov/pesticides/reregistration/rodenticides/finairiskdecision.htm

EPA Engages Chinese Students on Improving Health and Environment in Their Homeland

In Washington, D.C., on May 16th, 2008, *EPA Headquarters* had hosted Chinese students committed to improving public health and the environment in their homeland and around the world. Over the course of three days, EPA and the students had an opportunity to discuss environmental challenges facing both countries and solutions.

"The U.S. had worked for many years to achieve a growing economy and a healthy environment," said Rick Otis, deputy associate administer for EPA's Office of Policy, Economics and Innovation. "China faces a similar challenge, and we look forward to sharing our experience with its future leaders, as well as learning from them how to move both our nations toward a cleaner and more productive future."

EPA also hosted the third annual meeting of the Environment and Public Health Network for Chinese Students and Scholars (ENCSS). During the meeting, the students discussed the U.S. experience in protecting the environment, current environmental challenges in China, and the links between environmental and public health.

The students and scholars also participated in EPA's annual Science Forum. Many of the students presented research on topics ranging from antibiotic resistance to climate change adaptation in northwest China.

ENCSS is a network of mostly doctoral and post-doctoral students attending U.S. universities which has three goals:

- To connect Chinese scholars, students and others who are concerned about environmental and public health issues;

- To unite China and other countries in sharing information and discussing solutions for environmental and public health issues in China and the rest of the world; and
- To provide the supporting logic for wise environmental and public health practices

Working with ENCSS is part of EPA's long-standing efforts to assist the agency's Chinese counterparts in addressing international and domestic environmental issues. The U.S.-China Strategic Economic Dialogue, begun in 2004, has put a greater high-level focus on these environmental issues along with the integrity of trade, balanced economic development, energy conservation, financial sector reform, and advancing bilateral investment.

For more information on ENCSS, visit: http://www.encss.org

For more information on EPA's Science Forum, visit: www.epa.gov/ord/scienceforum/

Reno, Nevada Company Pays Over $80,000 for Toxic Chemical Reporting Violations

Reporting from San Francisco on May 6th, 2008 the U.S. Environmental Protection Agency reached an $80,080 settlement with a Reno, Nevada company for its failure to submit required toxic chemical reports, a violation of the Emergency Planning and Community Right-to-Know Act.

Electronic Evolution Technologies, Inc., located at Double R Road in Reno, Nev., failed to submit timely, complete, and correct reports detailing the amounts of lead processed at its facility from 2002 through 2005. EPA inspectors discovered the four violations as a result of a routine inspection in April, 2007 and a follow-up investigation. Obviously, many of the procedures and investigations by the EPA are exposing companies that have been negligent in doing business, whether it involves chemicals, or other products that are dangerous to the well-being of the people. More of this is needed, and hopefully, these examples will be followed in China.

"Facilities that process particularly toxic chemicals, such as lead, must follow reporting rules to ensure area residents and emergency response personnel are informed of possible chemical hazards locally," said Nathan Lau, Communities and Ecosystems Division Associate Director for EPA's Pacific Southwest region. "This penalty should remind others that we are maintaining a close watch over chemical reporting practices and are serious about enforcing community right-to-know laws."

Federal community right-to-know laws require facilities processing, manufacturing, or otherwise using more than 100 pounds of lead to report releases of this highly chemical on an annual basis to the EPA and the state. Although Electronic Evolution Technologies exceeded these thresholds from 2002 through 2005, it failed to submit reports to the agency for any of those years.

The facility uses lead in connection with its manufacturing of printed circuit boards. Although the facility's operations did not release lead into the environment, it was still required to report lead processing to the EPA because the facility was over the applicable reporting threshold.

Exposure to lead may result in high blood pressure, digestive problems, muscle and joint pain, nerve disorders, memory and concentration problems, increased change of illness during pregnancy, and harm to a fetus, including brain damage or death. Exposure to even low levels of lead can severely harm children under the age of six.

Each year, the EPA compiles the information submitted to it from the previous year regarding toxic chemical releases and produces a national Toxics Release inventory database for public availability. This TRI database estimates the amounts of each toxic chemical released to the environment, treated or recycled on-site, or transferred off-site for waste management, and also provides a trend analysis of toxic chemical releases.

For more information on the TRI program, visit: http"//www.epa.gov/tri

EPA's TRI program data, as well as other environmental databases, can be assessed at:

http://yosemite.epa.gov/opa/admpress.nsf/o/CF8ED9225B38FODA8525744100662624

Source: U.S. Food and Drug Administration / National Highway Traffic Safety Administration / U.S. Environmental Protection Agency

— 11 —

United States Food Safety and Inspection
Service Recalls

From March 14th, through May 21st, 2008 alone Washington had reported recalls that involved many companies throughout the country that placed high risk on poultry, meat, packages of chicken salad and other packages of food sold in stores, ground beef and sausages that initiated problems of E. coli and other infectious diseases and illnesses. These are but a few mentioned, but many more have slipped on by, causing potential human exposure and infections among consumers nationwide. Not only have products produced in China been the cause of such sicknesses, but those products manufactured right here in this country.

Alabama Firm Recalls Poultry Giblets That May Be Adulterated...
Cable's Inc., a Collinsville, Ala., establishment, had voluntarily recalled approximately 943,000 pounds of various fresh and frozen poultry giblets and fresh carcasses with giblets inserted that may be adulterated due to improper disposition of the giblets, the U.S. Department of Agriculture's Food Safety and Inspection Service announced. These included such products as:

- "Cagle's MRB Breaded Gizzards"
- "Cagle's Frying Chicken Gizzards"
- "Cagle's Frying Chicken Livers"
- "Our Premium Deli Pre-breaded Chicken Livers"
- "Cagle's Frying Chicken Hearts"

- "Cagle's Frying Chicken Skinless Necks"

Kansas Firm Recalls Cattle Heads That Contain Prohibited Materials...
Elkhorn Valley Packing LLC, a Harper, Kan., establishment voluntarily recalled approximately 406,000 pounds of frozen cattle heads with tonsils not completely removed, which is not compliant with regulations that require the removal of tonsils from cattle of all ages, the U.S. Department of Agriculture's Food Safety and Inspection Service announced. Tonsils are considered specified risk material (SRM) and must be removed from cattle of all ages in accordance with FSIS regulations. SRMs are tissues that are known to contain the infective agent in cattle infected with BSE, as well as materials that are closely associated with these potentially infective tissues.

New York Firm Recalls Meat and Poultry Products for Possible *Listeria* Contamination...
Gourmet Boutique, LLC a Jamaica, N.Y. firm voluntarily recalled approximately 286,320 pounds of fresh and frozen meat and poultry products that may have been contaminated with *Listeria monocytogenes,* the U.S. Department of Agriculture's Food Safety and Inspection Service announced. The following "Gourmet Boutique" products have been recalled:

> Curry Chicken Salad; Fruit and Nut Honey Chicken Salad Kit; Home Style Chicken Salad; Szechuan Style Chicken Salad; Buffalo Bob Twister; Chicken Burrito; Chicken Fajita; Chicken Chipotle Salad Twister; Chicken Parmigiana Twister; Hail Chicken Caesar Twister; Ham & Swiss Club Twister; Home-style Chicken Salad; Italian Stallion Twister; Turkey-Club Twister; plus Archer Farms and Jan's products.

The fresh meat and poultry salad products were produced between April 19 and April 24th, 2008, while the frozen products were produced between October 23, 2007 and April 23, 2008. Recalled products were sent to food service and retail establishments nationwide. Consumption of food contaminated with *Listeria monocytogenes* can cause listeriosis, and uncommon but potentially fatal disease. Healthy people rarely contract listeriosis. However, listeriosis can cause high fever, severe headache, neck stiffness and nausea. Listeriosis can also cause miscarriages and stillbirths, as well as serious and sometimes fatal infections in those with weakened immune systems, such as infants, the elderly and persons with HIV infection or undergoing chemotherapy.

Hawaiian Firm Recalls Ground Beef Products Due to Possible *E. coli* 0157:H7 Contamination...

Palama Holdings, LLC, a Kapolei, Hawaii firm, voluntarily recalled approximately 68,670 pounds of ground beef products because they may be contaminated with *E. coli*, the U.S. Department of Agriculture's Food Safety and Inspection Service announced. Some of the possible contaminated products include "May's Teriyaki Beef Patties," "May's Beef Picnic Patties," and "May's Beef Pattie, Layer Pack."

Consumers preparing ground beef products that may or may not be contaminated should heed the following advice:

- Wash hands with warm, soapy water for at least 20 seconds before and after handling raw meat and poultry. Wash cutting boards, dishes and utensils with hot, soapy water. Immediately clean spills.
- Keep raw meat, fish and poultry away from other food that will not be cooked. Use separate cutting boards for raw meat, poultry and egg products and cooked foods.
- Consumers should only eat ground beef or ground beef patties that have been cooked to a safe internal temperature of 160 degrees F.
- Color is NOT a reliable indicator that ground beef or ground beef patties have been approved and not spoiled.

New York Firm Recalls Ground Beef Products That May Contain Pieces of Plastic...

Fairbank Reconstruction Corp., an Ashville, NY establishment, voluntarily recalled approximately 22,481 pounds of ground beef products that may contain pieces of plastic, the U.S. Department of Agriculture's Food Safety and Inspection Service announced. Under the Shaw's label, some of the products include:

Fresh Ground Sirloin; Fresh Ground Beef; Fresh Ground Beef Patties; Price Chopper Fresh Ground Beef Sirloin Patties; Price Chopper Fresh Home-style Ground Beef Round Patties; Price Chopper Pub Style Ground Beef Chuck Patties; and Price Chopper Fresh Home-style Ground Beef Chuck Patties.

Illinois Firm Recalls Beef Products Due To Possible *E. coli* 0157:H7 Contamination...

JSM Meat Holdings Company, Inc., a Chicago, Ill., firm voluntarily recalled an undetermined amount of beef products intended for use in ground products because they may be contaminated with *E. coli*, the Department of

Agriculture's Food Safety and Inspection Service announced. The following products that were subject to recall included "Morreale Meat" beef products labeled as "Boneless Chucks," "Boneless Clods," "Flat Rounds," "Gooseneck Rounds," "Knuckle," "Heel Meat," "Scotties," "Trimmings 50," "Trimmings 60," "Trimmings 80," "Trimmings 85," or "Trimmings 90."

California Firm Recalls Pork Sausages For Possible *Listeria* Contamination...

Cecina Los Amigos, A Carson, Calif., firm voluntarily recalled approximately 290 pounds of pork blood sausages that may be contaminated with *Listeria monocytogenes,* the U.S. Department of Agriculture's Food Safety and Inspection Service announced. The following product has been recalled: "Cecina Los Amigos Pork Blood Sausage (Moronga).

The pork blood sausages were produced on May 14th, 2008 and were distributed to retail establishments in northern California. The problem was discovered by routine FSIS microbiological sampling. FSIS has received no reports of illnesses associated with consumption of products subject to this recall. Anyone with signs or symptoms of foodborne illness from this product or any other product that may or may not have been recalled should consult a medical professional.

Just How Safe Are Imports from China?
Just How Safe are those goods
manufactured in the U.S.A.?

As a country with many stringent rules and regulations placed on our goods to keep them safe for public consumption, we still have a long way to go. But why are we so much behind in safeguarding those imports from China and other countries? Why are only 5% of the goods being checked...inspectors being accused of taking payoffs to allow the goods to go through...and not taking action against the countries that ship bad products to our shores that may cause illnesses and death? Why are our Washington leaders not even concentrating on this horrific issue?

The truth is, following requests from certain officials in the United States, Chinese authorities are apparently now making closer checks on food exports. At least food is the most toxic and polluted products that can affect us more so than other types of imports. Chinese exporters have been asked to register with the government and adopt other measures in an attempt to provide greater assurance on the safety of their products.

The requests came after a series of problems with Chinese exports which have resulted in toxic materials being found in toothpaste, fish and pet food, as mentioned before. The Canadian Online Pharmacy had reported on Sunday, May 27th, 2007 that the list of potentially deadly products being exported to the U.S. and other countries seems to be growing on a weekly basis.

Food items such as proteins and glycerine must now be checked after a run of health scares involving tainted Chinese-made products and companies are now required to tell Chinese customs when they export or import glycerine, and have it inspected.

Concern has arisen following a number of pet deaths due to tainted wheat gluten and rice protein exported from China used in the animal feed; even more alarming is that toxins such as diethylene glycol, a toxic chemical used in engine coolants, has been found in tubes of Chinese-made toothpaste sold in Australia, the Dominican Republic and Panama. The toothpaste was supposed to contain glycerine. The imported pet food ingredients, it was found a month before, to be spiked with the industrial chemical melamine and related compounds. The scare prompted recalls of pet foods but the list includes dirty mushrooms, drug-laced frozen eel and juice made with unsafe color additives.

Five proteins, including casein which is used as a food binding agent, are also on the list, as are citric and tartaric acid, other widely used food additives, molasses, maple syrup and even ginger biscuits. Chinese imports are more often stopped at the border, more so in 2008, by the Food and Drug Administration than any other country's and experts say the problem with China is getting bigger and is appearing in different realms.

This book has covered many other products that have been tainted including leather, dinnerware, clothing, toys, car seats, tires and steel. The FDA has now stopped all imports of Chinese toothpaste and is warning consumers not to buy or eat imported fish labeled as monkfish because it might actually be pufferfish, which contains a potentially deadly toxin called tetrodotoxin. The FDA says that eating pufferfish that contains the potent toxin could result in serious illness or death.

At this time, I, as well as my family and friends, will not buy ANY FISH that has a label that says, "FROM CHINA!" We just do not trust any of the manufacturers in China any longer.

According to the FDA, 282-22-pound boxes labeled as Chinese monkfish that was distributed to Illinois, California and Hawaii has been recalled. For all I care, they may as well recall all other fish that has been exported from China and protect the lives of our American people.

Food safety has become an increasingly high-profile issue between the United States and China, and China is now under intense international scrutiny regarding its exports.

Imports from China have now caused more awareness in our country as more and more people are becoming aware of the inadequate products…and I say it mildly…that has reached our borders. Those who are aware of how dealing with China has affected our bad economy are now expressing their points of view. The impending recession in our country is related to what is occurring in China, their extensive use of oil which has been a part of the increase in oil prices, and the fact that we seem to be dependent on goods made in China because they are at least one third the price if the same goods were made in the United States. Whether or not all of this will change soon, it has brought more people publicly expressing their points of view and they are finally speaking out about this problem, although only a handful right now:

- "The World shouldn't complain too much. The U.S. was the engine that pulled the world out of its economic slump after WWII."
- "The U.S. is in the process of doing what every government does when it can't repay its debt…it lets inflation take care of it. Don't be fooled by the Fed's professional aversion to inflation. Like fire, you don't want to see it get out of control, but it can have its uses if properly handled."
- For several years, two rules have governed America's dollar policy. The first was that only the treasury security talked at length about the greenback. The second was that he repeated a vacuous mantra about a strong dollar being in America's interests, even as everyone knew policymakers quietly welcomed its slide.
- It is easy, but wrong to cite the US Government's debt as evidence of impending doom. Although the debt is higher than ever in absolute dollars, the correct measure of a country's debt is the amount of debt as a percentage of the GDP. Of course, the debt is bigger in absolute dollars because of inflation. But when using the real yardstick (debt as a percentage of GDP) we see that the debt is getting slightly smaller and not nearly at apocalyptic levels. The falling dollar is the global economy readjusting to the U.S.'s period of trade deficits.

China Isn't the Only Villain Behind Dangerous Imports

Having researched much of what is happening in this importing game, and the issue of problems stemming from the growth of China or our own failing economy, I can only express once again that we as a nation have lost our "Yankee Ingenuity." As reported in U.S. News and World Report just last September, 2007 there's plenty of bluster from Washington these days over imported toys and other products that might be dangerous. But for the typical consumer worried about unsafe imports, nobody has been able to answer the simple yet confounding question: *What can I do about it?*

Rick Newman was on the right track when he wrote about "The Business of Decisions" by alleging that China isn't the villain behind the dangerous imports. He hit the nail on the head.

For big-ticket products like cars and appliances, we're used to finding a trove of useful information on the Web that helps us make clear decisions about safety and performance. But for toys, food, medicines, and basic healthcare products, it's a much murkier picture. There are few third-party testers. We'd like to think that companies vouch for the quality of their own products, but huge safety recalls by Mattel, Fisher-Price, Thomas & Friends, and other brand-name companies have revealed gaping holes in quality control at far-flung multinational corporations.

At least we have an army of government regulators serving as a safety net, right??? Uh, nope!!! Ain't so, my friends!!! The New York Times and other publications have pointed out that the Consumer Product Safety Commission, responsible for enforcing safety standards, has been gutted in recent years, even as imports have been surging. The federal government, it turns out, spends more money monitoring the safety of animal feed than testing the safety of products used by children.

If you ask a number of industry experts the bottom-line question: *What can consumers do on their own to research the safety of toys and other products imported from overseas???* The answer you might receive, unfortunately would be...NOT TOO MUCH!!! But you will uncover a few basic principles along the way that can and will help consumers better understand what they're buying, and whether there's likely to be any risk.

Yep...you guessed it..."**Made in China isn't the only problem!**"

That's because the image of shoddy Chinese-owned factories hoodwinking naïve American corporations is largely a myth. Most big American companies importing products from China own the factories where those products are made or partially own them through a joint venture. I should know as my company, Global Communications personally had joint partnerships with Chinese companies as a distributor for over 15 years until I realized how they were putting my customers at risk through faulty products that did not work by the OEM (the manufacturer who assembled the components into finished products and only then did we realize that the parts were built erroneously). So the companies themselves are on-scene at the source of the problem-or should be-and they represent the first line of responsibility for dangerous components. That is why we got out of the business of joint relationships with Chinese companies and had to give credit to our customers once the products had failed.

Successful importers like British department store chain Marks & Spencer and Dutch electronics giant Phillips are well known for relentlessly checking and testing products while they're still on the assembly line-instead of relying on others to test, or waiting until products have already been shipped.

"It's the responsibility of manufacturers and distributors to check up on their suppliers," said Wharton Professor Marshall Meyer recently, who consults with many firms in China. "They need to go there and see what they're doing,"

That's a step the U.S. toy companies obviously skipped-and are not hustling to institute. But even if they chose to go to their Chinese facilities, what if anything would they find? Probably nothing! The reality is that the Chinese companies will constantly change their manufacturing program when you aren't looking. The real test of the products is when they are shipped to the distributors and sold to the outlets, then used by the end user. When the 'fit hits the sham' all hell breaks loose, and the products are not worth the price paid for them.

Yet, one might still consider…**Brand Names Still Matter!** Mattel is working 24-7 to repair damage to its reputation from the recall of several million Barbie accessories and other toys. Why? Because it has made a huge investment in its brand image, which will be wasted money if consumers decide Mattel toys aren't safe.

"Mattel's product quality will improve," insisted Merle Hinrich, CEO of Global Sources, a Hong Kong company that helps match corporations with international suppliers. The safety recalls, he argued, will ultimately lead to better products by forcing manufacturers to be more diligent about safety. And that happens only when a company has a brand name to defend. One startling bit of evidence is the toy industry's plea for more oversight by government regulators-a rare instance of corporate American inviting the kind of scrutiny it usually spends millions on lobbyists to avert.

Branding, of course, is about marketing, not safety, and there's nothing about a recognized brand name that guarantees quality. The connection begins to form only when safety questions affect profits, which is happening now. That's good for consumers.

The cheapest stuff is the riskiest. By the same logic, little-known distributors have a lot less to lose by selling flawed products, since they can just remarket their goods under another no-name brand while suffering little damage.

Consumers who shop at prominent retailers like Wal-Mart or Lowe's can still enjoy cheap stuff with a reasonable sense of security since the retailer's name is on the line. But it's probably not a good idea to buy unknown brands at fly-by-night discounters, especially ingestible products, toys with small pieces that could come loose or anything else with obvious safety implications.

Cheap imports are here to stay. Lawmakers can fume all they want about American-made goods being driven off the shelves by cheaper imported stuff, but it's not going to change. The world's economies are far too interconnected to try unraveling them. And while Communist China is always a ready bogeyman, Americans buy products from lots of other low-cost countries-such as Vietnam, Indonesia, and Malaysia-with home-grown standards no more stringent than those in China. If there's a safety problem with toys made in Indonesia, will politicians try to score points by blaming the Indonesian government? OR take the offending company to task instead?

It's also worth keeping in mind that over the past 30 years, there have been similar safety issues with products from Japan, Korea, and Taiwan-countries that are now considered first-rate trading partners that produce high-quality goods. Unless there's an ominous turn, the same thing will happen with China.

Imports remain a huge economic boon. Scary headlines about cheap imported goods obscure the benefits they bring. There are reasonable arguments on both sides about American jobs going overseas, but one thing that's indisputable is the cost savings that consumers enjoy from products manufactured at the cheapest, most efficient factories in the world. As imports from China and other low-cost countries have surged, the price of clothing, electronics, building materials, and a lot of other products have fallen, sometimes plunged.

Cheap stuff provides a massive benefit to low- and middle-income families, and many American consumers remain quite comfortable buying cheap imports, whatever the risk. But don't expect any congressional bearings about that.

As we close out 2007 and 2008 and enter 2009, we had seen many problems on the horizon. But the U.S. government did not act quickly enough, and the consumer did not make enough of a stink about the problems they encountered with the Asian products they had purchased. Either they took the products and returned them to the store, or just threw them away. In either case, they lost out. In order for the masses to understand what is going on with these failed imports, we, the people must make our voices heard... loud and clear!

Some Questions and Answers on Chinese Imports

In October, 2007, Jeffrey A. Bader, Director John L. Thornton China Center had described his take on American consumers at Brookings Institution. He indicated that there's been lot of individual talk of boycotts and consumers going to stores asking about whether items are made in China or not. In terms of the government reaction, so far the American regulatory agencies, principally the Food and Drug Administration, Customs, Consumer Product Safety Organization, the U.S. Department of Agriculture-are looking at their own standards. They're all short of the sources.

Frankly, they're not doing as much as they could, but they're all looking to do more. They also have been talking to their Chinese counterparts about what the Chinese can do to improve their own conformity with international standards. Now, this is not a problem unique to China. On a per dollar of imports basis, Mexican imports and Indian imports show just as many problems as Chinese imports do, but the differences is that our imports from China are many orders of magnitude larger in quantity than from India and Mexico-over somewhere between $250-$300 billion dollars in imported products this year. So, naturally, there is going to be a fair number of defective products.

Now why is China having these problems? On the food side, these are problems involving environmental difficulties, pollution, food additives. A lot of them come from the environment, which is just a huge problem in China. On the manufacturing side, there are multiple problems. One is that the manufacturing sector in China is highly fragmented. So you have tremendous numbers of producers, manufacturers, some of them quite small that don't have the same internal inspection safety standards as a large company would have. You also have a highly defective regulatory system in China. People think of China as a dictatorship where Beijing can tell everyone what to do in the provinces. It doesn't work that way, in reality. In the provinces, the capabilities are very poor.

I think that last factor that is particularly difficult for China to address is transparency and accountability. In the United States, of course, we have product safety problems ourselves and we have free media and the media expose a lot of those product safety problems. In China, media is geared toward the government plus they are reluctant to go after manufacturers of defective products particularly if they think they might run into a party official who is involved or protecting the enterprise.

That said, the Chinese leadership is said to be taking this issue quite seriously. Prime Minister Premier Wen Jiaboa has been personally very outspoken and vocal on it. The Chinese have done a number of things to try to address the problem. They've shut down a number of manufacturers of defective products; they have posted on websites such manufacturers; they have forbidden the use of certain products such as diethylene glycol that found its way into toothpaste that was going abroad. They are increasing the number of inspections; they have put in place their first recall legislation; they understand that they have a problem both domestically for Chinese consumers and with the acceptability of brand China overseas. For a country whose economic livelihood is largely dependent on exports, they know that's a problem that they have to take seriously.

—12—

Panic Spreads Over Food Imports From China

In January, 2008, the *Japan Probe* reported such stories relating to food imports from China. News broke out of insecticide-laden dumplings from China, and there was much media frenzy throughout Japan. Mainichi reported that 62 people claimed to be victims of the poison *gyoza*. Although few of the new victims had experienced anything more than diarrhea, one can be sure that the panic over the deadly *gyoza* will continue to grow.

The story was being picked up by the international media. Reuters did a pretty good job of covering the story:

"The food scare has triggered a nationwide probe into possible additional cases of food poisoning, while Japan's top government spokesman questioned China's attitude to food safety only weeks after the country said it had improved standards. Japanese media and opposition lawmakers have also suggested Japan's initial response to the problem may have been too slow.

"I have two children, boys aged four and two. They love dumplings. Japanese people love dumplings," said Democratic Party parliamentarian Yuichiro Hata. "This is something that threatens peoples' lives."

Japan Tobacco Inc. indicated that its subsidiary, JT Foods Co., would recall the frozen dumplings and other food made at the same Chinese factory, as television broadcasters flashed warnings to viewers not to eat the products.

Around 80 people in Japan have complained of getting sick from eating food made in China, TV Asahi said. Restaurants and schools took Chinese-made food off their menus, other media said. The scandal is the latest in a string of disputes over the safety of Chinese products from toys to toothpaste. Earlier, China declared that its campaign to ensure food and product safety had been a complete success. "I don't want to think that there is any difference among countries concerning food safety, but it seems there was a sense on the Chinese side that 'this is probably ok'," Chief Cabinet Secretary Nobutaka Machimura told a news conference.

According to the report reported in the Japanese news clip from CNN, at least 8,700 Japanese school children have been served school lunches containing items imported from China by JT Foods, the same company that sold the contaminated gyoza. While flipping through the channels on television, it was noticed that one channel had a special news ticker at the bottom of the screen informing viewers of schools and stores involved in the scandal.

Last year's Japanese/Chinese food scandals did not get to this level of coverage, but those scandals didn't involve levels of poison that put people in critical condition. Insecticide-laden food is a bit scarier than food past its expiration date.

As panic spreads, so does the number of people who believe they became sick from eating contaminated gyoza. The number of victims exceeded 450 at this writing, and seems to be growing. People acquired upset stomachs after eating at the Skylark Group Restaurant and are now convinced that tainted Chinese ingredients are to blame. A few media reports are placing some of the blame for this scandal on the Japanese government. The Japan Times had an article on Japan's Weak Food Inspection System, while the Yomiuri had an article revealing that the Tokyo Metropolitan Government received reports of tainted gyoza weeks before but was slow to act on the information.

The articles suggest that the poison was actually intentionally injected into the Gyoza which led to serious hospitalizations and it was also possible that the poisoning didn't occur in China. The proof was that a small hole was found in the packaging of dumplings that caused three family members in Hyogo Prefecture to fall ill, suggesting that a poisonous substance detected in the product was deliberately inserted, police said. The discovery had prompted police to consider forming a case on suspicion of attempted murder. They are continuing to investigate how the substance entered the package at this writing.

The World is Sending Us Their Junk

In March, 2008 inspectors checking Chinese seafood arriving at U.S. ports made some unsettling discoveries; fish infected with salmonella in Baltimore and Seattle, and shrimp with banned veterinary drugs in Florida. Meanwhile, a shipment intercepted in Los Angeles on March 19, 2008 and labeled "channel catfish" wasn't catfish at all, though records don't say what it was.

"A lot of those products coming in from overseas, you have no clue as to what is in them," said Paul Hitchens, an aquaculture specialist in Southern Illinois, where cut-rate Chinese catfish are threatening the livelihood of fish farmers. China rapidly has become the leading exporter of seafood to the United States, flooding supermarkets and restaurants. And while China agreed late last year to improve the safety of food exports, the inspectors' March findings were not isolated cases.

According to Food and Drug Administration records examined by the Post-Dispatch, inspectors turned away nearly 400 shipments of tainted seafood in a year's time from China. The records told a troubling tale, but even more troubling was what they didn't tell. Only a tiny fraction of imports are inspected at all, and even fewer are tested.

It's a challenge the United States is just starting to confront: With an increasingly globalized food supply, the government-using an antiquated inspection system-is unprepared to keep Americans safe from the dangers arriving at our ports.

"When you look at less than 1 percent of shipments, and samples and test maybe one-fifth of those, there's no way you can protect the American food supply," said Michael Taylor, a former FDA official who is professor of health policy now at George Washington University.

Seafood is considered one of the most risky imports, and those from China steadily have risen. When the FDA does turn away shipments, usually it is because the food contains veterinary drugs, among them nitrofurans, a family of antibiotics banned by the FDA because tests showed they cause cancer in animals. More than 100 of the shipments were rejected for being filthy, decomposed or otherwise unfit for consumption, according to the records.

In December, 2007, after disclosures about Chinese imports of poisonous pet food and lead-filled toys, the FDA and the Chinese government agreed on new procedures aimed at preventing tainted and dangerous food and drugs from reaching American shores. But skeptics question whether the new, voluntary arrangement has sufficient teeth.

Meanwhile, Chinese seafood is a prime target of legislation in Congress to revamp decades-old inspection mechanisms in hopes of protecting Americans in a globalized food system. FDA officials are requesting new authority, including the ability to license private companies to assist with inspections. But the Bush administration had signaled opposition to key provisions that would require regular inspections in foreign lands, and limit ports where food can arrive to docks with FDA labels. Former FDA officials argue that change is urgently needed.

William Hubbard, formerly the FDA's associate commissioner, noted in an interview that the FDA's inspection system was designed early last century when the big challenge was finding bugs or mold in arriving barrels of commodities such as flour or molasses. Now, the U.S. gets millions of shipments of foreign food each year from around the world.

Hubbard, who retired in 2005, recalled inspectors reporting particularly disturbing methods of Chinese aquaculture: raising chickens in cages kept above fish ponds-a potential source of the salmonella in seafood, he said.

"Increasingly, the world is moving in a better direction in food safety and we're falling behind," Hubbard said. **As our system becomes more antiquated and more ineffective, the world is sending us their junk.**

Soaring Imports...No Overnight Fix

Imports of seafood have surged dramatically in recent years and account for nearly 80 percent of the seafood Americans consume. Last year, that translated to 5.4 billion pounds of imported seafood out of estimated 6.75 billion pounds consumed.

Supermarket frozen food sections routinely are filled with imported fish fillets, shrimp and crab meat-which must contain country-of-origin labels on packaging. No such disclosure is required for fish served in restaurants, so people generally can't know with certainty the country of origin for the fish or shrimp they order.

Records at the National Oceanic and Atmospheric Administration show how surging Chinese imports are meeting the demand of seafood-loving Americans. For instance, between 2000 and 2007, imports of farm-raised tilapia from China-a staple in restaurants-soared nine-fold, to more than 240 million pounds. Imports of catfish have been especially vexing to U.S. seafood interests, given the whiskered bottom-feeder's popularity in parts of America.

In four years, imports of Chinese catfish-or fish so described-increased from 1.6 million pounds to more than 22 million pounds last year, posing stiff and sometimes crippling competition for U.S. catfish farmers. Jeff McCord, spokesman for the Catfish Institute, said that many of the more than 1,000 catfish-growers he represents saw their revenue plummet.

"It has led to many family farmers throwing in the towel and the loss of hundreds of jobs of farm workers and in fish-processing plants," he said.

In Southern Illinois, fish-farmers blame the 2003 collapse of a catfish processing plant in Pinckneyville on a flood of Chinese imports that they say nearly cut in half the price they could get. Even now, efforts in Illinois to build a successful industry with farm-raised prawns and bass are stunted by imports, said Hitchens, the aquaculture specialist at Southern Illinois University.

"We know we can't compete with them, so we're trying other angles," said Hitchens, who arranges sales of live, farm-raised seafood to markets in St. Louis, Chicago and as far away as Toronto.

Hitchens sounds a common refrain in the American aquaculture industry: "Here in Illinois, we're very conscious of trying to get out a fresh product that is natural and without antibiotics."

Echoes Brenda Lyons, whose family grows prawns in Sandoval, Ill.: "We're trying to compete with China. We're not going to grow a bunch of junk. We're selling live, fresh fish. And they can't supply that from over there."

It's usually impossible to track down the source of food-borne illnesses that, according to the Centers for Disease Control, occur 76 million times annually in the United States, resulting in 325,000 hospitalizations and 5,000 deaths. But fish-particularly uncooked or improperly cooked seafood-is a common source of problems. And the rapidly growing imports from China pose a new threat that needs attention, said Caroline Smith DeWaal, a food safety expert at the Washington-based nonprofit group Center for Science in the Public Interest.

In China and elsewhere in the developing world, "the ability to produce food and ship it globally far surpasses their ability to ensure it's safe," she said.

Experts agree that change is needed to protect Americans from dangerous imports. The question now is how much change Congress will demand and how much change the Obama administration and the FDA will be willing to accept. Last year, U.S. and Chinese officials began discussing changes amid disturbing revelations about dangerous products from poisoned pet food to shoddy tires.

In a "Memorandum of Agreement" reached by the FDA and their Chinese counterparts in December, 2007 seafood was accorded the status of "high-risk" because of ongoing problems. Now, says the FDA, both sides are pursuing initiatives that the FDA hopes will lead to an FDA office in China and an electronic certification system for imports arriving in the United States.

Dr. Murray Lumpkin, the FDA's deputy Commissioner for international and special programs, who helped negotiate the arrangement, said that the United States and China are in a "confidence-building" mode right now with both sides showing "commitment." Lumpkin, who traveled to China, noted that the Chinese have not yet said yes to an FDA office in Beijing.

"This is going to take some time," said Lumpkin, "but I think that both governments realize it is not helpful for either country to have tainted fish come in to the U.S. It doesn't help in terms of the safety we demand and it doesn't help the China brand."

Meanwhile, skeptics question the potential of an arrangement that lacks assurance that FDA inspectors will get access to production facilities and ponds where fish are grown. This is not going to be an overnight fix and the FDA needs to reinvent itself.

Should Our New U.S. President Adopt a Tougher Stance on Trade with Policy with China?

The 4th April, 2008 edition of *Council on Foreign Relations* had summarized a discussion that had taken place from March 31st through April 4th, 2008, between Robert E. Scott and Daniel J. Ikenson on the topic of the U.S.-China trade relationship, including a flashpoint for concern over the U.S. trade deficit, China's currency valuation, and Chinese intellectual property regulation. This relationship has been under especially keen scrutiny as the 2008 presidential campaign started to heat up in the U.S., with Democratic front-runners favoring punitive duties against China if it does not act to revalue its currency. Robert E. Scott, senior international economist at the Economic Policy Institute, and Daniel J. Ikenson, associate director of the Cato Institute's Center for Trade Policy Studies, debated whether the next U.S. president should get tougher with China on trade.

Robert E. Scott...

China is a protectionist state that has used all of its powers and resources to build an artificially competitive export powerhouse. The United States is the most important market for its exports. Growing U.S. trade deficits with China, and other countries are a major cause of the loss of 3.4 million U.S. manufacturing jobs since 2001, when China entered the WTO. China's export-led growth strategy was also very costly for its people.

We have been down this road before, and know how to deal with such situations. Two decades ago, Japan built an export powerhouse behind an artificially cheap currency and protected home markets. This continued until 1985, when it began to threaten the stability of the world financial system. The problem then, as now, was the U.S. trade deficit.

The Reagan administration, much like the Bush White House, doggedly ignored the over-valued dollar through its first term while millions of jobs disappeared and thousands of factories closed. Finally, Congress acted and passed a measure (HR 3035) which hit countries like Japan, Brazil, and Korea, that maintained large U.S. trade surpluses, with a 25 percent tariff. In a complete about-face, Treasury Secretary James Baker then negotiated the Plaza Accord with the G-5 (Japan, Germany, France and the U.K.), on September 22, 1985. The next day, the Federal Reserve and Central banks in Japan and Europe executed coordinated currency interventions that began to drive the dollar down. The dollar continued to fall until the Louvre Accord 16 months later, which stabilized its level again. The dollar fell 29 percent to 46 percent against the G-5 currencies in this period.

The U.S. never imposed a tariff in the Plaza era-HR 3035 never even became law. The mere threat, combined with concerns about a potential financial crises, were enough to get the deal done.

China has invested over $1.5 trillion in foreign exchange reserves in order to keep the yuan artificially cheap. Economists estimate that its currency, too, needs to rise by about 40 percent. Other Asian export economies, such as Japan, are following similar strategies and also need to revalue, but they can't do it alone. While the dollar has fallen sharply against the euro and other freely traded currencies over the past five years, it has barely budged against the yuan and yen. But this won't happen until we get tough with Beijing. We need to put some backbone in our trade policy to get multilateral currency talks started now.

Daniel J. Ikenson...

If a tougher stance means using the WTO Dispute Settlement Body (DSB) more systemically to achieve greater Chinese compliance with the vast obligations to which China agreed upon joining the WTO in 2001, the answer is "yes." If it means supporting or encouraging provocative legislation or taking unilateral administrative actions to compel or punish China in a manner that would violate our own WTO obligations or would benefit a few litigious industries at the expense of broader economic interests, the answer is "no."

In 2006, the USTR (Office of the United States Trade Representative) published its "Top-to-Bottom Review" of U.S.-China trade relations, in which it proclaimed the beginning of a new phase in the relationship, stating, effectively, that the honeymoon period (of reform implementation) was over and foreshadowing greater resort to the WTO dispute settlement system to achieve further compliance.

One month after publication of that report, USTR filed a WTO complaint alleging that certain China policies discriminate against imported automobile parts. Very recently, the dispute panel established to hear that case ruled in favor of the United States.

Before the auto parts case, only one complaint about Chinese practices had been lodged with the DSB. It concerned a value-added tax on integrated circuits that was allegedly applied in full to imports only. During the consultation phase of the dispute (and without need of formal adjudication), the Chinese agreed to change their practice and the dispute was resolved.

In 2007, the USTR filed three WTO cases against China. The first involved certain tax provisions that allegedly amounted to subsidization of Chinese exporters. In response to the allegations, China changed its tax rebate practices (although the dispute is not completely resolved yet as of this writing). The second concerned enforcement of intellectual property rights. The third concerned alleged barriers facing foreign traders and distributors of copyrighted materials like books, videos, and DVDs. A dispute panel was recently composed for the IP case, and the distribution barriers case is still in the consultations phase as of this writing. Earlier this month, USTR brought a sixth case, alleging discrimination against U.S. providers of financial services information in China.

Since the USTR's 2006 review, five cases have been filed with positive outcomes achieved in two (the others are pending). It is important to recognize that our trade relationship with China is mutually beneficial, and that unnecessary provocation could open a Pandora's Box of economic problems. There is no good reason to jettison a process that is working.

Robert E. Scott...

I'm glad that Dan thinks we need to get tough with China. We have ignored these problems for far too long. China provides vast and extensive subsidies to businesses making goods for export in many industries, artificially reducing the cost of their products. The U.S. government needs to develop new policies and institutions to enforce our fair trade laws and to ensure that the systems deliver broadly shared benefits to U.S. workers and businesses producing goods and services in the United States.

A recent study by Professor Usha Haley at the University of New Haven estimated that energy subsidies to the Chinese steel industry alone exceeded $27 billion between 2000 and mid-2007. China went from being a net steel importer a few years ago to the world's largest steel producer and exporter. China's share of U.S. steel imports increased six-fold.

Energy subsidies are rampant in China, and yet the U.S. Commerce Department refuse to authorize countervailing duties in recent trade complaints involving tires and coated paper imports, both energy intensive products. U.S. trade laws need to be toughened in this area to ensure that systematic subsidies that benefit all exporters are countervailed.

Beginning in 2001 with their tenth five-year plan, China targeted the auto and parts industries for rapid growth, and they have poured subsidies into this industry. U.S. auto parts imports soared from $1 billion in 2001 to $7 billion in 2007, resulting in massive layoffs and plant closures. These cases illustrate two key weaknesses in the U.S. trade policy enforcement system.

First, our system depends on manufacturing firms and agricultural producers to initiate the vast majority of all U.S. unfair trade complaints. The system makes it hard for them to win cases until they are on their last legs so many cases are never filed. The U.S. government has the right to initiate complaints, but rarely does. Second, only the USTR, which is part of the President's Executive Office, has the right to file trade complaints with the WTO. It often fails to do so for political reasons. For example, the big-three U.S. auto companies benefit from subsidized Chinese auto parts imports, and the USTR has refused to bring a WTO complaint until 2006, five years too late.

Congress should create an independent government agency with the resources and authority to file fair trade cases in the United States and at the WTO. We must insist that Chinese producers compete on a level playing field, and if we do, U.S. workers and businesses can win.

Daniel J. Ikenson...

The only substantive point of agreement between Rob and me about China is that it makes for a nice wedding gift.

To embrace Rob's perspective, one must assume away the reality of how the economy actually works and how it is structured. If the U.S. economy comprised only producers who were self-sufficient for their material inputs and who had no interest in selling products abroad, Rob's prescriptions, which subordinate the multitude of individual U.S. economic interests to manufacturers' interests, might garner some sympathy. But it is fantasy to characterize international trade as a contest between "our" producers and "their" producers. Not only has that line been blurred (thankfully) by foreign direct investment, cross-ownership, equity tie-ins, and transnational supply chains, but the fact is that the economy is composed of consumers, retailers, importers, shippers, designers, engineers, marketers, financiers, and producers who have great stakes in an open world economy, and who would be hurt by Rob's proposals.

The currency issue is far more complicated-and far less insidious-than Rob implies. Is a more-weakened dollar what American really needs as prices for essentials like oil and food continue to rise? Do we really want China to have 40 percent more spending power on account of Yuan appreciation when China's growing demand with a lower-valued currency explains much of the world's commodity price increases? Other countries are looking for ways to bolster their citizens' purchasing power by suspending tariffs and other import restraints, yet Rob thinks it's wise to reduce Americans' purchasing power by rendering dollars worth less.

I strongly disagree with Rob's assertion that the trade deficits are a major cause of the loss of 3.4 million jobs. Manufacturing jobs are in decline worldwide, even in perennial trade surplus countries like Japan and Germany, as well as in China.

It is worth noting that between 2001 (Rob's demarcation) and 2007, the increasing bilateral trade deficit has been accompanied by a 20 percent increase in real GOP, a 15 percent increase in manufacturing output, and the creation of 9.1 million net new jobs.

(NOTE: I don't know what planet Mr. Ikenson is on, but his figures are totally inaccurate).

With respect to trade remedies, let's summon the violins! Out of 263 U.S. anti-dumping and countervailing duty orders, there are 62 (24 percent) in place against Chinese imports. And the extremely prosperous U.S. steel industry-the victim in Rob's last post-accounts for 126 of the 263-nearly half! Rob's prescriptions are not only unnecessary; they are particularly ill-suited for the twenty-first century global economy.

Robert E. Scott...

If four low-wage workers are riding an elevator, the door opens, and Bill Gates gets on, everyone on that elevator becomes, on average, a billionaire. The economic benefits of U.S.-China trade, like the average net worth on that elevator, look good until you consider their distribution.

The gains from trade between the United States and China have flowed to a very small segment of both countries' elites. The gap between the value of what U.S. workers produce and what they receive has widened dramatically, partly because deregulated trade has suppressed the real wages of all non-college educated workers (about 70 percent of the labor force). Between 1980 and 2005, U.S. productivity rose 71 percent while real compensation (including benefits) of non-supervisory workers rose just 4 percent. This measure includes all the benefits of globalization received by these workers.

Most of the benefits of growth since 1980 have been captured by the top 10 percent, especially the top 1 percent, of U.S .workers. The problem is not trade, *per se,* but the current trading system which has encouraged a race-to-the-bottom in wages and labor standards.

The systematic suppression of workers' rights has reduced Chinese wages by 47 percent to 85 percent according to a recent labor-rights petition, and the problems are worsening. Occupational illness and injury rates have never been higher in Chinese manufacturing. Workers are frequently forced to go unpaid, and their complaints and protests are often met with violent government responses.

Fueling China's vast trade surplus with the United States is its very high savings rates, nearing 50 percent of GDP in recent years. Conventional wisdom is that Chinese workers save excessively because China's pension and public health systems are so poor. However, household savings recently declined to 16 percent of GDP. Business savings, on the other hand have soared to nearly 24 percent of GDP and government savings exceeded 10 percent according to the IMF.

Thus, globalization's benefits in China are reaped by an elite cadre who own and operate private and public enterprises. Their savings are piling up in the net worth of the rapidly expanding business empires under their control.

Getting tough with China about international trade and labor rights violations would help workers in both companies. The Bush administration has rejected two labor rights petitions submitted by the AFL-CIO and U.S. Representatives Ben Cardin and Chris Smith, and workers in both countries have suffered as a result.

China needs more spending on infrastructure, environmental clean-up, and public health and other social services. It needs fundamental improvements in labor rights and enforcement, which will raise wages, increase private consumption and reduce China's need to export. These win-win policies can help workers in the United States, China and all our trading partners.

Daniel J. Ikenson...

Space constraints preclude my rebutting each ad hoc, amorphous assertion made in Rob's last post, but I want to address some of the most outlandish.

If the current trading system encourages a race to the bottom, how does one explain the large and increasing foreign direct investment flows into the United States? Why is ThyssenKrupp building a $3.7 billion green field steel production facility in Alabama? Why do foreign nameplate automakers continue to invest in U.S. manufacturing? Why do the 5.1 million Americans employed by U.S. subsidiaries of foreign-owned companies earn on average 32 percent higher wages than workers at U.S.-owned companies?

Because there is no race to the bottom, that's why! There is a race to the top for skilled workers, for access to production facilities closer to markets, for investment in countries where the rule of law is clear and abided, where there is greater certainty to the business climate, where the specter of asset expropriation is negligible, where physical and administrative infrastructure is in good shape, and so on. Seems odd how the same sirens who decry the race to the bottom spend the rest of the day opposing foreign direct investment in the United States.

Are we to believe that America's elites are behind Wal-Mart's success? Seems to me Wal-Mart and other retailers have been a conduit of the benefits of trade, allowing ordinary Americans to tap into the division of labor, extend their budgets, and increase their families' access to clothing, food, and other everyday products. And American manufacturers and their workers are the beneficiaries of huge increases in exports to China-our fastest growing large export market since 2001. Beyond question, vast swaths of Americans and Chinese are benefiting from the expanding trade relationship.

With respect to U.S.-China trade, the next president should continue the tradition of this resort to the WTO dispute settlement system when the facts support doing so.

As President Obama reflects on the bilateral trade dialogue of the recent past, he should grant China market economy treatment in antidumping cases. While such a reform would take very little out of petitioning industries' hides, the gesture would win vast sums of goodwill from the Chinese, which will be needed to resolve more important issues going forward.

(NOTE: After listening to both men, one an economist, the other a director of trade policy studies, it appears to me that I would tend to agree more with Mr. Scott as he truly understands what has happened to our process of manufacturing and why so many goods are imported from China...including goods that are tainted and polluted, which Mr. Ikenson fails to make reference in his diatribe. It is true that the President Obama should adopt a tougher stance on the way manufacturing has changed in our country and to have a tougher trade policy with China because of the tainted and polluted products that are exported by China. Nothing is worse than putting peoples' lives at risk because of bad products that are manufactured by nations, including our own, who do not care or refuse to change their way of production. We are all to blame).

Who's Going the Wrong Way?

The pursuit of being the low-cost producer has been and will continue to be the primary focus of many successful businesses. In the June, 2008 issue of *CEO (Chief Executive Magazine)*, the article…written by William E. Rothschild, author of "The Secret to GE's Success" and CEO of Rothschild Strategies Unlimited LLC, and Stephen M. Rothschild, President and CEO of Provox Technologies…brings into perspective why many major multinationals from some countries are leaving China even as U.S. Countries aggressively move in.

Over the past few decades, companies have targeted low-cost labor areas, with governments that were willing to sacrifice the environment and even the welfare of its people to attract investors. In the 1960s, American companies moved from the unionized and high-cost Northeast and Midwest to the "right-to-work" south. Then it was Japan, Korea and Taiwan. But in each case, the costs increased and the journey continues.

In the 1980s the Chinese government sought to attract multinational companies via the combination of incentives and its huge, low-cost labor force. According to the Financial Times, some 30,000 South Korean companies had taken advantage of China's tax incentives to invest in southern China by the late 1980s, and by 2003. Korean companies had invested 41.4 percent of its investment into China. Other countries, like Japan and Taiwan, followed a similar pattern. China was clearly their preferred manufacturing nation. U.S. companies lagged but in recent years have accelerated their Chinese investments and have even been willing to transfer some of the research and development into China.

But, as in the past, many companies have found that China is not as attractive and are leaving the country for other "lower cost, hungry locations." For instance, the number of Korean companies in China has been reduced by two-thirds, from 30,000 to 10,000, and between 2003 and 2006 total investment declined from 41.4 percent to 31 percent. Japanese and Taiwanese companies are also leaving China.

Why the exodus? It is believed that there are four major reasons that Korean, Japanese and Taiwanese companies are leaving China: *cost, security, flexibility and complexity.*

Rising Costs…

The cost of doing business in China is rapidly increasing due to a number of factors, including:

Accelerating Inflationary Rates. According to the *Financial Times*, "The (Chinese) February inflation rate of 8.7 percent was the highest in 12 years and is expected to be deeply worrying for a government that has spent a lot of energy recently trying to talk down consumer and business concerns about inflation."

Taxes, stricter enforcement of environmental standards and over-all manufacturing cost increases. Prices for plastics, steel and other materials have climbed 30 percent or more, and electricity rates are surging, too," reports *The International Herald Tribune*.

Environmental and Product Standards. We all know about the lead issue in children's' toys and problems with drugs being exported from China. In addition, we know that China has enormous health and safety issues. Air pollution and water pollution are common. A recent *Economist* article reported that in 2006, "70 percent of 2 million annual cancer deaths were pollution related." Factories are unsafe. At some point the Chinese government will have to address these issues and stop sacrificing their own people's lives. Since China has over a billion and half people and only a small portion pay income taxes, the best, most obvious place to get money to fund these programs is to tax foreign companies.

Unique/Expensive Benefits. "Companies operating in China are required by the government to chip into a housing fund that's available to their Chinese employees, who also make a contribution," reports *Business Week* magazine. "When employees are ready to buy a home, they can draw from the funds to help. About 20 percent of the multinationals currently chip in more to the housing fund than required."

Scarcity of Talent. The *International Herald Tribune* reports that "despite its huge pool of unskilled rural laborers, China's supply of experienced, skilled talent falls far short of demand. The gap has pushed wages up by 10 percent to 15 percent a year." China has not trained its middle and upper management to lead companies and it is now very difficult for companies to find these people. If and when they do, they must compete for them and then expect a constant turnover and need to replenish the supply. Many companies are being forced to export their management training overseas, which is costly and difficult to do.

Infrastructure. China has embarked on a very rapid, some say too rapid, building of power plants, water systems, sewerage roads, railroads and highways, along with buildings. One of the major problems is that this construction was not centrally planned and implemented. Provinces have overbuilt and are competing among themselves. Ultimately there will be overcapacity and, even worse, much damage to the environment and physical assets of the nation. Again, the Chinese will increase the burden on its "foreign" companies.

Lack of Security...

The cost of doing business in China is not just restricted to the ordinary cost of labor, materials and taxes; it must also include the violation of patents, copyrights and other intellectual properties. This is a major issue with the Chinese.

China has never signed the International Copyright and Patents agreements, and does not protect copyrights or patents. A 2005 *Time* article called "The Idea-Stealing Factory" reported that "in a country where government-controlled companies comprise the industrial base, piracy is not derived from commercial callowness; it appears to be official policy."

The music/Entertainment/Publishing industries have lost billions because their protected materials are stolen and sold at a fraction of the list price, of which they get nothing. In fact, the last two books of Mr. Rothschild were translated and sold illegally in China. The CIA asserts that China has an elaborate spy system in the U.S. to steal commercial and military technologies. And a quick Google scan of articles about industrial espionage yields more than 15 incidences of companies either suing the Chinese for pirating or companies leaving China because of their inability to protect their patents and copyrights.

For example, **Cisco Systems** filed a suit against Huawei Technology of China, accusing the company of copying software and infringing patents. And former Lucent Technology scientists Hai-Lin, Kai-Xu and Young-Oing were indicted by a federal grand jury for allegedly conspiring to steal trade secrets from Lucent Technologies.

The Wall Street Journal summarizes the current situation this way: "Though China is working hard to repair its reputation as a place where theft of intellectual property is rampant...the truth is that counterfeiting and piracy remain common."

What's more, since foreign companies must train their Chinese managers, Professionals and workforce, they are, in essence, developing their own new competition.

There have been reports of companies who built factories in China and within a few years the employees left to build a competing factory across the street. In all of the major Chinese growth areas, such as wind power, electrical systems, transportation and water purification, new Chinese companies are being formed not only to serve the Chinese markets, but to sell offshore, especially in developing nations. In fact, in March 2008, China reportedly announced that it was creating a new company to design, produce and sell jetliners big enough to carry more than 150 passengers, which could eventually pose a threat to Boeing and Airbus.

Security issues extend beyond just the loss of intellectual properties. The travel of senior management and professionals as they visit and interact with their employees in China also presents huge security issues and requires an expensive infrastructure.

Declining Flexibility...

A third layer of costs deal with a company's ability to hire and fire workers to meet its strategic and financial needs and to make acquisitions or mergers if and when it makes economic sense. Both of these rights are limited in China.

A new labor law passed by China that would "substantially increase labor costs and reduce flexibility" was roundly protested by foreign companies, who warned the Chinese government that the new regulations would force them to move operations out of China. "Foreign executives said they are especially worried about the new labor regulations because their companies tend to comply with existing laws more rigorously than some of their Chinese competitors do," reported *The New York Times.* "Their competitive disadvantage could increase sharply, they said, if the new rules put fresh burdens on foreign companies that their local counterparts ignore."

Some provisions of the new law include:

- Requiring employers to provide written contracts to their workers, restrict the use of temporary laborers and make it difficult to lay off employees.
- Moving China closer to European-style labor regulations that emphasize fixed-and open-term employment contracts enforceable by law, and requiring that employees with short-term contracts become full-time employees with lifetime benefits after a short-term contract is renewed twice.
- Giving the state-run union and other employee representative groups the power to bargain with employers. When more than 50 employees are to be laid off, for example, the company must negotiate an agreement with the labor union on all employees.

Foreign companies are limited in what companies they may acquire. They are able to purchase "small Chinese companies that the central government is not interested in managing; large, state-owned enterprises that suffer from financial difficulty, provided the foreign investor agrees to restructure the purchased company, and non-majority interest in strong, successful Chinese companies, but only if there is some added benefit, such as transfer of technology, advanced management or access to foreign markets," according to *China International Business* magazine. Of course, it must also be kept in mind that China is and wants to remain a Communist state and may not hesitate to nationalize companies and seize investments if they believe it is to their benefit.

Continued Complexity...

Doing business in any foreign nation is complex and China is no exception. There are language, nationality and cultural differences, as well as different accounting and financial requirements. For instance:

Languages. There are between 6 and 12 main regional groups of Chinese languages with 13 sub-languages.

Nationalities and Cultures. The Han Chinese is the largest ethnic group, representing 91 percent of the population, but China recognizes 55 other "nationalities" or ethnic groups.

Different Accounting and Financial Laws and Regulation. Each country has its own unique accounting and financial laws and regulations. The Chinese accounting regulations and policies are very different from U.S. requirements and add complexity and cost to the company.

The New Frontier?

Because of increasing costs and complexity of doing business in China, the Koreans, Japanese and Taiwanese are moving to other low-cost countries like Vietnam, Cambodia and North Korea, as well as the U.S. Going to Vietnam, Cambodia and North Korea follows the same pattern as the past. These are developing nations, with large low-wage work-forces and governments willing to make major concessions to get new industry. Companies will benefit from these concessions for a few years and then experience higher wages and more government interference.

There are also many examples of companies moving into the U.S. Nissan recently opened a $1.4 billion vehicle assembly plant in Canton, Miss., expected to employ about 5,300 workers. BSH Home Appliance Corp. recently opened two plants in New Bern, N.C., employing about 1,200 American workers. Hyundai Motors and Kia Motors recently established a joint design and technical center in Irvine, Calif., and Eco-labels is adding 400 engineers at its research and development center in Eagan, Minn.

Why the U.S.?

The U.S. is still a very large, affluent and growing market for many of the products and services these companies provide. It has a low inflationary rate; stable government and legal system; a large skilled, highly productive workforce; and protects patents and copyrights. Pros include:

Stable wages and benefits. Wages and benefits in the U.S. become increasingly more competitive as unions and workers accept that they will not get pensions, must have their own 401 (k) plans, and, in many cases, pay more toward health care.

Strong infrastructure. The U.S. has increasingly focused on improving the quality of air, water and preserving natural resources. Quality of life is far superior and, while infrastructure has been neglected, it is still competitive and will improve in time. Information/communications networks are second to none.

Abundant management and productive workforce. The university and professional schools in the U.S. are still among the best. There are an ample supply of qualified business graduates and, despite declining enrollments, science and engineering programs remain competitive and can be increased with the right incentives.

State and local governments competing for jobs and investment. Major locations in the U.S., such as Michigan, New York, Massachusetts and Connecticut, are aggressively soliciting companies to build plants in their states with tax incentives and other support.

Security. U.S. laws protect copyrights and patents. Its workforce can be more loyal to their companies than to the nation. Travel is easier, safer and not as complex. It is easier to protect facilities and key people in the U.S. than in a developing, often unfriendly country.

Stable and consistent financial requirements. The U.S. has a strong heritage of sound financial and accounting practices that are more stable and understandable than China or other developing nations.

The Right Strategy...

Just because some companies have decided to de-emphasize China, seek new low-cost nations and re-invest in the U.S., doesn't mean this is right for everyone. Many clients have been counseled by the two writers to make global decisions based on three factors: nature of market or industry, time horizon, and strategic drivers.

If, for example, your company participates in a commodity and highly price-competitive market and industry, clearly you must seek out the lowest-cost areas to produce or outsource your products and services. Therefore, nations eager to provide low-cost labor and ignore the environment are the places to look. This may require moving from the coastal, increasingly expensive areas to the western, rural areas of China. Or it may mean moving to Vietnam, Cambodia or North Korea. However, some American states may still be low-cost manufacturing locations. Obviously this will require careful strategic evaluations and possibly moving again in time.

Deciding when a business requires adding value and quickly adapting to change will require focusing less on lowest costs and more on the skills and responsiveness of the workforce. Normally, this would mean being close to the customer and being able to respond rapidly. In this case, you want to be near the market you are targeting. So if you are targeting China or India, it may make sense to stay in these countries and not worry as much about the increasing cost. This is the main reason so many European and Far East automobile companies are building factories in the Southern part of the United States.

Finally, technologically innovative companies must protect their patents, copyrights and intellectual properties, now and in the future. They can't afford to lose their competitive edge and create their own competitors. In this case, it is strongly recommended that companies invest first in their own R & D and not fragment or jeopardize their technical skills.

. American companies should focus on the United States, European companies on their home countries and so on. It is not the cost of labor that is key to these businesses and their ability to implement their strategies and succeed, but their ability to control and protect their "crown jewels." Moving to nations that are not secure, even if they have low-cost technical skills, makes no strategic sense.

The message is clear. Winners are selective, adaptive and internally, strategically consistent. They have a long-term, balanced view of the world and refuse to just follow the herd, and most of all they protect their "crown jewels."

China-Gulf Economic Relations

In June of 2008 the *Council on Foreign Relations* reported on the trade relations between China and the six countries of the Gulf Cooperation Council (GCC) that have broadened dramatically over the past decade. The relationship has been dominated by oil, and growing Chinese energy demand had made it likely that large-scale oil flows between the two sides will continue to expand. China and the GCC states are also diversifying their bilateral economic relations beyond oil, a process accelerated by swelling foreign exchange reserves.

Yet experts also caution against overly heady trade estimates, at least in the short term. Factors including mutual cultural wariness and infrastructural shortcomings continue to limit the speed at which economic expansion takes place, no matter how eager business leaders might be to develop relations. In the long run, however, experts say a "New Silk Road" could emerge as a force to be reckoned with economically-and perhaps also politically.

What is the scope of China-GCC economic relations?
Total capital flows between the GCC and China tallied around $32 billion in 2006, the last year for which this data is available. Those numbers are somewhat higher now, but remain small in the context of either side's economic relations with the United States. According to data from the U.S. Census Bureau, total Chinese trade with the United States amounted to roughly $386 billion in 2007 (with Chinese exports accounting for over $321 billion of that sum), while U.S.-GCC trade amounted to a little over $72 billion.

Still, China-GCC trade is notable for its rapid growth. Since 2000, Chinese exports to the GCC have increased more than seven-fold, while trade flows the other way have increased five-fold. By contrast, GCC exports to the United States have grown about three-fold during the same period. The consulting group McKinsey predicts that by 2020, total trade flows between China and the Middle East will climb to between $350 billion and $500 billion, with China-GCC trade accounting for much of that run-up.

What are the trade interests of each side?
China ranks fifty-fourth, globally in per-capita oil reserves, according to 2005 data from the U.S. Central Intelligence Agency. A burgeoning population and rapid industrial development, meanwhile, have brought a spike in demand. The most recent data available, from 2005, shows that China relies on imports for roughly half of the 6.5 million barrels of oil it consumes every day.

By contrast, the four countries with the highest per-capita oil supplies are all GCC states (Kuwait, the United Arab Emirates, Qatar, and Saudi Arabia). These rankings are inflated, to a degree, given the large number of non-citizens living in each of these countries. Still, the fact remains that the GCC has large oil surpluses. China also seeks to import energy-intensive goods like phosphate and aluminum, which the GCC states can produce more cheaply. The process of aluminum smelting, for instance, requires large amounts of oil.

The GCC states are most interested in China's bustling labor market and the products the country can manufacture cheaply, such as textiles. Just as

GCC states have large energy surpluses, China has large labor surpluses; this dynamic has driven the rapid expansion of China-GCC trade. "The theory of comparative advantage would lead to a situation where energy-intensive goods from Saudi Arabia are traded for labor-intensive goods from China," says Dr. Abdallah E. Dabbagh, the president and CEO of Ma'aden, the Saudi Arabia national mining company. Given the strong synergies to be gained by either side, McKinsey predicts GCC oil exports to China will grow by an average of 3.7 percent per annum through 2030.

What other sorts of exchange exist beyond this core trade?
China and the GCC states are making capital investments in one another's markets. Often, these investments are targeted at improving the effectiveness of pre-existing trading relationships, or catalyzing new ones. Dabbagh noted that Chinese direct investment has helped to enhance the competitiveness of his company's mining projects, in turn bolstering the quantities of commodities the firm is able to export to China. Timothy Gray, the CEO of HSBC Saudi Arabia, said that such arrangements now exist. Gray noted two recent joint ventures forged by Saudi Aramco, the Saudi state oil company, Sinopec, one of China's biggest oil firms, and the U.S. firm Exxon Mobil.

In March 2007, the three companies agreed to a deal in which Exxon and Aramco would help fund a Chinese petrochemical refinery, in exchange for export rights (for Saudi) and rights to operate 750 gas stations in China (for Exxon). As part of separate working arrangements, Chinalco, China's state-run aluminum manufacturer, is now funding phosphate projects in northern Saudi Arabia, and plans to set up a production facility in Jazan Economic City, also in Saudi Arabia. Experts say these sorts of capital investments hold particular promise given the large capital reserves currently held both by China and the GCC states, which are boosted by rising energy prices and bilateral trade imbalances with the United States.

What factors could undermine rapid China-GCC economic expansion?
Despite the surge in trade since 2000, experts note a slew of factors currently slowing expansion, from mutual suspicions to a lack of developed business relationships. "We're talking about capital plus," says Victor Chu, the chairman of First Eastern Investment Bank, the first Chinese bank authorized to do business in Dubai. "That plus must include the relationship."

Chu indicated that both China and Saudi Arabia have business environments in which friendships and confidences, built over a long period of time, can make or break deals. "One underestimates the importance of values and culture in both regions," he said, particularly given that such factors play a less prominent role in western business culture.

Gray added that businesses from either side don't always know what to expect when they venture into the other: "Going into the (Saudi) economic cities, companies like Chinalco wonder who's in charge. Is it the Bin Laden Group? Is it the central government? Is it the regional government?"

When large amounts of money are on the table, these unknowns become very real business risks, he said. Local companies are often able to work around these market eccentricities and skirt bureaucracy through connections, but it takes time to develop these relationships and to garner the trust that makes them work effectively.

China and the GCC states are working to broaden bilateral business and cultural ties, but experts say they face a number of fundamental problems, such as language barriers,. Very few Chinese companies have employees who speak Arabic, and vice versa.

"Big investments into China from the (BCC) region have only started over the last ten years," said Sameer al-Ansari, the chairman and CEO of the UAE-based investment firm Dubai International Capital. "People are much more familiar with the United States and Europe."

To deepen familiarity, Chu has encouraged new partnerships between Chinese and Arab universities, improvements in language training, and other forms of exchange. In the short term, however, experts say there simply aren't enough qualified consultants with in-depth knowledge of the two regions' respective business cultures to bring the sides together; this could limit the pace of economic expansion.

What are the implications of a re-emerging "Silk Road"?

The most profound effect of a new "Silk Road" between China and GCC states is likely to be greater Chinese energy security, experts say. China's huge demand for oil, natural gas, and other commodities present a significant challenge and potentially a serious political risk for the country's leaders. While poverty rates have dropped dramatically over the past two decades in China, some analysts fear a combination of skyrocketing wealth and growing income inequality could lead to internal strife in the country of more than 1.3 billion people. An energy pinch would likely exacerbate these risk factors.

That said, the China-GCC relationship brings risks of its own. A briefing from the Washington-based Institute for the Analysis of Global Security points out that China has never before faced a situation in which it is overwhelmingly dependent on another part of the world for its energy needs. The International Energy Agency predicts China will import 70 percent of its oil from the GCC by 2015, as compared to less than 50 percent today. By contrast, as of 2007, less than 20 percent of U.S. crude oil imports came directly from GCC states. Increasing dependency on GCC states from oil exports could mean that Chinese political and economic stability would become dependent on the political and economic stability in the GCC.

Some groups also fear China's relationship with its energy providers could undermine political reforms in the GCC. Beijing has been criticized for propping up regimes that support terrorist activity, including the Sudanese government. Saudi Arabia and other Gulf states have met criticism on similar counts, and some experts fear an influx of Chinese oil money could effectively shelter GCC states from U.S. and European political pressures, muting hopes for political reform on those countries. According to the advocacy group Freedom House's 2007 Freedom Index, which rates countries based on an array of indicators, Saudi Arabia ranks among the least "free" nations in the world, and all six GCC states rank below the global average. Beijing counters that it remains committed to a "peaceful rise" philosophy aimed at embracing economic globalization and improving relations with other countries.

Finally, some Western analysts worry that broadening China-GCC economic relations could hamper developed economies by sucking away trade opportunities the United States and Europe might otherwise have in the region. But experts like Chu say that enhanced China-GCC ties will not necessarily come at the exclusion of other parts of the world. Indeed, China's need for natural resources is so profound that broadened China-GCC could have positive auxiliary effects for developed economies.

Firms in the United States and Europe still dominate the market in project-management skills, and these skills will be in high demand from firms in China or the Gulf region seeking joint ventures with one another. New York, London, and other financial centers could also prove useful intermediaries for companies in the Middle East, and particularly in China, seeking to raise money on capital markets.

Dubai International Capital's Ansari says China is swelling with small-to medium-sized companies that might seek to go public in the near future, but which will be limited by the country's underdeveloped capital markets. He estimates roughly one hundred thousand companies will seek an initial public offering in the next ten years, but says China's capital system, as it stands now, can only handle about one thousand such offerings per year.

China Imports, Factory Inflation Rise on Commodities

Also in mid June 2008, *Reuters* reported that China's imports in May grew at their fastest rate since 2004, driven by surging commodity prices, but its exports were also unexpectedly strong as buoyant emerging markets compensated for sluggish U.S. demand.

Higher raw material costs also pushed up China's factory-gate inflation to 8.2 percent in May, the highest in nearly four years, suggesting price pressures in the pipeline that could limit any moderation in consumer inflation in coming months.

China's trade surplus in May hit $20.2 billion, down 10 percent from a year earlier, after imports grew more strongly than exports, as they have done every month since October apart from one. The surplus was close to expectations.

The evidence that the surplus is cresting will offer some relief to Chinese policy makers who will hold high-level talks with their counterparts in the United States. But the surplus is not shrinking quickly enough to relieve the headache facing the central bank, for cash flooding into the country from exports is one of the root causes of inflation.

May's imports soared 40 percent, beating forecasts. But the 28.1 percent rise in exports also far surpassed the market's 20 percent projection.

"If export growth holds up and the trade surplus remains at these elevated levels, forex reserve accumulation continues," said Dwyfor Evans, an economist at State Street in Hong Kong. China's foreign exchange reserves, already the world's largest, grew a record $74.5 billion in April, adding to the vast pool of liquidity that threatens to push prices still higher.

China Jan-May Crude Oil Imports 75.97 Mln Tons Up 12.7 Pct Year-on-Year Customs

Forbes reported on June 11, 2008 that China imported 75.97 minimum tons of crude oil in the first five months, up 12.7 percent year-on-year, the General Administration of Customs said. Imports of oil products in the first five months rose 17.3 percent year-on-year to 17.34 mln tons.

Coal exports in the first five months dropped 18.1 percent to 18.8 mln tons while iron ore imports stood at 190 mln tons, up 19.6 percent, with an average import price of 130.9 usd per ton, up 78.8 percent. Soybean imports rose 20.4 pct to 13.65 mln tons in the first five months. Automobile imports rose 59.1 pct to 171,000.

Machinery and electronic products imports rose 18.9 pct to 219.05 bln usd, while exports of machinery and electronic products rose 26.1 pct to 320.48 bln usd. High-tech exports in the five months totaled 161.74 bln usd, up 22.2 pct.

China May Trade Surplus Down 10 Percent on Imports... China's Exports Soar, But Trade Surplus Falls

Associated Press, on June 11th, 2008 announced China's trade surplus shrank 10 percent in May from a year earlier, the second straight monthly decline, as the value of imports of crude oil and other raw materials surged.

The $20.2 billion surplus for May was still relatively large-up from a $16.7 billion gap in April and $13.4 billion in March, 2008-larger than analysts had predicted. Imports ballooned 40 percent to $100.3 billion, the General Administration of Customs said.

Exports, meanwhile, rose 28 percent to $120.5 billion-still strong amid speculation that the slowdown in the U.S. economy would significantly erode export demand. "It suggests that those saying that exports are collapsing are wrong," Stephen Green, an economist at Standard Chartered Bank in Shanghai, said in a report. While exports of manufactured goods remain strong, weakness is showing up in textiles and other industries.

However, China's trade gap with both the United States and the European Union grew in May compared with a year earlier. That's likely to rankle both trading partners, who have pushed for China to open itself up to more imports and make its currency more flexible. Critics claim authorities are keeping the yuan artificially weak to give Chinese exporters an advantage.

China's gap with the U.S. came to $14.3 billion in May, up from $12.6 billion in the same month a year ago. Imports from the U.S. jumped 26.3 percent to $6.9 billion, but they were far exceeded by China's $21.2 billion in exports, a 9.1 percent increase over May, 2007.

China's surplus with the EU surged 28 percent to $12.7 billion from $9.9 billion a year ago. But China's deficit with Japan nearly doubled in May to $3.1 billion. The trade surplus for the first five months of the year was $78 billion, down 8.6 percent from the $85.7 billion surplus in January-May 2007.

The Economic Times also recorded that China's export growth unexpectedly accelerated in May, easing concern that a strengthening yuan and a slowdown in U.S. demand will trigger an economic slump. TCL, China's biggest electronics maker, said mobile phone exports soared 62% in May from a year earlier. "Export growth held up partly because the U.S. economy appears to be recovering better than expected," said Shen Minggao, an economist at Citigroup in Beijing."

The central bank cautioned on June 3rd against exaggerating the risk that weakening global demand would lead to a hard landing for the world's fourth-largest economy. Machinery and electronic exports climbed 59% from a year earlier. Trade with India surged 70% in the first five months, the quickest gain among China's top 10 trading partners.

U.S. Treasury Secretary Henry Paulson said that a more flexible currency could be a "valuable tool" to help China cool inflation.

US / China Trade Imbalance Driving Dollar Lower and Gold Higher

DO DEFICITS MATTER? Right around the time that English missionaries produced the first Bible in Chinese, the British Empire found itself with a trickier kind of translation problem. Exporting the English language to China-and a little Protestant godliness besides-was proving much easier than exporting British-made goods.

Imports from abroad, in contrast, just kept on growing as the industrial revolution steamed ahead at home, sucking in the new consumer favorites-tobacco, sugar, coffee, calicoes, porcelain and silk. And that was just the beginning of global trade as we know it today!

By the early 19th century, of course, Britain owned the plantations of the West Indies and the factories of Bengal. So those deficits didn't even exist, let alone matter. But "the British were spectacularly unsuccessful in finding trade goods that the Chinese wanted or needed," as Jonathan Spence, professor of history at Yale, noted in his Reith Lectures for the BBC.

Thus "there was the problem of trade imbalances," And stuck for consumer items to ship back across the oceans, London's merchants were forced to pay in cash. For the British, money meant gold, just as it did until the last gasp of the Gold Standard one hundred years later. But the Chinese wanted silver. (They never did get around to using gold, in fact. And while Britain recovered early from the Great Depression by abandoning gold for credit-money in 1931, one theory holds that China side-stepped it entirely by sticking to the silver standard).

Translating English pounds into Chinese yuan in the 1830's meant selling gold for silver, and that meant dealing on Europe's precious metals market. Paying a commission to the bullion dealers of Paris or Prussia-as well as shipping it all back and forth-only added further to the transaction costs of running up that yawning trade gap.

What to do? A little of the British Empire's raw cotton found a market in China, but it wasn't nearly enough to close the trade gap. Gold bullion continued to flow out of London, aggravating the "bullionist" school of economists and policy-makers. They feared a shortage of coin in the domestic British economy, plus a fall in the Pound Stirling's international value...as well as giving work to foreign laborers, and paying profits to their foreign masters…while leaving the London exchequer impoverished should it ever need to fund a military defense of the home front.

And so, "It was this melancholy failure of the balance of trade that led to the under girding of the opium business in China," explained Professor Spence. Opium grown in India "started to be sold to the Chinese by British traders, and later by American traders, because the West simply could not find enough products to attract the Chinese in a sort of barter exchange at the time."

Widespread dope-smoking and the social breakdown it can invite rarely chimes with government policy-not domestically, at least. Opium had long been banned by imperial decree from Nanjing. But after ten years of trying to fend off Britain's drug dealers without damaging the inflows of silver, the Qin authorities finally cracked and made a stand, seizing 20,000 chests of the drug-some 1,200 tonnes-landed in Guangzhou.

London responded first with a gun-boat, and then the all-out Opium War of 1839. It ended three years later with the Treaty of Nanjing. Britain's military might won the island of Hong Kong, plus reduced trade tariffs, freedom from Chinese law for its ex-pats, as well as "most-favored nation" status.

Whatever trading rights or concessions China would grant in the future, the British Empire would also gain as well. Opium was then forced on the Chinese, and the trade gap closed without the need for hard money payments.

In today's market, we still don't make much that the Chinese want to buy. The United Kingdom's trade deficit with China rose 8% in 2008 through April of this year, as Chinese imports swelled by more than 10%.

But most clearly, here in the 21st century, it's America's turn to fumble around for a way of settling its debts with China. Yes, the value of Chinese imports to the U.S. fell slightly during the first four months of 2008 compared with the first third of 2007. But U.S. exports to China fell faster still, according to the Census Bureau's latest data. So the trade gap widened again, to rack up a deficit three times the size of America's debt to Canada or Mexico, the United States' number one and number three trading partners respectively.

Canada and Mexico just happen to share a land border with the U.S., whereas, China sits on the other side of the Pacific. As the British Empire's gun-boat diplomacy of 1839 attests, however, distance means little when consumers choose to buy luxury goods overseas. The United States, of course, ships dollars and bonds back across the Pacific, rather than silver or gold bullion. But are dollar bills and treasuries what China rally wants, anymore than it wanted 1,200 tonnes of dope in 1839?

The People's Bank of China just raised the required reserves ratio-the amount of cash which private banks must keep in reserve-to a massive 17.5%. That should drain something like $58 billion from the domestic lending markets, reckons the RGE Monitor, as the Chinese authorities set about "treating the symptoms of excess liquidity."

Spooked by the risk of a further slump in the over-heated Shanghai stock market, however, the PBoC continues to hold its key interest rate below the rate of consumer-price inflation. That makes cash a losing asset class in China today, just like it is in the U.S. and U.K. as well. The Chinese would still rather buy and hold precious metals apparently. China's retail investment demand for gold rose 63% during the first quarter of 2008, reports the GFMS consultancy, amounting to 15.1 tonnes. Gold jewelry sales grew by 9%-"one of the few examples of demand increasing over 2007 levels" during the global spike to $1,000 per ounce-reaching 86.6 tonnes.

China now represents the world's second-largest gold jewelry market after India, over-taking the United States in 2007. But even at a total of 420 tonnes last year, total demand for gold from mainland China, Hong Kong and Taiwan combined remains almost negligible on a per capita basis. That's not to say it's sure to keep rising; but with Chinese goods now accounting for 13% of America's imports each month-more than Mexican goods and only just less than Canada's (including petroleum)-we wouldn't be surprised to see ever more of that wealth swapped for silver and gold bullion.

Because deficits do matter after all, despite what Vice President Dick Cheney had claimed back in 2002 as the dollar's 40% decline got started. No least, trade deficits matter to those countries that sit on the other end of the shipping route.

Note: Thanks to Adrian Ash, city correspondent for the Daily Reckoning in London and a regular contributor to MoneyWeek magazine.

China to Import Grain as Economy Grows...
Progress on Product Safety in China...
Four Major Obstacles to Chinese Foreign Trade

China could be forced to become a major grain importer to feed its increasingly wealthy population at a time of record global good prices. As one of the world's top grain producers, China imports little wheat or corn, but may soon have to buy from abroad as citizens change their eating habits, said Lester Brown, president of the Earth Policy Institute.

Brown, an influential environmental scholar, said that four billion people worldwide are seeking to switch from grain-based diets to meat-based diets, which demand more farm resources. "I don't anticipate much increase in China's grain production and I expect China to move into the international market," Brown told reporters in Beijing. "If China imports only 10 percent of its grain needs, it will become the world's largest importer of grain."

Dwindling water resources in China, and a fall in crop yields brought on by global warming, will also force the world's most populous nation to tap foreign grain markets, he said. "China's 1.76 trillion dollars in foreign reserves will bolster its capacity to import more grain."

Brown however debunked Western media reports that blame China's rising appetite for resources as fueling global food inflation, saying the real culprit was the Western drive to produce more biofuels for their cars. "China's consumption of more meat, milk and eggs as it moves up the food chain is resulting in a two-million-tonnes increase of grain consumption per year. But grain fuel for the production of ethanol (biofuel) in the United States in 2007 amounted to 20 million tonnes," Brown said.

According to the World Bank, global food prices have nearly doubled in three years, with experts blaming factors such as rising oil prices and the growing use of biofuels. Sky-rocketing commodity prices in the past year have battered developing countries, where food takes the lion's share of household income. Rising food prices have sparked deadly unrest and rising malnutrition, and a number of countries have put limits on exports to try to feed their own populations.

"We are in the midst of the most serious food-price inflation ever witnessed," said Brown.

With regards to the safety problems in the exporting of products from China, Meglena Kuneva, the European Union Commissioner for Consumer Protection commended in Beijing on June 11th, 2008 on China's progress in eliminating safety problems with export products, but said that there was still 'no room for complacency.'

"I am pleased to tell you that I see that genuine progress has been made and we had very positive discussions looking at how to take forward work on key issues such as traceability standards, education and enforcement."

Kuneva traveled to the southern city of Guangzhou, the capital of the key export-oriented manufacturing province of Guangdong, where she planned to meet Chinese customs and quality-control officials. Concerns over product safety mushroomed last summer after about 1 million toys were recalled worldwide by U.S.-based Mattel because of potentially harmful lead content in paint. Several more U.S. and E.U. recalls of Chinese-made toys ordered by Mattel and other firms followed the withdrawal in August, 2007 of plastic toys marketed in the U.S. under the Fisher-Price brand. In early November, China said inspectors had suspended or revoked the export licenses of 764 toy factories in Guangdong.

But a row between China and the European Union over product safety erupted later in November, when visiting EU Trade Commissioner Peter Mandelson said shoddy import goods from China were 'unacceptable' and urged the governments to tackle its 'tidal wave of counterfeit goods.' Chinese officials had defended their record and said that less than 1 percent of exports to Europe had possible health risks.

"But Europe imports half a billion euros worth of goods from China every day...so even 1 percent is not acceptable," Mandelson said at a product safety forum in Beijing. "Some of those products-fake medicines, fake car parts, fake aircraft parts-carry huge risks when they are faulty or just plain fake," he said.

Mandelson's comments drew an angry response from Chinese Vice Premier Wu Yi. "We disagree with biased, incomplete media reports and pure condemnation that are blind to the facts, and we are opposed to trade barriers set for food safety issues and politicizing the issues," Wu said at the same forum.

Four Major Obstacles to Chinese Foreign Trade...
People's Daily Online had issued a statement on June 27th, 2006 that the period of the 11th five-year plan is very important for China. According to Zhang Lichuan, a Director with the Statistical Department of General Administration of Customs of China, to be a recognized trading power, China must commit to the search for solutions to emerging issues in foreign trade. She also said that the Chinese government should focus on four major hurdles in the field of foreign trade:

- Firstly, China should deal with pressure from international markets that are gradually becoming saturated. In 2005, the volume of Chinese exports ranked third in the world, making up 7.3 percent of the world's total volume, 3.4 percentage points up from 2000. In 2005, ranked among the world's top ten countries in terms of export volume, China has been growing much faster than the nine other countries. The growth rate of Chinese exports exceeds the world's average rate of 13 percent. As a result, the growth of Chinese exports is increasingly subjected to international markets.
- Secondly, the cost of Chinese exports is increasing, partly because of the higher cost of labor and environmental protection. Cheap labor is the foundation of the Chinese economy. However, the

worker shortage apparent in some areas of China indicates that it is inappropriate to sacrifice workers' welfare for the sake of low export prices and the Chinese government should change the situation. In recent years, China has tightened restrictions on the export of products that consume a lot of energy, create a lot of pollution or use a lot of resources in their production. Limited resources and the environment have become major obstacles to the growth of Chinese exports.

- Thirdly, increasing international trade protection has caused China to stumble into difficult territory. China has been involved in the world's largest number of anti-dumping cases in recent years.

- Finally, the trade imbalance between China and other countries is getting worse. As the Renminbi appreciates, Chinese enterprises will face greater exchange risks in import-export trade. Increasing pressures from the appreciating Renminbi will create new requirements and challenges for Chinese enterprises engaged in import-export trade.

Economy: What to Look for in the Trade Deficit Data... Federal Reserve Board Chairman Ben Bernanke Aggravated Trade Deficit Risks

Professor Peter Morici, of the Robert H. Smith School of Business at University of Maryland had reported in June, 2008 that the Commerce Department was going to report the April trade deficit, only one month after they reported the March deficit on goods and services...which was $58.2 billion. For April, the consensus forecast was close to $60.0 billion. The March deficit on trade in goods was $68.6 billion and was partially offset by a $10.4 billion surplus on services.

The key data to watch for will be the deficits on petroleum and motor vehicles, the deficit with China, and the progress of U.S. exports. Especially critical for signs of an export led economy recovery would be exports of capital goods. Together, the deficits on petroleum, on motor vehicles and with China totaled about $60 billion in March, or equal to the entire trade deficit on goods and services.

The deficit on petroleum products was expected to rise from $33.1 billion in March to $34.7 billion in April. According to the Labor Department report on import and export price data, petroleum import prices rose 4.4 percent in April. Commerce and Labor Department pricing data do not always coincide, because the Labor Department reports prices earlier and its data are more preliminary. Energy Department data indicate the volume of oil import volumes increased about 0.5 percent in April; the same caveats regarding Labor Department pricing date apply to Energy Department import volume data.

The trade deficit on motor vehicles was $10.7 billion in March, down from $11.4 billion in February. Sluggish new car sales in the U.S. have pulled down this deficit a bit; however, the shift from truck-based vehicles to small cars favors import brands.

In addition to high oil prices and the shift to smaller motor vehicles, overvaluation of the dollar against the Chinese yuan continues to push up the trade deficit. China has permitted the yuan to rise 16 percent since July 2005, or less than 5 percent a year. However, thanks to rising productivity, the underlying value of the yuan rises much more than 5 percent a year. This is evidenced by the fact that China has been forced to increase its currency market intervention to sustain its controlled exchange rate for the yuan. In 2007, it purchased $462 billion in dollars and other foreign currencies, as compared to $247 billion in 2006.

The Chinese yuan is at least 40 percent undervalued against the dollar. In 2007, the U.S. deficit with China hit a new record and was $16.1 billion in March. Consumer purchases of Chinese goods have been slowed, in recent months, by rising gasoline prices, which sap household income, and a trend toward diversification in sourcing for imported consumer items. The quality problems and safety risks associated with Chinese imports are playing some role. However, China's undervalued currency continued to provide a 35 percent subsidy on Chinese exports to the United States.

Since February 2006, monthly exports have risen $34 billion to $148.5 billion, thanks to a weaker dollar against the euro, pound and other market determined currencies. This has moderated the deficit on trade in non-petroleum products and the overall trade deficit.

U.S. exports compete with EU exports in nearly every category, and a weaker dollar against the euro helps boost U.S. sales in Europe and elsewhere around the world. However, oil is priced in dollars and a weaker dollar has pushed up, somewhat, the price of oil and the U.S. petroleum trade deficit. Further, many other Asian governments follow China's lead by intervening in foreign currency markets and maintaining undervalued currencies and this limits U.S. export gains in Asia.

Exports of agricultural commodities and industrial materials have performed well because of strong demand in Asia and a weaker dollar. However, during the second quarter of 2008, exports of capital goods have stalled. These were $37.7 billion in March, and down from $40.1 billion in December. If exports are to significantly lift the U.S. economy from recession, this category will have to perform better. Whatever the final trade deficit figure, it will be close to 5 percent of GDP, which is too large to be sustainable.

The foreign borrowing to finance the deficit is about $50 billion a month, as only about 11 percent of the deficit is financed by new direct investment in productive assets. Debt to foreigners now exceeds $6.5 trillion, and this flood of greenbacks abroad is driving down the dollar, heightening concerns about the solvency of U.S. financial institutions, pushing up the price of gold, and exacerbating the recession.

The stubbornly large trade deficit heightens the risk of recession. The deficit subtracts about $250 billion from GDP, and that amount could double if the economy slips into a prolonged recession.

Let's review this again as the growing U.S deficit on trade in goods and services, rising on US$60.9 billion in April from $56.5 billion in March, has heightened the risk of recession and surging unemployment. The recent comments by Federal Reserve Board Chairman Ben Bernanke about oil-driven inflation only serve to distract attention from these issues and aggravate risks.

The deficit, announced by the US Commerce Department this month and substantially larger than the $59.5 billion consensus forecast, was driven up by higher prices for imported oil and a dramatic surge in imports from China. At 5.1 percent of gross domestic product, these pose a significant drag on the economy.

Simply, money spent on Middle East oil and Middle Kingdom consumer goods can't be spent on U.S. made goods and services. The drag on aggregate demand is every bit as important as the credit crisis and housing adjustment in driving up unemployment. The combined effect of oil imports, the trade deficit and housing adjustment are pushing the economy into recession and breaking the inflation on non-energy products. That is why core inflation, prices less food and energy, stays in check.

Bernanke in recent comments has emphasized that Western central banks stand ready to resist oil-induced recession, when in fact oil price increases are far beyond the control of the Federal Reserve and other central banks to affect. This is causing markets to factor in Federal Reserve increases in the federal funds rate by the end of the year, just as the economy is sliding into recession.

China is subsidizing oil imports, without regard to spot prices in international markets, and controlling domestic gasoline prices with the dollars it purchases with yuan. It undertakes the latter purchases to keep the yuan undervalued against the dollar and boost exports. Hence, consumers in the country contributing most to growing demand for oil are wholly insulated from rising oil prices. As oil prices rise, the Chinese drive prices even higher with their subsidies. Bernanke should talk about that if he wants to do something about oil driven inflation.

Instead, Bernanke's words caused markets to believe the Fed will raise interest rates as we travel into a recession and this drives equity prices down, compounding the panic created by rising oil prices. Raising interest rates now would be the kind of policy the Federal Reserve pursued in 1929. Is that the kind of signal a central banker and student of the Great Depression wants to send to fragile markets?

If Bernanke wants to do something about both the recession and inflation, he should focus on Chinese purchases of dollars with yuan, which boost exports to the United States, and Chinese subsidies on oil imports with those dollars, which drive up global oil prices. Together, these are driving up the trade deficit, exacerbating the recession and driving up US gas prices.

Were the Chinese yuan problem solved, the trade deficit could be cut by a third, and that would boost U.S. gross domestic product (GDP) by about $250 million to $500 billion.

Breaking down the deficit…
Together, petroleum, China and automotive products account for nearly the entire U.S. trade deficit, and no solution to the overall trade imbalance is possible without addressing these segments. Let's talk about each of them separately:

Petroleum products accounted for $34.5 billion of the monthly trade gap, on a seasonally adjusted basis, up from $30.2 billion in March, 2008. Since December 2001, net petroleum imports have increased $30.0 billion, as the average price of a barrel of imported oil has risen from $15.46 to $96.81, and monthly imports have increased from 353 million to 388 million barrels.

Returning conventional gasoline engines and transmissions, hybrid systems, lighter weight vehicles, nuclear power, and other alternative energy sources could substantially reduce U.S. dependence on foreign oil. These solutions require national leadership, but both Republican and Democratic Party leaders have failed to champion policies that would reduce dependence on Middle East oil.

In 2007, the Congress managed to push through the first increase in automobile mileage standards in 32 years but don't cheer loudly. The 35 mile-per-gallon standard to be achieved by 2020 is far less than what is possible.

The bill also requires the production of about 2.4 million barrels a day of ethanol. Along with other conservation measures, the 2007 Energy Act could reduce U.S. petroleum consumption by 4 million barrels a day by 2030. Over the past 23 years, petroleum consumption has increased by about 5.5 million barrels a day, despite improvements in mileage standards, automobile and appliance technology, and conservation.

Being optimistic, in 2030 the United States will be just as dependent on imported oil as before without stronger conservation and alternative fuel policies. Factor in falling production from U.S. oil fields, the situation gets worse.

China accounted for $20.2 billion of the April trade deficit, up from $16.1 billion in March and $5.5 billion in December 2001. The bilateral deficit is rising because China undervalues the yuan, and this makes Chinese exports artificially inexpensive and U.S products too expensive in China. U.S. imports from China exceed exports to China by a ration of 4.5 to 1.

China revalued the yuan from 8.28 to 8.11 in July, 2005 and has permitted the yuan to rise less than 5% every 12 months. Modernization and productivity advances raise the implicit value of the yuan much more than 5% every 12 months, and the yuan remains undervalued against the dollar by at least 40%.

China's huge trade surplus creates an excess demand for yuan on global currency markets; however, to limit appreciation of the yuan against the dollar and drive its value down against the euro, the People's Bank of China sells yuan and buys dollars, euros and other currencies on foreign exchange markets.

In 2007, the Chinese government purchased $462 billion in U.S. and other foreign currency and securities. This comes to about 14% of China's GDP and about 35% of its exports of goods and services. These purchases provide foreign consumers with 3.5 trillion yuan to purchase Chinese exports, and create a 35% "off-budget" subsidy on foreign sales of Chinese products, and an even larger implicit tariff on Chinese imports.

In addition, China provides numerous tax incentives and rebates, and low interest loans, to encourage exports and replace imports with domestic products. These practices clearly violate China's obligations in the World Trade Organization, and it agreed to remove those when it joined the trade body.

Automotive products account for about $11 billion of the monthly trade deficit. Japanese and South Korean manufacturers have captured a larger market and are expanding their U.S. production. However, Asian manufacturers tend to use more imported components than domestic companies, and GM and Ford are pushing their parts suppliers to move to China.

GM, Ford and Chrysler still carry a significant cost disadvantage against Toyota plants located in the United States, thanks to clumsy management and unrealistic wages, excessive fringe benefits and arcane work rules imposed by the United Autoworker contracts. Recent negotiations improved the Detroit Three's cost position but did not wholly close the labor cost gap with Toyota and other Asian transplants.

Recently negotiated labor agreements should reduce, but not eliminate, these cost disadvantages. Even with retiree health care benefits moved off the books and a two-tier wage structure, the cost disadvantage will remain at least $1,000 per vehicle.

Also, the Bank of Japan has aggressively stepped up sales of yen and won for U.S. dollars and other securities to keep its currency cheap against the dollar. This discourages Toyota and others from moving more auto assembly and sourcing more parts in the United States.

Deficits, debt and growth...
Trade deficits must be financed by foreigners investing in the U.S. economy or Americans borrowing money abroad. Direct investments in the United States provide only about a tenth of the needed funds, and Americans borrow about $50 billion each month. The total debt is about $6.5 trillion, and at 5% interest, the debt service comes to about $2,000 per US worker each year.

High and rising trade deficits tax economic growth. Each dollar spent on imports, not matched by a dollar of exports, shifts workers into activities in non-trade competing industries such as department stores and restaurants.

Manufacturers are particularly hard hit by this subsidized competition. Through recession and recovery, the manufacturing sector has lost 3.7 million jobs since 2000. Following the pattern of past economic recoveries, the manufacturing sector should have regained more than 2 million of those jobs, especially given the very strong productivity growth accomplished in technology-intensive durable goods industries.

Productivity is at least 50% higher in industries that export and compete with imports. By reducing the demand for high-skill and technology-intensive products, and U.S.-made goods and services, the deficit reduces GDP by at least $250 billion a year, or about $1,750 for each worker.

Longer-term, persistent U.S. trade deficits are a substantial drag on growth. U.S. import-competing and export industries spend at least three times the national average on industrial research and development, and encourage more investments in skills and education than other sectors of the economy. By shifting employment away from trade-competing industries, the trade deficit reduces U.S. investments in new methods and products, and skilled labor.

Cutting the trade deficit in half would boost U.S. GDP growth by one percentage point a year, and the trade deficits of the last two decades have reduced U.S. growth by one percentage point a year. Lost growth is cumulative. Thanks to the record trade deficits accumulated over the past ten years, the U.S. economy is about $1.5 trillion smaller. This comes to about $10,000 a worker.

The damage grows larger each month, as the George W. Bush administration dallied and ignored the corrosive consequences of the trade deficit.

China May Trade Surplus Down 10 Percent on Imports

The Associate Press reported on June 12th, 2008 that China's trade surplus shrank 10 percent in May, from a year earlier, the second straight monthly decline, as the value of imports of crude oil and other raw materials surged, the government said Wednesday in Shanghai, China.

The $20.2 billion surplus for May was still relatively large-up from a $16.7 billion gap in April and $13.4 billion in March-and larger than analysts had predicted. Imports ballooned 40 percent to $100.3 billion, the General Administration of Customs said. Exports, meanwhile, rose 28 percent to $120.5 billion-still strong amid speculation that the slowdown in the U.S. economy would significantly erode export demand.

"It suggests that those saying that exports are collapsing are wrong," Stephen Green, an economist at Standard Chartered Bank in Shanghai, said in a report.

While exports of manufactured goods remain strong, weakness is showing up in textiles and other industries, he added.

However, China's trade gap with both the United States and the European Union grew in May compared with a year earlier. That's likely to rankle both trading partners, who have pushed for China to open itself up to more imports and make its currency more flexible. Critics claim authorities are keeping the yuan artificially weak to give Chinese exporters an advantage.

China's gap with the U.S. came to $14.3 billion in May, up from $12.6 billion in the same month a year ago. Imports from the U.S. jumped 26.3 percent to $6.9 billion, but they were far exceeded by China's $21.2 billion in exports, a 9.1 percent increase over May 2007.

Were We Suckered to get China into the WTO???

There was a very interesting essay by Robert Cassidy, the former Assistant U.S. Trade Representative for Asia and for China (tip of the hat to Howard Richman at his blog Trade Wars.) Mr. Cassidy was the lead U.S. negotiator for China's 1999 Market Access Agreement that paved the way for China's accession to the World Trade Organization.

Titled "The Failed Expectations of U.S. Trade Policy" and appearing in *Foreign Policy in Focus* (June 4th, 2008 edition), Mr. Cassidy's essay begins with his current unease with his own handiwork:

> **"As the principal negotiator for the landmark market access agreement that led to China's accession to the World Trade Organization (WTO), I have reflected on whether the agreements we negotiated really lived up to our expectations. A sober reflection has led me to conclude that those trade agreements did not."**

Why didn't the trade agreements work? Mr. Cassidy concludes that in the Clinton Administration's haste to get China into the WTO, the 1999 Market Access Agreement didn't address a number of critical issues. Specifically, he points out that the 'Clintonistas' overlooked the topic of currency manipulation (China deliberately maintains a significantly undervalued currency so as to encourage exports and discourage imports). They also chose to ignore a variety of tax and other internal commercial policies that continue to prevent U.S. exports from penetrating the Chinese market.

According to Mr. Cassidy, the power of these factors to distort "free trade" is obvious if you compare our economic relations with China to our economic relations with Canada and Europe:

> **"In order to join the WTO, China made unilateral concessions to reduce and, in some cases, eliminate barriers to entry for U.S. goods and services...U.S. exports to China have increased and, as the U.S. Trade Representative (USTR) often emphasizes, at a higher rate than to any other country. But such claims distort the real truth that exports grew faster because they grew from a very low level. In absolute terms, the increase in U.S. exports of goods to the EU was almost 70% greater than the increase in exports of goods to China. Likewise, the absolute increase to Canada was 40% more than to China. Neither of those trading partners made any trade concessions to the United States during this period."**
> **"Conversely, on the U.S. import side, the United States made no concessions to China, yet U.S. imports from China were more than triple the pre-accession levels; to**

> $321 billion in 2007, almost matching imports from the
> entire European Union. In contrast, increases in imports
> from Canada, our largest trading partner, rose by $82
> billion and imports from the EU increased by $134
> billion."

So it would appear that the *formal* barriers to free trade that China gave up
to get WTO membership had a much lower impact on its trade balance than
the *informal* barriers (currency manipulation and a series of internal barriers
to both imports and consumer spending generally) that it kept.

So why were we such, well, for want of a better term, suckers? Mr. Cassidy
gives some broad hints:

> "The beneficiaries of the agreement with China fall into
> two groups: multinational companies that moved to
> China and the financial institutions that financed those
> investments, trade flows, and deficits. Foreign direct
> investment (FDI) in China accelerated at a time when
> such investment to other parts of Asia was declining
> and, in 2001, even matched FDI to the United States.
> Sourcing from China, whether from direct investment or
> through licensing arrangements, has allowed companies
> to cut costs and increase profits, as reflected in increased
> corporate profits and the surge in the U.S. stock market."
> "Conversely, it is doubtful that the U.S. economy or its
> workers are better off. U.S. manufacturing jobs declined
> by more than 2.5 million since China joined the WTO
> in 2001. While service jobs increased during this period,
> with the exception of telecommunications, non-tradable
> jobs accounted for the most significant portion of that
> increase. Wages have been stagnant and real disposable
> income for three- quarters of U.S. households has been
> stable or declining. Only the top quartile of families has
> seen significant increases in real disposable income."

The U.S. government was looking out for the welfare of the people so it seems,
who make campaign contributions and not for Joe Sixpack! I'm shocked,
simply shocked to see that happen. What, therefore does he recommend for
the future? Well, he's suggesting we might do better to ignore the siren's song
spun by the powers-that-be:

"With the current financial and recessionary crisis, many 'traditionalist' thinkers will likely pull out the old premises, arguing to conclude the Doha Round and pass legislation enacting recently signed free trade agreements as a means of alleviating the crisis. Once again, multinational companies and financial institutions and their think tanks will lead the charge since they would be the primary beneficiaries. Before we blindly accept trade agreements that will simply result in lost jobs, the next administration needs to also comprehensively address the disparities in international monetary and competition policies that prevent our trade agreement from delivering the results that Main Street was promised and deserves."

The comments on Mr. Cassidy's article were numerous including many who agreed or simply disagreed with his logical...or illogical...points of view. Some indicated that the Chinese tend to invest most of their money back in the West, allowing for lower interest rates...while others think that the concept of having China in the WTO favors export industries at the expense of Chinese consumers. Others commented that our current trade regime is clearly designed to serve some of our citizens and not, shall we say, the general public.

China may be giving us a discount on all of the products that it sells to us, but then again, are all of the products suitable for consumption? Have we witnessed sicknesses and deaths because of some of the imports from China? Is China truly trying to take care of the polluted fish and the hallow steel or the leaded toys it has sent to us? Or are they in the business to try to destroy this country by importing imperfect goods?

We may be getting cheaper goods (which devalue to zero), while millions of jobs and huge productive assets, like factories, flow out of the country! And the sword of currency revaluation and dumping our US government bonds can fall anytime the Chinese probably wish. It is possible that our so-called economists are either brain-washed or outright liars. We got suckered into this program because people wanted to make lots of money from it.

China's Trade Surplus Dips as Exports, Imports Lift

China publications read the news differently than the United States. As posted in the June 11th, 2008 'Business in China Foreign Trade Publication' it states that China's trade surplus in May dropped 9.9 percent from a year earlier to US $20.2 billion after both export and import growth accelerated, the General Administration of Customs said.

Exports increased 28.1 percent in May, 2008 to US $120.5 billion, compared to growth of 21.8 percent a month earlier, while imports climbed 40 percent to US $100.3 billion, roaring past the 26.3 percent April growth.

"Thanks to many companies' swift shift to higher-value-added products and stronger demand for low-priced products under a battered world economy, China delivered strong export growth in May," said Zhu Jianfang, an analyst with CITIC Securities Co.

Stephen Green, an economist with Standard Chartered Bank (China) Ltd., said the nation is benefiting from its yuan, which is appreciating against the United States dollar, the currency in which oil and other raw materials are priced.

"China is gaining buying power and the accelerating export growth that suggests the notion that China's exports are collapsing is wrong," said Green. "The faster expansion of imports is partly due to higher prices of crude oil and iron ore on the global market."

The yuan has risen 19 percent since China dropped the peg to the greenback in July, 2005. It has gained 5.3 percent so far in 2008, compared to an overall 7 percent increase in 2007. The mechanical and electrical-equipment sector was the star performer among exporters. In the first five months of 2008, sales in the sector jumped 26.1 percent to US $320.5 billion, accounting for 58.8 percent of the total products sold abroad.

In imports, the purchase value of primary products rocketed 69.4 percent due to higher costs. For example, the average import price of crude oil swelled 64.1 percent to US $689.9 per ton, while the volume of imported crude oil rose 12.7 percent to 75.9 million tons. The overall trade value in May grew 33.2 percent to US $220.8 billion. It sent the nation's trade figure in the first five months this year to US $1.01 trillion, a growth of 26.2 percent.

The trade surplus through May cooled 8.6 percent from a year earlier to US $78 billion.

During the first five months, the European Union remained China's largest trading partner with bilateral sales of US $166 billion, advancing 27.9 percent. It was followed by the US and Japan, whose bilateral trade values rose to US $130.5 billion and US $106.5 billion respectively.

Emerging markets posted much faster growth in trade with China. India's bilateral trade has surged 70.3 percent so far this year to US $24.2 billion.

Here we are in mid 2009 and the economy in the United States is horrifying to say the least. We were once the capital of the world in business, in exporting, and in "Yankee Ingenuity." But we have lost much ground in the past ten years or more since allowing China into the WTO. That was not the reason of course, as we allowed to give away the bank to China and that is now hurting us financially and economically. We need to turn this around and soon. Yet, we have opened up a Pandora's Box. Pretty soon, we will have to cope with Vietnam and Korea.

Is Vietnam The Next China?

As reported in *Forbes* by Donald H. Straszheim, vice chairman of Roth Capital Partners in Los Angeles and former global chief economist at Merrill Lynch, Vietnam's government has been working hard in recent years to reform its economy in ways reminiscent of the successes of her neighbor to the north, China. Straszheim has been bullish on Vietnam for many years, and remains so for the long term. But, in the short term, real economic trouble is brewing that threatens a major economic disruption.

Here is the essential background. After the American war (as they call it), and years of internal conflict, the Vietnamese government launched a so-called "doi moi"-economic revival-in 1986. The economy was opened up, in steps, to foreign investment. Vietnam joined the Association of Southeast Asian Nations in 1995, a U.S.-Vietnam trade pact was signed in 2000 and Vietnam became a member of the World Trade Organization in 2007. Selected state-owned enterprises are being privatized, and new equity markets were launched, letting market forces start to work in the economy.

The very positive results are no surprise to those of us who believe in free enterprise. Vietnam has been the second-fastest growing economy in the world the last half-decade, behind only China. The people have never been better off. All they want to do is work, earn and consume. But too much of a good thing is turning into a bad thing.

Inflation is surging. In May, 2008 Vietnam's prices were 25.2% higher than a year earlier. This was up from 16% in March, 13% in December 2007 and 8.4% in May, 2008. The economy has gotten overheated. With commodity and energy prices spiking everywhere, Vietnam's inflation rate is likely to go even higher. The history of developing economies in Asia over the last quarter-century is that they rarely come back from inflation this high without experiencing a severe economic setback. That is exactly what is happening.

Hanoi is trying to slow inflation via a series of little steps-limits on key exports, tariff reductions on some imports, public-sector construction cuts and more. Really, only tighter monetary and fiscal policies will work, and Vietnam has no track record here. In addition to inflation, Vietnam has a trade deficit and a budget deficit that are both in the range of 6%-7% of gross domestic product. These are also reliable signs of spreading economic trouble.

The most visible sign is a young equity market that is plunging. The Ho Chi Minh Stock Exchange (HOSE index; $11 billion market cap) is down 67% from its March 2007 peak and down 60% year-to-date. Volumes are down 95% over the last year. Domestic investors are dispirited, and foreign investors can't get their money out of the market fast enough.

In an effort to slow the market's decline, daily trading-band limits were imposed on all stocks of 1% in March of 2008. This was the wrong step by a government that knows little about markets. Those limits were raised to 2% in April. But what has been happening? The market opens-and the price of virtually every security traded on the exchange opens down the daily 2% limit. Trading essentially stops at that level, and the next day the market opens limit-down again in a perfect stair-step fashion, now repeated for 23 days in a row. That's really ugly.

Vietnam's currency, the dong, has been gradually depreciating against the dollar in recent years. By the middle of June 2008, Hanoi announced a 2% depreciation of the currency as part of its basic economic repair medicine. But with inflation currently at 25% and headed higher, a mere 2% depreciation on the currency is far from sufficiently to keep Vietnam's export industries competitive. And the declining currency has the added feature of making equity market participation uneconomic for foreign investors. It also makes foreign imports of essential commodities more important, aggravating the inflation problem.

Vietnam's rapid economic ascent over the last decade has been impressive indeed. But the near-term outlook is not so rosy. The government has recently reduced its 2008 economic growth forecast from 8.5% to 7.0%, a figure that may be considered unrealistically optimistic. It will take months of unambiguously better statistics on trade, the budget deficit and inflation to convince investors that Vietnam is back on the right track. A significant devaluation on the order of 33% is also an ingredient in Vietnam's economic rebound. But until that time, the current slow-motion crash in Vietnamese equities is likely to continue unabated.

By and large, the country is beautiful. The people are well-educated, entrepreneurial and energetic. Vietnam is positioned in the middle of the fastest growing portion of the world, right next to China. But when an economy gets off the track, due to bad luck or bad policy, it usually takes a fresh start to get it back on the track. In that circumstance, the first round of investors often loses out, and the second or third round of investors get to pick up the pieces and capitalize most profitably.

China's Exports Soar...But Trade Surplus Falls

At the same time, China's export growth unexpectedly accelerated in May 2008, easing concern that a strengthening yuan and a slowdown in U.S. demand will trigger an economic slump. The *Economic Times* reported that overseas sales rose 28.1% from a year earlier, after gaining a revised 21.9% in April. Exports to the U.S. accelerated, withstanding a 10% gain in the yuan against the dollar in the year through May. Imports jumped 40% because of soaring raw-material costs, supporting the central bank's case that inflation is a bigger threat than weakening global demand. "This is very good news for the central bank, backing up their argument that exports are not collapsing," said Stephen Green head of China research at Standard Chartered Bank in Shanghai.

The trade surplus was $20.2 billion, down from $22.4 billion a year earlier. For the first five months, the surplus has narrowed 9% from a year earlier. Surging prices for iron ore, crude oil, oil products, coal and soybeans drove the biggest increase in imports in almost four years, according to the customs bureau. The gain was 26.4% in April.

TCL, China's biggest electronics maker, said mobile phone exports soared 62% in May from a year earlier. "Export growth held up partly because the U.S. economy appears to be recovering better than expected," said Shen Minggao, an economist at Citigroup in Beijing.

The central bank cautioned in June against exaggerating the risk that weakening global demand would lead to a hard landing for the world's fourth-largest economy. Machinery and electronic exports climbed 59% from a year earlier. Trade with India surged 70% in the first five months, the quickest gain among China's top 10 trading partners. U.S. Treasury Secretary Henry Paulson indicated that a more flexible currency could be a "valuable tool" to help China cool inflation. Producer prices rose 8.2% in May, the biggest increase in more than three years indicating consumer-price inflation may rebound. Consumer prices rose 7.7% in May 2008, government officials had stated and that April's 8.5% was the fastest in almost 12 years.

— 13 —

Deadly Chinese Blood Thinner Found in 11 Countries

China remained in the news mostly because of the media hype leading up to the summer Olympic Games in Beijing. But what the Chinese government surely hoped would be a months-long love-fest for the world's fastest-growing economy which hadn't developed. Instead, an increase of access for the Western press had resulted in a torrent of news stories exposing China's shortcomings on the environment, human rights, and other issues.

On a personal level, I am pleased to hear about this. I do believe that the Chinese government had been allowed to slide for far too long. Too often, China's misdeeds are swept beneath the rug in the interest of trade or politics. There is a seemingly endless line of toxic and deadly goods (from toys to toothpaste) that are churned out by China's factories and foisted on American consumers. And yet, no matter how many times these dangerous goods are exposed...from 2006 to 2007 and now continuing on into 2009... nothing seems to change-there's always another incident somewhere happening, some place, somewhere, and to someone.

The FDA has kept warning a Chinese pharmaceutical manufacturer about contaminated heparin-a blood thinner that's been traded to one of their plants. This tainted blood thinner has been linked to 81 deaths up to this writing, in the U.S. and what's more, the FDA believes it's present in the drug supplies of ten other countries.

In total, federal regulators have identified a dozen Chinese companies that supplied these corrupted doses to Australia, Canada, Denmark, France, Germany, Italy, Japan and the Netherlands, New Zealand and, of course,

China (the Chinese rarely discriminate with their deadly goods; in fact, it's likely that Chinese consumers get most of the dangerous Chinese goods because of their country's lax safety standards).

According to the FDA, the contaminate in question is a "cheap fake additive"-oversulfated chondroitin sulfate-which can only be detected with sophisticated tests. And that's not all: U.S. inspectors also allege that the Chinese plants used unclean tanks during the manufacture of the drugs, incorporated raw materials from an "unacceptable" vendor, and had no process in place to remove the impurities.

And how do the Chinese respond to these allegations? Deny, deny, deny. According to a secretary of the Chinese embassy, "We don't have strong evidence to show that it is heparin or its contaminant that caused the problem."

The Chinese even had the unmitigated gall to insist that Chinese inspectors be allowed to inspect the U.S. pharmaceutical plant where the final stages of the drug's production took place! Talk about trying to put the victims on trial...Unfortunately, our problems with China are just getting started.

The 21st century could belong to the Chinese in the same way that the 20th century belonged to Americans. Because China floats on a veritable sea of cheap labor, they've been able to transform their country from a backwater to a robust industrial giant in an incredibly short span of time. And, much like the growing United States of the 19th century, they are plowing forward without paying much attention to standards.

It is time for government agencies to do more than merely point out the many Chinese safety missteps. The time has come for a restriction on Chinese imports-ESPECIALLY pharmaceutical imports. When patients are DYING as a result of the poor hygiene standards in Asia, it's time for action.

What's at work here is "Profit Motive!" Chinese heparin is far less expensive that the American made variety, which is why Big Pharma is happy to import it. When Big Pharma spends less on making the drugs, they can pass the savings on to the consumer. Right? Just kidding of course...as any savings Big Pharma companies realize from the manufacturing of drugs go into their pockets and only increases their profits.

So what's an American to do? Basically, it would be wise to purchase as few Chinese-made goods as possible. If you shop at Wal-Mart, this is nearly impossible. But at the very least, you should try to find out as much about the origin of the ingredients that are in any prescription drugs you take.

Let's Look at this picture...
700 Toys Export Licenses Revoked

Seven hundred toy factories have had their export licenses revoked following a nationwide inspection campaign of all 3,540 of China's export-oriented toy firms that began in August, 2007 a senior official had stated in June of 2008. The figures were released by Li Changjiang, director of the General Administration of Quality Supervision, Inspection and Quarantine after meeting visiting EU Consumer Commissioner Meglena Kuneva in Beijing.

The licenses were revoked because the firms "failed to meet safety standards" Li said without elaborating. "After the inspection, the overall situation regarding the production of toys for export has been greatly improved," Li said.

Kuneva said the UE is impressed with the huge strides China has made in solving its product quality problems. China, which launched its own crackdown on shoddy products and manufacturers following a number of safety scares in 2007, has upped its game when it comes to cooperating with Europe, she said.

Kuneva's visit was her third since July, 2007 when the safety of Chinese-made products was in the global spotlight. She once threatened to ban imports from China if it did not act more aggressively to stop the manufacture of shoddy goods. EU-Chinese cooperation on consumer was now paying dividends, she said. However, the EU will keep up its guard against shoddy products, and toys remain its top concern, she said.

"Our worries are very much evidence-based. Toys are a primary concern and we are addressing the situation through a road map to improve production from design to sales," she said. "The next issue is electrical goods, especially those with low voltages, and we also have some worries about cosmetics, and bicycle tires," she said.

The latest figures show that RAPEX, Europe's rapid alert system for dangerous consumer products, reported 833 cases concerning Chinese goods last year, of which 400 involved toys. Dangerous chemical content and injuries caused by small parts were the major problems.

China exports some 22 billion toys globally every year, a quarter of which go to Europe. I also feel that revoking is a good thing as it may prevent further safety hazards.

USA and China: Re-Colonizing Africa?

Much of Africa's history has been detrimentally affected by people from outside its shores. It's nearly impossible today to imagine the brutal hardships centuries of slave trading inflicted on the continent's population and we are still living with the legacy of the colonial era, when empire-building Europeans carved up the land to better facilitate the extraction of its riches for the benefit of elites from Lisbon and London to Brussels and Paris, all under the pretence of delivering civilization and Christianity.

The article in the *Antidote* on June 13th, 2008 elaborated on this topic by explaining that things didn't improve a whole lot once most of Africa's countries had nominally liberated themselves from their European masters. The United States and the USSR found the continent a suitable terrain-sufficiently remote from their domestic populations and press-to stage their sometimes overt, but often secret Cold War machinations, propping up agreeable dictators here, deposing of less cooperative ones there and all the while fuelling bloody civil wars with weapons and military aid. After the fall of the Soviet Union, the industrialized world with the U.S. at its helm has continued to treat Africa as both a developmental basket case and a valuable source of raw materials.

None of this is to deny that Africa hasn't been plagued by many internal problems or that all of its woes can simply be blamed on outsiders. Far from it, but it does make one wonder what the rest of the world has in store for us in the 21st century.

Many observers believe that the stage is set for a massive period of geopolitical posturing between the U.S.A., currently the planet's only fully-fledged super power, and the not-so-new kid on the block, China. It seems inevitable that Africa with its wealth of natural resources and continuing trouble spots will play a strategic role in this showdown.

Both countries have upped their involvement in the continent's affairs in recent times and although their methods and motivations often appear literally worlds apart, the end results may not be all that different. Are we witnessing the beginning of a new era of political and economic colonialism in Africa? Will Africans benefit or suffer from the fallout of the looming power shuffle?

In 2007, the U.S. caused some controversy in diplomatic circles when it announced that all of its African military interests (with the exception of Egypt) would in future be consolidated under a single new control centre called Africa Command, or AFRICOM. In the past, U.S. military matters in Africa were steered from three separate units: the European, Central and Pacific Commands.

Officially, the main function of the new body is to help Africa "achieve a more stable environment in which political and economic growth can take place" and according to U.S. Assistant Secretary of Defense for Africa, Theresa Whalen, AFRICOM's mission is to promote economic humanitarian and diplomatic aid for African countries.

There are, however, several other reasons for establishing AFRICOM which the U.S. government is less vocal about. The new command will help to safeguard continued American access to African natural resources, most crucially oil-Africa is forecast to supply a quarter of all U.S. petroleum imports by 2015. It will also facilitate the continent's incorporation into America's "War on Terror" and put the U.S. in a strong position to compete with China in the new scramble for Africa.

Opponents of AFRICOM insist that it needs to be seen within the context of what they call the "militarization of U.S. policy in Africa." According to Beth Tuckey, Associate Director of Africa Faith and Justice Network (www.afjn.org), "developments like AFRICOM reveal that the Bush Administration's national security strategy relied on putting soldiers at the front of nearly all foreign operations."

In recent years, the U.S.A. has established, financed and enlarged military, intelligence and counter-terrorism bases and programs in several African countries, including Djibouti, Mali, Chad, Niger, Mauritania, Ghana, Gabon and Senegal and trained and equipped local troops for peacekeeping activities in numerous others. In 2009, legal commercial sales of military weapons and equipment by U.S. companies in Africa are projected to reach $92 million, an increase of 80 percent from 2006. The oil rich Gulf of Guinea is reported to be under nearly continuous U.S. naval patrol from Angola to Guinea.

That AFRICOM is more than simply a military entity is evident from the fact that it will coordinate the activities carried out by all U.S. governmental agencies, including for example the U.S. agency for International Development (USAID), which previously operated independently of the army. Marie Clarke, Deputy Director for Africa Action (www.africaation.org), a Washington-based African affairs organization, points out that "the projected structure [of AFRICOM] would place humanitarian work under the auspices of the Department of Defense."

Perhaps the most scathing criticism of AFRICOM has come from the U.S. National Conference of Black Lawyers, which believes that it "infringes on the sovereignty of African States", is "designed to violate international law standards" and "is also likely to become a device for the foreign domination and exploitation of Africa's natural resources". A number of African countries and regional bodies, including South Africa and the Southern African Development Community have expressed concern about AFRICOM and the United States' growing military footprint on the continent. Despite considerable diplomatic maneuvering, only Liberia has thus far publicly expressed a willingness to support AFRICOM which is expected to have its temporary headquarters in Stuttgart, Germany for the foreseeable future.

While the United States is significantly beefing up its military activities in Africa, its economic and development programme for the continent has been in place without major modifications for some time. On his 2008 state visit of Benin, Ghana, Liberia, Rwanda and Tanzania, President Bush reiterated his country's commitment to help Africa promote literacy, fight HIV/AIDS, malaria, corruption and "radicals and extremists associated with groups like al-Qaeda" and grow its economy through foreign direct investment, trade, and aid.

For the most part, however, this help has only come within the framework of what has been called the Washington Consensus, and economic doctrine largely administered via international institutions including the World Bank, the international Monetary Fund and the World Trade Organization that have been disproportionately influenced by U.S. policymakers. In exchange for financial and material developmental assistance, the governments of African (and other Third World) countries have been required to open their fragile economies to global markets, stop subsidies to domestic industries and agriculture, reduce social spending and privatize public assets. Many believe that rather than predominantly resulting in positive effects, these measures have contributed to the impoverishment of Africa.

Although the U.S.A. spends billions of dollars in support of African countries it also stands accused of supporting illegitimate and corrupt regimes that are willing to provide preferential access to resources or support for the unpopular "War on Terror". Examples include military aid supplied to Rwanda, a country that has been involved in armed conflict in the DRC and is alleged to have committed human rights violations directed at Hutus, as well as Equatorial Guinea's President Teodoro Obiang Nguema, whom U.S. Secretary of State Condoleezza offered military assistance, trade, investment and aid, .are still worried over the involvement of the U.S. and Europe.

What clearly has the Americans worried thought is the rate at which China has been expanding its influence in Africa. As a relatively resource-poor nation, China is increasingly looking to Africa to supply its burgeoning manufacturing sectors with raw materials and also for new markets for its cheap consumer goods...ones that may inflict danger to health as it has done in the United States and in Europe and the rest of the countries.

Africa already provides 25 percent of China's oil requirements and overall trade between China and Africa quadrupled to $39 billion from 2000 to 2005. It is expected to reach the $100 billion mark by 2010. Among other projects, China is smelting copper in Zambia, logging rainforest in Gabon, building roads in Kenya, farming in Zimbabwe, mining cobalt in the DRC and producing oil in Sudan, Angola and Nigeria. Unlike the U.S., however, it has not as yet sought to establish any military footholds on the African continent.

Chinese aid to African countries comes in the form of infrastructure projects such as building schools and hospitals, loans, investment, debt cancellation, trade agreements and scholarships to Chinese universities. Like the United States, China claims that its assistance is aimed at improving human rights and economic development as well as alleviating poverty.

The Chinese government claims to have a strict policy of non-interference in other countries' internal affairs and its aid comes without requirements such as economic reforms or commitments to improving human rights, democracy or environmental affairs. In juxtaposition to the Washington Consensus, these aspects of China's foreign policy are frequently described as the Beijing Consensus.

Although its hands-off approach is favored by many African governments, development assistance from China doesn't come without any strings attached. Chinese aid is often tied to trade and investment agreements and frequently used to negotiate favorable access to natural resources such as fishing rights in Sierra Leone and Gabon, or oil concessions in Sudan and Angola.

Like the U.S.A., China has been strongly criticized for maintaining friendly ties with discredited and authoritarian African leaders such as Mugabe and for not putting enough pressure on the Sudanese government to work towards peace in Darfur. In addition, Chinese construction projects in Africa are often carried out by imported Chinese workers, resulting in neither a transfer of much needed skills or job creation. Chinese logging and mining operations are often accused of showing scant regard for workers' rights or environmental concerns and in a number of cases, cheap Chinese imports have all but destroyed local industries, something the South African clothing and textile industry can attest to.

Clearly both the United States and China are ramping up their involvement in Africa and the continent with its wealth of strategic resources is bound to be caught up in the political brouhaha that will undoubtedly ensue as China challenges the U.S.A.'s status as the single dominant global power as the Americans prepare to defend their turf.

The threat of increasingly colonial relationships becoming entrenched between China and the U.S.A. on the one hand and the African countries on the other is certainly real. Is there any merit in African countries backing either one of the two participants in this contest? Unless they can negotiate truly equitable and mutually beneficial relationships for the first time in history, past experiences and current evidence suggest the choice would merely be one for the better of two evils.

China's Internal Dilemma

On June 14th, 2008 it was reported in *the Journal,* a blog Archive that the problem of China, rooted in geopolitics, is economic and it presents itself in two ways. The first is simple: **China has an export-oriented economy. It is in a position of dependency.**

No matter how large its currency reserves or how advanced its technology or how cheap its labor force, China depends on the willingness and ability of other countries to import its goods-as well as the ability to physically ship them. Any disruption of this flow has a direct affect on the Chinese economy.

The primary reason other countries buy Chinese goods is price. They are cheaper because of wage differentials. Should China lose that advantage to other nations or for other reasons, its ability to export would decline. Today, for example, as energy prices rise, the cost of production rises and the relative importance of the wage differential decreases. At a certain point, as China's trading partners see it, the value of Chinese imports relative to the political costs of closing down their factories will shift.

And all of this is outside of China's control. China cannot control the world price of oil. It can cut into its cash reserves to subsidize those prices for manufacturers but that would essentially be transferring money back to consuming nations. It can control rising wages by imposing price controls, but that would cause internal instability. **The center of gravity of China is that it has become the industrial workshop of the world and, as such, it is totally dependant on the world to keep buying its goods rather than someone else's goods.**

There are other issues for China, ranging from a dysfunctional financial system to farm land being taken out of production for factories. These are all significant and add to the story. But in geopolitics we look for the center of gravity, and for China the center of gravity is that the more effective it becomes at exporting, the more of a hostage it becomes to its customers. Some observers have warned that China might take its money out of American banks. Unlikely, but assume it did. What would China do without the United States as a customer?

China has placed itself in a position where it has to keep its customers happy. It struggles against this reality daily, but the fact is that the rest of the world is far less dependent on China's exports than China is dependent on the rest of the world.

Which brings us to the second, even more serious part of China's economic problem. **The first geopolitical imperative of China is to ensure the unity of Han China.**

The third is to protect the coast. Deng's bet was that he could open the coast without disruption of the unity of Han China. As in the 19ᵗʰ century, **the coastal region has become wealthy. The interior has remained extraordinarily poor. The coastal region is deeply enmeshed in the global economy. The interior is not. Beijing is once again balancing between the coast and the interior.**

The interests of the coastal region and the interests of importers and investors are closely tied to each other. Beijing's interest is in maintaining internal stability. As pressures grow, it will seek to increase its control of the political and economic life of the coast. The interest of the interior is to have money transferred to it from the coast. The interest of the coast is to hold on to its money. Beijing will try to satisfy both, without letting China break apart and without resorting to Mao's draconian measures. But the worse the international economic situation becomes the less demand there will be for Chinese products and the less room there will be for China to maneuver.

The second part of the problem derives from the first. Assuming that the global economy does not decline now, it will at some point. When it does, and Chinese exports fall dramatically, Beijing will have to balance between an interior hunger for money and a coastal region that is hurting badly. **It is important to remember that something like 900 million Chinese live** in the **interior while only 400 million live in the coastal region.** When it comes to balancing power, the interior is the physical threat to the regime while the coast destabilizes the distribution of wealth. The interior has mass on its side. The coast has the international trade system on its. Emperors have stumbled over less.

Geopolitics is based on geography and politics. Politics is built on two foundations: military and economic. The two interact and support each other but are ultimately distinct. For China, securing its buffer regions generally eliminates military problems. What problems are left for China are long-term issues concerning northeastern Manchuria and the balance of power in the Pacific.

China's geopolitical problem is economic. Its first geopolitical imperative, maintain the unity of Han China, and its second, protect the coast, are both more deeply affected by economic considerations than military ones. Its internal and external political problems flow from economics. The dramatic economic development of the last generation has been ruthlessly geographic.

This development has benefited the coast and left the interior-the vast majority of Chinese-behind. It has also left China vulnerable to global economic forces that it cannot control and cannot accommodate. This is not new in Chinese history, but its usual resolution is in regionalism and the weakening of the central government. Deng's gamble is being played out by his successors. He dealt the hand. They have to play it.

The question on the table is whether the economic basis of China is a foundation or a balancing act. If the former, it can last a long time. If the latter, everyone falls down eventually. There appears to be little evidence that it is a foundation. It excludes most of the Chinese from the game, people who are making less than $100 a month. That is a balancing act and it threatens the first geopolitical imperative of China: protecting the unity of Han Chinese.

China Talks Introduce World of Import Controls

The June 14th edition of *USA TODAY* spoke about "a toy dog, an electric train and a blond-haired doll that would bring smiles to most American homes during Christmas. When the giver is the Chinese government, and the recipients are visiting U.S. trade officials, the meaning is more pointed than simple festive cheer."

"It's a lot of fun. The gift is very nice," said U.S. Commerce Secretary Carlos Gutierrez in Beijing according to state news agency Xinhua, when he accepted a life-size toy dog from the chief of China's product quality watchdog.

What this means is that worries about the safety of Chinese imports have defined the booming but often fraught Chinese-U.S. trading relationship in 2007. During bilateral talks with Gutierrez that she described as "heated," Chinese Vice Premier Wu Yi, leader of a nationwide quality-raising campaign, complained that U.S. media had "hyped the product safety issue, causing serious damage to the image of Chinese products and China's national reputation."

Tensions surfaced in the spring of 2007, when thousands of American dogs and cats were poisoned by eating pet food made with tainted ingredients imported from China. A subsequent cascade of quality problems has included toxic toothpaste, unsafe tires, chemical-laden seafood and millions of lead-painted toys. Just in the month of June, 2008 Home Depot recalled about 64,000 Chinese-made festive figurines because of the lead paint hazard, reported by the U.S. Consumer Product Safety Commission.

Product safety "engages at a deeper, more visceral level than other issues," said U.S. Secretary of Health and Human Services Mike Leavitt, who was also in the Chinese capital during this meeting. The globalized marketplace, in which the U.S.A. imported $2 trillion worth of goods in 2007, means "you can't inspect your way to product safety. There's just too much of it," Leavitt said. "We are not just scaling up existing processes, we are inventing them."

Leavitt had unveiled what he saw as the new world of import controls. With Chinese counterparts, he signed two "strong and action-oriented" agreements to enhance the safety of food and feed, plus medical devices and drugs that the U.S. imports from China. Leavitt promised the new pacts would "enhance the safety and quality of products that Americans use every day" and "form the framework for agreements that will exist all over the world."

The new registration and certification requirements, which include Chinese importers of food, feed, medical devices and drugs, require registration with the Chinese government and to achieve certification, they must meet U.S. Standards. If, within 48 hours, a health risk is forecast, each side must inform the other and provide necessary tracking information. China has resisted giving U.S. regulators such access in the past. Leavitt promised that the new system should provide great comfort to American consumers and that problems can be traced back to the grower if necessary.

Such items that are watched carefully include Juices (about $10 million worth of goods to the U.S.; kids-oriented BellyWashers and Tummy Tickler brands that are sold at Wal-Mart and 7-Eleven Stores; as well as pet food, toys and other products that raised questions in 2007.

To improve product quality, 47,000 illegal food factories have been shut down and 500 tons of highly poisonous pesticides have been confiscated along with melamine-laced pet food and other products that U.S. retailers should still be cautious of carrying in their inventory.

Overcoming Problems When Importing Goods from China... Or Just Eliminate the Chinese Labels Altogether

The prospect of importing goods from China is both exciting and terrifying for many sellers. On one hand, there is huge potential for making money from reselling wholesale goods purchased very cheaply. But on the other hand, language and cultural barriers present a number of difficulties to sellers. The main issue that everyone is worried about...aside from good quality products...is payment. How do I pay? Will my money disappear?

The difficulty lies on the fact that most Chinese wholesalers will only accept Western Union and wire transfer payments. These are not secure payment options so they must be treated with caution. However, the main reason why these are the only payments accepted is that they are in fact the only payment methods available to the Chinese. Getting a credit card in China is an extremely difficult task with a lot of government regulations and strict criteria for getting a card.

Despite the risks involved with using Western Union and wire transfer, these are the methods one uses if you want to import from china with most suppliers. To minimize this risk, it is recommended to start with a fairly small shipment of goods so you are not standing to lose too much money if everything falls apart. Then, as trust is established, gradually build up your order over time. On the whole, most Chinese suppliers are genuine, hard working people who want to establish a long-term relationship with you. They need your business, so it's unlikely they'll try to deliberately screw you over. It is difficult to trust many of the companies in China.

Yet it happened to this writer as president of Global Communications. They did try to screw us over…and we had terms of net 40 days with them just in case our customers complained of the products they had received. About 40 days after receipt of the products, we sent wire transfers to our suppliers. Sometimes, we found that the OEM, the original manufacturer had a failed product because the printed circuit boards that we had supplied were not good. Thus, we had to give credit to our customers and deducted the amounts that we owed to the manufacturers in China. Eventually, we found other manufacturers. This had happened to us many times in 14 years we were dealing with companies in China, Taiwan and Hong Kong.

We decided to work with agents or the general managers of these manufacturing companies overseas who could speak English very well and were able to communicate with us at any time. It can be extremely daunting trying to negotiate complex business issues when communication is so difficult. Working with people who understand what you were saying certainly makes life much easier especially when there are problems.

We also make it our business to always chat with our contacts on line and by telephone so you can build up a better relationship. This also gives you a direct point of contact instantly if you cannot find an agent who will work with you. Once communication is established, you can proceed to ask questions and get them to send pictures of stock, samples and contracts. For any genuine company, this will not be a problem and it allows you to see the quality of the product first hand.

Quality is always a major concern for sellers who often have difficulty telling whether a brand name product is genuine or not. Basically, the vast majority of brand-name goods that come from China are either replicas or fakes. eBay is always trying to crack down on people selling fakes. Chinese suppliers are best suited for cheap generic goods that can be sold at higher rates in Western countries. For example, some of the latest trends are pocket bikes, scooters and generic electronic goods. These goods do not have to have a brand name in order to sell well and they can be purchased wholesale at very good prices if you are serious about importing from China.

Basically, one should do his homework and research the companies you deal with and ask for a list of customers they sell to in the U.S. Always keep an open mind, ask questions and do your research as best as you know how!

Rising Costs Affect China, Plus Firms That Import

As if skyrocketing oil and food prices weren't enough, Americans might soon find they're paying more for another item on their shopping lists: Chinese imports!

As reported in the *San Diego Times-Union* in the summer of 2008, thanks to the global spread of inflation, Chinese toys, electronics, plastics and other goods were starting to get a bit pricier. Rising factory wages, shipping costs and exchange rates were starting to add to the price tags of Chinese products-and the costs of U.S. companies that have moved their production and supply lines to China.

The rising cost of doing business in China was a hot topic at a round table held by the World Trade Center in June, 2008 and the local chapter of the American Electronics Association. About 15 high-level executives from local manufacturing firms listened as Scott Wang, who heads the China desk at the San Diego World Trade Center described China's rising costs, tighter lending policies and declining export subsidies.

"Prices on some raw materials have increased 20 percent over the past year," Wang warned. "Because of a new labor law, labor costs are going up 5 to 10 percent, depending on the industry. Beijing is also phasing out its export subsidy, which means that exporters will get 5 percent less money from the government."

China is experiencing its worst bout of inflation in 12 years. Chinese consumer prices in May 2008 were 7.7 percent higher than a year before, despite generous government subsidies that keep the price of fuel relatively inexpensive for consumers. Food costs jumped more than 22 percent. The Chinese government is responding by pushing companies to raise salaries-a contrast to the Federal Reserve policy of guarding against so-called wage inflation.

A recent study by the Booz Allen Hamilton consulting firm found that wages in China rose 9.1 percent for white-collared managers and 7.6 percent for blue-collar workers over the past year. That compares with an average raise of 4.3 percent in San Diego County.

"China's advantage in labor costs is diminishing at the same time that the cost of transportation is increasing," said Simon Croom, executive director of the Supply Chain Management Institute at the University of San Diego.

Wang said local companies are complaining that the rising salaries in China are making it harder to find and retain qualified workers. "Loyalty to companies is not high in China, so workers often jump to other firms where they are offered better incentives," he said.

The good news is the rising prices in China could inspire some U.S. manufacturers to keep their production lines at home. And even before the recent rise in prices, some manufacturers were having second thoughts about China. Vanimen Manufacturing, which makes dental equipment in Fallbrook, shifted part of its production line to China in 2002 to save money. But the company brought the production back to San Diego County in early 2007.

Don Vanimen, who heads the company, cited several reasons for his move: "There were shipping delays, security hassles and poor quality control. If you order a thousand widgets in four shipments, three shipments might be all right, but the fourth might be totally wrong. In the U.S., a supplier would jump through hoops to fix that kind of problem, but in China it could take six months to work out the details."

In addition, rising costs in China as well as more efficient manufacturing techniques in the United States erased much of the price gap between the two countries. Vanimen said that six years ago, the cost of producing his components in the United States was as much as 50 percent higher than in China. Now, it's only 5 percent higher-a premium that he's happy to pay.

Vanimen still gets some supplies from China, but his suppliers are saying that they will have to raise their prices 10 percent because of the rising cost of metals and transportation.

Michele Nash-Hoff, president of ElectroFab Sales, a contract manufacturer in San Diego, said two of her manufacturing clients have recently brought production lines back from China to their bases in San Diego and Riverside counties. The primary reasons, she said, were that their Chinese subcontractors were using low-quality materials and had problems handling complex assembly procedures. This is exactly why this writer had gotten out of the printed circuit board business after 14 financially, successful years. When costs start to climb working with offshore suppliers, it might make better sense to work with your own suppliers here at home as they too want the business and that is how we are going to get back into the manufacturing business once again.

Then again, rising wages and a Chinese crackdown on pollution were adding to the cost of doing business in China. Oil prices were also making shipping too expensive. "As energy costs go up, transportation costs rise, and the distance that goods travel begins to matter," said Paul Bingham, a trade and transportation specialist at Global Insight, a financial analysis firm in Massachusetts.

"For low-value products that take up a lot of space, like furniture, for example, transportation costs can get quite high," said Bingham, who gave a talk on logistics in San Diego in June, 2008. "And if you're not saving enough money from using low-cost labor, it makes sense to bring your production lines closer to home."

Beyond the rising cost of oil, one reason that Chinese goods are getting more expensive is that Beijing-after years of criticism from the United States-is finally allowing its currency to strengthen against the dollar. The yuan grew 7 percent against the dollar in 2007 and has risen more than 4.5 percent in 2008. By the end of 2008, the yuan will have risen a total of 8 percent, some economists project.

Beijing has a pragmatic reason for wanting higher wages and a stronger currency. History shows that if prices shoot up without salaries keeping pace, it can lead to social unrest. One reason for the Tiananmen Square protest in 1989 was that wages were outpaced by inflation, which was then rising at a slower pace than today.

Allowing the value of the yuan to rise further would give Chinese citizens greater power to buy consumer goods while keeping up their strong savings rate.

"China's not going to be able to accomplish what they want to accomplish if they don't have a currency that's more reflective of underlying fundamentals," U.S. Secretary Henry Paulson said in June 2008, pushing for a stronger yuan.

A rising yuan means further jumps in the price of Chinese-produced goods. It also means a shrinking market for U.S. securities, which the Chinese have been buying to keep their exchange rate artificially low. But at lease we might have a slightly better chance of keeping our factories from crossing the ocean.

Treasury Secretary Henry Paulson
Sees Progress in U.S.- China Ties

The *New York Times* reported on June 18, 2008 that during the intense economic talks between the United States and China, Treasury Secretary Henry M. Paulson declared that despite recent tensions over trade, investment and food and product safety, ties between the two countries were "growing in a positive direction."

"The United States and China don't always agree on economic issues," Mr. Paulson said at the U.S. Naval Academy on the Severn River in Annapolis, Md., "yet, sometimes we may even disagree quite strongly. But we keep talking."

Seeking to smooth the way for the discussion, Mr. Paulson said that while China faced many economic difficulties, so did the United States. One reason that China does not import more American goods, he said, was that its savings rate was so high. In the United States, he said the savings rate was too low. The last round of talks in December, 2007 in Beijing set up a 10-year goal of cooperating on energy and the environment, and Mr. Paulson said he hoped that the two countries could take additional steps in that area.

"As the two largest net importers of oil, China and the United States face similar challenges as demand for energy increases, and the global production capacity has remained relatively flat for the past 10 years," he said.

In the last several months, Mr. Paulson said there has been progress on issues like monitoring the safety of food and other products imported from China.

Now he said, China needed to do more to crack down on piracy and counterfeiting of American goods, including software and movies, and opening its markets to American investments and goods. The trade deficit between the United States and China topped $250 billion in 2007, causing some anxiety in Congress.

The Chinese side opened the talks with pledges of cooperation, but also pointedly raised again its criticism of the United States as being partly to blame for the credit crises and other world economic problems.

Wang Qishan, a Chinese vice premier and its lead envoy at the talks, said he intended to raise the issue of the fallout from the American subprime mortgage crises, saying that a solution to that problem would benefit the economic stability of the United States, China and the world. These comments came the morning after Chinese and American businesses, seeking to overcome mutual suspicion of foreign investment, announced $14 billion in new deals.

The deals involve $8 billion in Chinese investments and purchases of aircraft engines, telecommunications equipment, semiconductors and electronic components, said Chen Deming, minister of commerce in China. Another $6 billion involved American purchases and investments in China. Among the American companies signing deals were Chrysler, Cisco Systems, Ford Motor, General Motors, I.B.M., Motorola, Sun Microsystems, Qualcomm and Texas Instruments.

In an interview, Mr. Paulson said the meetings were not meant to resolve specific disputes but to discuss how to overcome economic downturns and deal with impending crises in energy and the environment. "The tone will be one of constructive engagement," Mr. Paulson said. "We're going to be dealing with some of the most fundamental economic issues there are. I know some people would like to see quick fixes. But the most important issues don't avail themselves to quick fixes."

The Annapolis talks are the fourth in a twice-a-year series that Mr. Paulson started when he left Goldman Sachs to become Treasury chief in 2006. The biggest issue at the time was American irritation over China's intervention in currency markets to purchase dollars and keep the value of the dollar high in relation to China's currency.

Since mid-2005, China has allowed its currency, the yuan, to appreciate nearly 20 percent, easing at least some of the criticism in Congress. The Bush administration continued to accuse China of raising barriers to foreign investment, and China has increasingly complained that its attempts to invest in American often provoke an outcry.

Mr. Paulson said that, although China had made only limited reforms in its economy and taken limited steps to open its market to American goods and investment, the "strategic economic dialogue," known as the S.E.D., produced more progress than otherwise would have been the case.

"I would argue that the reason we've made progress is that the S.E.D. is a mechanism for convincing China that certain things are in their interest," he said, citing American efforts to get China to open its economy to foreign investment and to lift government subsidies of export industries.

In recent months, the Chinese government has pushed back with demands that the United States do more to open its economy to Chinese investments and to halt the depreciation of the dollar against European and other currencies, a trend many economists say has helped drive up oil and food prices.

China's Economic Growth Will Rise at 9.8 Percent

The World Bank, on the same day as the economic talks with China, had revised upwards its projection of China's economic growth from 9.4% as forecast earlier to 9.8% in 2008. In its quarterly update, the Bank said despite less buoyant investment, the domestic economy was "holding up well" in China, where the economic activity had moderated in line with the global economy's showdown.

However, it said, the real growth of exports and imports remained robust, sharply higher import prices were inflating import values and bringing down Chinese trade surplus, even as the contribution of net trade to growth remains positive.

The devastating earthquake in southwest China on May 12 expected to have only a "moderate impact" on the wider economy with a direct economic loss of $58 to $73 billion, the report released at a news conference. Over a discussion of rising prices which has emerged as a major worry to the government, the Bank said the headline inflation was receding even as non-food price pressures emerge, and added, "Food price increases are already starting to fade from consumer price data." The report noted that some spill-over from the higher food prices was flowing into wages and some other prices, while new impact from recent industrial commodity and oil price hikes was in the pipeline. Spill-over to consumer prices remained limited and headline consumer price inflation tipped to recede gradually.

China Sends More Defective Junk-Valve Stems

No matter what kinds of safe-guards China has promised, the defective products keep coming into our country, sometimes unnoticed until it is too late and have caused harm to the users. Remember the poisonous pet food, lead paint on children's toys…how could we not forget?

The latest potentially defective Chinese import to hit American shores: tire-valve stems, the rubber shafts that allow motorists to fill their tires with air. There are at least 36 million of the imported valve stems on tires on American roads. Any of them could cause dangerous tire failures anytime, anywhere.

Already, a law suit has blamed a defective tire-valve stem for a crash that killed a Florida driver. One U.S. importer issued a formal recall in June, 2008; another alerted the National Highway Traffic Safety Administration (NHTSA), which had begun an investigation. Earlier in June, the federal agency issued an advisory to motorists to check their tires for wear but said nothing about valve stems. Most of the valves in question, which are said to crack prematurely, appear to be on tires sold between September 2006 and June 2007.

The extent of the problem won't be known until NHTSA completes its investigation, said an agency spokesman. But some independent safety experts say motorists should be warned to inspect the tire-valve stems immediately.

"The company [that imported most of the tires] has issued a technical bulletin, but nobody seems to know about it," said Sean Kane, an auto-safety consultant with Safety Research & Strategies in Rehoboth, Mass., which issued its own public warning. "We need to know because the public is entering the high-risk summer season, and this is a real problem that potentially affects millions of vehicles."

The investigation appeared to stem from a law suit filed after the fatal crash in November of 2007 of Robert Monk of Orlando, Florida. In March, 2008, his widow sued Dill Air Controls Products, blaming its tire-valve stem for causing the right rear tire of her husband's SUV to fail, precipitating the vehicle's rollover. Shortly after the suit was filed, the Oxford, N.C., company approached NHTSA with a report of "a potential defect." The agency last month began investigating the valve stems the company distributes in the United States.

Some 30 million suspect valve stems were manufactured over a five-month period in 2006 for Dill by Topseal, a subsidiary of Shanghai Baolong Automotive Corp., based in Shanghai, according to NHTSA's preliminary summary of its investigation. In May, Dill issued a technical bulletin to its customers: **"We have received a number of parts showing surface cracks on the outside of the rubber near the rim hole…Out of an abundance of caution, we are recommending that when customers return to your stores for regular service, you inspect the valve stems on vehicles who received valve stems during the period September 2006 ~ June 2007."**

The Orlando attorney for Mr. Monk's widow said that more should be done.

"They talk about an 'abundance of caution' but aren't really following through," said Richard Newsome. "With summer vacation coming up and families taking trips, the right thing to do for consumers is issue an order to check valves and look for cracks."

Several calls and an e-mail by a reporter to Dill's general manager were not returned. Mr. Kane, the auto-safety consultant, said that the valves could deteriorate and crack in as few as six months. Dill's suspect valves were manufactured more than 1 ½ years prior to the accident, from July through November 2006, according to the company.

On June 2nd, another auto-parts importer, Tech International of Johnstown, Ohio, issued a formal recall notice for 6 million valve stems made by a Chinese company with nearly the same name-Shanghai Baolong Industries Co., Ltd.-and the same address. Dates of manufacture of the defective product are also the same.

In its recall notice, Tech said, "the defect is such that after the valve has been in service approximately six months or more, the rubber compound may undergo cracking," resulting in loss of tire pressure. It blamed the defect on "improper mixing of the rubber compound in the manufacturer's facility." Calls to Tech International and an attorney representing the company were not returned. For its part, NHTSA said the Tech recall is a good enough reason for consumers to have fire valves checked. But until the Dill investigation is complete, there was not enough basis for a national alert.

"We monitor all forms of vehicle equipment, and we're always on the lookout for abnormal rates of failure," said Rae Tyson, a NHTSA spokesman. "We are looking at every aspect of these valve stems...We can't presume defects until we've completed an investigation."

In response to pubic outrage over contaminated pet food and lead paint on toys made in China, Congress moved, in 2007, to bolster the U.S. Consumer Product Safety Commission. But a bill to boost commission funding and force it to notify consumers of unsafe products more quickly has not yet passed. **The agency does not oversee tires.**

"Congress and whatever agency [involved in overseeing Chinese imports] don't do much," said Peter Navarro, a business professor at the University of California at Irvine. "It's very hard because they're understaffed and under-budgeted."

The Sham Dialogue with China

The Fourth Strategic Economic Dialogue (SED) as reported prior, between the United States and the People's Republic of China, that took place at the U.S. Naval Academy in Annapolis and other venues in Washington the middle of June, 2008 was basically a series of cabinet-level summits that were established by President George Bush and Chinese President Hu Jintao in August, 2006. They meet every six months, alternating capitals. Though top officials from many departments and agencies take part, the Treasury is the leader on the American side.

As expected, nothing came of this grand gathering in terms of helping American industry compete against Chinese producers. It was another installment of the "chit chat" diplomacy conducted by the business side of the Bush Administration with is meant more to smooth over problems to avoid Congressional action. Indeed, using the term "dialogue" instead of "negotiation" was a purposeful choice to lower expectations, and to project an air of cooperation rather than confrontation as reported by the SED.

Treasury Secretary Paulson's opening statement this year was very bland, marking the downward spiral of these events. One of the great success stories of these large, high-level meetings he cited was the opening of non-stop flights from Atlanta to Shanghai. But at least he did not make the same mistake he made last December in Beijing. There he said, "The United States welcomes the rise of a stable and prosperous China," leaving out the third adjective "peaceful" found in most U.S. documents. This crucial third term is meant to convey America's concern that Beijing will translate its economic gains into military power aimed at the U.S. and its allies. China, of course, is known for always doing this.

As William R. Hawkins, Senior Fellow for National Security Studies at the U.S. Business and Industry Council in Washington, DC put it so eloquently, instead, Paulson has attacked the very concept of national interest in economic policy. At the Third SED he said, "Whereas trade was once largely a source of stability in U.S.-China relations, it has recently become a source of tension, and not only because of safety concerns. Worries about the effects of foreign competition-through trade or through foreign investment-have led to a rise in economic nationalism and protectionist sentiments in both our nations...many people in the U.S. are not sure...that the benefits of trade are being shared fairly." This is an understatement! The current trade imbalance runs 5-1 in Beijing's favor.

It should be remembered that before he became Treasury Secretary, Paulson was CEO of Goldman Sachs, which called itself a global investment banking firm. He made a fortune working with the Chinese on profitable business deals, including raising money for the Communist regime itself.

Beijing's currency manipulation, supposedly the main issue behind the creation of the SED, has not ended. The Chinese renminbi (RMB) has risen about 20% in nominal terms since July 2005, but the United States still ran a record trade deficit with China of $256 billion in 2007. The Chinese have been slowly testing where to set their currency's value. As prices rise for the oil and raw materials that China imports, there is a desire to increase the RMB's purchasing power, but Beijing's first priority remains strong exports to bolster its economic growth.

The RMB will not be allowed to rise to a level where it hurts exports. This will be especially true if China's trade surplus falls due to a slowing U.S. economy. Beijing will not want to add to that decline by losing the competitive advantage it gets from an undervalued currency. Indeed, as the euro appreciates against the dollar and the RMB, China has been able to rapidly expand its trade surplus in Europe as well as in America.

The only business group Paulson seemed concerned about is his own, the banking and financial services industry. He has been pushing hard to get Beijing to open its financial sector to foreign interests. Beijing might offer larger minority shares to outside investors to get their money, but China has made it clear that it will never give foreign interests control over any important segment of its financial system. Paulson's argument that American bankers can teach the Chinese modern business methods has lost its appeal in the wake of the subprime mortgage-derivatives meltdown.

Paulson hailed the opening of a branch of the China Merchants Bank in the United States. He had assured China that its banks, brokers and investment advisors would be given "national treatment."-meaning that they will have all the rights of an American-owned enterprise to operate in the United States. No reciprocity is required. China Merchant Bank has 64% of its shares held by state-owned entities, and a majority of its directors come from "large, state-owned enterprises" according to the bank's 2006 annual report.

Beijing often makes small, symbolic gestures before a major meeting to look like it is being flexible. Once the meeting is over and the press releases filed, it goes back to its old behavior. For example, just before the SED opened this year, there was the usual flurry of announcements of American firms landing export deals in China, but these will not narrow the trade gap. That Ford will get to sell 30,000 U.S.-made cars in China next year is hardly a drop in the bucket.

The Treasury seems eager to appease Beijing's demand that the United States weaken its national security restrictions on trade and investment. Treasury Special Envoy Alan Holmer told a Chinese audience on May 21st that new rules had been issued by his department to "reinforce strong open investment principles" in reviews conducted by the Committee on Foreign Investment in the U.S. (CFIUS), a multi-agency group chaired by Treasury which has the power to block or modify business deals that threaten American security.

Speaking at Wuhan University, Holmer said "we often hear concerns from China about the U.S. investment review process and whether the United States truly welcomes Chinese investment. U.S. legal authority in this area is narrowly targeted to address acquisitions that raise genuine national security concerns, not broader economic interests or industrial policy factors."

One of the first things the 110th Congress did was strengthen and expand the CFIUS process by passing the Foreign Investment and National Security

Act of 2007. This legislation passed unanimously in the House and by voice vote in the Senate. It was signed by President Bush. Unfortunately, it still left Treasury in the CFIUS chair, despite a warning from the Government Accountability Office (GAO) that the process "in protecting U.S. national security may be limited because Treasury-as Chair of the Committee on Foreign Investment in the United States-has narrowly defined what constitutes a threat to national security."

The first successful test of the improved CFIUS process involved a Chinese firm. Huawei Technologies tried to purchase a stake in 3Com, a U.S. firm that makes computer network security software for the Pentagon. When it became apparent in March that CFIUS was not going to approve the deal, due in part to objections raised by the Director of National Intelligence (who had been named as an advisor to CFIUS in the 2007 law), the offer to buy 3Com was withdrawn.

But three months later, Treasury was trying to assure Beijing not to worry about security reviews in the future! Indeed, at this latest SED, the groundwork was laid for the U.S. and China to negotiate an investment treaty, which would take precedence over CFIUS procedures and kick the American door wide open to Chinese money (and influence).

Treasury seems oblivious to the fact that Beijing and Washington are geopolitical as well as economic rivals. China has used the gains from trade and investment to strengthen its capabilities. It has been foolish to allow Beijing to amass its currency hoard ($1.6 trillion and growing) through an unequal trade policy. It would be even more irresponsible to allow Beijing to use its money any way it pleases to support ambitions which are at odds with American strategic interests.

—14—

Most Low Quality Imports From China: Commission

While the SED meetings were underway, it was reported in the Taipei Times that unsafe foods identified last month came from Thailand, the U.S. and Vietnam, while the PRC accounted for most subpar commercial goods.

The commission published on its Web site 66 warnings about unsafe imported goods and other foreign goods in May, 2008. Of these, 36 concerned products were made in China, CPC section chief Liu-Ching-fang had stated. The commission inaugurated the Web site last August as part of its efforts to inform local consumers about unsafe and substandard products.

The total number of reports in May increased by 11 from listings in April, Liu said. Sixty-two of the 66 warnings concerned goods classified as commercial products. Twenty of the 66 concerned chemical industrial products, 11 concerned toys, 18 named electronics products and 13 named other goods of substandard quality, Liu said.

The commission gathered information about substandard commercial products in part from announcements released by U.S. companies that have recalled toys, clothes for teenagers, electronic heaters, gas stoves and sleeping bags over the past month. However, many of the products recalled in the U.S. were not sold in Taiwan, Liu said.

The remaining four warnings published on the Web site fell into the category of food and agricultural products and the substandard foods were imported from Vietnam, the U.S. and Thailand, and were found to contain excessive amounts of bleach and preservatives.

No matter what kind of deals are made with the SED or other governmental agencies, unsafe food and other household products are still being made and distributed to countries all over the world. When will the governments finally crack down on this problem instead of playing "who's got the upper-hand" at these phony meetings. This is what is important in the world, not who controls banks and companies. So much wasted time and still, we have people at risk world wide.

Why We're Suddenly Paying Through the Nose for Gas

Michael T. Klare, national defense correspondent and professor of peace and world security studies at Hampshire College had written a good piece on the increase of oil and gas and I totally agree with his logic on how all of this came about.

As the pain induced by higher oil prices, spreads to an ever-growing share of the American (and world) population, pundits and politicians have been quick to blame assorted villains-greedy oil companies, heartless commodity speculators and OPEC. It's true that each of these parties has contributed to and benefited from the steep run-up. But the sharp growth in petroleum costs is due far more to a combination of soaring international demand and slackening supply-compounded by the ruinous policies of the Bush Administration-than to the behavior of those other actions.

Most, if not all, the damage was avoidable. Shortly after taking office, George W. Bush undertook a sweeping review of U.S. energy policy aimed at expanding the nations' supply of vital fuels. The "reality is the nation has got a real problem when it come to energy," he declared on March 14th, 2001. "We need more sources of energy."

At that time, many of the problems evident were already visible. Energy demand in mature industrial nations was continuing to grow as the rising economic dynamos of Asia, especially China, were beginning to make an impact. By 2002, the Energy Department was predicting that China would soon overtake Japan, becoming the world's second-largest petroleum consumer, and that developing Asia as a whole would account for about one-fourth of global consumption by 2020. Also evident was an unmistaken slowdown in the growth of world production, the telltale sign of an imminent "peaking" in global output.

With these trends in mind, many energy experts urged the White House to minimize future reliance on oil, emphasize conservation and rapidly develop climate-friendly alternatives, especially renewables like wind, solar, geothermal and biofuels. But Dick Cheney, who was overseeing the energy review, would have none of this. **"Conservation may be a sign of personal virtue," the Vice President famously declared in April 2001, "but it is not a sufficient basis for sound, comprehensive energy policy."**

After three months of huddling in secret with top executives of leading U.S. energy companies, he released a plan on May 17th that, in effect, called for preserving the existing energy system, with its heavy reliance on oil, coal and natural gas.

Because continued reliance on oil would mean increased reliance on imported petroleum, especially from the Middle East, Bush sought to deflect public concern by calling for drilling in the Arctic National Wildlife Refuge and other protected areas. As a result, most public discourse on the Bush/ Cheney plan focused on drilling in ANWR, and no attention was paid to the implications of increased dependence on imported oil-even though oil from ANWR, in the most optimistic scenario, would reduce U.S. need for imports (now about 60 percent) by just 4 percent.

But this produced another dilemma for Bush: Increased reliance on imports meant increased vulnerability to disruptions in delivery due to wars and political upheavals. To address this danger, the Administration began planning for stepped-up military involvement in major overseas oil zones, especially the Persian Gulf. This was evident, for example, when then-Defense Secretary Donald Rumsfeld gave early priority to enhancement of American "power projection" to areas of instability in the developing world.

Then came 9/11 and the "war on terror"...giving the White House a perfect opportunity to accelerate the military expansion and to pursue other key objectives. High on the list was the elimination of Saddam Hussein, long considered the most potent challenger to U.S. domination of the Gulf and its critical energy supplies.

But the invasion of Iraq-intended to ensure U.S. control of the Gulf and a stable environment for the expanded production and export of its oil- has had exactly the opposite effect. Despite the many billions spent on oil infrastructure protection and the thousands of lives lost, production in Iraq is not higher today than it was before the invasion. Iraq has also become a rigorous training ground for extremists throughout the region, some of whom have now migrated to the oil kingdoms of the lower Gulf and begun attacking the facilities there-generating some of the recent spikes in prices.

Then there is the dilemma posed by Iran. With Saddam out of the picture, the Islamic regime in Tehran is viewed in Washington as the greatest threat to U.S. mastery of the Gulf. This threat rests largely on Iran's ability to attack oil shipping in the Gulf and ignite unrest among militant Shiite groups throughout the region, but its apparent pursuit of nuclear weapons has inflated the perceived menace significantly. To restrain Tehran's nuclear ambitions, Washington has imposed economic sanctions on Iran and forced key U.S. allies to abandon plans for developing new oilfields there. As a result, Iran, having the world's second-largest reserves after Saudi Arabia, is producing only about half the oil it could-another reason for the global constriction of supply.

But the Administration's greatest contribution to the rising oil prices is its steady stream of threats to attack Iran if it does not back down on the nuclear issue. The Iranians have made it plain that they would retaliate by attempting to block the flow of Gulf oil and otherwise cause turmoil in the energy market. Most analysts assume, therefore, that an encounter will produce a global oil shortage and prices well over $200 per barrel. It is not surprising, then, that every threat by Bush/Cheney (or their counterparts in Israel) has triggered a sharp rise in prices. This is where speculators enter the picture. Believing that a U.S.-Iranian clash is at least 50 percent likely, some investors are buying futures in oil at $140, $150 or more per barrel, thinking they'll make a killing if there's an attack and prices zoom over $200.

It follows, then, that while the hike in prices is due largely to ever increasing demand chasing insufficiently expanding supply, the Bush Administration's energy policies have greatly intensified the problem. By seeking to preserve our oil-based energy system at any cost, and by adding to the "fear factor" in international speculation through its bungled invasion of Iraq and bellicose statements on Iran, it has made a bad problem much worse.

What can be done to reverse this predicament? There was no realistic hope of substantially increasing the supply of oil-drilling in offshore U.S. waters, as favored by then President Bush. It is now up to the Obama Administration and whatever program they come up with. It is only by reducing demand that fundamental market forces can be addressed. This is best done through a comprehensive program of energy conservation, expanding public transit and accelerating development of energy alternatives. It will take time for some of these efforts to have an impact on prices; others, like reducing speed limits and adding bus routes, would have a more rapid effect. And if this new Administration truly wants to spare Americans further pain at the pump, there is one thing it could do that would have an immediate effect: declare that military force is not an acceptable option in the struggle with Iran. Such a declaration would take the wind out of the sails of speculators and set the course for a drop in prices.

Another Way to Reduce Oil Prices...
Break the Oil Cartel?

Posted on the *All News Blog* back on June 22nd, was the article written by Michael Avari on "Break the Oil Cartel?" Should "break the cartel" therefore be a rallying cry of our energy policy? We do not tolerate cartels at home; we should not tolerate them in a strategic commodity.

The U.S. imports over 13 million barrels of oil per day. Nearly 6 million barrels per day, 45%, comes from the Organization of the Petroleum Exporting Countries (OPEC)-Algeria, Angola, Ecuador, Indonesia, Iran, Iraq, Kuwait, Libya, Nigeria, Qatar, Saudi Arabia, United Arab Emirates, and Venezuela. That is too much leverage over price and supply policy, not only for the U.S., but the world. Looking at this list, one can also make a strong national security argument to divest OPEC of control.

OPEC's stated mission, based on OPEC's very own Web site (www.opec.org) "...is to coordinate and unify the petroleum policies of Member Countries and ensure the stabilization of oil markets in order to secure an efficient economic and regular supply of petroleum to consumers..."

"Stabilization" and "economic" are not words that have characterized oil markets in the last two years. OPEC has failed! In fairness, the blame is shared by purchasing countries. High prices are partly attributable to overheated demand seeking limited supply. China's growing economy created much of that increased demand, and to exacerbate matters, their subsidies and price controls encourage over-purchasing and discourage efficiency. In mid June, China agreed to lift prices on fuel, and oil prices dropped $5/barrel on world markets. The U.S. for its part is neither an efficient consumer of energy. Both countries can do more.

Does speculation cause high prices? The answer may not be satisfying. *The Economist* argues that commodity traders do not actually hold oil. They buy and resell futures contracts-"paper barrels"; i.e., "hoarding" of oil is not their business. Ultimately, contracts end up with the companies who must sell real oil to their customers, so we are back to the demand problem. Analysis of oil company profit margins, in spite of the recent profits in absolute dollars, shows a *decline* in the last ten years; just the opposite of what one would expect if they were "gouging".

What about the supply side of the equation? That is infinitely more promising. Some economists believe ethanol subsidies contribute to higher food prices. The Arctic National Wildlife Refuge (ANWR), may have enough oil to displace the volume we import from Saudi Arabia, even though 75% of Alaskans approve of drilling on a footprint, as George Will pointed out, the size of Boston's Logan Airport (2000 acres)...from Potential Oil Production from the Coastal Plain of the Arctic National Wildlife Refuge: Updated Assessment, EIA. ANWR is almost 20 million acres!

Senator McCain had called for 45 nuclear power plants to be built before 2030, and pointed out that it will solve both the energy and pollution problems. Judging from the French experience, his was correct. France generates over 86% of its power from 58 nuclear plants. Combined with hydropower, wind, and solar they claim that 95% of their energy production emits no carbon dioxide (Electricite de France).

Most interesting is the abundance of oil shale. The Energy Information Administration estimates, "The global resource of oil shale base is huge-estimated at a minimum of 2.9 trillion barrels of recoverable oil, including 750 billion barrels in the United States. The U.S. resource, if fully developed, could supply more than 100 years of U.S. oil consumption at current demand levels.

A charming, if not altogether constructive, characteristic of America is that we are most effective when faced with an adversary. $4/barrel gas could be an ephemeral adversary because Americans are good at adapting. Besides, Congress' machinations will dull over senses to that pain in short order. On the other hand, OPEC-busting presents an opportunity to take control of a vital primary input of economic production while disabusing potential rogue states from exerting unearned leverage over American production.

— 15 —

The Decline and Fall of the American Economy: Off-shoring Our Security

We started by saying that the tainted and counterfeit imports are enough to make you sick. But it goes beyond dangerous imports and how the FDA failed to stop these products from reaching our shores. A significant percentage of U.S. imports, especially those from China, is the offshored production that U.S. corporations sell to us at home. When a corporation closes facilities located here and moves them to China in order to benefit from lower labor costs, our GDP goes down, and China's goes up. When the products manufactured offshore are brought back into America, imports rise by that amount. By offshoring their production for U.S. markets, American corporations have simultaneously increased U.S. imports and reduced U.S. goods available for export.

Offshoring has reduced the availability of good-paying jobs for middle-class Americans. It is not only manufacturing jobs that are being moved abroad, but software-engineering jobs, IT jobs, and a wide range of other professional occupations. Consequently, the ladders of upward mobility are being dismantled. Many of the professional jobs that remain are being filled with foreigners, especially engineers and IT professionals from India, who are brought in on work visas and paid less by U.S. employers, who falsely claim worker shortages. Many thousands of U.S. employees are discharged after being forced to train their foreign replacements. The pursuit of lower-cost foreign labor is eroding consumer purchasing power in the United States.

In the 21st century, all net new U.S. jobs have been in non-tradable domestic services, such as waitresses and bartenders, healthcare and social assistance, and wholesale and retail trade. The U.S. labor force is taking on the characteristics of a Third World economy. In 2007, we lost 374,000 jobs in goods-producing industries. Job growth was confined to domestic services. Waitresses and bartenders accounted for 29 percent of the 1,054,000 net new private-sector jobs in 2007. Healthcare and social assistance accounted for 45 percent of them. Wholesale and retail trade, together with transportation and utilities, accounted for 17 percent.

As of the beginning of 2008 the economy started to enter into a recession. With consumers pressed and jobs declining, Americans today do not have enough discretionary income to afford a tax increase. The Republicans were determined not to increase taxes but we now have a Democratic Congress and an Obama Administration that may very spend trillions of dollars and will most likely tax the people who truly cannot afford to pay more. The unemployment rate is over 8% and climbing and more and more people are being fired. The full cost of the wars in Iraq and Afghanistan is now a staggering three trillion dollars and climbing.

Foreigners have been financing our trade deficit by using export earnings to purchase existing U.S. assets, acquiring ownership over a larger percentage of U.S. equities, companies, bonds, and real estate. They have even acquired long-term leases (99 years) on the revenues from several state toll roads. The Chinese have purchased U.S. iron deposits. With each passing year, the United States owns less of herself. By acquiring our assets, foreigners also acquire the income streams generated by them-profits, capital gains, rents, dividends, tolls, and interests. These diverted income streams, in turn, increase the U.S. current-account deficit.

The idea that the United States is a "superpower," when she is dependent on China and Japan to finance her wars in Afghanistan and Iraq, is nonsensical. The United States is too dependent on foreign finance to retain her role as holder of the world's reserve currency, an important source of U.S. power.

Libertarians and free-market economists mistake offshoring for free trade and, therefore, assume that offshoring is beneficial. Offshoring is not trade at all; it is international labor arbitrage. Trade takes place when, for example, U.S. industries compete against Chinese industries in domestic and foreign markets. Free trade is based on different countries specializing in areas in which they have comparative advantage.

Offshoring is based on the desire for absolute advantages by achieving lowest factor cost. U.S. corporations move their production to China in order to maximize profits by minimizing labor and compliance costs.

Offshoring was not possible on a significant scale until the collapse of world socialism and the advent of high-speed internet access, which opened large excess supplies of Chinese and Indian labor to First World corporations. Today, Many American brand-name manufactured goods are made abroad in whole or in part for U.S. markets, and a wide range of professional services can be supplied to U.S. offices from foreigners via the internet and H1B, LI, and other work visas. Young people from Russia, Ukraine, Rumania, Thailand, and elsewhere are brought in on short-term J9 and J4 visas and supplied as contract labor to supermarkets, resort-area cleaning services, and restaurants. It is becoming increasingly difficult for Americans of all ages to find a job of any kind.

Offshoring, the internet, and work visas have forced American labor into direct competition with foreign labor. This is different from trade competition in which U.S. labor competes with foreign labor in manufactured product markets. In foreign trade, U.S. labor, working with better technology and business know-how, was more productive than foreign labor and remained competitive despite higher U.S. wage rates. Today, offshoring provides Chinese or other foreign labor with the same technology and business acumen. This gives the advantage to the lower-wage countries and has halted growth in U.S. real wages despite productivity growth.

In pursuit of higher profits, Wall Street pressures corporations to move facilities offshore, and in pursuit of price advantages, large retailers, such as Wal-Mart, pressure their U.S. suppliers to go offshore. Some economists tout Wal-Mart's lower prices as the payoff to Americans for their lost jobs. However, when the lower prices are offset by lower incomes and the dollar's decline, the overall effect of offshoring is adverse. Wal-Mart's "always low prices" can only last so long as China keeps her currency pegged to the U.S. dollar. Sooner or later, if the dollar continues to decline, China may abandon the currency peg (Beijing has recently adopted a moving peg and is allowing its currency to appreciate gradually against the dollar), and the United States will find herself dependent on expensive foreign-manufactured goods she cannot afford.

Very interestingly, before his resignation in March of 2008, David M. Walker, head of the U.S. Government of Accountability Office, revealed that the unfunded liabilities of the U.S. government total $53 trillion. Our declining economy has no possibility of paying such an enormous sum. Hubris has blinded Washington to the severity of our economy problems. In truth, it owes the world.

So, based on what Mr. Walker stated, he believes that socialism vanished leaving wide-open the doors (at least for a while) of offshoring; and we may be too big to be a country or nation and NO LONGER can we even secure our own borders.

Personally I feel that we are heading into a socialist catastrophe with Obama as president and he is now CEO of General Motors; has taken over the banking institutions; wants to nationalize healthcare; and spread our wealth around by taxing the rich and giving more to the poor. Unless we can stop this madness, then we may very well not be virtual and no longer be a nation that we once were. If we owe everyone else in the world money and have to borrow to put the parts in the rifles of our soldiers in some remote part of the world rather than even being able to secure our own borders then we are not a 'superpower,' any longer. But as an American who believes in our country…there is hope!

Outsourcing To China Not So Cheap Anymore

The China Price used to be the global standard for low-cost manufacturing. It shut thousands of factories across North America, put tens of thousands of Canadians out of work and drove down the price of consumer goods around the world. Now China's cost is being eroded by soaring oil prices, rising wages and an appreciating currency. Canadian companies that outsource their manufacturing to China are already feeling the pinch and some are even bringing production closer to home.

As reported in the June 27th issue of the *Canada.com network*, could globalization be reversed in an era of high oil? What would that mean for Canadian companies that have come to depend on the China Price?

In the latter part of June, Levon Afeyan flew to China to find out the answer to these questions for his mid-size Montreal Company. He's the president of Seatply Products, Inc., a manufacturer of molded plywood for use in commercial seating.

About half of Seatply's products originate in China and Malaysia and he's becoming increasingly uneasy about soaring freight costs that have seen the price of a shipment of a standard container from China hit as much as $6,000 from $4,000 a year ago.

"People are taking a second look at everything because the costs are becoming prohibitive," said Afeyan, whose company's efforts to cut costs through lean manufacturing techniques were featured in The Gazette in 2006. "It goes right to the bottom line."

On his trip, Afeyan tried to get price concessions from his Asian suppliers to help cover his rocketing freight costs. But he did not expect an easy time because his suppliers have their own problems and want to raise prices.

Inflation has already risen 8 percent in 2008 in China and the government just lowered subsidies on gasoline, resulting in an increase of roughly 20 percent at the pump. Meanwhile, the Chinese currency has jumped about 17 percent against the U.S. dollar, making exports more expensive. And wages are rising fast as well. Depending on the industry and skill-level, wages are up by 10 to 25 percent a year and labor shortages have developed in some regions.

Having had 15 years in the distribution of products made offshore, I had seen the rise of shipping costs by freight forwarders because of increased fuel costs and security costs that arose from 9/11. The shipping costs had just about doubled in 15 years and the cost of doing business with offshore companies made it more difficult. There were times when it paid to use local manufacturers in the states where there were no shipping costs that added to the cost of the products which made them non-competitive.

And of course, another reason for higher costs was the fact that the freight forwarder had to book space on the planes weeks ahead just to make sure that the goods would be shipped out on time. If the order was cancelled, sometimes the freight forwarder or logistic company would have to pay for the space anyway. It was all a matter of price and it was getting more and more difficult to claim that it was cheaper to outsource than to do the manufacturing stateside.

CIBC World Markets economists, who predict oil is heading to $200 U.S. a barrel...at this writing, oil had dropped $15 a barrel to $130 a barrel... believe the cost of maintaining a supply chain that reaches to the other side of the world is outstripping the benefits for many North American sectors.

"In a world of triple-digit oil prices, distance costs money," CIBC economists Jeff Rubin and Benjamin Tal wrote in a report at the end of May. "Soaring transport costs, suggest trade should be both dampened and diverted as markets seek shorter, and hence, less costly supply lines."

Rubin and Tal note there remains a huge differential between Chinese and North American wage rates but have found evidence that companies are already looking for production closer to home in capital-intensive manufacturing such as steel where there's a high rate of freight costs to final selling prices. "Furniture, apparel, footwear, metal manufacturing and industrial machinery-all typical Chinese exports, incur relatively high transport costs."

The CIBC economists expect Mexico with its maquiladora plants along the U.S. border to be a prime beneficiary of the high freight phenomenon as companies seek low-wage centres closer to home. Competition Pools, Inc. has already moved a third of its production of pool accessories and fixtures from China to a new plant in Mirabel. The rising price of shipping, along with lower tax credits on exports and rising Chinese currency is making it uneconomical to move bulky products like pool filters from China, said Mario Lampron, co-founder of Competition, a firm that ships pool products to 40 countries.

"Importers and distributors will have to relocate their supply chain," Lampron said. "It's already happening."

Myer Deitcher of Montreal steel trading firm Novosteel North America said his firm has imported more than 50,000 tonnes of steel product from China in some years, but freight costs have almost doubled, making foreign steel too expensive to import.

Jayson Myers, president of Canadian Manufacturers and Exporters, said that the cost of producing goods in China has risen 30 to 40 percent for many Canadian companies over the last couple of years. "A lot of Canadian manufacturers are going to have to reassess their outsourcing strategies," Myers said. "What we may be seeing for some industries and companies is a contraction of supply chains back to North America."

But Myers added many companies will just have to find ways of absorbing the cost increases because they have no immediate alternative to Asian factories. That's a bitter pill to swallow at a time when raw material prices are also soaring and the economy is slowing. "There's been a rapid swing in prices around the world," he said. "When you're a business, you can't move that quickly."

Other economists cautioned that the impact of higher costs in China will slow, but not stop, the outsourcing trend for mass production of goods although some companies are moving to even lower wage countries in the region, notably Vietnam. "People might rethink their plans for outsourcing, but I don't think we're at a point of reversing the outsourcing phenomenon," National Bank Financial economist Stefane Marion said. "The foot is coming off the accelerator."

Yuen Pau Woo, president of the Asia Pacific Foundation of Canada, said there was a slowdown in the torrid pace of Asian shipments to North America last year and 2008 was the year of the start of the decline. But he didn't foresee a large scale return to outsourced manufacturing to Canada and the U.S., noting investments and expertise in such industries as consumer electronics will not be easily displaced.

"The infrastructure and production networks in Asia are well established and represent a significant investment that will not be dismantled in a hurry."

Indeed, China received almost $83 billion U.S. in foreign industrial investment last year, tops in the world. It's not clear that companies now outsourcing to Asia will want to make investments to ramp up manufactured capacity in North America in response to what may turn out to be short-term factors, Woo said.

But rising costs in China will give a push to manufacturers in North American who make advanced, high-value goods that require rapid product cycles or have a high design or marketing requirement, he said. The way ahead for Canadian manufacturers looks difficult.

Recalls Rise in Imported Foods Highlight Strain on Inspection System

As reported in the *Dallas News* on June 29th, day after day, Mexican trucks line up as far as the eye can see for entry to the U.S. at the World Trade Bridge in Laredo, carrying everything from raw tomatoes, broccoli and fresh basil to frozen seafood,. They also bring in salmonella, listeria, restricted pesticides and other food poisons.

Customs and Border Protection officers take less than a minute per truck to determine which products enter the U.S. and find their way into grocery stores and restaurants across North Texas.

Most trucks are waved through. The avalanche of imported goods-especially food from Mexico-is too much for the limited number of inspectors at the nation's 300 ports of entry to effectively screen, critics say. And the sheer volume makes it impossible for them to carry out their mission: protecting the U.S. food supply and American consumers.

Concerns about the nation's food inspection system are gaining urgency-especially as the U.S. Food and Drug Administration looks at Mexico as a likely source of salmonella-tainted tomatoes that have sickened more than 800 people in two months alone. The FDA in the last week of June, 2008 sent inspectors to three Mexican states-Jalisco, Sinaloa and Coahuila-and Florida to check farms and packing plants.

The great majority of the food that crosses the southern U.S. border is safe, U.S. officials say. But a surge in imports in recent years means that the system of border inspections is badly strained and in urgent need of repair, the officials acknowledge. Inspectors at the border are tasked with enforcing hundreds of regulations from more than 40 government agencies. And just a tiny percentage of agricultural products, seafood and manufactured goods is actually inspected, say the critics.

"We have this huge growth in imports, this huge growth in trade; at the same time we have severely cut back on our regulatory agencies and their ability to do their job, especially the food portion of the Food and Drug

Administration," said Jean Halloran, director of food policy initiatives for Consumers Union, which publishes *Consumer Reports* magazine.

"If they are only checking 1 percent of the stuff and finding lots of problems, then...there are a lot of problems that are never caught," she said.

What is getting stopped, critics say, is representative of what is getting through. Overall, about 15 percent of the U.S. food supply and 60 percent of fresh fruits and vegetables consumed are imported, according to the U.S. Department of Agriculture's Economic Research Service.

Mexico is the second-largest foreign source of agricultural products and seafood for the U.S.-moving to No. 1 during the winter months and filling about 60 percent of the supermarket produce aisle. And it's the worst offender when it comes to food shipments turned away at the border by U.S. inspectors, a review of food rejections shows.

An Overwhelmed System - In Laredo, trucks sent to a dock for inspection are greeted by a hired crew that unloads samples of broccoli, tomatoes and dried corn husks used for wrapping tamales. Customs and FDA inspectors move quickly, checking for poisons or pests that could damage U.S. agriculture. On another dock, manufactured goods are hauled out of rigs by forklift and inspected for safety issues, such as lead in toys. Even tigers on their way to a U.S. circus tour are checked for potential health risks.

"Whatever is put in front of you, you are going to make sure it meets all of the regulations in order to be introduced into the country," said Mucia Dovalina, a veteran inspector and public affairs liaison for Customs and Border Protection.

The problem, officials and analysts say, is the result of sometimes substandard agricultural practices south of the border, and a U.S. food inspection system that has become so overwhelmed that President Bush endorsed a 50-step plan that would put more emphasis on inspections in the countries of origin.

The in-country system would put U.S. inspectors in foreign countries or use third parties to check products before they are shipped to the U.S. It also would give the FDA mandatory recall powers over food products. Currently, the agency negotiates "voluntary" recalls.

"For many years, we have relied on a strategy based on identifying unsafe products at the border," Mr. Bush said late 2007. "The problem is that the growing volume of products coming into our country makes this approach increasingly unreliable."

Both consumer groups and an internal FDA study group said the proposed Bush plan during his presidency, to fix the current system "within available resources" was far too modest and have yet to hear what the Obama Administration has planned.

"We can state unequivocally that the system cannot be fixed 'within available resources,' the agency's subcommittee on science and technology said in a report late in 2007 and again in 2008. The subcommittee called the inspection rate "appallingly low."

More Eyes on Imports – In fairness to Mexico, U.S. food producers were the subject of far more expansive recalls last year than foreign producers, including recalls of California spinach that tested positive for E. coli and was blamed for three deaths, and of 22 million pounds of frozen beef hamburger patties, also because of a dangerous strain of that common bacteria.

"I must emphasize that by and large, the food traded is very safe," said Suzanne Heinen, the USDA's counselor for agricultural affairs at the U.S. Embassy in Mexico City. "We have very few problems, especially when you consider the volume of trade that crosses the border every day."

Still, food imports remain on Washington's radar-particularly in light of the latest salmonella outbreak. As a matter of fact, U.S. Health and Human Services Secretary Michael Leavitt announced plans recently to open a food safety monitoring office in Latin America, similar to three being planned for China. He did not say which country might house the office, but he did say that a March salmonella warning against Honduran cantaloupes, along with the tomato scare, showed the need to be on the ground in exporting regions.

"What it demonstrates is that when these incidents occur, we need a quick response," he said in late June as U.S. and Mexican inspectors combed farms and packing houses in Mexican tomato-growing states for signs of the source of salmonella. Another recent recall targeting Mexican agriculture is an example of what consumer groups say is wrong with the system.

In December 2007, officials took a sample for testing from a 5,500-pound load of Mexican basil moving through the Otay Mesa border crossing in San Diego. The basil continued on to its destination and was sold to restaurants and other customers in California, Texas and Illinois the next day. When the test results came back two weeks later, they suggested salmonella contamination sparking a late recall. Mexico has been the subject of other recent recalls as well.

- In February 2007. the FDA recalled 672 cartons of Mexican cantaloupes after a sample analysis found salmonella, which can cause fever, diarrhea, nausea, vomiting, abdominal pain and arterial infections
- In September 2007, the FDA recalled a hard, dry cheese from Mexico that it suspected was contaminated with salmonella
- And in early December 2007, the Texas Department of State Health Services announced the voluntary recall of several Mexican candies

after tests showed high levels of lead. Lead can harm the mental and physical development in children and unborn babies. California had banned the candies in August of 2007.

Many of Mexico's problematic goods are especially dangerous for children and the elderly, who can't fight off illness as well as healthy adults.

Non-pasteurized cheese-which can carry listeria and even tuberculosis, Mexican officials say-is often brought into the U.S. by border-crossers who are allowed to bring in up to 22 pounds "for personal consumption." Often, the cheese makes its way into flea markets and restaurants, most in the Latino community. The toll in Texas from non-pasteurized cheese over the last five years: four miscarriages or stillbirths, one newborn death, and four deaths of adults who weren't pregnant. All but two were Latino.

A top Mexican health official acknowledged that some Mexican food producers cut corners to boost their profits or have simply not adopted modern safety measures, although they've made great strides in recent years. For example, chile peppers are often spread out to dry on the ground, where they can pick up lead or pesticides only approved for other crops.

"In Mexico, we have a lot of work to do," said Maria Esther Diaz Carrillo, a chemist and food technician at Mexico's Federal Commission to Prevent Sanitary Risks, part of the Health Ministry, "We also have producers who are very conscientious…of the risks associated with their products and truly dedicated to public health. In some cases, it's ignorance."

Increasing Vigilance – Still, Mexico is not China when it comes to the breadth of the U.S. recalls last year-including those of pet food that killed hundreds of animals, toothpaste tainted with diethylene glycol, a poisonous chemical used in antifreeze, and millions of Mattel toys with dangerous levels of lead in their paint.

"I don't think we've reached those extremes," said Ms. Diaz. "Our vigilance and ability to respond has been increasing,"

For example, Mexican and U.S. health authorities jointly inspect slaughterhouses in Mexico certified to export meat to the U.S. Two of eight slaughterhouses were suspended from exporting to the U.S. after an inspection in late 2006, according to an inspection report. In one case, the facility was not properly testing for E. coli. As of today, both are back in operation.

The panel that came up with Mr. Bush's import safety plan also detected a series of problems with the current inspection system. Those include government computer databases involved in import safety that can't communicate with each other, as well as a practice called "port shopping," in which a shipment rejected at one port of entry can get through another. Mr. Leavitt, the health and human services secretary, said there is no estimate on what it would cost to upgrade computer systems, put more U.S. inspectors abroad and carry out the report's other recommendations. But in recent testimony before a Senate committee, Mr. Leavitt said there is a sense of urgency in improving import safety as foreign foods and foreign goods become a staple of American life.

"U.S. imports are large and growing rapidly. American consumers like the variety and abundance of consumer goods and the competitive prices that result from global trade," he said. "The American people, however, have reasonable expectations that the products they buy for their families will be safe. We can and must do more to honor that trust."

Food Rejections Just in April of 2008 Alone...

Compiled by Laurence Iliff from the FDA's OASIS database and released by the *Dallas News*, food safety advocates say one way to get a glimpse into what is getting through the food safety inspection system is to see what is getting caught. The Food and Drug Administration's Operations and Administrative System for Import support, a database of information on refused import shipments, highlights some of the problems and their severity. Mexico routinely is number one in refused food shipments, according to the database.

- In April 2008, Mexico, the number two provider of agricultural and seafood exports to the U.S., valued at $9.8 billion in 2007, had 48 food-related shipment rejections
- China, at number three, with $4.1 billion in agricultural and seafood exports to the U.S., had 44 rejections
- And Canada, at number one, with $15.6 billion in agricultural and seafood exports, had nine rejected food shipments

Here's a look at some examples of rejected items from April 2008, a fairly typical month for the United States' top foreign food suppliers:

CANADA.
Item: Decorated gingerbread cookie
Violation: "Unsafe Col"-appears to contain an unsafe coloring
Item: Black currant juice concentrate
Violation: "Pesticide"-appears to contain a pesticide chemical that is unsafe
Item: Frozen dry-pack lobster meat
Violation: "Lacks Firm"-lacks the proper label of producer or distributor

Item: Kinder Surprise chocolate eggs
Violation: "Imbed Objt"-appears to contain a non-nutritive imbedded object

MEXICO.
Item: Spicy Peanuts
Violation: "Salmonella"-appears to contain a poisonous substance
Item: Honey-filled pacifiers
Violation: "Poisonous"-appears to contain a poisonous substance
Item: Pumpkin Seeds
Violation: "Aflatoxin"-appears to contain mycotoxin, which may render it injurious to health
Item: Mennonite Cheese
Violation: "Bacteria"-appears to contain a poisonous substance

CHINA.
Item: Frozen, dusted shrimp
Violation: "Vetdrugres"- appears to contain a new animal drug that is unsafe
Item: Pickled yam, powdered
Violation: "Filthy"-appears to consist in whole or in part of a filthy, putrid or decomposed substance
Item: Chinese ginseng
Violation: "Pesticides"-appears to be adulterated because it contains a prohibited pesticide chemical
Item: Salted Olive
Violation: "Unsafe Add"-appears to contain a food additive that is unsafe

The Maggots in Your Mushrooms

E.J. Levy, a professor of creative writing at the University of Missouri had submitted an article to *The New York Times* that was reported in the middle of February of 2009, stating that the Georgia peanut company at the center of one of our nation's worst food-contamination scares had officially reached a revolting new low; a recent inspection by the Food and Drug Administration discovered that the salmonella-tainted plant was also home to mold and roaches. You may be grossed out, but insects and mold in our food are not new. The FA actually condones a certain percentage of "natural contaminants" in our food supply-meaning, among other things, butts, mold, rodent hairs and maggots.

Now get this: among the booklet's list of allowable defects are "insect filth," "rodent filth" (both hair and excreta pellets), "mold," "insects," "Mammalian Excreta," "rot," "insects and larvae" (which is to say, maggots), "insects and mites," "insects and insect eggs," "Drosophila fly," "sand and grit," "parasites," "mildew" and "foreign matter" (which includes "objectionable" items like "sticks, stones, burlap bagging, cigarette butts, etc.")

Tomato juice, for example, may average "10 or more fly eggs per 100 grams (the equivalent of a small juice glass) or five or more fly eggs and one or more maggots." Tomato paste and other pizza sauces are allowed a denser infestation-30 or more fly eggs per 100 grams or 15 or more fly eggs and one or more maggots per 100 grams.

Canned mushrooms may have "over 20 or more maggots of any size per 100 grams of drained mushrooms and proportionate liquid" or "five or more maggots two millimeters or longer per 100 grams of drained mushrooms and proportionate liquid" or an average of 75 mites" before provoking action by the FDA.

Sauerkraut on your hot dog may average up to 50 thrips. And when washing down those tiny, slender winged bugs with a sip of beer, you might consider that just 10 grams of hops could have as many as 2,500 plant lice. Yum!!!

Giving new meaning to the idea of spicing up one's food, curry powder is allowed 100 or more bug bits per 25 grams; ground thyme up to 925 insect fragments per 10 grams; ground pepper up to 475 insect parts per 50 grams. One small shaker of cinnamon could have more than 20 rodent hairs before being considered defective.

Peanut butter...that culinary cause celebre...may contain approximately 145 bug parts for an 18-ounce jar; or five or more rodent hairs for that same jar; or more than 125 milligrams of grit. And in case you're curious: you're probably ingesting one to two pounds of flies, maggots and mites each year without knowing it, a quantity of insects that clearly does not cut the mustard, even as insects may well be in the mustard.

The FDA considers the significance of these defects to be "aesthetic" or "offensive to the senses," which is to say, merely icky as opposed to the "mouth/tooth injury" one risks with, for example, insufficiently pitted prunes. This policy is justified on economic grounds, stating that it is "impractical to grow, harvest or process raw products that are totally free of non –hazardous, naturally occurring, unavoidable defect."

The unsettling reality is that despite food's cheery packaging and nutritional labeling, we don't really know what we're putting into our mouths. "Waiter, there's a fly in my soup"...would be, to the FDA, no cause for complaint.

We then go back to the fact that if we are having problems here in our own country, why is it not so different from the problems we are having with products that are imported from China or elsewhere? No matter what kind of salmonella or maggots are found in food produced in the U.S. or if the drywall and pet food, or fake brands from China are causing delirium to everyone, everywhere, either we continue to work with China by correcting their mistakes or tend to correct ours and forget this country even exists.

Dirty Engines from China Pollute U.S. Air

From Washington, *STL-today* reported on June 30th of 2008 that not only is food dangerous from China and Mexico, but with costly new anti-pollution rules looming for lawn mowers, boat engines and many other small motorized devices, U.S. manufacturers are pressing the government to halt the imports of "dirty" equipment from China.

The environmental Protection Agency and U.S. customs agents already have stepped up enforcement efforts, seizing or turning away thousands of motorcycles, generators, water pumps and other Asian-made outdoor power equipment illegally imported under existing rules.

"We see everybody from major corporations to mom-and-pop stores trying to import everything from generators to chain saws to weed-whackers to ATVs," said Adam Kushner, the EPA's director of air enforcement, "It if moves and blows smoke, it's being imported."

The stakes are about to grow higher for U.S. and foreign manufacturers alike. A new EPA regimen of rules for small engines will require catalytic converters and other design changes aimed at reducing exhaust pollutants by millions of pounds in coming years. With the rules supposedly due out by July 2008, American manufacturers are mounting a late campaign pressuring the government to step up enforcement of the Clean Air Act at American borders and write in provisions to discourage the arrival of more polluting equipment.

The recent flood of Chinese imports, legal and otherwise, presents competitive threats for U.S. companies such as Milwaukee-based Briggs & Stratton. Last year, Briggs, which has two plants in China, closed its Rolla, Mo., gasoline engine manufacturing plant, which employees 800 people. The company's other Missouri plant is in Poplar Bluff.

"The tip of the iceberg," was how Briggs & Stratton described a recent government seizure of imported equipment in a letter in June to the EPA demanding better enforcement. Briggs, John Deere, Stihl and other companies with American plants are pushing the EPA to insert liability provisions, registration requirements and other wording in the new rule as a means stem the flow of Chinese equipment.

John Foster, product compliance manager for Stihl Inc., noted in his recent letter to the EPA that his company invests millions of dollars to comply with EPA rules. But foreign manufacturers, he wrote, "are becoming ever more sophisticated and brazen as they implement fraudulent schemes," to avoid such costs. Foster's company had reason to be pleased when the EPA closed a major case this spring. A Taiwanese manufacturer and three U.S. companies accused of importing 200,000 dirty-engine chain saws agreed to pay a $2 million civil penalty.

But it fell short of a complete victory. The chain saws already had been sold across the country, some by Sears, a failure that will result in 268 tons of carbon missions pumped into the air during the saws' lifetimes. "Unless they are caught by U.S. Customs before they enter the United States, there's a good chance that they will hit the market," Foster said in an interview.

Rising Import Tide – As with such problematic Chinese imports as tainted seafood, poisonous toothpaste and leaded toys, the arrival of dirty small engines is a recent problem.

Five years ago, the EPA had no cases stemming from illegal Chinese equipment arriving at U.S. borders. But by 2005, 44 of the 50 EPA dirty-engine import cases were Chinese.

The trend has continued, and most of the recent cases settled by the government also involved Chinese imports, EPA officials said. Among them were two cases this spring that prevented distribution of more than 700 motorcycles and ATVs that arrived illegally at East Coast ports.

The rising tide of Chinese imports has much to do with the ease of conducting commerce over the internet, officials say. Simply by supplying a credit card number, a company, broker or an individual can arrange for the arrival of a shipping container of equipment at any U.S. port from China's burgeoning manufacturing sector.

The new EPA emission regulations will increase the burden on border agents to intercept those dirty engines. The long-debated rules evolved after a successful effort by Senator Christopher "Kit" Bond, R-Mo., to prevent states from adopting California's strict rules. Bond argued that the emission rules would be an unfair burden on U.S. manufacturers.

Three years later, the American companies are supporting the new rules and making investments to meet them despite concerns that non-complying imports will have an unfair market advantage. EPA officials declined to discuss what specific wording might be written into the regulations but said by e-mail that "we intend to include discussion and new provisions in the upcoming final rule to further address this issue."

Environmental advocates such as Frank O'Donnell, of the nonprofit Clean Air Watch in Washington, are supporting the industry's demand after battling manufacturers for years over the scope of the rule. All those dirty Chinese engines, O'Donnell said, "are a significant source of our smog."

Our Endearing Competitive Edge

What could be reassuring about killer Chinese toothpaste, toys and tires? Hard to believe, but there's a silver lining. The rash of product recalls reveals that China is not the manufacturing juggernaut we fear-and that America has an edge we tend to overlook. Sure, greed factors into why Chinese suppliers make defective, even harmful products. But often it's because of just plain ineptitude. If you visited a typical Chinese factory, you'd see why. It lacks capital, technology and know-how. Its workers place obedience over quality. And it sits along an endless chain of middlemen. Believe it or not, the Huffington Post had written an article on this topic.

On average, it takes China 17 separate parties to produce a product that would take us three. Unlike Japan in the 1980s, little companies drive China's economic growth, not big ones. China's industries are composed of hundreds of thousands of tiny factories and farms-plus traders, brokers, haulers and agents, all of whom take control of the goods and materials but add little value to the product. With every additional player in the chain, the cost, risk, and time grow. Effective quality control in this environment is difficult.

So is effective cost control. Despite cheap labor, making goods in China is often more expensive than in the U.S. Far from being a bottomless ATM of cheap consumer goods, China is a risky, costly and time-consuming place to do business.

Yet polls show a majority of Americans believe China has mastered basic manufacturing-and it's now barreling into our high-tech backyard. That's false. As the product recalls demonstrate, China can barely make low-value goods reliably, much less higher-value ones. The problems are structural, not the result of a few bad apples.

To compete head-to-head with the American economy, China will have to revolutionize the very way its industries are organized. It must shake out the thousands of low-value middlemen and integrate the tiny factories into larger, competitive companies. It must train a workforce in modern technology and business practices. And, it must instill transparency and a uniform rule of law. Such an effort could span generations.

Meanwhile, we're expected to believe that Americans will import Chinese passenger cars in just two years. Making products that live up to international standards requires more than simply modern production lines. Your entire corporate culture, along with that of your suppliers and buyers, must be focused on minimizing errors and defects. Rattle around in a Chinese-made car and you'll see tangible proof of why they've had to delay their launch into the U.S. market again and again-and just how far China still has to go before it can make a car Americans will buy.

Made in China isn't a label you'll see on a vehicle anytime soon. But if you've had your car worked on lately, there's a small but growing chance that your mechanic will be using Chinese-made parts. Indeed, these imports have risen sharply to $8.5 billion in 2007-up from $1 billion in 1998. There's still a small fraction of the $286 billion car-parts business, but Chinese-made components comprise a big chunk of the parts used in the so-called aftermarket, especially in car repairs. According to consulting firm McKinsey, an estimated 80 percent of Chinese parts brought to the U.S. are used as replacements. China is also the largest exporter of tires to the United States and we know what happened there.

Because Chinese parts are generally cheaper, they do keep repair costs down….welcome relief in this economy. But after a string of disturbing incidents, safety experts are raising concerns about the made-in-China movement, including recall of 450,000 Chinese-made replacement tires that lacked a gum strip, making them prone to tread separation.

The National Highway Traffic Safety Administration has also received reports of Chinese engine fuses that could spark an electrical fire, windshield glass that could shatter into large shards and poorly welded wheel rims that could separate from the wheels at highway speeds. All those parts have been recalled, along with 2 million potentially defective rubber valve sterns, after a deadly accident traced to this tiny part.

Chinese companies aren't the only one with manufacturing black eyes. More than 600 automotive recalls occur every year, and every major carmaker has to one point issued one. Even safety experts say the concern is largely anecdotal, since the U.S. doesn't track recalls by country of origin. Meanwhile, companies that import Chinese parts say they have good quality controls in place and that parts meet industry and governmental standards. Indeed, upgraded facilities have led to "tremendous improvement" in Chinese manufacturing in the past decade, says Lee Kadrich of the Automobile Aftermarket Industry Association, a lobbying group.

But fair or not, Chinese manufacturers are facing an image issue these days. Their factories have been linked to lead-tainted toys, contaminated pet food and defective pharmaceuticals, while the Chinese government had admitted in 2007 that one one-fifth of its products didn't pass inspection. Even Chinese business representatives say their factories need to do better. "We've seen improvement in Chinese products. But this problem won't go away," said Siva Yam, president of the U.S. – China Chamber of Commerce.

Most drivers, of course, have no idea where parts come from or even bother to ask. Certainly, most have noticed that repair bills have escalated as cars have become more high-tech. But few are aware of the cutthroat competition among replacement-part makers, especially in today's slumping auto market. People fight over tenths of a penny at times as Chinese companies compete among the lowest-cost producers. Then it takes months for a defective part to be recalled. And even then, most consumers may not find out about it.

The U.S. economy, on the other hand, can efficiently produce a wide variety of goods and services. In most industries, we're decades ahead of China. And, huge swaths of our economy-like the services sector and high-tech manufacturing-don't even exist in China yet. America possesses this competitive edge at the precise moment when Chinese consumers are buying more than ever before. China's middle class already outnumbers the combined populations of the United Kingdom and France. And it's expanding at a rate not seen since the industrial rise of the U.S., Europe and Japan.

Chinese consumers want modern homes, schools and hospitals, as well as advanced technologies and infrastructure. Local sources can't keep up with demand. So China imports most of the higher-value goods, materials and services it needs. As a result, China is increasingly buying American and growing five times faster than any other market for U.S. exports.

Nearly all sectors of the U.S. economy are experiencing unprecedented Chinese demand. And while most Americans fear the flood of cheap Chinese goods, many of these products are, in fact, composed of U.S. raw materials and components. The Chinese apparel that lines our shelves is made from American cotton; the housewares from American steel; the computers from American technologies. So as Chinese imports to the U.S. surge, American exports to China surge, too. China is buying from large U.S. companies as well as small ones, and China is the fastest-growing export market for small business.

We should take another hard look at the "China Century." China's rise need not drive America's fall. By tapping into its expansion and capitalizing on our strengths, America's companies have a once-in-a-century windfall opportunity to build value, make money and create jobs here at home-not shutter the shop.

Putting near-term gains aside, though, the next century will not be led by the country that can make the cheapest copy of a spark plug. It will be led by innovators and entrepreneurs, America's unrivaled assets. Innovation-not imitation-will create jobs and maintain America's economic primacy in the century ahead.

The scope of the product recalls will surely widen as we start to scrutinize what we're importing from China. Remember, these recalls tell us as much about China as they do about America. The silver lining is our inherent strength...it's called "YANKEE INGENUITY."

FDA Food Protection Plan Shows Significant Progress

In the first of July 2008, it was reported in Washington that the U.S. Food and Drug Administration's Food Protection Plan Progress Report...in conjunction with the Interagency Working Group on Import Safety Action Plan Update... showed significant areas of activity to further improve the safety of America's food supply since unveiling its Food and Protection Plan in November 2007. The improvements highlight the agency's efforts to address domestic and global changes in our food supply to help keep consumers enjoying one of the safest food supplies in the world.

"The Food Protection Plan is the comprehensive framework the agency needs to enhance the protection of our nation's food supply," said Commissioner of Food and Drugs Andrew C. von Eschenbach, M.D. "Implementing the strategic approaches outlined in the plan is essential if we are to enhance our ability to respond and intervene in food-borne outbreaks. But there is much more that needs to be done. We are hopeful that Congress will support these efforts by providing the proposed new authorities that we requested in the Food Protection Plan."

The FDA Food Protection Plan focuses on prevention (building safety in from the start); intervention (using targeted risk-based inspections and testing); and response (responding rapidly when problems are identified).

The FDA has been working collaboratively across the agency and with Federal, State and Local Partners as well as foreign governments to execute a number of the action steps laid out by the Food Protection Plan. Listed below are select accomplishments of the plan:

PREVENTION.

- In an effort to increase foreign capacity, the FDA "Beyond our Borders" initiative is underway
- FDA is implementing its landmark China Memoranda of Agreement (MOA)
- FDA has provided registration materials to the Chinese government, identified points of contact for the MOA, and drafted the first five-year work plan

- FDA held its first bilateral meeting in March 2008 in Beijing, China. The meeting solidified the relationship with the General Administration of Quality, Supervision, Inspection, and Quarantine (AQSIQ). Verbal agreements were made to focus the present efforts in fulfilling the MOA to aquaculture (five species plus Tilapia) and ingredients (wheat gluten, corn gluten, and rice protein)
- FDA is moving forward to establish an FDA presence in China
- FDA delegation visited Indian counterparts to discuss requirements for an FDA presence in India
- In 2007, FDA began working in collaboration with the State Health and Agriculture departments in Virginia and Florida, several universities, and the produce industry on a multi-year Tomato Safety Initiative. As part of the initiative, FDA has led assessments of grower practices focusing on the factors believed to be associated with contamination of tomatoes with Salmonella. FDA has conducted assessments in Virginia and began assessments in Florida in April
- FDA is exploring current existing third-party certification programs
- FDA is developing ingredient, processing, and labeling standards for pet food. We are also developing ingredient and processing standards for animal feed

INTERVENTION.

- FDA is working with the New Mexico State University to develop a prototype system for improving electronic screening, using open-source intelligence, of imported products offered for entry into the U.S. The evaluation of the prototype system, PREDICT (Predictive Risk-Based Evaluation of Dynamic Import Compliance Targeting) has been completed and the final pilot evaluation document is under review
- FDA has developed a rapid detection method using flow cytometry to identify E. coli and Salmonella in food. This system is being used in poultry processing facilities to detect and prevent bacterial contamination during food processing
- FDA has completed a three-year plan to increase state inspections and will hire at least an additional 130 employees to conduct food field exams, inspections and sample collections using FY 2008 appropriated dollars
- FDA plans to conduct an additional 327 state contract food inspection in FY 2009 over the FY 2008 estimate

- In FY 2009, FDA also will conduct an additional 20,000 food import field exams above the FY 2008 performance goal

RESPONSE.

- FDA is working with industry to identify best practices for traceability
- FDA is collaborating with other Federal agencies; State, Local, Tribal, and foreign governments and industry to develop the science and tools necessary to better understand the current risks of the food supply and to develop new detection technologies and improved response systems that rapidly react to food safety threats
- FDA issued a Request for Applications (RFA) for funding to establish state Rapid Response Teams to investigate food-borne illness outbreaks, perform trace backs of implicated foods and evaluate data from investigations to identify trends
- FDA is currently exploring the use of multiple and targeted channels to quickly alert consumers of a threat to food safety

Related Links.

To view all the accomplishments listed in the Food Protection Plan Progress Report:
www.fda.gov/oc/initiatives/advance/food/progressreport.html and the FDA's Food Protection Plan
www.fda.gov/oc/initiatives/advance/food/plan.html.
For additional information on FDA's activities under the Action Plan for Import Safety:
www.fda.gov/oc/initiatives/advance/imports/activities.html
Article link: http://www.infozine.com/news/stories/op/storiesview/sid/29190

German Firms Pull Out of Chinese Fluff Teddy Production

Berlin reported on July 7th 2008 that in the end, it was a sneaking suspicion that the eyes had lost their iconic melancholy look that made Steiff realize that if you want top-quality teddy bears, there's no place like home. Before that, it was the three-month wait for 80,000 cuddly white polar bears to arrive just as "Knut", Berlin zoo's real life star, was gracing the cover of Vanity Fair and demand was exploding.

For the German soft toy maker, which started life in the late 18ᵗʰ century before teddy bears were even called teddy bears, with a wheelchair-bound woman making elephant-shaped pincushions, trying to produce in China was no picnic. In an effort to cut costs, Steiff began outsourcing production to Chinese factories in 2004, and even sent 300 workers there to make sure the bears were up to scratch.

But this week, Steiff called time on its Chinese adventure!

"We are withdrawing from China step by step. For toys of high quality, China is simply not a reliable source," the Stuttgarter Nachrichten newspaper quoted chief executive Martin Freshen as saying.

But for this privately owned company, whose teddies sell for up to 120 euros (190 dollars) each, and which is trying to win back market share for its trademark bear with a button sewn into its ear, quality is everything. The multi-billion dollar toy industry has been at the forefront of the massive shift of manufacturing to China where it can pay workers a fraction of what it pays them in the west. Four out of five toys sold in Europe were made in a Chinese factory, and China exported 32 billion of them in 2006.

But problems with quality and a series of scares about safety has made firms a lot more wary. In the most high profile episode, U.S. toy giant Mattel recalled 21 million toys like Barbie dolls and Batman action figures last year over concerns about toxic lead paint and small magnets that children could choke on. Mattel admitted later its problems were down to design more than manufacturing flaws, and Chinese authorities have since tightened quality controls and have cracked down on factories producing dangerous toys.

But safety and quality problems remain, and stricter import laws are having the effect of reducing the cost of advantage of going east, firms say. "There are going to be new regulations in the European Union," said Ulrich Brobell from the German toymakers association DVSI, so it is set to be "easier and cheaper to manufacture in Germany or in nearby countries."

The story is the same in other industries, as textile firms attest.

"We are feeling that there is a movement in this direction," of "returning," Silvia Jungbauer from the industry's federation in Germany told AFP. "Geographical proximity is playing a predominant role again, quality too," Jungbauer said, and most importantly "costs in China have risen sharply in recent months."

Wages for Chinese workers are going up and up, and oil prices above 140 dollars (which has dropped since this report was made) a barrel are also making it significantly pricier for container ships full of Teddies and radio-controlled mini-helicopters to sail around the world.

Convincing Consumers Your Food is Safe

If you are like me, you have always enjoyed shrimp, have grilled it, ordered it in a restaurant, or sampled it as a party hors d'oeuvre. In June of 2007, the U.S. Food & Drug Administration temporarily halted the import of some Chinese shrimp and other fish (BusinessWeek.com, 6/28/07) because they contained carcinogens and antibiotics-probably the result of what they were fed in huge cramped fish farms. The FDA continues its "Import Alert," and as of April of 2008, had detained and tested nearly 3,000 shipments of aqua-cultured seafood from China, releasing less than half into the U.S.

China isn't the only exporter of shrimp to the U.S.-it comes from dozens of other countries-and I figure other countries use similar fish-farming techniques. The nonprofit Fishwise recommends sticking with U.S. farmed and wild shrimp only. Unfortunately, waiters in restaurants and the guys behind the fish counter generally don't know, or care, where the shrimp they scoop for you come from, and it's not considered good form to ask the host at a party where the shrimp platter originated. Easier just to do without.

Apparently I'm not alone in abstaining. Shrimp sales in the U.S. were off 7% last year, according to a report prepared by trade organization Infopesca for the U.N.'s Food & Agriculture Organization, with much of the decline coming in the second half of the year, apparently because of the FDA's action. But the July 7th edition of BusinessWeek truly covered this topic quite well.

Now consider this...what do you do if you're in the business of importing shrimp, and you've taken pains to ensure your shrimp isn't contaminated and you've had it certified as organically raised and free of chemicals and antibiotics? How do you let the marketplace know your product isn't like everyone else's?

That's the challenge facing John Battendieri, founder and CEO of Blue Horizon Organic Seafood, a three-year-old company that sells shrimp imported from special farms in Ecuador where, according to Battendieri, the shrimp is raised in pristine low-density conditions much different from most of the world's fish farms. "We know the folks who raise our shrimp personally," says Battendieri. "We can trace a bag of shrimp back to the pond in which it was grown."

While Blue Horizon has expanded its markets and sales to take advantage of the fears around Chinese shrimp, Battendieri thinks sales could be a lot better, except for two big problems associated with trying to sell eco-friendly shrimp. First, there are no official U.S. standards for organic fish, as there are for other organic foods, such as fruits and vegetables. In fact, California passed a law in 2005 that says, among other things, you can't label fish you sell as organic until federal standards for such labeling are set, and those are still a way off.

Second, you don't get much opportunity in the fish section of most supermarkets to explain what makes your fish special. That's because the supermarkets pretty much determine how the fish are displayed in the fish counter, and most don't provide a lot of background about where the fish came from or how they are raised.

To get around the organic-labeling problem, Blue Horizon uses respected outside organizations to certify its shrimp, such as Naturland, a German organic farming association. That helps in selling to stores, but still doesn't give you the "organic" label to put on the fish you sell to consumers.

Educating the Public

The case of tainted and polluted shrimp is a common matter now facing many companies such as Blue Horizon who is now shifting to selling more pre-packaged frozen shrimp, for which it has control of the packaging design and wording. "For us, the message is our product certification by three different certifiers to be free of the chemicals (that have been associated with Chinese shrimp), "says Battendieri. The company is also working to educate grocers so they'll provide consumers with more information about the distinctive qualities of his company's shrimp.

Guys behind the counter at supermarkets tend not to be interested in providing a lot of background where fish came from or how they are raised…and the fish buyer only sees a multi-colored flyer from Blue Horizon promoting "Certified Eco-Farmed Bulk Shrimp." And the consumer likely will only see a sign say "Shrimp - $12.99 lb."

Blue Horizon's attention to differentiating itself in a suspect crowd is paying dividends. Battendieri is expecting sales to at least triple in 2008, to $6 million or more, up from sales in 2007 of $2 million. Future growth "is all about education at this point," said Battendieri.

— 16 —

What's Worse...Tainted or Counterfeit Products???

Counterfeit products have long been widely available in Thailand, but the people responsible for their production, distribution and sale today are dealing with the same kinds of competitiveness problems as their legitimate peers. In the past, Thai counterfeit products were not only sold locally but also exported to other countries. Most of the products were low-tech, low quality and low priced.

Intellectual property (IP) rights were infringed, for example, by simply copying famous trademarks and applying them to low-quality products such as T-shirts and jeans. Infringing activities were straightforward. Counterfeit products were made in small factories, transferred to and kept in warehouses, distributed to retailers per order, and finally openly sold by retailers throughout the country.

Relatively recently, things have started to change. Fewer and fewer counterfeit products are being produced in or originate from Thailand. Cost benefits can be gained by outsourcing production to places where labor and material costs are lower than the local market. Thus, like mainstream industries, counterfeiters are relocating or outsourcing production to countries where there are clear cost benefits from doing so.

One such country is China, which also has the added advantage of having a massive market of its own, with a voracious appetite for counterfeit brand name goods. Millions of competitive counterfeit products are being produced in China and shipments are arriving in Thailand on a daily basis.

These Chinese fakes are very different from those made in Thailand in the old days.

They are much better in terms of quality and price per unit. Thus, those counterfeiters that did not outsource or relocate simply stopped producing their own goods and started to import cheaper ones from suppliers in China, among others. They had no option as they were no longer customers. This trend will be a huge problem for IP owners in the future because Chinese counterfeiters are now not only copying well-known brands, but also pirating the technology needed to produce more technologically advanced counterfeit products. It seems to be a catch 22 situation.

High-tech industries seeking cost benefits are outsourcing production overseas but in doing so are also having to transfer their technology to enable such production. This transferred technology appears to be falling into the hands of the counterfeiters, who then go to produce fake goods that compete directly with those produced by the originators of the technology. Sometimes you just can't win.

While the demand for counterfeit products in the Thai market has remained stable over the years...constantly high in other words...Thai people and tourists are focusing more on purchasing better quality and technologically more advanced produced, which are the same price or only slightly more expensive than the lower-quality products made locally. Thus, the more "traditional" Thai counterfeit products are being replaced by these better quality imports.

That is not to say that Thailand does not have a major role to play in the supply of counterfeits, just that it tends to have a greater focus on particular markets, namely, counterfeit low-end clothing, automobile and motorcycle parts and a few other items.

While the source of counterfeit products has changed as a result of market trends, economic feasibility and technical know-how, the methods of bringing those products to the market have also changed considerably. The whole counterfeit market and trade in Thailand is much better organized that it was. In the past, organization was very relaxed, if it existed at all. Now it is a well-oiled machine of illicit activity.

There is so much more to be gained and lost in the counterfeit business nowadays that infringers have had no alternative but to improve their organizational and business practices. Strategies have been introduced for maintaining sufficient inventory to meet demand while at the same time reducing the risk to the holder of the inventory.

Who would ever have thought that infringers would have started to use supply chain and inventory control economic models for carrying out their illegal activities? They may not know the correct terms to use for what they are doing, although some certainly do, but they assuredly are taking advantage of such business models.

Aside from counterfeit products, as much as the financial world comes to realize the extent of our economic woes and the possibility of catastrophic consequences, reports on the scope of the oil crisis are coming at bewildering speed, killing any hopes of share-market rises daily.

The suggestion that China may soon be dead in the water is so unthinkable that it should be imprintable. NOT SO FAST! Even the *Telegraph* in Australia reported that "Asia's exporters are suffering as global demand weakens," which quotes a Deutsche Bank estimating that 20% of China's low-end exporters will go belly-up this year. China's official inflation rate may be about 7.7% but it has started rolling back domestic subsidies for fuel-and fertilizer, the price of which has increased about 300% recently. The Chinese government has realized a bit late that its energy inefficiency puts it at a competitive disadvantage; ending the subsidies as seen as necessary to force businesses to become more efficient energy users. This will be a painful process.

Energy subsidies have disguised the damage. China has held down electricity prices, though global coal costs have tripled since early 2007. Loss-making industries are being propped up. This merely delays trouble. The true impact of the shock will only be revealed over time, as subsidies are gradually being rolled back. The Asian outsourcing game is coming to a close.

The China Watch...Problems in its Economy

You don't have to be an expert on Chinese economies or to have studied the statistics of a country to know what people expect to prophesize events and conditions in that region. In my opinion, and that of many journalists, documentary writers, financial consultants and investors, the Chinese economy will continue to grow for a bit and then slow down. At that point the Chinese economy will continue to be important in the world, but much of its current activity will shift southward to Indonesia and Vietnam.

This assumes of course, that catastrophes such as civil war or economic collapse do not occur. Then again, I think such things are possible but most likely are not going to happen. There is a parallel between China now and Japan and its economic boom in the 1980s. Other journalists like David Hirst says that China's days as the world's manufacturing base may be numbered.

As much of the financial world comes to realize the extent of our economic woes and the possibility of catastrophic consequences, reports on the scope of the crisis are coming at bewildering speed, killing any hopes of share-market rises daily.

The Dow, buoyed by the current falling oil prices was buffeted and continued to take water when Freddie Mac and Fannie Mae began to flounder. Those two organizations, if one can use the word loosely, are the bears' best friends, and a mention of them is enough to send the indices into troubled water.

But along with the publicized Bank of International Settlements reports, and apparently unreported outside of Europe, is an extremely dire study (on which the BIS reports may be partly based) that finds that banking losses have skyrocketed to US $1.6 trillion) with total debt of US $26.6 trillion, which has stunned European financial authorities.

And perhaps more frightening is a report published by the London Telegraph that China oil prices threaten the "blowing-up" of the Chinese economy and the demise of the Chinese economic model, as distance from markets threatens to impose a harsh tyranny. "The great oil shock of 2008 is bad enough for us," writes the Telegraph, citing some very solid sources. "It poses a mortal threat to the whole economic strategy of emerging Asia."

China's economic model is, like most economic models, based on oil prices far below what they are today. Even the ships that transport the basic goods to be assembled in China, and then freighted around the world are built assuming cheap oil. And its super-mass production relies on very slim profit margins. And, before we take heart in the hope of cheaper oil, China's banks, controlled as they are by the Communist Party, are not exactly models to follow, except for those elements in the U.S. Government that seem to be uncovering new and exciting ways to nationalize or socialize that country's banking system. Freddie Mac and Fannie Mae are likely starters for formalizing such, but more of that when we have digested the problems to Australia's north.

In Peter Huston's report on July 9th, he reported that a U.S. web site posted a translation of a German newspaper report from Marco Zanchi, a noted European writer and editor of Finaz und Wirtschaft of Zurich, commenting that his "dire" predictions for world markets had "echoes of Japan written all over it, with the spectre of zombie banks slowing the U.S. for years" unless its mess was cleared away.

The report, titled "The large financial crisis has just begun", opens with the statement: "Those that assume the misery is coming to an end are wrong. When it comes to write-downs, losses and raising fresh capital, the crisis has only just begun for banks. Losses are expected to reach $1.6 trillion, only a fraction of which have been uncovered."

"But that is not everything," the study continues. "While banks give their word of honor that no further capital is needed, the paper by Bridgewater Associates says: 'We have big doubts that financial institutions will be able to obtain enough new capital in order to cover the losses. This will worsen the credit crunch.'"

Along with news of the huge strains Vietnam is experiencing...I believe no share-market in history has, like Vietnam, fallen every day for a solid month...the news out of China might result in a blow to the lucky country's glass jaw. The Asian outsourcing game is over...it's not just about labor costs any more; distance costs money.

Now, other unexpected problems have risen to once again place the boom of China's exports to the U.S. and other countries in more jeopardy. We are talking about more recalls of beef, drugs and the link of Salmonella to tomatoes. But not all of the imports are from China as Mexico is running a close second. Still, the U.S. Government and the FDA as well as the people... the end users...are keeping a close watch on the imports coming from these countries and the purchasing of these products are beginning to show a major decline as people are becoming more aware and are afraid of getting sick and dying.

China may be poised to surpass the U.S. economy by the year 2035, and to double its size by 2050, as they are basing their booming economy on what is occurring today, its economy is likely to be sustained over the next two years before gradually declining to around three percent, the rate at which the U.S. economy is projected to grow over the same period, by 2070.

By then, however, China's economy, currently estimated at only about one-third of the U.S., will have built up such momentum that its total amount of gross domestic product (GDP) will reach the equivalent of nearly 180 trillion 2005 dollars, dwarfing the 80-trillion-dollar U.S. economy projected for the same year, according to the study, entitled "China's Economic Rise-Fact and Fiction."

And while important obstacles to that growth...including possible social unrest, corruption, and macro-economic mismanagement...clearly loom on the horizon, it is argued that China's leadership appears prepared to overcome them based on the record it has compiled in dealing with related problems, particularly over the past decade. Of course, the global implications of such an economic powerhouse are enormous and that China's financial clout alone will spill into every conceivable dimension of international relations.

China's high growth rates are more likely to be sustained, moreover, because it started at such a low level of development when it first implemented economic reforms in the late 1979s. Compared to Japan and South Korea, China is still at a relatively early stage of economic and political development. Unlike their two neighbors that protected their key industries at a comparable period in their development, the Chinese economy has been much more open to global competition, ensuring that leading sectors import and use the latest technology, thus enhancing their own competitiveness. By 2035, per capital GDP in China could reach about one third of U.S. GDP, and roughly one half as measured by Purchasing Power Parity (PPP).

Beef Recall Expands to 5.3 Million Pounds

MSNBC reported in the beginning of July that Nebraska Beef Ltd. expanded a recall announcement to include all 5.3 million pounds of meat produced for ground beef between May 16 and June 26, 2008. Federal investigators have linked Nebraska Beef's products to an outbreak of E. coli illnesses that has sickened 40 people in Michigan and Ohio. The USDA's Food Safety and Inspection Service said in a statement that these products may have been produced "under unsanitary conditions." Kroger Co. expanded its voluntary recall of some ground beef products to its stores in more than 20 states, saying the meat may be contaminated with E. Coli.

The nation's biggest traditional grocer also urged customers to check the ground beef in their refrigerators and freezers to determine whether it is covered by the recall. The warning comes as federal investigators try to pinpoint the source of a separate salmonella outbreak linked to tomatoes that has sickened nearly 900 people, raising more questions about the nation's food safety system. While insisting that tomatoes remain the leading suspect, investigators are looking at other produce but remain mum on exactly what vegetables are getting tracked.

Kroger indicated that as a precaution, it removed from stores all ground beef supplied by Nebraska Beef marked with sell dates of May 21 or later. "Ground beef in stores comes from other suppliers not involved in the recall," Kroger spokeswoman Meghan Glynn said.

The Cincinnati-based company initiated a recall June 25 for Kroger stores in Michigan and in central and northern Ohio. The expanded recall includes ground beef sold at Fred Meyer, QFC, Ralphs, Smith's, Baker's, King Soopers, City Markets, Hilander, Owen's, Pay Less and Scott's with overlapping sell-by dates from mid-May through mid-July.

In some stores, the recall included products in Styrofoam tray packages wrapped in clear cellophane or purchased from an in-store service counter. It did not include ground beef sold in 1-, 3-, or 5-pound sealed tubes or frozen ground beef patties sold in the frozen food section.

Kroger can track purchases by customers who use the company's loyalty card, which entitles customers to certain discounts. Sometimes those customers receive information about products the next time the card is used and a receipt is issued. In other cases, Kroger is able to call customers who used the loyalty card to purchase a tainted product, and it is doing that with the ground beef recall.

Symptoms of E. coli infection can include severe stomach cramps, diarrhea, vomiting and fever. It can potentially be deadly, but most people recover within five to seven days. Health officials urge people to thoroughly cook hamburger and, if possible, use a digital thermometer to make sure meat has been heated to at least 160 degrees. They also recommend that people wash their hands with warm water and soap for at least 20 seconds before and after handling food.

Consumers who have questions about the recall may contact Kroger toll-free at 800-632-6900 or online at http://www.kroger.com/recalls.

Salmonella Toll Tops 1,000; Peppers Perhaps Source… U.S. Rechecks Cause of Salmonella Outbreak… Experts See Flaws in Law

The *Associated Press* reported on July 9th 2008 in Washington that more than 1,000 people have become ill from Salmonella initially linked to raw tomatoes, a sobering milestone that makes this the worst food-borne outbreak in at least a decade. Adding to the confusion, the government is warning certain people to avoid types of hot peppers as well.

Certain raw tomatoes…red round, plum and Roma…remained a chief suspect and the government stressed that all consumers should avoid them unless they were harvested in areas cleared of suspicion. But people at highest risk of severe illness from salmonella also should not eat raw jalapeno and Serrano peppers, the Centers for Disease Control and Prevention urged during this epidemic. The most vulnerable are the elderly, people with weak immune systems and infants. Raw jalapenos caused some of the illnesses, conclude CDC investigators of two clusters of sick people who ate at the same restaurant or catered event.

But jalapenos cannot be the sole culprit-because many of the ill insist they didn't eat hot peppers or foods like salsa that contain them, CDC food safety chief Dr. Robert Tauxe told the Associated Press. As for Serrano peppers, that was included in the warning because they're difficult for consumers to tell apart.

In some clusters of illnesses, Jalapenos "simply were not on the menu," Tauxe said. "We are quite sure that neither tomatoes nor jalapenos explain the entire outbreak at this point, … We're presuming that both of them caused illnesses."

That has Food and Drug Administration inspectors looking hard for farms that may have grown tomatoes earlier in the spring and then switched to pepper harvesting, or for distribution centers that handled both types of produce. An ongoing investigation includes fresh cilantro, because a significant number of people who got sick most recently say they ate all three-raw tomatoes, jalapenos and cilantro.

"I understand the frustration" that after weeks of warnings, the outbreak isn't solved, Tauxe said. "But we really are working as hard and as fast as we can to sort out this complicated situation and protect the health of the American people."

"Added FDA food safety Chief Dr. David Acheson: "It's just been a spectacularly complicated and prolonged outbreak."

The outbreak isn't over, or even showing any sign of slowing, said Tauxe-with about 25 to 40 cases being reported a day for weeks now, to a total of 1,017 known since the outbreak began on April 10, 2008. Illnesses now have been reported in 41 states...and even four cases in Canada, although three of those people are believed to have been infected while traveling in the U.S. and the fourth is still being probed.

At least 300 people became ill in June, 2008 with the latest falling sick on June 26. Two deaths are associated with the outbreak-a Texas man in his 80s, and another Texas man who died of cancer but for whom salmonella may have played a role-and 203 people have been hospitalized.

The toll far surpasses what had been considered the largest food-bourne outbreak of the past decade, the 715 salmonella cases linked to peanut butter in 2006, Tauxe said. In the mid-1990s, there were well over 1,000 cases of cyclospora linked to raspberries, and previous large outbreaks of salmonella from ice cream and milk.

The CDC acknowledges that for every case of salmonella confirmed to the government, there may be 30 to 40 others that go undiagnosed or unreported. "The outbreak could actually be tens of thousands of people rather than 1,000 people," agreed Caroline Smith DeWaal of the consumer advocacy Center for Science in the Public Interest. "It's certainly a disturbing event to have this many illnesses spanning this many months."

Salmonella Probe Frustrates Top Health Official

At the same time the Health and Human Services secretary asked Congress for more funding and stronger legal powers for food import safety agencies. Former President Bush's administration's top health official expressed frustration that the salmonella outbreak from tainted tomatoes hasn't been solved as yet. More than 800 people have been sickened since April 2008, and investigators said that they were no closer to finding the cause.

Adding to tomato confusion, the government started to test numerous other types of fresh produce in the hunt for the source of the nation's record salmonella outbreak-even as it insisted that tomatoes remain the leading suspect. Investigators were mum on exactly what other vegetables are getting tracked.

Items commonly served with fresh tomatoes was the only hint Food and Drug Administration food safety chief Dr. David Acheson had given, calling it "irresponsible" to point a finger until he had more evidence that some other food really deserved the extra scrutiny. "Tomatoes aren't off the hook," he stressed. "It's just that there is clearly a need to think beyond tomatoes."

Still, Acheson widened FDA's probe, activating an emergency network of food laboratories around the country in anticipation of lots of additional samples to test. The reason is that the outbreak continues, with 869 people now confirmed having taken ill. Most troublesome, at least 179 of them fell ill in June, the latest on June 20, 2008. That is more than two months after the first salmonella illnesses appeared, meaning the outbreak was continuing weeks longer than food-poisoning specialists had expected-and suggesting the culprit was still on the market.

During the first week in July, disease detectives with the Centers for Disease Control and Prevention began interviewing people sickened in June to find out what they ate and to compare their diets with those of healthy relatives and neighbors. Officials wouldn't reveal early findings, except to say they supported the investigation's new move.

Among the possibilities FDA is exploring is whether tomatoes and other products are sharing a common packing or shipping site where both might become contaminated, or whether multiple foods might be tainted while being grown on adjoining farms or with common water sources.

Pressure is increasing on the FDA to solve the case, with the tomato industry suffering millions of dollars in losses and pushing for Congress to investigate how the agency handled the outbreak. But Acheson said that there's a growing misconception in the public that if tomatoes really were to blame, the outbreak would only have lasted six weeks. That's not true, he said, pointing to farms that rotate harvests so as to keep producing tomatoes for months.

Tomatoes first became a suspect because of what are called "case-control" studies rapidly conducted in New Mexico and Texas, the outbreak's center, CDC food-poisoning specialist Dr. Robert Tauxe said.

Those kinds of studies compare the sick to people who are otherwise similar-in income, lifestyle, where they live-but healthy. In those initial studies, about 80 percent of the ill reported eating certain types of fresh tomatoes, far more than the healthy group did, Tauxe said. Statistically, the association was too strong to think it a coincidence.

Some food-poisoning experts say the CDC missed a key step in not taking those studies a step further and trying to trace why some of the healthy ate tomatoes without harm.

For now, the FDA continues to urge consumers nationwide to avoid raw red plum, red Roma or red round tomatoes unless they were grown in specific states or countries that the agency has cleared of suspicion. You may find out data on this on the FDA's Web site: http://www.fda.gov.

Continuing under fire are tomatoes because they are usually sent through multiple repacking and distribution sites around the country, even to Mexico and back, regardless of where they're grown.

Even Health and Human Services Secretary Michael Leavitt expressed frustration that the case isn't solved. "Nothing happens fast enough when you have a problem like this," Leavitt said as he asked Congress for more funds and stronger legal powers for food and consumer safety agencies. Still, "I feel confident we will find the solution to this problem."

Acheson did follow up by saying that it is possible that tomatoes being harvested in states considered safe could be picking up salmonella germs in packing sheds, warehouses or other facilities currently under investigation. FDA inspectors spent many weeks chasing the best clues to date in the CSI-like hunt for the outbreak's source, but leads are growing cold.

Inspectors tested for traces of salmonella on farms in southern and central Florida and in three Mexican states, farms suspected to have harvested at least some of the tomatoes involved in the outbreak's earliest weeks. They also are following the path tomatoes took from along those farms to packing houses and other distribution stops, testing water supplies and equipment.

Salmonella bacteria live in the intestinal tracts of people and animals. Food outbreaks typically are caused by direct contamination with animal feces or use of contaminated water on foods eaten raw or not fully cooked. Fever, diarrhea and abdominal cramps typically start eight to 48 hours after infection and can last a week. Severe infection and death are possible if not treated.

The key message is to keep looking at all possibilities and to re-examine all of the information that may relate to packing houses that handled suspect tomatoes from Florida and Mexico may now be handling freshly harvested tomatoes. It becomes an on-going problem.

Drug Industry to Announce Revised Code on Marketing

On July 10th, the *New York Times* announced that the pens, pads, mugs and other gifts that drug makers have long showered on doctors will be banned from pharmaceutical marketing campaigns under a voluntary guideline. The industry's Code on Interactions with Health Care Professionals will ask the chief executives of large drug makers to certify in writing that "they have policies and procedures in place to foster compliance with the code." The code was written by the Pharmaceutical Research and Manufacturers of America, the industry's trade association.

But the code provides no definite limits on the millions of dollars spent on speaking and consulting arrangements that drug makers have forged with tens of thousands of doctors. Nor does it ban the routine provision of office breakfasts and lunches, or the occasional invitation to educational dinners at fancy restaurants.

"Informative, ethical and professional relationships between health care providers and America's pharmaceutical research companies are instrumental to effective patient care," said Richard T. Clark, chief executive of Merck and chairman of the trade association. Some industry critics praised the new rules.

"We've been pushing to see reforms like this for some time now," said Senator Herb Kohl, a Democrat from Wisconsin. "Consumers will undoubtedly be the beneficiaries of these industry changes." Mr. Kohl has co-sponsored a bill to require drug and medical device companies to publicly disclose payments to doctors of $500 or more.

Other critics dismissed the new rules, which are entirely voluntary. "It strikes me as an attempt to persuade people against doing anything that's serious," said Sharon Treat, executive director of the National Legislative Association on Prescription Drug Prices.

A growing number of states have passed or are considering legislation requiring drug makers to disclose payments to doctors. Minnesota has banned gifts to doctors valued at more than $50, including food; Massachusetts is considering a similar ban.

Earlier in 2008, Christopher A. Viehbacher, now president for North American pharmaceuticals at GlaxoSmithKline, wrote to Governor Deval Patrick of Massachusetts and Speaker Salvatore F. DiMasi of the state's House, suggesting his company might not invest as much in Massachusetts if "political development" worked to "devalue" its assets there.

Mr. Viehbacher said that the proposed gift ban would make Massachusetts "the most hostile state in the nation when it comes to biopharmaceutical sales."

But after years of opposing state efforts to require disclosures of payments to doctors, Pharmaceutical Research and Manufacturers of America recently announced support for the legislation to create the national registry of such payments, sponsored by Mr. Kohl and Senator Charles E. Grassley, a Republican from Iowa.

During the second week of July 2008, Attorney General William H. Sorrell of Vermont released that state's annual report on pharmaceutical marketing efforts. As in past years, the state found that drug makers gave more money to psychiatrists than to doctors in any other specialty. Eleven psychiatrists in the state received an average of $56,944 each.

Seven of the ten most marketed drugs in Vermont treat psychiatric conditions. The report found that 84 drug companies spent more than $3 million in the 2007 fiscal year to market their products in the state, a 33 percent increase over reported expenditures the year before.

The new marketing code requires drug makers to set annual limits on the amounts they will pay doctors to deliver educational lectures to colleagues, although the code does not specify what the limit should be. Such a cap will require drug makers to track across divisions the amounts paid to doctors, which could make complying with a national registry far easier.

The drug industry last updated its marketing code in 2002, when it banned "dine and dash" events in which drug makers provided free take-out dinners, Christmas trees and gas to doctors who agreed to listen to brief sales pitches. The earlier code also banned golf outings and free tickets to sporting events, bans which remain in effect. The new code takes effect in January.

But neither the earlier rules nor those expected to be announced apply to biotechnology or medical device makers, many of which continue to give expensive gifts and resort vacations to high-profile physicians.

Billy Tauzin, president of the drug industry trade association, said, "This updated code fortifies our companies' commitment to ensure their medicines are marketed in a manner that benefits patients and enhances the practice of medicine."

Solution to World Food Crisis Lies in Revealing Real Truths... While China's Farm Produce Trade Deficit Up 14.3 Times, China's Auto Import Growth Slows Down

As reported from Beijing in mid July 2008, the unrelenting rise in food prices has become a matter of grave concern for many countries. A recent report in the British newspaper The Guardian revealed a secret World Bank report which said that from 2002 to February 2008, food prices had risen by 140 percent, 75 percent of which was "contributed" by bio-fuels, thanks to vigorous promotions by the United States and the European Union (EU).

In contrast, increases in energy and fertilizer prices pushed up food prices by only 15 percent. The World Bank's conclusion sharply contradicts some nations' claims that higher demand from newly emerged markets such as India and China has led to higher food prices.

However, as different sides argue about the causes of the global food price hike, the World Bank report offers evidence on the true causes behind the international price surge. The severe impact of high food prices is being felt around the world, with some developing countries facing food shortages, hunger among the poor, increases poverty and social unrest. Uncovering the truth behind the food crisis is a step toward finding feasible solutions at an early date.

The World Bank report studied the food price movement in recent years, analyzing the connection between the food price surge and biofuels on a monthly basis. It came to the conclusion that the EU and the United States' drive for biofuels has had by far the biggest impact on food supply and prices.

On the other hand, the rapid income growth in developing countries had not led to large increases in global grain consumption and was not a major factor responsible for the large price increase, the report said. It is only logical that the results of a study by an institution such as the World Bank should be recognized by all parties concerned and fully employed to seek ways to resolve the food price crisis.

However, government officials, media and experts from some countries are bent on denying the huge impact of biofuels on world food prices, rather preferring to insist on exaggerating the effects of increasing food consumption by some so-called newly emerged markets. The explanation for such a reaction lies hidden in those nations' own interests.

The violent surge in oil prices on international markets has heavily burdened major import countries like the United States and the EU nations. They need to use their rich agricultural resources to switch to biofuels, so as to ease the cost burden of and reliance on imported oil. It also allows them to play the green energy card.

Therefore, they choose to refrain from mentioning the dire consequences of large-scale biofuel production. It could eat up global wheat and maize stocks, diminish food supply, push up food prices, and plunge millions into starvation. The rising food prices have already pushed some 100 million people across the world below the poverty line, the report estimated.

To reveal the truth behind the world food crisis is not aimed at seeking a scapegoat, but rather at uncovering the real picture and finding the real problems, so that corresponding solutions can be found. For example, biofuel itself is green energy and, as the World Bank report pointed out, some crops such as sugar cane can be used to manufacture biofuels, as Brazil does, without creating the risk of higher food prices.

But the United States uses almost one-third of its maize production and the EU about half of its vegetable oil production to make biofuels, while millions, most of them in developing countries, face starvation. The choice between filling up stomachs or filling up tanks could not be more obvious. The global food crisis needs a comprehensive and rational evaluation, so that its real causes are discovered, and practical solutions arrived at.

The article in the Guardian pointed out that the World Bank report was finished in April but was not published earlier to avoid embarrassing the U.S. government. On issues such as this, which are affecting the entire world, revealing the truth and informing the public must get top priority, so that people, governments and organizations can jointly look for feasible solutions to end the crisis.

Around the first of July, United Nations Secretary-General Ban Ki-moon called on the international community to take urgent steps to address the global food crisis. He has stated in a speech at the China Foreign Affairs University that the pledges of world leaders of 6 billion dollars in emergency aid to feed the poorest and to develop long-term solutions to the crisis must be reflected in immediate food assistance, as well as seed, fertilizer and irrigation for small-holder farmers in countries worst affected. He also stated that at a time of high energy and transportation costs, food production needed to be boosted in areas of hunger.

On July 13th, it was reported in Beijing, that China's trade deficit in agricultural products rocketed 14.3 times on the year-earlier level to 7.57 billion U.S. dollars in the first five months of this year, sources with the Ministry of Agriculture said. Foreign trade in agricultural amounted to 39.93 billion U.S. dollars in the five month period, a growth of 36.1 percent year-on-year.

The total included 16.18 billion dollars in export value, up 12.2 percent, and 23.75 billion dollars in import value, up 59.2 percent. The five moths saw the nation's net cereal exports decline drastically and trade deficit in animal by-products increase rapidly.

Between January and May, China exported 1.19 million tons of cereals, down 76.6 percent from the year-earlier level, but imported 911,000 tons, up 14.2 percent. The net exports stood at 276,000 tons, down 93.5 percent.

In the five months, 1.65 billion U.S. dollars worth of animal by-products were sold abroad nationwide, up 10 percent, while 3.28 billion dollars worth were imported, up 35.9 percent. The trade deficit was 1.63 billion dollars, up 78.6 percent.

Meanwhile, the country imported 3.58 million tons of edible vegetable oil, up 11.2 percent. The total included 1.13 million tons of soybean oil, up 7.6 percent, 98,000 tons of rapeseed oil, down 12.8 percent, and 2.33 million tons of palm oil, up 17.1 percent.

It was reported on July 13th from Beijing, the growth in China's auto imports slowed down in the first five months of 2008, thanks largely to a compulsory coding system for standardizing vehicle purchases from abroad, according to General Administration of Customs. The new import management system, which became effective in April, denies refitted and stolen motor vehicles access to the Chinese market.

Chinese customs said between January and May, China bought 171,000 motor vehicles from abroad, a growth of 59 percent of the same period last year. The arrivals were valued at 6.26 billion U.S. dollars, up 74.9 percent. The import growth rate, however, was 15.7 percentage points lower than the first quarter level.

The total imports included 71,000 motor vehicles bought from Japan, up 100 percent, and 57,000 from the European Union, up 54 percent. The growth rates were 19 percentage points and 13 percentage points, respectively, lower than the first quarter level.

The January-May period saw off-road vehicle imports soar 91 percent to 87,000 units nationwide, or 50.9 percent of the total auto arrivals. The growth rate was 32 percentage points higher than that for the total imports, while the proportion was up from the 42.4 percentage level, a year earlier. Car imports went up 29.6 percent to 65,000 units, or 38.2 percent of the total, down 8.7 percentage points.

…The Realities of China – U.S. Trade
The Realistic Effects of China Trade and Is Our Food Really Safe?

It was reported in the *Dissident Voice* by Jack A. Smith, editor of the Activist Newsletter and a former editor of the Guardian (US) radical newsweekly on July 16th , that China is being blamed by members of Congress and some labor leaders among others for the loss of good jobs in the U.S. and our country's enormous balance of payments (trade) deficit.

Much of the mass media uncritically echoes the views of the economic China bashers on these matters. But the business press, which is more inclined to level with its readers because their money is involved, is more nuanced on the question of jobs, the trade deficit, and the value of China's currency.

U.S. – China's trade is taking place within an economic construct championed and enforced by the U.S. through the World Trade Organization. China thus plays by American rules, or it would not be allowed in the game.

The rules are based on neo-liberal globalization, the contemporary modus operandi of American corporate capitalization and its bodyguard, the U.S. government. Neo-liberalism prefers a free trade orientation, deregulation of markets, privatization, and government non-interference. Globalization facilitates the current unprecedented internationalization of business. This is not to say Washington practices what it preaches. About neo-liberalism: it is quite interventionist on behalf of big business and protective of its trade when though necessary.

Corporate and financial wealth in the U.S. has one overriding objective: the acquisition of more wealth. Reducing the cost of labor is a key means of increasing profits.

Many years ago, owners of factories in New England closed shop and moved to the poorer, non-union South. In the current era, corporate leaders are moving throughout the world to take advantage of the lower wages paid in the post-colonial economies of developing Asia, Latin America and Africa. This window of opportunity will not last forever because workers in time are going to demand increasingly better compensation.

American multinationals operate in many such countries in quest of higher profits, and threaten to move elsewhere if wages rise. The largest number have been investing, building production facilities, and subcontracting to thousands of factories in China for over 20 years, all with Washington's encouragement and understanding that a byproduct of this policy would be an increase in the trade deficit. The move to China, and the great profits that the corporations earn there, was considered worth the higher deficit. As *Foreign Affairs* magazine commented in 2002:

"U.S. multinational corporations are using China as an export platform in the face of unrelenting global competition. An increasing percentage of the products these affiliates export from China is destined for the U.S. market. These goods count as Chinese exports to the United States – even though they are shipped by U.S. – owned entities – and they contribute to the ever-widening American trade deficit. European and Japanese multinationals are following a similar strategy of manufacturing in China for export, further adding to America's import bill from that country. Together, the delivery of U.S. goods through affiliates and the increasing use of the mainland as an export base by the world's leading multinational corporations could inhibit any significant improvement in the American trade deficit with China."

And of course it has. In 2007, the total U.S. trade deficit was $738.6 billion, a 9% decline from 2006 due to the weaker dollar (which increases demand for lower-priced American exports) and slowing economy. Some U.S. politicians convey the impression that China causes the entire deficit but about $400 billion of the 2007 total was because of ever increasing oil imports. By comparison, America's petroleum import bill was only $48 billion a decade ago. China accounted for $256.3 billion of the U.S. trade deficit in 2007.

At least 30% of the "Made in China" goods exported from that country to the U.S. actually are produced by subsidiaries of American multinational companies – and this accounts for a considerable portion of the deficit. (If American companies stayed in the U.S., and paid a decent wage, there wouldn't be a big China deficit, and many jobs would have remained back home, but corporate profits would be smaller.) Another chunk of the China deficit is from imports of goods manufactured by subsidiaries of corporations from other advanced capitalist economies.

These U.S. and foreign corporations make the big bucks. American consumers of modest income tend to get cheaper prices from items imported from China, in many cases to partially compensate for lower wages or joblessness. China benefits, but gets the blame in Congress and from some unions for "stealing" American jobs causing the deficit. The China bashers act as though our country's runaway corporations and a complicit Washington are innocent bystanders, and that it was not in the ingrained nature of capitalism to put profits before the needs of the people.

The anti-Beijing coterie suggests China doesn't buy American goods, but Commerce Secretary Carlos Gutierre recently called China America's "fastest growing market for U.S. exports." China would import more, but the de-industrializing U.S. now produces far fewer goods than yesteryear, and many of them made in America are not competitive. Look at how the mighty U.S Auto industry deflated its own tires. In addition, a range of costly high technology items that Chinese buyers want to purchase are withheld for "national security" reasons.

China's critics attribute some of the deficit to Beijing's undervalued currency, the yuan. According to Ramapo College (NJ) professor Behzad Yaghmaian in early May, 2008: "Conceding to American pressures, China relinquished the decade-long policy of pegging the yuan to the dollar in July 2005. The yuan rose by more than 5% in the first year, 12% by the end of 2007, and 14.3% by March, 2008. Meanwhile, the trade deficit with China continued to swerve more than 15% percent."

The U.S. wants China to increasingly strengthen the yuan, but Beijing responds that it must proceed gradually with its own economy stumble. The stronger the yuan, the tighter the profit margins for a multitude of small and medium export-oriented Chinese companies, causing reductions in wages and layoffs at a time when the Communist Party is already concerned about worker protests.

On June 5, 2007 the *PRC Customs Administration* reported that for the first time in five years, "China's trade surplus is likely to shrink in 2008." It fell 7.9% in the first four months of 2008 against a similar period in 2007. One of the factors was a "clear acceleration" in the value of the yuan against the dollar, plus increased global protection and a reduction in exports to the U.S. due to the apparent recession. The agency also forecast China's "imports" to keep picking up speed. This will result in a reversal of the swift growth in the trade surplus and in the trade imbalances." In the wake of the American financial downturn, the European Union has now become China's latest export market.

A significant problem behind the trade deficit is that the U.S. is simply spending much more money on importing than it has in the bank, and its trading partners (China and Japan mainly) have been lending Washington great sums of money for deficit financing. Much of America's consumer and government spending is based on debt as well, and it is one of the symptoms of our country's decline.

As far as jobs and wages for American workers are concerned, big business for the last few decades, has been carrying out a campaign to eviscerate the labor movement, to deprive workers of the fruits of increased productivity, to lower wages and benefits, and to oppose government intervention on the side of the working class/lower middle class and the poor. Shifting jobs overseas and turning the screw ever tighter on American workers at home is what's causing job loss, not China.

As Business Week wrote a few years ago, "One reason politicians are whipping themselves into a frenzy over China is because it's an easy way to explain the constant din of layoff announcements that show little sign of slowing. Much of America's industrial base that has not gone abroad for super profits has failed to keep up with the foreign competition (except in the production and export of weapons of war, where the U.S. is without peer). As progressive writer James Petras wrote a couple of years ago, "China bashing is merely a response to the loss of competitiveness. Nationalist demagogy in a declining global power is a compensatory mechanism."

Contrary to many of the arguments seeking to blame China for some of the problems afflicting the U.S. economy and American workers, we think such difficulties were generated within our country's capitalist system itself, compounded by the policies of neo-liberalism and corporate globalization.

As reported in the middle of July of 2008 before any of the bailouts actually did occur, the announcement by US Treasury Secretary Henry Paulson together with Federal Reserve Chief Bernanke, that the US Government will bailout the two largest guarantors of housing mortgage debt-the Fannie Mae and Freddie Mac-far from calming financial markets, has confirmed what had been said repeatedly: **"The Financial Tsunami which began in August 2007 in the relatively small "sub-prime" high risk US mortgage securitization market, far from being over, is only gathering momentum. As with the Tsunami which devastated Asia in wave after terrifying wave in December 2004, is a low amplitude, long-wave phenomenon of trillions of dollars of financial securities being unwound, defaulted on, dumped on the market. But the scale of the latest wave to hit, the collapse of confidence in the two Government-Sponsored Entities, Freddy Mac and Fanny Mae, is a harbinger of worse to come in what will be the most devastating financial and economical catastrophe in the United States history. The impact will be felt globally."**

'And guess what, for two months, no...two years, the government under the leadership of President Bush did not keep us in the loop. They tried to hide the obvious! Then they tried to force the bailout down our throats!'

The United States economy may only be in the early phase of its worst housing price collapse since the 1930's. No end is in sight. Fannie Mae and Freddie Mac, as private stock companies, have gone to excesses in leveraging their risk, most as many private banks did. The financial market bought the bonds of Fannie Mae and Freddie Mac because they bet that the two were "Too Big To Fail,' i.e. that in a crisis the Government, that is the U.S. taxpayer, would be forced to step in and bail them out.

The two, Fannie Mae and Freddie Mac, either own or guarantee about half of the $12 trillion in outstanding U.S. home mortgage loans, or about $6 trillion. To put that number into perspective, the entire 27 member states of the European Union in 2006 had annual GDP of slightly more than $12 trillion, so $6 trillion would be half of the GDP of the combined European Union economies, and almost three times the GDP of the Federal Republic of Germany.

In the meantime, the Buffalo News and Dallas Morning News reported that Day after day, Mexican trucks line up as far as the eye can see for entry into the United States at the world Trade Bridge, carrying everything from raw tomatoes, broccoli and fresh basil to frozen seafood. They also bring in salmonella, listeria, restricted pesticides and other food poisons.

The United States is getting it from both ends...financially and economically...from the banks and mortgage holders to the exporters who don't care who gets hurt, sick and may just die.

Customs and Border Protection officers take less than a minute per truck to determine which products enter the country and find their way into grocery stores and restaurants. Most trucks are waved through. The avalanche of imported goods-especially food from Mexico-is too much for the limited number of inspectors at the nation's 300 ports of entry to effectively screen, critics say. And the sheer volume makes it impossible for them to carry out their mission: protecting the U.S. food supply and American consumers. In essence, we are getting screwed either way.

Concerns about the nation's food inspection system are gaining urgency-especially as the U.S. Food and Drug Administration looks at Mexico as a likely source of salmonella-tainted produce that has sickened more than 800 people in the last two months. The FDA last month sent inspectors to three Mexican states-Jalisco, Sinaloa and Coahuila-and Florida to check farms and packing plants.

The great majority of the food that crosses the Southern U.S. border is safe, officials say. But they acknowledge that a surge in imports in recent years means that the system of border inspections is badly strained and in urgent need of repair.

Inspectors at the border are tasked with enforcing hundreds of regulations from more than 40 government agencies. And just a tiny percentage of agricultural products, seafood and manufactured goods is actually inspected, critics say.

"We have this huge growth in imports, this huge growth in trade; at the same time we have severely cut back on our regulatory agencies and their ability to do their job, especially the food portion of the Food and Drug Administration," said Jean Halloran, director of food policy initiatives for Consumers Union, which publishes Consumer Reports magazine.

"If they are only checking 1 percent of the stuff and finding lots of problems, then...there are a lot of problems that are never caught," she said.

What is getting stopped, critics say, is representative of what is getting through. Overall, about 15 percent of the U.S. food supply and 60 percent of fresh fruits and vegetables consumed are imported, according to the U.S. Department of Agriculture's Economic Research Service.

Mexico is the second-largest foreign source of agricultural products and seafood for the United States-moving to number 1 during the winter months and filling about 60 percent of the supermarket produce aisle. And it's the worst offender when it comes to food shipments turned away at the border by U.S. inspectors, a review of food rejections shows.

China's Christmas-toy Industry Suffered After Olympic Visa Crackdown

In Yiwu, a city that makes Christmas Kitsch for the West, trade has slumped as a result of the government security drive.

Jin Zhixun sits alone in a booth stuffed from floor to ceiling with plastic Father Christmases climbing walls, playing saxophones and dangling from parachutes. The foreign buyers, who used to snap up 50,000 Santas at a time, are nowhere to be seen. He cannot remember a worse year. This has nothing to do with it being a steamy 37C (100F) outside, and about as un-Christmassy as you could imagine. It is because of the Olympic Games.

Mr. Jin's problems are shared by the hundreds of booths selling Christmas goods-plastic trees, decorations, tinsel, stockings, inflatable snowmen-that stretch away down labyrinthine corridors in one of the ten vast multi-storied halls of the world's biggest, small commodities market (the Christmas booths run out where the red lanterns of the Chinese New Year section start). Each of these booths is a wholesale shop-front for a factory somewhere in the teeming metropolises of eastern China, and in July and August they would normally be packed with Western buyers.

In the summer of 2008 however, the buyers were scarce because China had cracked down on foreign visitors lest they disrupt the Olympics. Indeed, the West faces a shortage of kitsch this Christmas because the bulk of its decorations and many of the cheap toys exported from China are bought in Yiwu, and unless the orders would be placed during these months, it would be too late. July and August came and went. The expected orders were not placed. Mr. Jin, 31, complained: "Normally, there are many foreigners. This year, there are very few."

Among those who had inspected the Christmas stock were a New Zealand couple who had slipped in with tourist visas and a Russian lady, Dasha Shaykhutdinova, whose multiple entry visa was issued before the crackdown. Colleagues back home were still waiting in vain for single-entry visas, she said.

"Beijing Welcomes the World" was one of the original Olympic slogans, but after the spring's violent protests over Tibet and some unspecified terrorist threats, it appeared to have been supplanted by a new one: "Olympics Without Incident."

The authorities were determined that nothing would disrupt China's great coming-out party-certainly not troublesome foreigners. Since April before, they had virtually stopped giving multiple-entry visas, or the six-month "investor" visas used by teachers, artists and freelance writers. They had made it far more difficult for businessmen and tourists to secure 30-day, single-entry visas by demanding letters of invitation, proof of hotel bookings and return tickets. Foreigners already living in China have been subjected to spot checks at home or in the streets. Thousands-especially students-have been forced to leave the country after being denied extensions to their residence or work permits.

The Olympic organizers had even issued a nine-page book of rules warning foreigners against "Illegal gatherings, parades and protests", "shouting or displaying of political or religious slogans at events" and the import of materials "harmful to China's politics, economics, culture and morals". The consequences of the crackdown were apparent widely. Hotel occupancy rates in Beijing, Shanghai and other cities had fallen sharply.

In May, there were 14 per cent fewer foreign visitors to the capital, and Beijing's hotels were far from full, even during the games. Business meetings, seminars, and conferences had been cancelled. Western quality control and factory inspectors were not able to enter the country. Language schools had lost teachers and students. Foreign chambers of commerce had protested vigorously but to no avail. The Foreign Ministry insisted that the restrictions were necessary to keep out "hostile forces" and were no worse than those of Western countries.

For China's rulers, the success of the Olympics was paramount and if that hurt cities such as Yiwu that depend entirely on foreign trade-so be it. Yiwu, 200 miles (320km) southwest of Shanghai, was a rural village until the 1980s. But thanks to its road and rail links, and it proximity to the ports of Shanghai and Ningbo, it took off after the local authorities set up an open-air market in 1982.

Today, Yiwu has a population of more than a million living in endless rows of new apartment blocks, and if China is the factory of the world, this city has become its showroom. Here, about 60,000 vendors flaunt an estimated 400,000 items in 1,700 categories to buyers from 180 nations. It is reckoned that at least 1,000 container-loads of goods are shipped out daily and about 7,000 foreign businessmen have set up shop in the city.

Half are from the Middle East, including many Iraqis who have fled the violence of their homeland. An empty clothing factory is now a giant mosque. In a district dubbed "Exotic Street" there are Jordanian, Egyptian and Iraqi restaurants, signs in Arabic, women in headscarves and men cooking kebabs or drinking sweet, black tea on the pavements.

The crackdown on foreigners has affected everyone in Yiwu. "It's getting more and more difficult," complains Hussein Abdulihim, 25, as he watches Arabic television in the largely empty Alazem restaurant, which he opened after a bomb killed 60 people outside his Baghdad restaurant. Hotels and taxi drivers lament the lack of foreign custom. Export agencies are sending out fewer containers. Language schools have lost foreign students.

It is particularly bad for vendors of Christmas goods such as Mr. Jin. By September, when the Olympics were over, it was too late for the factories to fulfill new orders and ship the goods to Western shops in time for the Christmas rush. Dong Shaochen, 36, whose tinsel factory in Tianjin has cut its workforce by a third, said: "We have 50 percent fewer customers than last year."

Li Siyi, who sells remote-controlled cars and helicopters for a factory in Guangdong province, added: "Our imports are down about 60 per cent."

Rois Zhang, 19, sat in a booth stuffed full of ceramic dolls-all with Western features. Her factory, Maiqimoppet, had halved its workforce, she said. Thanks to the Olympics, she added, "there will be fewer Chinese dolls in Western shops this Christmas."

But here is the curious thing: nobody really minds. The people of Yiwu, like Christmas people everywhere, are immensely proud that their country was staging the games.

Mr. Jin said: "It's the big wish of 1.3 billion Chinese to have the Olympics. It's something that happens every thousand years, if the West has fewer Father Christmases this year, it's worth it."

On China and What the World Didn't See During the Olympics...
From arrests to surface-to-air missiles

- Chinese authorities detained 82 suspected terrorists in Xinjiang in 2008 who, they claimed were planning to attack the Olympics
- Five Uighur separatists were killed in Urumqi as part of an operation to foil an attempt to sabotage the Olympics
- 1,500 members of the Falun Gong spiritual movement have been detained in China in the run-up to the games, the group claimed in April
- Close to 1,000 Tibetans were arrested in Lhasa in March as protests in the city turned violent. Tibetan exiles claimed as many as 100 people were killed

- After the earthquake in Sichuan province in May, the Government tried to stifle criticism by parents whose children had been killed when schools collapsed. Police prevented parents and journalists accessing the schools, and broke up protests
- Both China and Nepal banned climbers from ascending Mount Everest as the Olympic torch was taken to the summit in May. Details of the ascent were kept secret due to fears of sabotage attempts
- Surface-to-air missiles had also been installed around Olympic venues as part of a 100,000-strong counter-terrorism operation, which included large cash rewards for tip-offs about terrorist plots

Speaking philosophically, we as a nation love to worry, don't we? In the 1970s, it was the fear that Russia (well, back then it was referred to as the USSR) was going to bury us as we decayed morally and depended dearly upon easily-interrupted foreign oil-of which the Russians had supposedly unlimited quantities.

In the 1980s it was Japan, Inc. Japan was buying American. The Chicken Littles in the U.S. ran around squawking that the sky was falling because Japan's inherently organized society, its keiretsu, its cooperation between government, industry, and banks, and its automation workforce were so much better than the U.S. Why, it was an unstoppable juggernaut. Remember when the Japanese investors were stupid enough to buy a hotel they had to get $600 per room per night for...in 1980s dollars...and have 88% occupancy just to break even? It was predicted then that they would sell it back to Americans at 50 cents on the dollar. But guess what...they sold it back to Americans at 28 cents on the dollar.

With the silly certainty of hindsight, many scoff at both notions as if we've learned so much since then. No, we have not! The same people scoffing now were buying up copies of Japan, Inc...titled books just a few years ago. And the new bogeyman is China. If you believe the press, China, with over a trillion U.S. dollars in their coffers, is going to buy up all our oil companies (indeed, has already bought many Canadian ones), will be a peer military rival, will be the economic leader of the 21st century, and will eclipse American as a world leader...especially having Obama as the new president. So they think!!!

But wait! Hold the phone!

China, like every nation, has prospects...and problems. Too many people, and way too many investment advisers, are putting the cart before the horse, looking only at China's potential and none of the pitfalls and pratfalls. This had never been more evident than the media picture that emerged during the Olympic games. But the Olympic games did, in fact, change many things.

China's pre-emptive grab recently for Unocal is an object lesson in China's strategy to dominate the world's energy supplies...if it ain't nailed to the floor, China will scoop it up. The reports from Brazil, Venezuela and the Northwest territories of Australia have been dense and many inches thick, but the bottom line in each case had been summarized as follows: There's not a ship leaving these three areas that isn't headed for a Chinese port...and we are making money hand-over fist from China's determined attempt to ransack the world for energy...Brazil has been turning 60% of its sugar crop into ethanol for the China market. Venezuela started to break ties with the U.S. and diverting its tankers to the East...to all of which we say is "Horse-feathers!"

Every battle, every scourge, every advance, every strategic retreat, is subject to a myriad of factors that can radically change the outcome. The key to all of this is the fact that China has 1/5 of the world's population. If life were fair, it would 1/5 of the world's water. It doesn't...of course. China has just 1/14 of the world's water supplies, and much of that is rank, dank, and polluted, increasing population will not help...yet you think oil is important? Try living without water. Or with water too polluted to drink.

Thanks to *Earth Trends Country Profiles*...we can compare the amount of Internal Renewable Water Resources (IRWR) on a per person basis from country to country. Even with some of the world's most powerful rivers, China has just 2,173 cubic meters IRWR per person. By contrast, Japan, also a rather densely populated nation, has 3,372 cu M per capita, and Vietnam has 4,568.

Russia has a surfeit of riches with 30,001 (with much of this concentrated in Siberia just north of an expansionist China...). The U.S. has nearly 10,000... not bad, considering we are ransacking the aquifers that took millions of years to fill in order to create false oases in the desert so this generation can have swimming pools in Las Vegas and Phoenix. With this kind of developer-fueled profligacy, our grandchildren will reap the dust-bowl rewards. But, for now, we are whistling past the graveyard.

Water is essential to life...and China walks a thin line keeping enough of it flowing. In order to grow, it also needs oil...and most estimates say China's currently-known fields, all in decline, will run dry in the next 15 years, meaning they will have to import somewhere close to 100% of their oil. China produces the most coal of any country, mitigating its imports of oil and gas...but it is a distant third to the U.S. and Russia in terms of coal reserves. It's burning reserves at an incredible rate...and that leads to another major problem in China: massive environmental degradation. Add to this the crushing burden of over-population, the wrenching rural poverty, the flight to cities unprepared to provide basic services, and the massive unemployment, which leads to political unrest and political corruption as all jockey for guangxi (connections).

Now, a clearer picture emerges. China is a nation with great potential... and equally great pitfalls in terms of water, oil, coal, the environment, population displacement, health care and a host of others. To navigate a course to the future will require skill, intellect, and a massive infusion of good luck and foreign capital. Many companies headquartered in the U.S. and other markets will benefit. For starters, look with hungry eyes at some of the beaten-down infrastructure giants that have the wherewithal to provide the massive engineering efforts that China will need to engage in as they repatriate some of those dollars like General Electric, Microsoft, General Motors and Wal-Mart.

China's Economic Growth Cools to Slowest Since 2005... China Loses its Competitive Edge in Clothing and Other Areas

Bloomberg reported in July 2008 that China's economy grew at the slowest pace since 2005 in the second quarter, prompting speculation the government will slow the yuan's gains to protect export jobs. Gross domestic product rose 10.1 percent from a year earlier, down from 10.6 percent in the first quarter, as exports weakened and the government curbed lending. Consumer prices rose 7.1 percent in June 2008, slowing from 7.7 percent in May.

The yuan fell 0.2 percent, against the dollar, paring a 7 percent advance in 2008 that made it Asia's best performer. Some Chinese officials were pressing for slower currency appreciation in July of 2008 to protect jobs as cooling global demand threatened to trigger a slump in shipments from the world's fastest-growing major economy. "A slowing pace of appreciation would have meant breathing room for the export sector," said Jing Ulrich, JPMorgan's chairwoman of China equities. As things started to change in July, the yuan closed at 6.8213 against the dollar in Shanghai. Recession was on the rise. The world was going to experience a huge downturn.

GDP growth cooled for the fourth straight quarter. The median estimate of 18 economists surveyed by Bloomberg News was for a 10.3 percent expansion. The U.S. economy grew 2.5 percent in the first quarter.

Up to this point, China's growth was still the fastest of the world's 20 biggest economies and was helping to sustain the global expansion in 2008 as a housing slump and credit-market turmoil started to threaten to send the U.S. into a recession.

"This was considered to be an orderly slowdown, not a dramatic one," said Kevin Lai, a Hong Kong-based economist with Daiwa Institute of Research. But things were getting a lot worse.

The trade surplus for the second quarter narrowed 12 percent from a year earlier to $58.14 billion as import costs climbed and U.S. demand faltered. Expert prospects had deteriorated, with Federal Reserve Chairman Ben S. Bernanke having said in July of 2008 that the U.S. faced 'significant downside risks to the outlook for growth.' But the "Fit didn't Hit the Sham' until September when Bernanke, Paulsen and Bush asked for a $700 billion bailout, which became a disaster as every bank, car company and government agency wanted a piece of the action.

Rising prices, constraints on agricultural output, lagging rural incomes and global financial market turmoil became problems for China's economy, and the Ministry of Commerce had urged China's cabinet to rein in currency gains and raise some export rebates. The yuan would gain only another 2.6 percent against the dollar by year end, according to the median estimate of 26 currency analysts surveyed by Bloomberg. It had risen 21 percent since the government scrapped a fixed exchange rate in July 2005.

Most textile companies were unprofitable in the first five months of 2008, and as many as 45 million workers had been earning their livings in export-oriented sectors. The salespeople had cried out that "We will all be dead if the government doesn't increase tax rebates and slow the appreciation."

Inflation may have eased from February's 12-year high of 8.7 percent on smaller gains in food prices but it still remained above the central bank's 4.8 percent annual target and rising commodity costs would surely keep the prices elevated. Morgan Stanley had raised its inflation forecast for the year to 7 percent from 6.5 percent, citing the likelihood of energy-price increases. Besides using the currency to cool inflation, China had imposed lending quotas and ordered banks to set aside a record 17.5 percent of deposits as reserves to soak up cash flooding the economy from trade, foreign direct investment and investors betting on gains by the yuan. The central bank hadn't raised interest rates in 2008 to avoid attracting capital inflows. The China Banking Regulatory Commission had warned against higher bank reserve requirements because they had already damaged the industry's ability to repay debt.

Government efforts to boost consumption at home started to pay off. Retail sales rose 23 percent in June from a year earlier, the fastest pace since at least 1999. Urban disposable incomes rose 14.4 percent to 8065 yuan for the first half from a year earlier. Rural cash incomes rose 19.8 percent to 2528 yuan. The surprising thing had been the strength of the domestic economy... consumers still had a lot of cash and in that sense it was difficult to be too pessimistic about the domestic economy. Investment jumped amid rebuilding after the Sichuan earthquake in May and they would try to keep the economy growing at 10 percent even if there was going to be a sharp slowdown elsewhere in the world.

But China started to lose its competitive edge in textiles and clothing and started to face mounting costs on several fronts. In the first quarter of 2008 alone, U.S. apparel imports from China declined by nearly 10% compared with the corresponding period of 2007, reaching U.S. $4.43bn. In terms of China's currency, the renminbi, the fall was an even greater 17%.

China's drop in competitiveness had stemmed from mounting costs on several fronts. Apart from higher costs of energy and raw material...which manufacturers face all over the world ... Chinese textile mills faced greater costs in having to comply with growing environmental legislation. At the same time, Chinese apparel factories had to cope with new regulations on working conditions.

Furthermore, firms wishing to invest were finding it harder to obtain finance as the Chinese authorities had tightened credit in a bid to limit inflation...Chinese exporters had been hit by lower export tax rebates. Labor costs became a particularly serious issue for Chinese firms. At least seven major exporting countries in Asia were now offering lower labor costs than China.

Apparel exporters in Vietnam and Pakistan were able to benefit from labor costs as low as US $0.38 and US 0.37 an hour, respectively, whereas China's labor costs started to reach US $1.08 an hour in certain areas of the country's coastal provinces. In Cambodia, labor costs were only US $0.33 an hour, and in Bangladesh they got as low as US $0.22 an hour.

Victim of its Own Success...

In many ways, China had become a victim of its own success. Rising wages were a direct consequence of the economic boom in the country, especially in coastal regions where it was easier to export goods to the world's major markets. The boom also led to upward pressure on China's currency, the *renminbi*.

Although the Chinese authorities had not taken the risk of allowing the currency to float freely, they have accepted that it is not possible to keep a lid on it. On July 21, 2005 they unpegged the renminbi from the US dollar and since then its value had been allowed to increase by about one fifth. As a result, the U.S. market had become less lucrative for Chinese suppliers.

The fall in competitiveness of Chinese apparel exporters could not have come at a worse time.

Their problems have been compounded by poor economic conditions in the U.S. market where the subprime lending crisis has had a knock-on effect on the housing market, on consumer confidence and on the economy as a whole.

During the first quarter of 2008, U.S. consumer expenditures on clothing and footwear (on an annualized basis) were 0.2% lower than in the first quarter of 2007-after growing by 3.7% in 2007, 4.5% in 2006 and 5.1% in 2005.

One of the main beneficiaries of the drop in U.S. imports from China is Vietnam.

In the first quarter of 2008, sales of Vietnamese apparel in the U.S. market were up by over 30% compared with the corresponding period of 2007. As a result, Vietnam increased its share of the U.S. import market significantly during that period.

Chinese exporters are expected to enjoy a brief resurgence in the U.S. market in the first quarter in 2009, after safeguard quotas have been removed by the U.S. authorities at midnight on 31 December 2008. Admittedly, the quotas affect only 34 product categories but many of these products sell in large volumes and China had already proved that the will be supplying them.

Basically, like the United States had started to lose its Yankee Ingenuity, it is now safe to say that China is losing its competitive edge in Textiles and clothing, as well as other products. The reports during the middle and latter part of 2008...and with the recession hitting all countries plus a stock market that had been cut in half, losing trillions...are becoming increasingly common.

It should be noted that "A rising yuan (renminbi) and higher raw material and labor costs are negatively affecting China's competitiveness.

WELCOME TO CAPITALISM!!!

– 17 –

Enough to Make You Sick:
Most Imports Are Not Inspected

As reported in *Reporternews' Health Search* on July 26th, 2008, the FDA may have the responsibility for overseeing the safety of all domestic and imported food with the exceptions of meat, poultry and eggs. But are they truly looking after our well-being per se? Let's look at the mission of the FSIS, the CDC and the EPA and see what is really going on here.

The United States Department of Agriculture Food Safety and Inspection Service: The mission of FSIS is to serve as "the public health agency in the U.S. Department of Agriculture responsible for ensuring that the nation's commercial supply of meat, poultry, and egg products is safe, wholesome, and correctly labeled and packaged."

The Centers for Disease Control and Prevention Office of Food Safety: The Foodborne Disease Outbreak Response and Surveillance Team conducts national surveillance on food-borne infections and outbreaks of food-borne illness.

The Environmental Protection Agency: The Office of Prevention, Pesticides and Toxic Substances is charged with protecting public health and the environment from potential risk of pesticides and toxic chemicals.

Sources: USDA, FDA, Trust for America's Health Web sites.

From spinach to tomatoes, every few years a new food-related health concern sends government officials and private individuals scurrying for solutions. A 2007 poll by consumer group Trust For America's Health found that 67 percent of Americans are worried about food safety...ranked higher than concerns about pandemic flu, biological or chemical terrorism, and natural disasters. And there is cause for concern.

About 76 million Americans...one in four...are sickened by food-borne illnesses every year, according to the organization. Much attention in investigations such as the recent salmonella outbreak is given to the quality and standards of imported foods, which make up 15 percent of food consumed in the United States.

Each year, the average American eats about 260 pounds of imported foods. The Associated Press reported in 2007. But only about 1 percent of imported foods the Food and Drug Administration oversee...including fruits and vegetables...is inspected, according to Trust for America's Health. An estimated 85 percent of known food-borne illness outbreaks are associated with FDA-regulated food products, compared with 15 percent of such outbreaks being associated with meat, poultry and eggs-items regulated by the U.S. Department of Agriculture's Food Safety and Inspection Service.

"We need to recognize that Americans are getting 13 to 15 percent of their diet from imported food products," said Sarah Klein, staff attorney with the Center for Science in the Public Interest's food safety program. "When you think about how much that is, and how little the FDA is inspecting, it is somewhat alarming."

The FDA regulates $417 billion worth of domestic food and $49 billion worth of imported food each year, according to its Web site. Questions sent to the FDA were not immediately answered. The organization has been systematically stripped of the funding it needs to adequately oversee food safely, Klein said.

The FDA's Center for Food Safety and Applied Nutrition has lost 20 percent of its science staff and about 600 inspectors in the past three years, according to TFAH's April 2008 report, "Fixing Food Safety: Protecting America's Food Supply From Farm-to-Fork.."

The organization has 1,700 field inspectors, versus 7,600 for the USDA, and the FDA's budget for fiscal year 2007 was $563 million, versus the USDA's $1.02 billion. Patty Lovera, assistant director for consumer group Food & Water Watch, said that while for years her group has focused on the USDA, the FDA is responsible for much more of the U.S. food supply, both imported and exported.

"We have a split system, and many people are shocked when they realize how much the FDA doesn't do," she said. "Many more people are familiar with the concept that the USDA is in there. That's their legal mandate...to be in the plants."

The FDA relies solely on point-of-entry inspections of imported food. The USDA, on the other hand, works with the importing establishments' governments to verify that other countries' regulatory systems for meat, poultry and egg products, are equivalent to that of the U.S. and that products entering the U.S. are safe.

The FDA's inspection requirements are company-specific, meaning companies must register with the FDA before importing food products. The USDA is in many ways "doing a much better job than the FDA," but the organization also imports fewer products and has more resources, Klein said. The United States Department of Agriculture inspected about 16 percent of imported foods in fiscal 2006. The Associated Press reported last year.

There are inherent difficulties in dealing with any agricultural products from other nations, Lovera said. "If you're talking about things like salmonella in produce, chances are you're talking about something that was spread through contaminated water," she said. "That's an example of a challenge in other countries."

Items such as fish have an enormous number of challenges, including being kept at the proper temperature. "There are logistical issues in just moving some of this stuff around the planet and keeping it at the temperature it needs to be," she said. "There are so many things that can go wrong. The FDA import model is one of voluntary guidance," she said.

"They tell the industry, 'Here are our suggestions for how to do things safely,'" Lovera said. "When it comes to the inspection resources they have and the size of the industry they're supposed to be regulating, they're just really outgunned."

But according to a 2007 U.S. Government Accountability Office report, federal oversight of food is on general fragmented, with 15 agencies collectively administrating at least 30 laws related to food safety.

"None of these agencies has ultimate authority or responsibility, so accountability for the total system is limited," according to TFAH. "No one person in the federal government has the oversight and accountability for carrying out comprehensive, preventive strategies for reducing food-borne illness," the report says.

America's food safety system includes the government, which ideally serves as a regulatory agency, and the food industry, which produces, processes, distributes and sells food, according to the report, which said that most producers take safety seriously. Historically, innovations in food safety come from within the industry. The FDA does not have the authority, in this country or elsewhere, to take an overly active role, Klein said. The FDA has had problems with tainted imports including pet foods, seafood and produce in recent years, she said.

"One of the things we saw during the pet food outbreak last year was that the FDA had to basically make a request to China to go inspect facilities that had been importing tainted wheat glutens," Klein said. "We'd like to see the FDA go over and certify these systems before they accept product from them."

While much attention had been paid to potential overseas problems, domestic outbreaks can be just as deadly and hard to track, Lovera said. Two years ago, a domestic E. coli outbreak in spinach made people in "almost the entire country sick" from something that happened in one county in California, she said.

The Center for Science in the Public Interest wants a comprehensive traceability system, similar to tracking systems used by shipping businesses such as UPS, Klein said. "When you mail a package, you're given a bar code that allows you to go online and track your package," Klein said. "It will show you that your package went from the UPS center where you dropped it off to the distribution center where it was sorted to an airplane, where it was sent to another distribution center and sorted again."

In CSPI's vision, a farmer would affix a label to an item of produce, similar to stickers already seen on foods at some supermarkets.

"We're just saying, why don't we do a standardized number?" she said. "On that sticker would be a number that stays with that commodity whether it was repacked, what kind of packing house or distribution it went through, so that in the event of an outbreak like the one we're experiencing now, the FDA would be able to track it right back to its source."

Jaydee Hanson, policy analyst at the Center for Food Safety, said some have proposed other solutions such as laser-inscribed tattoos on the skins of fruits. But determining who should run such a tracking program is difficult, Lovera said.

"We think it should not be an industry-run system," she said. "We need more than what we have now...I think we're living through an example of that. But right now, I don't think that just a traceability system is all we need to do. That's a system for dealing with a problem, and we would also like to put as much energy into preventing problems."

Ideally, government agencies should implement farm-to-fork tracking to prevent drawn-out searches for the source of tainted goods when it happens, while trying to create better practices to ensure safety before the food reaches them, Klein said.

In 2004, the FDA came up with what Hanson called a good food safety strategy but didn't ask Congress for the money to implement it. "The FDA has come up with some good designs, but it hasn't asked Congress for the resources to build the house," he said.

The Bush administration released its import Safety Action Plan which was integrated with the FDA's Food Protection Plan, according to the TFAH report. "The Food Protection Plan discussed the need to build safety into the entire food supply chain-including imported food," according to the report. It is essential to stress that the U.S. wants food that meets its higher standards.

Trade Talks Collapse as U.S. Feuds with China and India... America's Increasing Propensity for Importing

As reported in the *Associated Press*, trade officials reported in the latter part of July of 2008 that a high-level summit to salvage a global trade pact collapsed, after the United States, China and India failed to compromise on when poor countries could raise import tariffs on farm products. Trade officials from two developed and one emerging country told The Associated Press that a meeting of seven commercial powers broke up without agreement at the World Trade Organization. The officials, who asked not to be named because the news was soon to be announced to a larger meeting of countries, said a U.S. dispute with China and India over farm import safeguards had effectively ended any hope of a breakthrough.

Two officials said WTO chief Pascal Lamy had informed ministers that an agreement slipped away after nine days of talks aimed at a comprehensive deal to lower the tariffs and subsidies that hinder international trade. The meeting had been working on a broad compromise that, in short, would have let poor countries sell more produce to rich countries while giving the developed world greater market access in developing countries for services and manufactured goods.

U.S. Trade Representative Susan Schwab appeared downcast as she began to brief reporters. She said negotiations were "so close..." but then stopped speaking. Asked if the entire Doha trade round was over, she said, "I didn't say that" and walked away.

Negotiators were hoping for a deal on farm and industrial trade, so that crisis-ridden WTO talks could be saved. They were launched in 2001, but have repeatedly stalled amid deep divisions between rich and poor nations. Some officials had described this meeting at the WTO's Geneva headquarters as a last chance for the trade round launched in Qatar's capital seven years ago, noting that U.S. and other national elections would make negotiations difficult over the next couple of years.

Without a final deal, Europe will not be required to open up its farm markets to emerging powers in Latin America and elsewhere. Brazil, China, India and other fast-growing developing nations won't have to ease access to manufacturing imports from the rich world. And the U.S. will not have to make any tough decisions on the billions of dollars in farm subsidies it pays out each to American growers of cotton, soybean, rice and other staples.

The debate over farm subsidies has taken on added significance amid the recent spike in food prices around the world. Poorer nations say the payments distort global farm markets and hinder the development of sustainable agriculture in the Third World.

Talks had occurred that had brought consensus on many of the challenging problems that scuttled major trade meetings in Cancun, Mexico, in 2003, and in Hong Kong two years later. A number of trade officials described the debate pitting the United States against China and India as one of principle-and not just hard economics. Others blamed a lack of courage for the standoff.

"It is a jump in the dark," Brazilian Foreign Minister Celso Amorim said before final efforts were made. "You can't calculate until the very last situation all the hypotheses. If you do that (the round), will never finish. It will take two years, three years. It will probably be for a new generation."

The issue concerned a "special safeguard" developing countries led by China and India have demanded to deal with a sudden surge of imports or drop in prices. While farm import safeguards currently exist in rich and poor countries, they are rarely used. The dispute over the current proposals concerns the threshold for when developing nations could sharply raise their tariffs, and how high those taxes could rise. The United States had accused the two emerging powers of insisting on allowances to raise farm tariffs above even their current levels. That violates the spirit of the trade round, the U.S. and other agricultural exporters argued, because it is supposed to help poorer countries develop their economies by boosting their exports of farm produce.

After a Year of Executive and Congressional Investigations, Testimony and Posturing... Are We Any Safer?

By now, most Americans are well aware of America's difficulties with ensuring the safety of imported products...a problem that a string of high-profile product recalls highlighted. The recalls sparked government scrutiny, but are imports today any safer than when the recalls...some, disturbingly, of children's products...occurred?

Unfortunately, America has an increasing propensity for importing... an enormous appetite for imports. According to government estimates, in 2007, over 825,000 U.S. companies imported more than $2 trillion of products through 300 ports of entry. That's an average of over $63,000 of product imported into the U.S. every second of every day…and the number is growing. By the time you finish reading this book (assuming it takes you a few days), nearly $1 billion plus of products will have been imported into the U.S.

This staggering amount equates to over 20% of the U.S.'s GDP (ranked #1 in the world), nearly half of Japan's GDP (ranked #2), over 60% of Germany's (ranked #3) and China's (ranked #4), and nearly all of the United Kingdom's (ranked #5). If the value of our imports alone represented the GDP of a single country, that country would rank eighth in the world… above Spain, Canada, and Brazil.

Of the $2 trillion in imports last year (including oil), a total of $321.5 billion (16% of total imports) came from China. (That's a huge expansion from 2006, when the figure was $240 billion. The change represents an increase of 34% from 2006 to 2007). Of the China imports, over $56 billion comprised of computers and accessories; $27 billion, toys; and $25 billion, video and telecommunications equipment. Unfortunately, China-manufactured products continue to top the list of recalled consumer products and that list has grown.

The President's Interagency Working Group on Import Safety's Action Plan Update

Mark H. Allenbaugh's article in *'FindLaw'* on July 30, 2008 continued to state that in reaction to the massive recalls of consumer products manufactured in China, President Bush created a cabinet-level Interagency Working Group on Import Safety (www.importsafety.gov). Its mandate was to review the problem and provide suggestions for improving the security and safety of the international supply chain. The Group issued an "Action Plan Update" in July after a year of investigations, testimony, and trips to foreign countries that export consumer products to the United States.

According to the *Update*, the Working Group has largely spent the last year traveling to several foreign countries…including China…to discuss bilateral or multilateral agreements to improve import safety. In addition, the Working Group had met with some industry associations to obtain insight into ways to improve product quality control.

The Update proudly boasts that between November 2007 and May 2008, about 8,500 products were refused admission into the U.S. due to appearances of unsanitary conditions. Likewise, the government "detected and took action" against approximately 2.4 million pounds of meat that appeared to violate health standards (a drop in the bucket compared to the 180 million pounds of meat we consume a year). And, about half a dozen companies have been federally indicted for violating various importing regulations.

All these efforts apparently come under the rubric of the Department of Homeland Security's (little-known) Operation Guardian, which "represents a multi-agency approach to import safety operation."

Frankly, Operation Guardian appears by its own reporting to be a woeful failure at improving import safety. They obfuscate the critical need to work directly with overseas manufacturers, and especially to understand the rather unique dynamic that businesses encounter when importing products from China.

The Consumer Product Safety Commission Reform Act

Unfortunately, Congress seems to have succumbed to the same fundamental misunderstanding of the primary issue facing import safety that has plagued Operation Guardian. Congress, too, has failed to focus on the need for U.S.-based importers to travel to China and train their overseas manufacturers in China as to how to comply with U.S. safety regulations.

The bipartisan Consumer Product Safety Commission Reform Act, H.R. 4040 ("The Act"), was set to pass any day during the middle of 2008. The law is intended to "establish consumer product safety standards...and to reauthorize and modernize the Consumer Product Safety Commission." Among the many action items the Act proposes to improve safety are these three: (1) require third-party certification of children's products; (2) require the replacement of tracking labels on children's products; and (3) require U.S. importers, retailers, and distributors to identify their manufacturers.

Will these measures be effective? They are not really "carrots"...for they do not incentivize importers to improve their import safety processes and procedures. Not are they really "sticks," imposing penalties...although many importers will have concerns about revealing their manufacturers out of concern that their key suppliers of imported goods may then quickly be usurped by their competitors and even by customers who want to cut out the middle-man.

What does function like a very heavy stick...indeed, a lead bat...are the penalties for violating relevant provisions of the Act.

As is typical with so much fix-it legislation, Congress has shown in the Act that it is addicted to addressing problems through threats of onerous punishment. Many civil fines have increased by orders of magnitude...rising from, in some cases, $1.25 million to a massive $20 million. Likewise, the Act increases criminal penalties from misdemeanors to federal felonies potentially triggering five years' imprisonment.

These penalties, however, will have very little real-world effect. Very few violators ever will be caught, let alone prosecuted or fined…as the statistics cited by the Working Group's Update regarding the massive volume of imports clearly indicate. The sheer flood of products being imported into this country is simply beyond the means of any government agency or network of agencies to effectively police.

Though Trade, Here and Overseas, are Ideal for Training… the Government has Failed to Take Advantage of Them

But our government remains silent…or, worse, unaware of these opportunities. Nowhere in the Working Group's three reports on in H.R. 4040 is any such training or cooperation mentioned. That's a serious omission: While meetings with government officials and trade groups provide excellent photo ops, they do nothing to assist the actual manufacturer or importer in improving the safety of products along the entire supply and demand chain.

Our trade with China will soon become far more bilateral than it is now, as its middle class continues to grow (now outnumbering the entire U.S. population), and as the renminbi continues to grow in value relative to the weak U.S. dollar. By working with overseas manufacturers as partners and in a spirit of camaraderie (as opposed to a necessary evil), U.S. importers will come to far better understand the enormous potential of the Chinese market, and the opportunities that lie there for U.S. businesses as exporters as it did for me and my company.

Congress sent Bush Bill Banning Lead in Toys… Congress Decided to Stop Playing Games with Toy Safety

Around August 1st, the *AP* announced that the Senate passed and sent to the White House legislation that would ban lead from children's toys, seeking to ensure that chemicals posing possible health problems would not end up on toys and articles that kids chew on and play with.

The Senate, stymied by partisan differences over the energy crisis, put aside those differences momentarily to vote 89-3 for the Consumer Product Safety Improvement Act. The House passed the bill 424-1, a reflection of the national outcry over a rash of recalls last year of toys and children's products contaminated by lead and other dangerous elements.

"We are going to make a big, big difference in the American marketplace," said Senator Mark Pryor, D-Ark, a sponsor of the bill.

The administration had objected to parts of the bill, but White House spokeswoman Dana Perino stated that President Bush would sign it. "We are ensuring that the products that come into America are safe for consumers and that the regulating agencies have what they need to do their job," she said.

The bill would impose the toughest lead standards in the world, banning lead beyond minute levels in products for children 12 or younger. Lead paint was a major factor in the recall of 45 million toys and children's items in 2007, including Cookie Monster toys and Tommy the Tank Engines. Many came from China. It also bans, either permanently or pending further study, children's goods containing six types of a chemical called phthalates that are widely used to make plastic products softer and more flexible. The chemical industry insisted that Phthalates have been used for decades and there is no evidence they pose health risks to humans.

But consumers advocacy groups pointed out that the European Union has banned the six phthalates and that tests on rats have revealed possible reproductive problems and cancer. "Toxic chemicals like lead and phthalates have no business in our children's toys," said U.S. PIRG Public Health Advocate Elizabeth Hitchcock. Some major retailers, including Wal-Mart and Toys-R-Us, have already taken steps to phase out phthalates.

The legislation bolsters the Consumer Product Safety Commission, a 400-staffer agency that took the brunt of criticism in 2007 over the massive recalls and the failure of the government to better test and monitor toy imports before they reach store shelves. The bill would double the agency's budget, to $136 million by 2014, and give it new authority to oversee testing procedures and impose civil penalties on violators.

Another key provision requires pre-market testing by certified third-party laboratories of children's products for lead and for compliance with safety standards. American Academy of Pediatrics President Renee R. Jenkins lauded the "extraordinary effort" of Congress. "Safety testing and certification for such hazards as powerful magnets before products are sold, a ban on lead and phthalates and more, will helpfully put an end to the recalls of children's products and the horror stories that lead to those recalls."

The bill also:
- Provides whistle-blower protections to employees who report consumer product hazards. The provision was championed by Senator Claire McCaskill, D-MO.

- Requires the CPSC to set up a user-friendly database where consumers, government agencies, child care products or doctors could report incidents of injury, illness, death or risk related to products.
- Makes more products now covered by voluntary industry standards subject to mandatory standards. With that, more toy hazards, including goods containing small magnets that were included in products recalled in 2007, would be subject to third-party testing requirements.
- Bans the three-wheel all-terrain vehicles and strengthens regulations of other ATVs.

The three senators opposing the bill were Republicans Tom Coburn of Oklahoma, Jim DeMint of South Carolina and John Kyl of Arizona. Rep. Ron Paul, R-Texas, was the lone House member voting against the measure.

On August 3rd, the Los Angeles Times reported that Enrique Barajas was poking around the little shops of the Toy District in downtown Los Angeles with his 4-year old daughter and 1-year old son. The store shelves were packed with inexpensive imports, most from China. Barajas, 27, said he liked buying toys for his kids, but he found it hard to know what was safe and what potentially could harm them. "The government should be doing more," he said. "It's never enough, what they do."

That was about to change.

After months of wrangling, congressional leaders finally came to terms in August on landmark legislation that represents the most sweeping overhaul of U.S. product-safety rules in decades. The Senate approved the bill after a similar vote by the House of Representatives a day earlier. President Bush was expected to sign the legislation into law.

"This is a huge deal," said Rachel Weintraub, director of product safety for the Consumer Federation of American. "It's going to change the products in the market place."

Not immediately though. The various provisions of the bill would be enacted at different times over the coming months. That meant shoppers will have to remain vigilant when buying toys and other goods during holiday season. But by 2009, the product-safety landscape would be very different. Among other things, the legislation would:

- Beef up the Consumer Product Safety Commission with new funding and resources. The commission is responsible for overseeing the safety of 15,000 product categories, including items as varied as toys, cribs, power tools and kitchen appliances.

- Require mandatory third-party testing of products for kids age 12 and under. Most such products are now subject to a mix of regulatory standards and frequently make it to store shelves without being tested in advance.
- Ban the sale of children's products containing lead and certain types of phthalates, which are chemicals used to soften plastic that have been linked to long-term health problems.
- Provide safeguards for whistle-blowers who alert authorities to unsafe products and industry practices.
- Establish a searchable database of all reports of deaths, injuries or illnesses related to consumer products.

The legislation would increase the penalty cap for civil fines to $100,000 from $5,000 for individual penalties and up to $15 million for violations involving multiple products. It also would require tracking labels that would allow officials to trace a product back to its factory in the event of a recall. More than 45 million kids' products...most produced in Chinese factories... were recalled in 2007.

El Segundo's Mattel Inc., the world's largest toy maker, was responsible for about 20 million recalled toys. Some, like a die-cast vehicle depicting the Sarge character from "Cars," were found to have lead in the paint. Others had small magnets that posed a risk of internal injuries if swallowed. Then, there was Hasbro Inc.'s Easy-Bake Oven, nearly a million of which had to be recalled after dozens of little girls were burned or had their hands caught in the oven's door. One 5-year old had to have a finger partially amputated.

Even though manufacturers and retailers vowed to crack down on defective products, the number of recalls of toys and children's products increased 22% in the nine months ended June 30th from a year earlier, according to a government aid.

"The 22% increase suggests strongly that what the toy industry called 'last year's problem' remains very much today's problem," said Ami Gadhia, policy counsel for Consumers Union. Jim Neill, a spokesman for the National Association of Manufacturers, said businesses generally supported strengthening the Consumer Product Safety Commission but were wary of other aspects of the legislation.

He said that his organization was particularly concerned about the whistle-blower provision and the database of potentially unsafe products, both of which, he said, could lead to "unintended consequences," Neill also said a provision authorizing state attorneys general to help enforce federal safety laws "may blur the lines on national uniform standards."

At this point, consumers need all the help they can get. The Consumer Product Safety Commission has been a decidedly low priority for the Bush administration. The three-person commission has been without a chair since July 2006, when Bush appointee Hal Stratton left to take a job with a law firm that specializes in shooting down class-action lawsuits filed by consumers. In March 2007, Bush nominated Michael Baroody, a leading manufacturing industry lobbyist, to head the commission. Baroody withdrew from consideration after lawmakers demanded copies of his severance agreement with the National Association of Manufacturers. It now appears likely that no one will be appointed to the long-vacant post until Obama chooses a chairperson.

Meanwhile, consumers' distrust of imported toys and the sour economy have taken a severe toll on many Toy District merchants. A number of shops have closed in by the middle of 2008. Others were barely hanging on. "There's no business," said Michael Chang, a salesman at W.T. Toys on 4th Street. "Many stores are closing."

Unfortunately, the new product-safety legislation won't make those toys…Chinese-made dolls, action figures and remote-control cars…any safer. But it would go a long way toward ensuring that future toy shipments meet much higher standards.

China Stealing More Money, Jobs Than You Think… China's Booming Economy Shows Signs of Weakening

Local manufacturing firms such as Okay Industries and Arkadia Plastics haven't been too concerned about the threat of Mainland China's ever-widening influence in the global economy. As Arkadia's Georgia Georgacopoulus explained, "Show me a Chinese company that can match us in knowledge or in our speed in developing products." But maybe they should be.

Until recently, Chinese manufacturing conjured up images of over-crowded sweat shops grinding out low-skill, low-margin products such as lead-based toys and mass produced pens. So when in August of 2008, the Economic Policy Institute released a study showing that between 2001 and 2007, 2.3 million American jobs were lost, some economists shrugged their shoulders.

However, contrary to the stereotype that these lost jobs were predominantly in low-skill, low-pay industries, EPI insisted that the trade deficit with China has, in fact, forced workers from better-paying jobs to lower-paying sectors. More than half (55.6 percent) of the displaced jobs were in the top half of American wage earners. Nearly a third (31 percent) of the jobs lost were among workers with a college degree. Growing China trade deficits have contributed to the loss of 200,000 scientist and engineer jobs within the manufacturing sector, a 10.7 percent drop.

The jobs lost range from those in traditional manufacturing to newer technology sectors. The largest states lost the most jobs since 2001... with California losing over 325,000, Texas nearly 203,000 and New York about 127,000. Eleven states lost more than 10,000 jobs in 2007 alone. Connecticut lost 26,000 jobs between 2001 and 2007, including 5,400 jobs in the state's electronics and computer manufacturing sector, because of the trade imbalance.

More than two-thirds of the lost jobs were in manufacturing, which generally pays better wages and benefits. The type of manufactured goods imported, however is changing. "China is rapidly diversifying its export base and expanding into higher, value-added commodities such as computer and electronic products, aircraft, and auto parts and machinery," the report said. Some economists believe that China is trying to emulate Japan and South Korea. Both nations were successful in evolving from low-skilled to high-skilled manufacturing to high technology services and the creation of global brands.

According to the New York Times, the Chinese government is now using incentives to encourage companies to innovate while discouraging low-end manufacturers from proliferating. Contrary to the Olympic spirit, China's President Hu Juntao called on scientists to challenge other countries in high technology. "We are ready for a fight," he told The New York Times, "to control the scientific high ground and earn a seat on the world's high technology board. We will make some serious efforts to strengthen our nation's competence."

How did this sit with Frank Johnson? Not too well. Johnson is president/ CEO of Waterbury-based Manufacturing Alliance of Connecticut, Inc., a special interest group "preserving, promoting and protecting manufacturing in the state." Its members and affiliates range from Acme-Monaco Corp. in New Britain to Yarde Metals in Bristol.

"From the beginning, China had intended to work its way up the value chain," Johnson said. "Their aggressive pursuit of U.S. technology is an indicator of that."

Johnson said that companies in Connecticut standing up to the China threat are in the aircraft assembly, medical device and food industries. Look what happened when the Chinese tried to export toothpaste," he said. (Toxic chemicals were found in toothpaste sold in the Dominican Republic and Panama.) "Still, the Chinese will try every inroad they can. They have an enormous population plus an appetite for growth."

On the opposite side, Johnson believed some commodity work has returned from China. "Transportation costs between China and the U.S. are higher than they used to be," he said. "More and more companies here are working on the just-in-time basis where they get parts exactly when they need them. Chinese workers are beginning to rebel at some of the [working] conditions that exist there. So, between the added fuel costs, the inability to deliver on time and the lack of quality, some of that work has made its way back to the U.S."

Nevertheless, globalization has taken its toll.

"The direct impact on incomes, more than $8,000 per displaced worker per year on average, is catastrophic for the individual workers and the most single most visible cost of globalization for American workers," said EPI economist Josh Bivens. "But, it's also critical to recognize the indirect impact of trade on workers. Trade with less-developed countries has reduced the bargaining power of all workers in the U.S. economy who resemble those displaced workers in education, credentials, and skills. Annual earnings for workers without a four-year college degree are roughly $1,400 lower today because of this competition and this group constitutes a large majority (70 percent) of the entire work force. China, the source of nearly 40 percent of our non-oil imports from less-developed countries, is a chief contributor to this downward wage pressure."

Department of Labor Economist John Tirinzonie acknowledged that China is a fierce competitor and that the U.S. has lost jobs to Asia but cites his own studies that show Connecticut has gained 23,000 jobs from 2001 through 2007.

"Connecticut's exports to China beginning in 2006 have increased almost 53 percent and account for $546 million worth of goods and services to China," Tirinzonie said. "Our manufacturing sector is high tech and research oriented and shouldn't be affected for now. Still, we always need to keep a step ahead of them…whether we come up with different technologies or a more advanced one."

By August 7th, the International Herald Tribune through the Associate Press reported that the Changshu Zhongjiang Import-Export Co., a clothing exporter in Suzhou, west of Shanghai, was accustomed to 'double-digit' annual revenue growth in the past. In 2008, with its key U.S. export market limping, sales had fallen an alarming 10 percent.

Changshu, with 580 employees, had avoided layoffs, but profits were down as much as 85 percent from their 2005 peak, said Xue Jianfang, the company's vice president. "We are not going to switch to domestic sales, because the domestic market is even worse," Xue said. "There are still some profits in this industry, but they are squeezed."

China's booming economy, a bright spot amid global gloom, was starting to weaken in areas ranging from clothing exports to auto sales to manufacturing. Communist leaders who had spent a year fighting politically dangerous inflation were scrambling to change course and avert job losses by revving up struggling industries.

Growth concerns have definitely become more important," said Grace Ng, a JP Morgen Chase & Co. economist. "I don't think they have come to the definite conclusion that we are having a sharp slowdown in growth, but they are clearly cautious. They do not want to ignite inflation pressure."

The fact remained that companies were starting to suffer a triple blow from record-high costs for energy and raw materials, slowing foreign demand and a rise in China's currency, the yuan, which makes their goods more expensive for American consumers. A slowdown only produces a global impact if China buys less factory equipment from the United States and Europe or oil and raw materials from developing countries. It would set back hopes that as U.S. demand falters, China would fill the gap in global growth. But many unforeseen changes were beginning to take place throughout the world and they started to come fast and furious.

Analysts started to expect economic growth to fall as low as 9 percent by the end of 2008. That's well ahead of other major countries but a sharp decline from 2007's 11.4 percent. That worried Chinese leaders, who needed to create jobs and satisfy urban workers who had come to expect steadily rising living standards. Premier Wen Jiabao and other top economic officials would be politically damaged if they failed to scope with the problem. But the problem was getting way out of hand and no one had any answers at the time. There was a recession coming.

"I think there is a bit of gridlock and not a lot of consensus about what to do," said William Hess, chief China analyst for the consulting firm Global Insight. "For some senior leaders who have come out and taken personal responsibility for the issues, they face some career pressures."

With regards to oil imports, ending our reliance on oil from the Middle East and Venezuela really amounts to ending our import of foreign oil. It doesn't count to just pass a law saying that we won't buy oil from certain sources because they are politically incorrect. All that does is drive up the cost of oil to us. For example, let's say we don't want to buy oil from Saudi Arabia anymore so we pass a law that prohibits the import of oil from there. Since oil is a global commodity, Saudi Arabia will just sell their oil to a country like China. We will import more oil from a country like Nigeria or Libya. It will likely be more expensive to do this. China might save a little money here because they don't have the same political constraints. This doesn't solve the problem. It just increases our costs to pay for this oil diversion. We could also become more dependent on fewer foreign suppliers.

We currently produce about 5 million barrels of oil per day and consume about 18 million barrels per day. That means we have to either consume 13 million barrels per day less than we are using (72% reduction) or we have to increase our domestic production by 13 million barrels per day. There could be some combination or an increase in domestic production and a decrease in consumption, but that is a very large gap to fill in 10 years.

All of the automobiles in the country consume about 9 million barrels of oil per day. Heating oil for homes and diesel fuel for trucks and other heavy equipment are other big consumers of oil. Reducing consumption by 72% would be devastating if alternative energy sources were not available to provide an equivalent amount of energy.

Finding substitutes for oil will be difficult. We currently do not have the technology or infrastructure to produce alternatives for oil as this product is used mostly in transportation. Heating oil can be displaced by either natural gas or electricity. Electricity would be the preferred solution to displacing heating oil, especially if the electricity came from non-carbon polluting energy sources. A large percentage of our heating oil is consumed in northern, industrial states which are not the best places for wind power and solar power. Nuclear power is a strong contender for fuel oil displacement, but President Obama is opposed to nuclear power.

Again, we are looking at a politician delivering a lot of blue sky and sunshine in his talk, with little substance behind the vision. What Barack Obama might mean is that he wants to reduce U.S. oil imports by 3.5 million barrels per day (20 %) over the next ten years. Where are the details? T. Boone Pickens has a plan that calls for replacing oil with natural gas in cars.

His plan has a drilling component to supply all of our cars with natural gas. That is currently available in technology but is still a huge undertaking. $150 billion…the amount that Obama wants to reduce from our dependence on the Middle East in the next ten years…might sound like it could solve our energy problems. But we really need to find ways to invest 20 or 30 times that amount in alternative energy development. $15 billion per year is really a drop in the bucket. Now that Mr. Obama is president, let's see what he really does in the next four years.

America's Exports Are Now Growing Faster Than China's... Helping to Reduce the Strains in the World Economy

And as we look over the past decade, the world economy has been plagued by widening imbalances, most notably America's current-account deficit and China's surplus...both the largest in the world. There is not much to celebrate about the world economy at present, but at least it is becoming more balanced. Not only are trade gaps in American and China shrinking, but the composition of growth within countries is also looking healthier.

For the first time in years, China's exports are growing more slowly than America's. In the 12 month's to June 2008 (the latest figures at this writing), America's exports grew by 23%, well ahead of China's 17% (in dollar terms). Export volumes showed a similar trend. China's rose by 11% in the year to the second quarter, while America's climbed by 12%. Stephen Green, an economist at Standard Chartered, had expected China's real export growth to fall to zero by the end of 2008 and to turn negative in 2009.

In July, China's exports surged a mighty 27% from where they were a year before, but this did not alter the picture much. China's monthly trade figures were notoriously volatile and if exports were converted into yuan...the currency which matters for China's GDP growth...growth had fallen sharply to an average of 12% to July 2008, from 35% in early 2005. Meanwhile, import growth had quickened over the past year, due in part to higher oil bills. As a result, China's trade surplus in yuan terms in the first seven months of 2008 was almost 20% smaller than in the same period of 2007. Even in dollar terms it had fallen by 10%.

That is not to say that there will be a sharp drop in China's current-account surplus in 2008. In dollar terms, it remained roughly as big as in 2007 because higher income from its vast foreign assets offset the smaller trade surplus. But as a share of GDP, it did shrink because China's economy was expanding so rapidly. Mr. Green had forecast a current-account surplus of 9% of GDP in 2008 and 7% in 2009, down from 11.3% last year. Thus, China was able to claim that its surplus had fallen sharply, even as its critics, in America and elsewhere, continued to argue that it had barely budged in dollar terms. No one could dispute, however, that China's exports were growing much more slowly than its economy (which was galloping along at 20% in nominal yuan terms). This was occurring at the same time as America's export machine had revved up, which was bound to help trade imbalances upward.

Turning to American, the decline in its total trade deficit had been modest, because of the higher cost of oil imports. But the underlying improvement was more impressive. Excluding oil, the trade deficit had fallen by almost one-quarter since 2006. At the same time as exports had soared, real imports fell by 2% in the year to the second quarter, dragged down by weak domestic demand. If the recent drop in oil prices was sustained, the total trade deficit would have shrunk more rapidly in the second half of 2008 than it did in the first half. Meanwhile, America's overall current-account deficit had fallen to around 5% of GDP from a peak of 6.2% in the third quarter of 2006. Merrill Lynch forecast that it would drop to around 3.5% of GDP in 2009.

Bilaterally, it was the same story: America's exports to Chine were 20% higher in the first half of the year compared with the same period in 2007, while its imports from China were up only 4%. However, America's import bill for goods from China was so huge…four times that of exports…that the rising exports had not dented America's overall trade deficit with China. The changing patterns, buried beneath the headline figures, were very hard to spot.

What had caused the shifts? The cheaper dollar is one factor; until its rebound in the summer of 2008, it had about a quarter of its value on a real trade-weighted basis since its peak in 2002. That not only made American exports more competitive, it made exports into American less attractive. Probably of more importance, though, were the shifts in domestic spending. America's real domestic demand had stagnated over the past year. Whereas China's had risen by 10% as its citizens had picked up the baton from flagging American consumers. In dollar terms, which better measure China's ability to buy imports, its domestic spending had soared by a whopping 33%.

Global rebalancing requires a redistribution of growth within countries as well as redistribution between countries. Until last year, American's growth was driven by an unsustainable consumer boom; now it is being supported entirely by external demand. Without the boost from net exports, real GDP would have fallen since the third quarter of 2007.

Meanwhile, in China, consumer spending has been growing faster than exports. Retail sales jumped by 23% in nominal terms in the year to July 2008, and 16% in real terms. Dragonomics, a Beijing-based research firm, estimated that consumption contributed two-thirds of China's growth in the first half of 2008, up from 44% in 2007.

In America, weak consumer spending was likely to continue to dampen imports through 2009. Auguring tougher times ahead, the country's retail sales in July fell for the first time in five months. This was the beginning of a recession but no one truly recognized the signs or just acted stupid and let it ride through the fall of 2008 when all hell broke loose. Less clear was how strong America's export performance would remain, given the recent rebound in the dollar and slower growth in the rest of the world. It was election year…

no one talked about recession...but the fact remained that we were going to hell in a hand basket...not only the U.S., but the entire world.

The greenback remained cheap by many measures and so should have continued to support America's sales abroad. Slower growth elsewhere in the world was a more serious concern. Japan's economy fell by an annualized 2.4% in the second quarter, figures released had shown, after growing strongly in the first quarter. Growth in the euro area also seemed to have come to an end. But these two places accounted for only about 20% of America's exports; much more important were emerging economies which now buy more than half of its exports.

Economic growth in developing countries was likely to slow over the coming year. But what mattered far more for American exports was the growth in their domestic demand and hence their appetite for imports. Goldman Sachs had forecast that real domestic demand in the four BRIC countries...Brazil, Russia, India and China...would grow by over 9% in 2009, roughly the same as in 2007 and 2008. If so, this would be good for American exporters.

For all the improvements, trade imbalances were still too big. It was worrying that since mid-July China had stopped allowing the yuan to rise against the dollar; indeed, the country had since fallen by 1%. China had also increased some tax rebates for exporters. Brad Setser, of America's Council on Foreign Relations, a think-tank, argued that if China tried to bolster its GDP growth by supporting exports, it would hinder global rebalancing. Instead, with surpluses in its budget and current-account, China should have propped up growth by further stimulating domestic demand. That meant increasing spending on infrastructure, schools and health care.

To be fair, the yuan had not fallen in trade-weighted terms in June or July of 2008, but it was still undervalued and needed to rise further. Mr. Setser reckoned that given high oil prices and sluggish American demand, China's trade surplus should have fallen by more. Likewise, one might argue that without big tax cuts to prop up consumer spending, America's deficit would have shrunk further. If global rebalancing was to continue, America still needed to save more, and China to save less.

We were not finished with the tainted and polluted products that were coming from China. Between the increase of products that were going to be a problem in the U.S., and the economy going into the tank, the American people were in for a huge surprise. We still had a month or so to go before the recession became a reality and about two months before the election.

We should look at some of the problem products that were increasing, not only in the United States, but worldwide. And the people, rather than the governments were making a stand against what was going on. Let's look in on some typical stories of such products that were bogus.

Grim Competition with Counterfeiters... U.S. Firms Fighting Golf Fakes

On August 21 out of Boston, a story broke from the *Boston Globe*. It seemed that Jason Yao of Shanghai was living a dangerous life for a guy in the golf business. He was receiving death threats. He raided factories and markets. He had shaken down informants and hung out with private investigators. He also had ten aliases.

China is the focus of the worldwide war against counterfeit golf products, and Yao is on the front lines. His employer, Acushnet, located 7,000 miles away in Fairhaven, Mass., makes the world's most popular...and most copied...golf ball, the Titleist Pro V1, along with clubs, accessories, and shoes that counterfeiters mimic for sales around the globe.

As Chinese officials cracked down during the summer of 2008 on the sale of fake items to Olympic fans in Beijing, Yao was further south in that country, raiding factories that make ersatz Titleist clubs and golf bags. Acushnet is one of a growing number of merchants fighting the increasingly sophisticated counterfeit operations, which are diverting billions of dollars globally to the black market for everything from golf balls and brake pads to pharmaceuticals and luxury handbags. In its most recent report, the Paris-based International Chamber of Commerce estimated that counterfeit goods cost more than $600 billion annually in lost sales, tax revenue, and jobs. For Massachusetts, the largest U.S. exporter of golf balls, counterfeited Titleists could mean millions less in tax revenue.

Increasingly, Chinese fakes are being exported to the United States through online sales on such sites as eBay and Craigslist, where copycats see a chance to cash in on American consumers looking for deals. Technological advances make it easier to manufacture fake goods that look almost like the real products. About 81 percent of all counterfeit products seized in the United States came from China in 2006, up from 65 percent a year earlier, according to the latest U.S. government statistics. And the slow reaction by Chinese officials to the burgeoning business of rip-offs has forced brands such as Acushnet, Gucci, and Tiffany to largely take on the fakers on their own based on Globe.com of the Boston Globe.

Acushnet was spending more than $2 million a year to combat counterfeiting, a budget that didn't exist five years ago. The $1.4 billion company is training U.S. federal customs agents to recognize fakes...for example, to know that since Titleist balls are manufactured in America, all imports from China are counterfeits. Acushnet is paying for security services that monitor sites like eBay for fraud, a move that has allowed Acushnet to shut down 10,500 auctions of fakes since January, 2008. And it has hired Yao, a 35-year-old lawyer, and other investigators to ferret out wrongdoers in China and to lobby officials to pay more attention to their cases.

"I'm never going to stop the problem. I'm just trying to make it harder to do," said Lisa Rogan, Acushnet's trademark manager, who oversees the company's anti-counterfeit efforts. "We're not just protecting our reputation. We're trying to protect consumers who are getting fooled by these lesser quality copies."

Jimmy Rosen, of Harrisburg, Pa., was on of those consumers. He found what sounded like a bargain on Craigslist: $35 for a dozen Titleist Pro V1 golf balls in damaged boxes (typically $50 at stores). Rosen, 43, called up some friends who wanted in and negotiated for 42 dozen balls for $20 a dozen.

He met the alleged seller, Dallas Conrad, of Carlisle, Pa., and after giving the balls a cursory look, handed over $840 in cash. But when Rosen and his friends compared the balls to ones bought at a store, they saw they had been fooled. The counterfeit balls were a brighter white with a different font and had a visible seam.

"It didn't even occur to me that golf balls were being counterfeited and brought in from China," said Rosen, who filed a law suit against Conrad.

Conrad could not be reached for comment. Calls to several phone numbers listed for Conrad were disconnected. Rosen's 504 golf balls, meanwhile, are locked in his lawyer's office. Rosen sent photos to Acushnet, which is trying to track down links to different counterfeit rings.

While many factories make fakes for local markets in China, exporting products online is increasingly popular. A typical internet operation includes factories in China; middlemen shipping products to sellers overseas in small packages to elude customs; and sellers across the world listing hundreds of items on websites like eBay, Craigslist, and Alibaba. Records are rarely kept, delivery instructions are often given via text messages to avoid detection, and merchandise is moved quickly by courier out of factories to the middleman so raids turn up few goods.

MarkMonitor, a firm that helps companies track fraudulent auctions, estimates the amount of counterfeit products sold online almost doubled to a record $120 billion from 2004 and 2007. MarkMonitor identifies fraudulent goods online for businesses to review and automatically transmits the counterfeit listings to eBay. Auctions are typically shut down by eBay within 12 hours.

But frustrated retailers, which want eBay to do more, are taking their cases to the courts with mixed results: In the summer of 2008, a French judge fined eBay $63 million for failing to adequately prevent counterfeit items from appearing on its French site in a lawsuit filed by luxury merchant LVMH, which includes brands such as Louis Vuitton. eBay has said it plans to appeal the ruling. Several days later, a New York judge sided with eBay in a case brought by Tiffany, saying the high-end jeweler is responsible for policing its trademark.

Catherine England, an eBay spokeswoman, said the site tried to avoid counterfeit goods: "It's bad for sellers, bad for buyers, and has no place on eBay."

Fighting fakers on their home turf in China is even more challenging for brands that must try to convince judges and government officials that counterfeiting is a serious crime. In August of 2008, Yin Xintian, of the State Intellectual Property Office in China, played down the amount of Chinese counterfeits and blamed them on expensive copyrighted brands, which he said were driving consumers to buy fake goods.

In some instances, Chinese authorities have stepped up their efforts. They have raided factories and made arrests. During the Olympics, officials were conducting market sweeps in Beijing and targeting fans at the airport trying to bring back fake goods. And the government is playing a video titled "Say NO to counterfeiting and piracy" at airports featuring actor Jackie Chan posing as a customs agent who forces tourists to surrender counterfeit items.

Still, the complexity of tackling counterfeiters has led Acushnet to work with unlikely partners, rival golf businesses. Together, they share information and help fund investigations to target counterfeiters of multiple golf brands. Companies do much of the legwork…hiring investigators and cultivating informants among employees at suspected factories…before local authorities will get involved. But of the 40 factory raids, Acushnet has helped with over the past four years, only 9 have resulted in criminal cases. Chinese authorities rarely shut down factories permanently for making fakes, and some counterfeiters under investigation boldly keep up their illicit business.

"The police spend a lot of resources investigating, but then the prosecutor may not be supportive to police, and when cases are tried in court, sentences are usually a suspension or criminal fine," said Jack Chang, chairman of the Quality Brands Protection Committee, a lobbyist group in China representing 180 multinational companies.

Chinese markets are beginning to react. Hawkers of counterfeits, which fill the stalls at indoor silk markets in Beijing and Shanghai, have adapted. Many shop owners now present authentic goods on their floor, or show them in catalogs, but then sell fakes at lower prices. An authentic set of Titleist clubs costs about $2,200, but a customer can get the fake set for $175. At the market, many sellers admitted to a casual shopper recently that they sell copies, and even describe the difference between good and bad fakes.

One shop that moved into a Shanghai strip mall after an outdoor market was closed because its counterfeiting got creative. The store, Shanghai Zhizun Golf Sport Product, has a secret door that leads to a secondary-story warehouse, where the merchant keeps its stash of counterfeit goods.

Consumers in China have no reason to show loyalty to the authentic foreign brands. In some cases, residents and local officials tip off factories that make counterfeits before planned raids. In the Tong'an District of Xiamen, where an estimated 50 factories are suspected of counterfeiting golf products, villages have their own security teams which work with the factories and post video cameras at every entrance, Yao said. The security teams question and keep watch on every stranger who enters, making it impossible for the private investigators Acushnet sends to get information.

Even factories contracted to make authentic goods often do a side business in fakes or manufacture additional legitimate products to sell to unauthorized vendors. Yao discovered a driving range that was selling authentic Titleist club heads in June of 2008. But the company sells only clubs assembled completely, not in separate parts. Yao contacted the factory that manufactures the clubs in Zhongshan, and was told that a security guard must have stolen the club heads in an isolated incident.

"I just don't believe them," Yao said.

U.S. Assigns Safety Inspectors to Chinese Cities in October of 2008... China's Latest Dilemma... Challenging Demands its Leaders be Bold

In August of 2008, *Bloomberg* reported that the U.S. was going to station inspectors in three Chinese cities to scrutinize exports to the world's largest economy, responding to concerns over the safety of China-produced food, toys and pharmaceutical ingredients.

Up to 15 inspectors were to be assigned to Beijing, Shanghai and Guangzhou from October, U.S. Secretary of Health and Human Services Michael Leavitt said in an interview. China agreed in December 2007 to let the Food and Drug Administration establish China offices, among the agreements reached in its Strategic Economic Dialogue with the United States.

China's government "worked hard" at improving safety, Leavitt said in Beijing. "I don't think they've got the problem completely solved, but it was clear to them that the made-in-China brand was affected by product quality problems and they moved aggressively to begin making progress."

Concern over the safety of Chinese products in 2007 shifted the focus of the twice-annual U.S.-China strategic dialogue away from the pace of the yuan's gains. President George W. Bush in June boosted the FDA's budget by $275 million for the fiscal year starting October 1st 2008 to finance inspections of overseas plants that produce food and medicine for export.

Food-safety problems sparked a drop in exports to Japan and the U.S. in 2008. Contaminated consumer exports, including pesticide-laced frozen dumplings in Japan and tainted Heparin blood thinner in the U.S. had sparked international furor over the safety of Chinese-made products.

Mattel Inc., the world's biggest toymaker, recalled 21 million Chinese-made products in 2007. The Segundo, California-based company incurred $110 million in recall, legal, advertising and testing costs in 2007, after taking back Sesame Street vehicles painted with lead-tainted paint and Polly Pocket dolls with magnets that may detach and be swallowed by children.

Menu Foods Ltd., Wal-Mart Stores Inc. and five other companies sued by consumers in 2007 for selling tainted pet food reached a $24 million settlement in May of 2008 with plaintiffs.

A U.S. company, ChemNutra Inc., and two Chinese businesses were in February of 2008, charged by a federal grand jury in connection with the import of tainted pet food ingredients that may have killed thousands of cats and dogs in 2007. The dog and cat foods contained melamine-tainted wheat gluten that if ingested can cause kidney failure and death.

In February 2008, Las Vegas-based ChemNutra Inc. and the two Chinese businesses were charged by a Kansas City federal grand jury with illegally importing 800 metric tons of wheat gluten poisoned with melamine. ChemNutra had denied any deliberate wrongdoing.

"I don't think there is any question," that Chinese food and drug products are safer as compared to last year, Leavitt said. "Will there be problems in the future? Yes. Will there be as many of them? I don't think so."

For a while in 2007, it seemed the reports of tainted food, drugs, and toys flowing in from China would never cease. First came the pet food scare, in which a toxic additive killed thousands of animals. Summer brought vast recalls of lead-tainted Thomas trains and other name-brand toys, counterfeit Colgate containing antifreeze, salmonella-infected toddler snacks, and DDT-contaminated seafood. In the fall and winter, dozens of patients died after receiving bad batches of heparin, a blood-thinning drug produced in China by U.S. firms.

At the height of it all, then President Bush offered lip service. "The American people expect their government to work tirelessly to make sure consumer products are safe. And that is precisely what my administration is doing," he declared that July. He then issued an executive order directing Health and Human Services Secretary Leavitt to seek solutions. Two months later, Leavitt promised that U.S. agencies would pinpoint the riskiest imports and step up enforcement. And then nothing happened.

William Hubbard, a senior Food and Drug Administration official who retired in 2005 after serving under seven presidents, had seen it all before. In response to the 9/11 attacks, staffers at the FDA...which oversees some 80 percent of food imports (the USDA handles the rest)...had developed an Import Strategic Plan that revealed perilously weak controls on food imports. Unveiled in 2003, it was intended to boost inspections of risky cargo and slap greater penalties on importers of dangerous goods. It would have cost a paltry $80 million, but the administration had already made its wishes clear: no new programs. As Hubbard recalled, then-deputy FDA commissioner Lester Crawford "told us there's no money for this, and the White House wants to cut it."

Hubbard realized this spelled trouble! Chinese food exports to the United States had nearly quintupled in the past decade, from roughly $880 million to more than $4.2 billion, and the People's Republic, after Canada, has become America's second-largest seafood supplier. China's pharmaceutical exports to the U.S. had more than quadrupled in the past five years, and some 3,000 Chinese firms now sell medical devices in the States. Such is China's reach that American consumers would be hard pressed to find certain items, including vitamin C tablets or heparin, manufactured anywhere else.

Yet, the Bush administration, in its eagerness to expand trade, had relegated consumer safety to the backseat. FDA warning letters to companies fell off dramatically, Hubbard said, after the agency's general counsel, a Bush appointee, decided such letters should only be sent in cases where the FDA intended to sue the firm. According to the Government Accountability Office, inspections of overseas food factories declined by more than half from 2001 to 2007, and FDA inspectors routinely gave foreign drug makers a heads-up in advance of their visits, a courtesy not extended to American firms.

In some cases, oversight had even been outsourced to China. In June 2007, responding to an epidemic of Chinese seafood containing carcinogenic chemicals and banned antibiotics, the FDA announced that certain products would be held until cleared by lab tests, but allowed Chinese labs...notoriously unreliable...to do the testing. Six weeks later, the Associated Press reported that at least a million pounds of the targeted seafood had hit American plates and stores untested, despite the agency's directive.

Don't blame the inspectors. As it was reported in the New York Times September/October issue of *MotherJones*, by Joshua Kurlantzick a contributing editor, the administration waited until June 2008…after legislators from both parties had given the FDA commissioner a sound public flogging…to seek more funding for food safety. As of the spring of 2008 there were only about 300 inspectors, Hubbard said, to spot-check more than 13 million annual shipments. Only a fraction…7 percent of incoming drugs, for instance… got even a cursory glance. "We've known for years this is a huge problem," he said.

Indeed, FDA documents scrutinized by *MotherJones* show that officials had long known dangerous products were entering the country.. They knew it because some portion of the tainted, counterfeit, or mislabeled shipments were being intercepted and tallied in monthly lists that get passed around the agency. While the same products appear on the lists month after month, agency officials seldom warn the public until after Americans are hurt or killed.

For example, starting in February 2006, FDA inspectors routinely caught shipments of other Chinese seafood tainted by pesticides, illegal drugs, bacterial infections, and malachite green, a carcinogenic dye. But agency officials didn't sound a significant public alert until 16 months later, in June 2007. That same month, the FDA announced a recall of veggie Booty, a toddler staple, because its Chinese-made seasonings contained salmonella, but the warning came too late for 50 Americans, mostly young children, who were stricken with the bug.

Simply, Chinese-made heparin might have killed far fewer Americans had the FDA devised a better way to monitor deadly drug reactions. But because the reports trickled in months after the fact, the public wasn't warned until a spike in "adverse events" had left 106 people dead; 71 had symptoms suggesting a bad reaction to what later proved to be a counterfeit ingredient.

China isn't the only offender, of course, but the documents show it's consistently the worst. In May and June of 2008, for example, the FDA rejected nearly three times as many food shipments from China as from Canada, even though Canada sent five times as much food into the United States. As the world's top consumer of Chinese goods, the U.S. has the clout to sway China's behavior, but the administration had alternately ignored safety concerns and accepted assurances from the world's fastest-growing exporter that it will clean up its act. China had placed almost no environmental or safety controls on exports; its food safety problems will cost $100 billion to fix, according to AT Kearney, a leading consultancy.

If anything, the Bush White House had put Americans at greater risk. Its safety agreements with China tend to be non-binding, said Tony Corbo of the consumer group Food & Water Watch, and fail to hold Chinese goods to U.S. standards. Food safety was barely mentioned at the U.S.-China

Strategic Economic Dialogue in May 2007, according to a federal official privy to the proceedings. (The subject was addressed belatedly at the next meeting, that December, following nine months of import nightmares.) "This administration is more interested in promoting trade," the official noted.

Consistent with that agenda, the White House Office of Management and Budget, normally slow on regulatory matters, took all of one day to green-light U.S. imports of Chinese-processed chicken in April 2006. "We are trying to open up our beef trade with China," said Corbo. "The Chinese always say that they want the U.S. to import Chinese poultry in exchange for U.S. beef."

The decision came despite unsettling findings by the USDA team that had visited the Chinese poultry facilities two years earlier. At one point, inspectors had found paint from the ceiling "on the table used for edible product," while workers at another facility wiped down meat-handling areas with dirty cloths. Parts of a third factory, designated for sanitary operations, were contaminated with "grease, blood, fat, pieces of dry meat, and foreign particles." President Bush nonetheless presented Chinese President Hu Jintao with the new poultry-import rule during a White House visit last year.

Explained a congressional staffer, "It was a goodwill gesture."

The *TimesOnLine* from the Times had reported in September 2008 that by December, China shall reach a milestone more important by far than the Beijing Olympics. It will be 30 years since Deng Xiaoping set China on the course of "reform and opening up", effectively ditching the Maoist dogmas that had turned the hopes vested in the 1949 revolution into tragedy for tens of millions and unnecessary poverty for the great mass of China's people.

Time, then, to take stock...and it risks being awkward times. China's economy had expanded tenfold over this 30-year span, but it will be undeniable by December 2008 that the going is getting tougher. After a decade of double-digit growth that most Chinese under 40 think of as normal, momentum has slowed...from 11.8 percent in the past two years, to an expected 9.8 percent for 2008 and 8 to 9 percent in 2009.

To outsiders, 8 percent still looks awe-inspiring...and a success for the People's Bank of China's fight against overheating. Inside China, even 9.8 percent feels less like cook air than a spell in the freezer. The situation is complicated by inflation, a neuralgic political issue. The official CPI inflation index has cooled thanks to falling food prices, from 8.7 percent in February to 6.3 percent in July, 2008. However, inflation as most Chinese experience it is far higher and is reflected in social unrest and inflation-busting pay raises in key coastal export industries. It would be higher still had the Government not clamped price controls on grain, coal and utilities (exacerbating electricity shortages) and blown 1.2 percent of GDP on fuel subsidies, more than double central government spending on education.

Add to these concerns massive industrial overcapacity, and the urgency of tackling environmental degradation, and Liu Xiang, the Chinese hurdler whose injured Achilles tendon forced him to pull out of the Games, may be a more apt symbol of China's present condition than the 51 other athletes who took it to the top of the gold medal league.

Being the world's factory is China's boast, and its problem. Taking imports and exports together, China's National Bureau of Statistics reckons that 60 percent of its economy relies on foreign trade, and the terms of trade have deteriorated, trapping exporters in a severe profit squeeze. Excess capacity in shrinking markets prevents them passing on sharply higher input costs. Again, no one outside China would term this year's 10 percent fall in its trade surplus a disaster. Indeed, given the size of China's surpluses and the political tensions they generate, not least in election-year America, it was seen as a timely 'rebalancing'.

Still, China is not used to rebalancing; and it hurts. The sag in the U.S. housing market, for example, hits China's $80 billion furniture industry hard: America buys 40 percent of its $23 billion of exports. In Zhejiang's low-end manufacturing hub, the local trade commission stated that 10,700 enterprises, a fifth of the total, had lost money so far in 2008 and shall lose more in 2009. In Guangdong, where Deng's revolution began, the Federation of Hong Kong Industry said that a tenth of the province's 70,000 Hong Kong-owned factories were to close by December 2008 More closed by the beginning of 2009. Guangdong produces 30 percent of China's exports.

Despite mass layoffs, which hit remittances to poor rural families, domestic consumption is rising, but Rio Tinto earned the rubic of Rosy Tinto last week for declaring that demand in cities of China's interior would take up the export slack. Most Chinese remain almost excessively frugal. The British consume more than do 1.3 billion Chinese.

Wang Zixian, policy researcher at the Ministry of Commerce, fretted that China is vulnerable to a version of the 1997-98 Asian financial crisis. His forebodings may seem farfetched, given China's $1,800 billion reserves. Ordinary Chinese who uttered them would land in jail for scaremongering. Yet, remember the sources of that crisis: inflows of hot money; state interference in bank lending and accompanying favoritism, corruption and resource misallocation and, finally, property bubbles. China suffers all these ills...and danger signs abound. The Shanghai exchange has fallen 60 percent in 2008; a third of Beijing's downtown office space is vacant and only a dozen of the 1,500 spaces in Dongguan's South China Mall are filled. Not all "growth" is growth. Nonperforming loans, officially $600 billion, could be as high as $1,100 billion...either at, or well above, the fifth of GDP that, in Japan, triggered a decade's slump.

On July 25th, 2008 the Politburo abruptly altered course. Controlling inflation no longer comes first. The new slogan is: "Fast yet steady growth for a long time to come." Li Keqiang, the vice-premier, had been reportedly devising a 370 billion yuan ($54 billion) stimulus package. Bank lending targets, which are centrally set, had been eased.

Why would Beijing want to "stimulate" the economy when overcapacity is acknowledged as "a deep-seated problem"; when the infrastructure, despite hefty investment, is creaking; and when real lending rates are negative and so, importantly, is the interest on bank deposits where most Chinese save?

Politics is the answer. "Stability, stupid" is the card on every cadre's wall; the instinct is to go for growth and handle the consequences later. But these could be grave. China needs to move on from cheap energy and labor and zero attention to the environment, moving up the value-added curve. That, Mr. Li said in August of 2008, will require "innovation" and a freer "market system". In 1998, China's then premier, Zhu Rongji, responded to crisis by closing loss-making state enterprises...breaking Mao's "iron rice bowl" and throwing millions out of work. China's present leaders need to be equally bold...ditching distorting price controls and putting more disposable income in people's pockets by investing heavily in health, education and pensions. Deng might have done that. But Deng is dead.

Knockoff designer blue jeans are now among the biggest growth areas in the booming field of knock-off imports into the U.S. U.S. customs and legal experts say that luxury blue jeans such as True Religion, Joy's Jeans and Antik Denim are seeing big increases in counterfeiting, the Los Angeles Times reported.

"The counterfeiting problem exists with Rolex watches and high-end jeans because people want the cachet without spending the money. The opportunity to make money is greater when there's a much higher profit margin. Custom officials said they intercepted $18 million worth of counterfeit apparel, including denim, from China in 2007, marking a 29 increase from 2006

Facing Counterfeiting Crackdown, Beijing Vendors Fight Back

Any tourist who has stepped foot in Beijing's famous Silk Street Market can testify that it is home to some of the wiliest, most tenacious vendors who ever tried to palm off a fake handbag on a naïve foreigner. So when the market managers temporarily shut down 29 stalls over the course of a month for selling counterfeit goods, no one expected the merchants to acquiesce quietly to the loss of business. IntellecPro, a Beijing firm that specializes in intellectual property rights, represents five foreign luxury-brand manufacturers that have sued the market for trademark violations.

The *New York Times* reported on March 2nd of 2009 that many vendors had responded with the same ferocity with which they nail down a sale. Dozens of them had staged weekly protests against IntellecPro lawyers who were pursuing the trademark case, mocking them as bourgeois puppets of foreigners. The vendors confronted witnesses who proved evidence of trademark violations and filed countersuits asserting that only the government can shutter a business.

This proves that any successful products are likely to be illegally copied in China although China's government had pledged to crack down as it faces continual increasing pressure to show progress. But some doubt much will change until China graduates from manufacturing goods to designing them, and has more to lose than to gain.

While the branded merchandise manufacturers are saying that the government is not doing enough of a job to protect their intellectual property rights, the vendors have said that they are going overboard in protecting the intellectual property rights. Now, tourists guidebooks call the Silk Street Market, a seven-story glass box near Beijing's diplomatic quarter, one of China's most popular spots to buy cheap, good-quality imitations. With some 1,200 stalls, it attracts 15 million shoppers a year, two-thirds of them foreigners.

There are shelves bulging with fake handbags bearing the designs and tags of Coach, Dolce & Gabbana, Chloe and other famous companies. Fake Gucci and Louis Vuitton bags are still offered, but are hidden inside cupboards; buyers are invited to seal the transactions outside the building; and the vendors' lawyers try to portray their clients as too ignorant to distinguish fake goods from real or to recognize brand names. "They have no idea this says Louis Vuitton," Xu Shengzhong, a vendor's lawyer said, tapping a brown wallet with the brand's distinctive logo.

Realizing that these ordinary people have worked for decades, to their deaths, selling these counterfeit goods, the Silk Market must fundamentally change and shift its focus from counterfeit goods to genuine pearls, silks, homegrown brands and tailoring services. But then again, this would mean that the shoppers would also have to change their habits as well. The visitors want the knockoffs and you can see it in their eyes when they go to the Silk Market. That is the brutal reality.

— 18 —

Secrets That Restaurants Don't Want You To Know...
and
is The FDA a Broken Agency?

Restaurants have one major purpose: to stuff you with as much food as they possibly can. If they do that, they achieve their primary business goal, which is to lighten your wallet. But while they're doing that, they're also using their best marketing tricks, craftiest numerical switcheroos, and most dastardly dietary stratagems to swap unhealthy, cheap ingredients for more expensive, wholesome ones. The result: bloated bottom lines...for their budgets, and for their customers.

But we don't want to let that happen to you, which is why the *Men'sHealth* September 2008 issue had spent the last two years researching all of the ways restaurants try to sabotage your food choices. Listed is a sampling of the fruits of our long labor: some of the new secrets the restaurant-chain gang doesn't want you to know. They're only a few of the many ways restaurants fatten up their customers for the sales slaughter. Heed the warnings and you (and your family) can make it through the drive-thru alive. Here is a report from *Men'sHealth The Burn*:

1. **Baskin-Robbins doesn't want you to know that...**
    Sometimes a drink can have fruit in the title, but not in the cup. For instance, the top four ingredients in its Blue Raspberry Fruit Blast were Sierra Mist soda, water, sugar, and corn syrup. Since we

first called the company out on this fruitless horror, Baskin-Robbins discontinued the Blue Raspberry Fruit Blast. The company also began listing all nutrition and ingredient information online. We call that progress.

2. **Papa John's doesn't want you to know that...**
Unlike rival chains such as Domino's, it has made little effort to introduce healthier options. After we goaded them on their slow pace of innovation, Papa John's did introduce whole grain wheat crust pizzas in May of 2008. Now, if only Papa would toss a thin-crust version into the mix and alter the recipe for sides like cheese sticks, which are loaded down with more than 2,900 milligrams of sodium!

3. **Fuddruckers doesn't want you to know...**
The fat content of its 1-pound burgers. We contacted our local Fuddruckers restaurant and were told that the nutritional information was available on the chain's Web site (it's not). The corporate office later responded that providing such information would be "very extensive and timely." We're pretty sure he meant "very expensive and time-consuming." How's that for a Freudian slip?

4. **Panera Bread doesn't want you to know that...**
The synthetic food colorings in its pastries have been linked to irritability, restlessness, and sleep disturbances in children. And British researchers found that artificial food colorings and preservatives in the diets of 3-year-olds caused an increase in hyperactive behavior. The same ingredients appear in fast-food items like mayonnaise, M&M Blizzards, and McDonald's shakes.
    On Panera's Web site, you cans track down calories, fat, sugar, and other nutritional numbers. If you look hard enough you'll find ingredient lists, too...and note that a few items still contain artificial coloring. Disappointing. If you want to cut out the artificial stuff entirely, head over to Chipotle: The restaurant used no artificial colorings or flavorings. Just make sure you saw their burritos...which can have more than 1,000 calories...in half.

5. **Chevy's Fresh Mex doesn't want you to know...**
How its tortillas stack up nutritionally. The chain says it provides "nutritional information regarding calories, fat, protein & carbohydrates for some of our most popular item"...the chicken, steak, and shrimp fajitas, for example...on its Web site. But the numbers provided don't include the tortilla: an essential component typically bloated with fat and carbs. When we called a New York Chevy's for more information, a server told us he couldn't find

that info on the in-house menu, either, which would seem to be a violation of New York City regulations. He did direct us to the same misleading nutritional information on the company's Web site. Gee, thanks.

6. **Applebee's, IHOP, Olive Garden, Outback, Red Lobster, and T.G.I. Friday's don't want you to know…**
   The nutritional impact of their dishes. Despite the fact that we continued to pester each company, they all were mum about their nutritional information. So we had it nutritionally analyzed on our own. We may not be in this fix for long, however. New York City regulations that went into effect in July 2008 require all restaurants with 15 or more branches nationally to post calorie counts on their menus.

   After tracking down every last dish, we can see what they were hiding. At Friday's, no fewer than nine sandwiches and 10 appetizers topple the 1,000 calorie barrier; at IHOP, the "healthiest" entrée-size salad has a staggering 1,050 calories; and at Outback, even a simple order of salmon will wipe out 75% of your day's caloric allotment.

Basically, for more restaurant industry secrets that will freak the weight right off of you, check out other dubious restaurant secrets that are being hidden from you! And you can lose weight in record time by staying away from the unhealthiest drinks in America! They can be responsible for causing you to gain a few pound of fat…a month!

And now that you're aware of the danger, do us all a favor: if you notice other big fat restaurant lies, let Men's Health weekly magazine know. Likewise, if you've found ways to cut through the fast-food jungle without getting eaten, tell them as well. When it comes to the battle of the restaurant bulge, we're all in this together.

We would think that the FDA would protect us against tainted foods as well as grossly disturbing facts about how much fat content is in the foods we eat…tainted peanuts…unsterilized syringes…salmonella in Mexican chili peppers…a contaminated blood thinner from China that sent patients into life-threatening shock. Some say that the FDA is broken.

Representative John Dingall, D-Michigan had said that "You can bet yourself a new hat or a fine dinner that you are going to have a scandal a month. They are running around like a lot of headless chickens."

Because of a lack of legal authorities and inadequate resources, it's really hard to do the job and restoring the FDA's reputation will be a major challenge for the new Obama administration that strode into town promising competent government. "This agency is quite frankly either nonfunctional or dysfunctional, or maybe all of the above," said Dingell, who as the longest serving member of the House has investigated many agencies, including the FDA.

The decline didn't happen overnight. There's no single cause. In 2007, an independent group of science advisers concluded that the FDA was in danger of falling in its mission. American lives are still at risk. As the pharmaceutical and food industries went global, the FDA fell behind on inspections. Its legal powers failed to keep up with fast-changing industries. Its own scientists said it grew too cozy with drug companies and tuned out signals of safety problems. Money for research grew scarce. Internal computer systems were allowed to decay, although they are essential to monitoring drug safety trends or blocking shady imports.

The FDA drifted. During the Bush administration, it went long periods without a permanent commissioner who could be an advocate before Congress. Lawmakers piled new responsibilities on the agency, often without the funds to carry them out. This year's safety problems...homegrown and imported...illustrate the FDA's weakness.

Last winter, heparin from China contaminated by a mysterious ingredient prompted an international recall. The blood thinner was triggering life-threatening allergic reactions. Summer brought a salmonella outbreak blamed first on tomatoes and later on hot peppers as well.

The winter, it was salmonella again, in peanut products. A small company's apparent disregard for basic sanitation led to the recall of more than 2,800 foods that used its ingredients. More than 2,100 people were sickened in these incidents. At least nine deaths have been blamed on tainted peanuts alone.

Around the first of March, 1009, the Federal prosecutors in North Carolina obtained guilty pleas from two employees of AM2PAT, a company that manufactured syringes in unsterile conditions and covered it up with phony paperwork. Prosecutors said that hundreds of patients were sickened and five died. The feds are looking for the company's owner, who may have fled the country. Different products were involved in the incidents, but they shared some of the same FDA shortcomings: inspections, legal authority and technology.

Although the FDA is supposed to inspect overseas plants, the pharmaceutical factory in China that made the heparin was never visited, partly because the agency confused its name with a similar name belonging to another drug factory.

The tomato outbreak in the summer of 2008 underscored other kinds of gaps. Produce companies are not required to have a food safety plan. And the FDA lacks legal authority to require a system for tracing foods back to the farm.

In the peanut butter outbreak, FDA inspectors quickly focused on a small Georgia processing plant. But they didn't get the whole story immediately. The FDA had to invoke bioterror laws to get lab reports that ultimately showed the company shipped tainted peanuts. Meanwhile, the agency had no authority to order a food recall.

Congress has been pumping more money into the FDA. And the Obama administration seems willing to consider big changes. Let's see if these big changes do take place. I doubt it.

What we need is an overhaul of the entire agency no matter who the next FDA commissioner may be, whether he/she comes from within or outside the agency such as the health commission, a pediatrician or even a bioterrorism expert.

Source: The Associate Press – Inside Washington, March 5, 2009

– 19 –

**FDA Issues Warning on Imported
Chinese Baby Formula...
Worried Parents in China Wait for Answers on
Tainted Formula...
Tainted Milk Scare Goes Beyond China**

The *Los Angeles Times* first reported this story around September 12, 2008 when Federal officials warned consumers to avoid buying any infant formula imported from China, citing reports of dozens of babies in that country who fell ill with kidney stones after drinking a brand called Sanlu, resulting in at least one death. The warning was aimed at Chinese American communities across the United States, including Southern California, home to one of the largest ethnic Chinese populations in the nation.

Importing Chinese-manufactured baby formula into the U.S. is illegal, but federal officials said that they knew of at least one case in which a Chinese brand was found in a New York store in 2004.

"We're concerned that there may be some formula that has come in illegally and could potentially be in the ethnic Chinese markets," said Janice Oliver, a deputy director at the U.S. Food and Drub Administration's Center for Food Safety and Applied Nutrition in College Park, Maryland. There is no indication that tainted formula has made it onto U.S. store shelves.

The FDA has strict regulatory authority over baby formula and allows only six companies to distribute it in the United States. None of the firms import ingredients from China, Oliver said.

The six manufacturers are Abbott Nutrition, Mead Johnson Nutritionals, Nestle USA, PBM Nutritionals, Solus Products…which are all based in the U.S.….and SHS/Nutricia, based in Britain. The contaminant in the Chinese infant formula is melamine, the same substance found in tainted pet food that sickened or killed thousands of dogs and cats in 2007.

The addition of melamine, which is normally found in plastics, can make food appear, in testing, to have higher levels of protein. Ingestion of melamine can cause kidney failure.

Cat Chao, a Mandarin-language radio host for Pasadena-based KAZN-AM (1300), said the brand of the tainted baby formula, Sanlu, is popular in China, but said she didn't believe it was available in the U.S. "We do feel like those business guys who want to make money from this product, and sometimes you really get angry at those people," Chao said.

In the meantime, Sanlu company officials ordered a recall of its infant formula according to the China Daily, the Chinese state-run English newspaper. The recall came a day after the death of an infant in the northwestern province of Gansu province in 2008. There where no deaths reported in 2006 and 2007. Reports of kidney stones in infants had spread to six other provinces, according to Chinese media reports.

This is not the first time that problems had been identified with baby formula made in China. The FDA said that in 2004, Chinese-manufactured infant formula was found in an ethnic Chinese market in New York. There were no reported illnesses, but lab tests found low quantities of protein, fat, calcium and magnesium in the formula.

Earlier that year in China, at least 13 babies died and more than 170 suffered serious malnutrition when they drank fake milk powder in the impoverished eastern province of Anhui, which is one of the seven provinces affected by the current illnesses. Lab tests showed that the purported formula was made of starch, four and sugar.

On September 18, 2008 *The New York Times* reported that harried nurses at Children's Hospitals on the east side of Beijing sat behind a small desk, registering infants in a rapidly filling logbook. Anxious parents, fearing they might have unwittingly fed their infants tainted formula, waited for hours to determine if their babies had been harmed.

One father, Zhang Gaofeng, 35, had waited more than a day at the hospital with his wife, Wang Hui, and their 22-month-old daughter, Yue. The couple had fed Yue the Sanlu brand of baby formula now at the center of a nationwide food safety scandal that had left three infants dead and sickened more than 6,000 babies. Mr. Zhang, a migrant worker, blamed corporate greed.

"They are trying to make a profit off the people who are not rich enough to afford the imported brands," he said as he waited in the hospital parking lot with other families. "Poor people can only afford the low-end products like this one," He said the Sanlu product had cost about $3.20 for two days' worth of formula, compared with about $5 for the top brands.

The anxiety at Children's Hospital was just one snapshot of a scandal that has broadened every day since it became public and Health Minister Chen Zhu reported that more than 1.300 infants had been hospitalized and that 158 had suffered acute kidney failure after being fed formula contaminated with the industrial additive melamine.

With anger rising, the State Council, China's cabinet, pledged an overhaul of the nation's dairy industry, and government officials tried to reassure people by issuing a statement that "most" of China's baby formula was safe. But public confidence seemed shaken.

"What should we eat, then?" asked one person on an Internet discussion forum. "I'm furious! The milk powder is now exposed, but what about the other tainted food that we don't know about? What has the central government been doing every day?"

Melamine, the contaminant, is used to make plastics and fertilizers but banned from food production. In the past, it has sometimes been illicitly blended into agricultural products as a cheap way to raise protein levels. Milk producers sometimes inflate their supplies by adding water. But the diluted milk has lower nutrient levels, so melamine, high in nitrogen, is then added to restore those levels artificially to meet protein requirements. Infants who drink the formula for sustained periods can develop kidney stones and suffer kidney failure.

Initially, the contamination was thought to be confined to baby formula produced by the Sanlu Group, one of China's largest diary companies. But investigations have since discovered traces of melamine in batches of powdered formula made by 21 other dairy companies, including the biggest, Mengniu Dairy. Mengniu and other companies have recalled tainted products, even as government officials have promised to correct the problems so that big operators can resume or even expand production to meet demand.

"They can absolutely undergo a major overhaul in a short period of time," Li Changjiang, head of the General Administration of Quality Supervision, Inspection and Quarantine, said during a news conference carried live on national television.

A quick remedy might seem overly optimistic, given that China experienced a similar baby formula scandal in 2004. In 2007, after a string of food and drug safety failures, government officials promised to root out official corruption and strengthen regulation of the food and drug industries. Now, a group of lawyers is organizing lawsuits on behalf of parents against diary operations. The authorities have arrested four suspects, offered free medial care to ailing children and sent investigators across the country to inspect dairy operations. Four officials in Hebei Province were fired, including Tian Wenhua, chairwoman and general manager of Sanlu Group, based in Hebei. Ms. Tian was also fired from a post in the Communist Party.

Meanwhile, a nationwide inspection examined 491 batches of formula selected from the 109 companies that produce baby formula in China. The Sanlu brand contained the highest levels of melamine, according to state media reports. In all, 22 companies were found to have produced some batches of bad formula. Two of them, Yashili, which is based on Guangdong, and Suncare, based in Qingdao, export to Asia and Africa, but it was unclear whether those products contained melamine.

Public indignation seemed to deepen as the scope of the crisis became known. Several bloggers called for the resignation of Mr. Li, the top quality control official. People also complained that the government had taken greater precautions on food safety for athletes during the Olympics than for the public.

"Why are the dairy products supplied for the Olympics safe?" asked a blogger who used the name Absentminded. "Why are the dairy products exported to other counties safe? Why do the dairy products for ordinary Chinese people have problems?"

The government tried to mollify the public by providing information on how to look for symptoms of poisoning. A popular Internet chat room operated by People's Daily, the Communist Party's newspaper, offered a live question-and-answer session with a doctor and a government scientist.

At Children's Hospital in Beijing, nurses shooed away a foreign journalist who tried to enter a special clinic established for infants who may have ingested the tainted formula. One nurse said as many as 200 babies were brought for testing and the babies were undergoing two urine tests and an ultrasound to check for kidney stones.

Mr. Zhang, the migrant worker, said his daughter was still waiting for the second urine test. The waiting list was so long that her ultrasound was not scheduled for six more days. "I read a story in the newspaper," Mr. Zhang said, explaining how he learned about the danger. "I was stunned. My concern is whether or not people will be held accountable and whether they will be put in jail. They might simply buy their way out. I want to see them jailed or even executed for this."

Milk Off Shelves as China's Safety Scandal Grew

It was reported by the *Associated Press* that in Shijiazhuang, China by the latter part of September, that when China's food safety crisis widened after the industrial chemical melamine was found in milk, this prompted stores, including Starbucks, to yank milk from their shelves. The recalls came as evidence was mounting that adding chemicals to watered-down milk was a widespread practice in China's dairy industry.

The crisis was initially thought to have been confined to tainted milk powder, used to make baby formula that had been blamed in the deaths of four infants and for sickening over 6,200 other children. The apparently widespread contamination had rapidly become a political headache for a communist government that hoped to be basking in popular adulation over the successful Beijing Olympics. Instead, the government was being forced to scramble to regain public confidence. No tainted infant formula had turned up in the United States, where authorities had inspected more than 1,000 retail markets mainly serving Asian communities. China is an importer of liquid milk, so it's unlikely that milk from that country would have been shipped to the U.S.

It had been proven that Chinese farmers were cutting corners to cope with rising costs for feed and water. Before this incident, it was known that they had been adding organic stuff like animal urine or skin...basically anything that can boost the protein reading, said Chen Lianfang of the Beijing Orient Agribusiness Consultant Company. The farmers knew to add melamine to milk as the chemical is not water-soluble, and must be mixed with formaldehyde or another chemical before it can be dissolved in milk.

"The farmers are not well-educated enough to think of melamine," Chen said. "There must be people from chemical companies contacting them and telling them it's a good idea."

The crisis highlighted the growing influence of dairy products in the Chinese diet. Milk is not part of the traditional Chinese diet, but the country's economic growth and the increased availability of refrigeration had brought about a wide range of products, with flavored milk and sweetened yogurts among the most popular.

The crisis had raised questions about the effectiveness of tighter controls China promised after a series of food safety scares in recent years over contaminated seafood, toothpaste, and a pet food ingredient tainted with melamine that was blamed for the deaths of dogs and cats in the United States. In 2004, more than 200 Chinese infants suffered malnutrition and at least 12 died after being fed phony formula that contained no nutrients.

Starbucks Corp. said its 300 cafes in mainland China were pulling all milk supplied by Mengniu, though the Seattle-based company said no employee or customers had fallen ill from the milk. And in Singapore, White Rabbit Creamy Candy, a milk-based treat popular with children and adults here, had been found to be contaminated with melamine.

The candy joined two other brands-Dutch Lady Strawberry-flavored milk and Yili Choice Dairy Fruit Bar Yogurt Flavored Ice Confection-on the list of dairy products from China which the authorities here said are adulterated by the chemical normally found in plastics. In China alone, by the end of September 2008, four children had died from taking contaminated milk and another 12,892 warded for kidney problems.

Beside milk and milk products such as ice cream and yogurt, confectionary items such as chocolate, biscuits, sweets and anything that could contain milk from China came under its latest advisory, including Snickers bars, M&Ms, Nabisco Chicken in a basket, Dove chocolate bars, Mentos yogurt balls, Oreo wafer sticks, and Want Want Take One Baby Bites, all labeled 'Product of China' With cheap products, there is a chance it is made with milk from a country that sells milk cheaply, namely China. By the end of September the number had risen to 53,000 children who had fallen ill because the Chinese company, the Sanlu Group had failed to report complaints about the product for months, probably since December of 2007.

Many American shoppers keep asking the question, "Why are we still importing ANYTHING from China?" Some conscientious shoppers had reported reading labels from Wal-Mart that certain items "could" be imported from China or other various countries. Needless to say, many of these customers took the items back to Wal-Mart and got their money back. I therefore question why is there a need to import juice from China as well as any kind of food product...or any product at all if there are problems of being tainted? Is it all about making a lousy buck no matter the consequences? It seems that the companies, no matter who they are, do not care if they poison our children even in our own country. Even Japan's Marudai Food Company withdrew buns made with milk, supplied by Yili, and any products with Chinese dairy ingredients were being recalled in Japan.

Other countries that have banned or recalled Chinese milk products include Brunei, Singapore, Malaysia, Hong Kong and Taiwan which banned all mainland dairy products. The Chinese Ministry of Agriculture had stated that despairing farmers were dumping milk and killing cattle after companies stopped buying their supplies. It promised subsidies to help farmers.

The list of products caught in China's tainted milk scandal included cereal in Hong Kong and snack foods in Japan, while Taiwan reported three children and a mother with kidney stones in the island's first cases possibly linked to the crisis. The latest problematic foods were Heinz baby cereal and Silang House steamed potato wasabi crackers. The Hong Kong government said in a statement it found traces of melamine in the products, which were both made in mainland China.

The scandal is the most serious black market to date against the "Made in China" brand. Recent years have seen scares over seafood, dumplings and pet food, while toys, toothpaste and pharmaceuticals, have been revealed as substandard and dangerous. In Starbucks' 300 cafes around China, the baristas have switched to using soy milk in lattes and cappuccinos, and many customers seemed to be switching to black coffee or skipping their daily caffeine hit altogether.

Two baby orangutans and a lion cub at a zoo in eastern China had developed kidney stones from being fed tainted milk powder, while two gorillas at the same zoo, the Hangzhou Wildlife world in Zhejiang province, were also sick.

In the supermarkets, the food safety crisis had people asking whether other products out there, such as meat and vegetables, were safe or not, although the Xinhua news agency stated that shoppers were slowly buying dairy again after crisis management efforts.

Perhaps fearful the scandal was going to translate into wider social unrest, the Chinese media was chiefly focusing on the Shenzou-7 space walk, and China's food safety regulators said recent food safety problems had been brought under control.

The EU had banned the import of Chinese baby food that contains any traces of milk, while other food made in China or with Chinese ingredients such as toffee, biscuits and chocolate, would be tested. Sanlu, which is 43 per cent owned by New Zealand's Fonterra Group, is now facing bankruptcy and its chief executive is in jail. The Chinese company may be bought by Beijing Sanyuan Foods, whose products have not been found to be contaminated.

Until the next time...one can only hope for the best!

— 20 —

EU Bans Food Imports from China...
More Foods Getting Labeled as U.S. or Foreign Grown...
Time to Ban All Imports From China

By the beginning of October, The *Press Association* had reported that a Europe ban on all food for children coming from China had come into force. The European Commissioner's ban came amid growing concern over contaminated milk powder which had already caused infant deaths in China and affected thousands more in many countries.

Although there was no evidence of contaminated products from China in many of the European countries, the decision, under EU health and safety provisions, was announced and was formally adopted in the EU. Random testing of other foods which could be affected was considered and industry and FSA were well placed to take action if any contaminants were found.

Dairy farmers, milk collectors and dairy company employees in Inner Mongolia, the heart of China's dairy industry, told The Age that substandard milk had long been routinely accepted by China's two biggest dairy manufacturers Mengniu and Yili, but this had stopped after the melamine scandal broke. A Mengniu employee had stated that production was down because the scandal had forced the plant to stop accepting dodgy milk. "Before, there was no testing as strict as there is now," he said. "There was only standard, the milk was either qualified or not!"

Many milk collection owners professed ignorance of any underhand practices and that it was now a lottery whether the milk was accepted. It seemed that the dairy manufacturers were all aware of the problem, but they still took in tainted raw milk either because of the shortage of supply or because they were connected to the agents and accepted bribes.

Six of the 22 dairy companies whose infant formula was later found to be melamine-tainted, including Sanlu, had been exempted from regular inspections because they were deemed "famous brands" that could be trusted to ensure quality. One of the government's first actions after the scandal became public was to abolish the system of exempting famous brands from regular inspections. Obviously, the state-owned Sanlu Group had lied about problems with its infant formula for more than eight months, investigators sent by the State Council (China's cabinet) found. The investigators blamed local government officials in Shijiazhuang, Hebei's capital, for saying nothing to higher authorities.

Basically, the story was exposed publicly, in the "big-headed baby" scandal in 2004, when 13 babies in the poor province of Anhui were killed by the fake Sanlu brand powder. Sanlu confirmed that the milk powder was genuine, denied any problems but offered the parents refunds. One of the fathers posted the story online to try to get media interest. After the tainted milk scandal was finally exposed in September 2008, the father, Wang admitted he withdrew his online complaint after 10 days because Sanlu paid him 2500 yuan…in milk powder…and he felt powerless to keep going.

When the news broke, first of the cover-up of the problem having failed to report the matter to the New Zealand Government of bodies such as the World Health Organization…a Fonterra employee let drop at an NZ embassy Olympic cocktail party on August 14 that there was a problem. It took almost three weeks for the Prime Minister Helen Clark to learn this. Beijing, if not directly complicit in the cover-up, had made it clear to all levels of government and state media that it wanted no bad news, specifically citing food and product safety issues, aired in the lead-up to the Olympics.

The cover-up and later full exposure with the Government putting its considerable powers behind fixing the problem is chillingly reminiscent of what happened during the SARS crisis in 2003. Then the sensitive political issue was the transition of presidential power from Jiang Zemin to Hu Jintao. Officials ignored, suppressed and lied publicly about a dangerously infectious epidemic that was ripping through the country. When it became impossible to hide the SARS epidemic or its origins in southern China, Hu and his Premier, Wen Jiabao, took the gamble of coming clean. It paid off: SARS was quickly contained and public support for Hu's Government increased.

The political fallout from the tainted milk scandal was not so positive for the Government, which has been delicately juggling using censorship to avoid "social instability" (communist code for threats to its authority) while allowing public outrage to be vented. The real test will be not another overhaul of food and product safety standards…which were allegedly comprehensively overhauled a year ago after the string of scandals about contaminated toothpaste, seafood and pet food, but whether the Government will allow an unprecedented class action.

More than 100 lawyers had volunteered to represent aggrieved parents, but allowing a class action on tainted milk would create a troubling precedent for an authoritarian Government that had already shut down similar moves by parents whose children were killed in the Sichuan earthquake because of shoddy school construction.

On September 30, 2008 the Associated Press reported that 'No more wondering where your hamburger came from, or where your lettuce and tomatoes were grown: Starting this week, shoppers will see lots more foods labeled with the country of origin,"

It's a law years in the making but timely, as China's milk scandal and the recent salmonella-tainted Mexican peppers prompt growing concern over the safety of imported foods. Still, hold the import-bashing: Numerous outbreaks in recent years have come from U.S.-produced foods, like spinach grown in California.

Until now, shoppers have had little clue where many everyday foods… meats, fresh fruits and vegetables, certain nuts…originate. That's what the so-called COOL law, for country-of-origin labeling, changes. Those who want to buy local…or who prefer, say, Chilean grapes and New Zealand lamb… can more easily exercise their purchase power.

Those worried about tax safety regulations in certain countries can avoid those imports. And the next time tomatoes are suspected of food poisoning, consumers may be able to tell investigators they bought only ones grown in a certain region, speeding the probe.

"We do see it as an important step on the road to a more comprehensive system for tracing food items" during outbreaks, said Caroline Smith DeWaal of the Center for Science in the Public Interest.

"It will be a very good thing because we'll have a lot more information," added Jean Halloran of Consumers Union. But, "you can still be fooled by the COOL label."

How, you ask? There are bunches of exceptions. Fresh strawberries get a label but not chocolate-covered ones. Raw peanuts? Label. Roasted ones? No Label. Those popular pre-washed salad mixes? Sometimes!

My own comment on labeling foods, based on whether it is a single product like strawberries, or if they are multi-products like chocolate covered strawberries, we must label all products so that everyone can have the knowledge where they originated from and decide at that point whether to buy them or not.

It has been too long where people were deceived into thinking that many products have originated from the U.S. and they actually came from China or other countries like Mexico, South and Central America, Indonesia and the Philippines. Realizing that many products that originate in the U.S. may go to China for the inclusion of other ingredients, and then come back to this country for packaging, we must find a way to include this in the labels. If there is a recall, the consumer must be able to look at the labels on the products being recalled and determine if that product should be returned to the store where it was purchased. This could be an initial step in handling the tainted products that come from overseas.

Here are some common questions as shoppers navigate the change:

Q: What does the new law require?
A: That the retailers notify customers of the country of origin... including the U.S....of raw beef, veal, lamb, pork, chicken, goat, wild and farm-raised fish and shellfish, fresh or frozen fruits and vegetables, peanuts, pecans, macadamia nuts and whole ginseng. (The aim was big agricultural commodities; ginseng was added for fear of imports masquerading as U.S.-grown.)

Q: Where will I see the country of origin?
A: Anywhere it fits. The rubber band around asparagus; the plastic wrap on ground beef; the little sticker that says "Gala" on an apple. If a food isn't normally sold in any packaging...such as a bin of fresh green beans or mushrooms...then the store must post a sign.

Q: Aren't many foods already labeled?
A: Some fresh produce already uses origin labeling as advertising. "Fresh from Florida" or "Jersey Grown" or "Vidalia Onion" tags don't have to be changed under the new rules; the shopper should realize they're all U.S. products.

The COOL law mandating such labels first passed in 2002, but lobbying by grocery stores and large meatpackers led Congress to delay the U.S. Department of Agriculture from implementing it. Seafood labeling was phased in first, in 2005...a key change given recurring safety problems with fish and shellfish from certain countries, including China.

Q: What's the biggest exception?

A: The labels aren't for processed foods, meaning no label if the food is cooked, or an ingredient in a bigger dish or otherwise substantially changed. So plain raw chicken must be labeled but not breaded chicken tenders. Raw pork chops are labeled, but not ham or bacon. Fresh or frozen peas get labeled, but not canned peas. Raw shelled pecans, but not a trail mix.

Q: What if the foods are merely mixed together?

A: They're exempt, too. Cantaloupe slices from Guatemala get labeled. Mix in some Florida watermelon chunks, and no label. Frozen peas, labeled. Frozen peas and carrots, no label. As for bagged salads, USDA considers iceberg and Romaine to be just lettuce, so that bag gets a label. Add some radicchio? No label.

Q: Must all stores comply?

A: No. Meat and seafood sold in butcher shops and fish markets are exempt.

Q: What if companies buy food from various places...beef from both U.S. and Mexican ranchers, for instance?

A: That's a bone of contention between large U.S. meat producers and smaller ranchers that produce exclusively U.S. animals. Tyson Fresh Meats, for instance, says it's too expensive to separate which of its cattle came from which country. So in a July letter to customers, Tyson said it would label all beef "Product of the U.S., Canada or Mexico." The National Farmers Union is protesting. USDA is considering the complaints.

Q: Aren't country labels on some processed foods?

A: Yes, tariff regulations have long required that a food put into consumer-ready packaging abroad be labeled as an import; that doesn't apply to bulk ingredients.

Q: When does the change take effect?

A: The law was to go into effect the latter part of September, although the USDA won't begin fining laggards until spring of 2009. Violations can bring a $1,000 penalty.

Also around this time, Chinese biscuits were being recalled in the UK as officials admitted that the milk firm covered-up the tainted food. Thousands of packets of biscuits contaminated with industrial chemical melamine were ordered off shop shelves in the UK following an alert from the Food Standards Agency. Inspectors were dispatched to Chinese supermarkets and independent retailers across the country to remove and destroy the biscuits after officials in the Netherlands said 3,500 packets of contaminated biscuits had been shipped to Britain.

The alert marked the first case of melamine-contaminated food to arrive in the UK since the health scare in China, in which tens of thousands of babies have been taken ill and four have died due to kidney problems after drinking Sanlu infant formula containing the chemical. It was also revealed that the company at the heart of the scandal asked officials to help conceal the extent of the problem, according to China's state media.

The authorities had already said that officials in Shijiazhuang, Hebei, where Sanlu is based, sat on a report from the company for more than a month before telling provincial bosses. It was noted in the People's Daily, a city government spokesman, Wang Jianguo, said Sanlu asked for help in "managing" the media response to the case when the firm informed the authorities of the problem on August 2nd, 2008. Parents had begun complaining to the firm by the end of 2007.

According to the paper, Sanlu's letter asked the government to "increase control and coordination of the media, to create a good environment for the recall of the company's problem products. This was to avoid whipping up the issue and creating a negative influence in society."

Wang said his colleagues sent a team to investigate as soon as they became aware of the issue. But the People's Daily pointed out that they did not inform the provincial government until September 9th. "We mistakenly thought that taking necessary measures and raising product quality could mitigate the effect and reduce losses," said Wang.

Firms around the world have since been forced to withdraw a range of products due to health concerns. Britain's Food Standards Agency said the Chinese biscuits, which have not been distributed to major supermarkets, were being withdrawn as a precaution and were unlikely to pose a significant health risk.

Dutch authorities raised the alarm after tests on Koala brand biscuits, manufactured by Lotte China Foods Co., found the biscuits contained nearly twice the precautionary limit of melamine at 4.98mg a kilo. Import checks revealed that 168kg of the biscuits had been sent on from the Netherlands to Britain. The FSA had withdrawal alerts on four products: Koala chocolate cookies, Koala strawberry cookies, Koala yummy cookies chestnut and Koala melon cookies.

Reuters then reported on October 4th that South Korea's food watchdog had ordered China-manufactured snacks from Nestle SA and Mars Inc. to be taken off shelves after detecting melamine in their samples. The Korea Food and Drub Administration (KFDA) said 2.38 parts per million (PPM) and 1.78 ppm of the substance were found in M&M's milk chocolate snack and Snickers peanut Fun Size, both produced by Mars and manufactured in China. "We are urgently recalling the products due to melamine detection," KFDA said in a statement.

Mars said it was temporarily withdrawing the products from the Korean market because it was legally obliged to do so and that the melamine levels announced by the KFDA did not pose a health risk. Kit Kat bars from Nestle were also found carrying 2.89 ppm of melamine, bringing the total number of melamine-detected items to 10 in Seoul.

Nestle said the KFDA asked it to withdraw one batch of mini Kit Kat made in China from the market, after their tests detected minute traces of melamine in a single batch out of eight Nestle confectionery items tested No melamine was detected in the other seven products, the company said. "The company immediately complied with the authorities' request, even though this product is absolutely safe by recognized international standards," Nestle said in a statement.

"South Korea has no regulations on maximum levels of melamine in food, and the conditions under which the South Korean authorities conducted their tests are unclear," it added. Melamine, widely used in kitchen utensils, can pose serious health risks if consumed in large quantities. At least four children in China died after drinking tainted infant milk formula last year. At that time, KFDA said it was currently examining 428 processed products manufactured in China.

So now we must consider that it is possible that Melamine may be in everything that is imported from China and that there may be more of this coming...here's why!

As things started to unfold in 2008, there is a chance that China may not be entirely at fault for the melamine in the milk...at least we don't think that melamine had been deliberately added into the milk to fake the protein test.

But why Melamine? There are a thousand and one proteins out there that can probably fake a protein test (milk is periodically tested to ensure that there is sufficient amounts of certain proteins in it) and to use melamine probably requires some level of sophistication on the part of the China factory on hind sight. To suddenly find melamine in nearly every single thing imaginable means that the factories in China have syndicates all over the world, or that something went wrong in some fundamental food chain that led to the surfacing of melamine everywhere.

While the Chinese authorities have taken responsibility for the presence of melamine in the milk and that "the chemical was added to milk before being sold to dairy manufacturers in a bid to falsely boost protein reading" it is felt that there is more than meets the eye.

Melamine was also found in lactoferrin, one of the export products from New Zealand. Unless there is a worldwide conspiracy on the use of melamine in their products, it is unlikely that the factories in New Zealand have also added melamine into their products to fake a protein test. However, if you look at the common denominator of the products, the answer lies in the cows. To be more precise, it lies in the food of the cows.

Melamine is a by-product of cyromazine and is formed in the bodies of mammals that have ingested cyromazine. Cyromazine is a pesticide that is commonly used to control pests in plants. If cows have been given such plants as part of their diet, it could be possible that melamine is formed in their bodies and passed out in their milk and urine. This is particularly evident in the latest report of vegetables being tainted with melamine, which probably has no purpose when used on plants. However, it was also reported that cyromazine may also be converted to melamine on plants through photodegration, resulting in dealkylation and thus the formation of melamine. This can be found in Lim et. Al., 1990 L.O. Lim, S.J. Scherer, K.D. Shuler and J.P. Toth, Disposition of cyromazine in plants under environmental conditions, J. Agric. Food Chem. 38 (1990), pp. 860-864.

Thus, the real culprit at the end of the day may very well be the pesticide, cyromazine, through use of it leads to the metabolite, melamine being formed in milk, urine and on plants through photodegration. To this, it may be felt that the Chinese government was probably too quick to admit to the accusation that their factories could have played a vital role to fake protein tests. Of course, it may still be possible that the factories somehow managed to find out that melamine had always been present in milk and perhaps thought that it's an inexpensive way to boost their protein test results. The truth of it, will probably be known after a thorough investigation had been carried out.

One more thing about frozen foods...Keta Salmon is known by many names...Calico and Silverbrite among them. Keta is light in color with a very mild flavor. Trader Joe's has Wild Alaskan Keta Salmon from the new catch that's frozen just once and packed for them.

Are you confused by this "frozen just once" business? You didn't know that most wild salmon caught in American waters is processed and frozen twice? Let me explain. Most salmon is caught and quickly frozen, then shipped to China, where it is thawed and made ready for sale...boned, filleted, etc. It is then frozen again and sent back to the U.S. for sale in markets across the country. But Trader Joe's states emphatically that all frozen wild salmon sold in their stores are frozen only once. Now that is something worth looking into!

And finally...BRAND China is on notice according to a survey of Australians about their perceptions of the milk contamination scandal and food products bought more widely from the Asian region. A study, conducted by AMR Interactive for the Herald, showed 68 percent of respondents nationally said they were now worried about the quality of food sourced from China, 73 percent saying they would stop buying food products from China.

These results contain widespread implications for supermarket chains and local and multinational food brands in Australia, which have moved increasing amounts of production and product sourcing overseas. The supermarket house brands ranges at Coles and Woolworths, which have been powering along, will have to tread carefully, according to AMR. Sixty-five percent of respondents said they were now more likely to look at supermarket house brand labels to see if they were made in China. Another 81 percent said they were "more likely" to look at food brands in general to see if they were sourced from China.

The rising public concern in Australia about Chinese-made food products is reflected in another study published by *Nielsen Online*, which has been tracking the levels of online discussions about food safety across 14,000 Australian blogs and discussion threads on web sites such as essentialbaby.com.au, Yahoo!Messages, parent2parent.com.au, huggies.com.au, bellybellycom.au and aussiehomebrewer.com.

According to *Nielsen's online BuzzMetrics study*, concern about Chinese and Asian food products was the second most commonly discussed topic, behind food handling at home and in restaurants. There was a tendency to blame the public for poor food handling, but online discussions point to a belief there may be procrastination from Australian food regulators. There is a certain amount of trust which has been eroded and a very high awareness of the issue.

— 21 —

Wal-Mart Plans a Crackdown on Chinese Suppliers...
China Makes Wal-Mart Toe the Labor Line

On October 24th of 2008, *BusinessWeek* reported that after a series of scandals involving dangerous products, the Wal-Mart chain announced a strategy to enforce environmental and labor standards. If Wal-Mart is to be believed, the world's biggest retailer's latest slogan, "Saving people money, so they can live better," will soon need to be replaced with a greener, more socially conscious one. At a gathering of top company executives, non government organizations, and more than 1,000 suppliers in Beijing on October 22nd of last year, the Bentonville (Ark.) retailer announced an ambitious plan aimed at ensuring its products are made according to strict environmental and labor standards.

That, too, will help ensure the quality of its products and help meet a goal of ending all defective product problems by 2012, said Wal-Mart CEO Lee Scott at the Beijing conclave. "Meeting social and environmental standards is not optional."

Wal-Mart has good reason to show it is cracking down on wayward Chinese suppliers. The country has been rocked by a series of scandals involving dangerous toys, drugs, and food. Following news in September, 2008 of the hospitalization of tens of thousands of children sickened by milk tainted with an industrial chemical, governments have been banning imports of Chinese dairy and other food products. As a result of the scares, customers in the U.S. have shown growing concern about products made in China, where Wal-Mart sourced close to $10 billion last year. The company has also been feeling heat from the Chinese government, which has applied pressure on Wal-Mart through the state-controlled All China Federation of Trade Unions. Bowing to pressure from Beijing, Wal-Mart, which doesn't have a unionized workforce in the U.S., began allowing its 40,000 Chinese employees to open unions and even carry out collective bargaining agreements.

Beijing got the biggest big–box to go union which was a sign the government was paying attention to employees' issues, but it truly did not mean that the workers are on easy street. Wal-Mart stores may stiff-arm unions in the U.S., but not in China. The giant retailer had signed a new collective bargaining deal with the All China Federation of Trade Unions, the government-controlled union representing Wal-Mart's Chinese workers. Under the agreement, which for now only covers two Chinese cities (Guangzhou in the southeastern province of Fujian and Shenyang in China's northeast), Wal-Mart employees were to receive 8% pay raises this year and in 2009.

The deal is a victory for the government, which successfully forced Wal-Mart to unionize its 48,000 local employees in 2006. It's also a sign that employers in China, both local and foreign, are starting to take labor, safety and environmental issues more seriously. In part, that's because Beijing wants to improve China's image after the many made-in-China safety scandals in 2007. Multinationals like Wal-Mart that spend billions of dollars sourcing goods from Chinese factories also are feeling the heat from consumers at home concerned about allegations of abuse.

Chinese workers of course still have few rights: They can't form independent unions, for instance, and they criticize the government's labor policies at their peril. The Wal-Mart deal "looks like a pro-forma agreement that is simply imposed on the enterprise from outside rather than something that was negotiated by genuine representatives of labor," says Geoffrey Crothall, a spokesman for China Labor Bulletin, a Hong Kong group promoting workers' rights on the mainland.

The labor shortage does indeed help workers rights. Workers in China are benefiting somewhat from the new emphasis on corporate social responsibility, say experts in the region. "Anyone in the export supply-chain is being pushed to pay much more attention to labor issues," says Stephen Frost, executive director of CSR Asia, a Hong Kong consulting firm that works with Asian and Western companies. Some of the bigger export-oriented companies in China "have improved quite a bit on health and safety," he said. Employers also have gotten better regarding timely payment of wages, adds Frost.

One factor contributing to the improvement is the shortage of labor in some of China's top manufacturing zones. Factories in the Pearl River delta in southern Guangdong province, adjacent to Hong Kong, are having more difficulty hiring new workers or retaining existing ones; annual turnover rates for some manufacturers can go as high as 200%, said Frost. That's leading companies to raise wages and treat their workers better. When it comes to improving conditions for workers in China, he said, "a tight labor market probably did more than 10 years of CSR activism."

Foreign companies also need to be wary of aggressive local media eager to spotlight problems at multinationals. The Chinese press is highly restrained when it comes to critical reporting of the government but has a much freer hand in coverage of multinationals. That means reporters and bloggers can more easily write about companies that treat their workers poorly. "As the Chinese press becomes more active, bad news will be on the Web within 24 hours," said Melissa Brown, executive director of the Hong Kong-based Association for Sustainable & Responsible Investment in Asia.

No stranger to bad press, Wal-Mart bowed to government pressure to unionize its Chinese workforce and reach the new collective bargaining agreement. For local companies, Beijing uses other tools. For instance, the Shenzhen stock exchange now is encouraging listed companies to issue reports on their labor, safety, environmental, and other policies related to corporate social responsibility, or CSR. The Shanghai exchange has a similar policy regarding corporate governance. The central government's Audit Committee for State-Owned Enterprises, which oversees 160 state companies, now requires reports on environmental and social performance.

The government figures all of these moves will help China turn the page form the embarrassing news about dangerous sweatshops or poisonous toys. "China wants to build its reputation and the reputation of Chinese companies," said Martha Grossman, general manager in Shanghai for RepuTex Group, a Melbourne consulting firm focusing on corporate governance. "There's a perception outside China that Chinese companies are disgraceful. But that's not the case; there are companies that do really good work here."

Not everyone agrees on what it means for companies to be good corporate citizens, though. For state-owned China Construction Bank, which was among the first Chinese companies to start issuing a CSR report last year, it means making donations to art and culture groups, supporting disaster relief efforts such as those following the May 12 earthquake in Sichuan, and following government directives regarding loans to lower-income borrowers. "A company cannot just pursue profits," said bank spokesman Song Hailin, adding that the idea is starting to win acceptance locally. "Chinese companies are gradually starting to come around."

Crothall isn't so sure that will lead to much improvement for workers. "For Chinese, CSR is about philanthropy, doing good things in the community like building hospitals and schools," he said, rather than issues related to labor, safety, and the environment. "CSR as it's promoted in the West hasn't really translated yet."

Wal-Mart is now doing more to prove it is a good corporate citizen. While many of its suppliers currently don't obey all labor and environmental laws in China, Wal-Mart in January 2009 was scheduled to begin requiring its nearly 20,000 direct suppliers in China to certify that their factories meet the gamut of such laws. Among the other steps: Wal-Mart's top 200 Chinese suppliers will have to cut their energy usage by 20% by 2012; suppliers will have to provide the names of every factory they use in producing Wal-Mart goods; direct suppliers worldwide will have to source 95% of their production from factories that meet environmental and social standards set by Wal-Mart; and 30% of the company's 100-plus outlets will have to cut their energy usage in half.

To ensure compliance with these new rules, Wal-Mart is using both carrot and stick. The company claims that the environmental rules help pay for themselves, as suppliers can lower costs by using less packing and cutting energy use. But in case that doesn't persuade suppliers to get on board, Wal-Mart will expand its auditing of supplier factories to include both Wal-Mart-administered and third-party company-run audits.

None of this will be easy. Auditing of labor and environmental conditions in China's factories has been rife with corruption for years. Indeed, the situation has been so bad that many now see audits as more of a public relations and legal exercise than a serious attempt to "improve factory conditions." "Rather then make expenditures on fixing up factories, people instead go for fraud, deception and lying," said Stephen Frost, executive director of Hong Kong-based CSR Asia, a consulting firm that works with corporations and other organizations.

Because of the opaque nature of China's vast and fragmented manufacturing sector, where suppliers often turn to sub-suppliers who in turn use their own suppliers, it is hard to know the actual producer of a toy or piece of furniture. "The biggest China challenges are complexity and transparency [and] understanding where all the goods come from," said Andrew Hutson, a manager at the environmental Defense Fund, an NGO based in Washington that works closely with Wal-Mart. The company plans to consolidate the number of suppliers it uses globally to meet this challenge; it hopes that will make it easier to monitor others in the supply chain.

"If they are able to have a relatively small number of very big suppliers, that gives Wal-Mart much more clout," said CSR' Asia's Frost. "And then the audit becomes just one plant of a much more effective program."

The new rules may very well raise costs for Wal-Mart's suppliers, despite the company's assertions the measures will lead to savings. At least in the short term, gaining compliance on everything from lower factory emissions to shelling out legal overtime pay is instead likely to mean factories must spend more on production. With labor and input costs rising sharply in China, that will squeeze "already tight margins."

Even Wal-Mart suppliers who attended the Beijing summit have their doubts. "We can't accomplish this in one day," cautions Qin Yangjing, who manages the Wal-Mart business at Shenzhen Zuonmens Industrial, a maker and buyer of men's apparel that also sells to Bangkok-based Lotus Supermarket and Britain-based Tesco. While he hopes there won't be a big long-term impact, Qin believes his company's costs will definitely rise for now. "We will have to implement all of this step by step," he said.

Wal-Mart no doubt is hoping the push to make its suppliers greener and more socially conscious will win it big brownie points with Beijing. The company has more than 110 stores in China and owns a 35% stake in Trust-Mart Hypermarkets, a Taiwanese retailer that operates 100 stores on the mainland. Wal-Mart's major rival, Carrefour, has 118 outlets in China. Increasingly, China's government and people are demanding that foreign investors not just focus on the bottom line but also be good corporate citizens. After the May 2008 earthquake in Sichuan, critics in the Chinese media and on the Internet attacked both companies for allegedly not donating enough relief money. Carrefour also faced a backlash following reports in April that it supported Tibetan independence. With its latest sustainability push, Wal-Mart surely hopes to smooth the way for continued expansion in China.

At the same time, in the beginning of November of 2008 China's melamine woes were getting worse and the U.S. placed a ban on Chinese food imports.

First, a tainted product emerges, killing some and sickening many more. As Time reported, its origin was traced to China, where a combination of greed and negligence allowed the danger to slip into the food chain. The government downplayed and ignored the risks. Then the problem became so big that it could not be denied, leadership ordered inspections and promised to punish wrongdoers. The new vigilance led to other risky products being identified, but officials suggested that the problems weren't systemic…just the work of a few bad eggs. The state tightened inspections on imports and found a few tainted products from overseas, as if to say, "See, everyone has problems with food safety."

In late October, the scope of the scandal broadened when Hong Kong authorities announced that eggs imported from the mainland also contained melamine, the result of tainted feed given to chickens. Beijing ordered widespread testing of animal feed, and discovered 3,600 tons of contaminated product. The country's agriculture minister, Sun Zhengcai, called the tainted eggs an isolated problem. And the state press trumpeted news that sauces tainted with toxic chemicals were imported from three Japanese factories.

Change some of the details above and you could have the Chinese Product Safety Scandal of 2007. That round was touched off when the death of more than 100 Panamanians was traced back to cough medicine tainted with dietheylene glycol from China. Then hundreds of pets in North America were killed by eating food made from Chinese raw ingredients, also tainted with melamine. As the 2007 scandal spread, problems were found with Chinese-produced toys, tires, seafood and toothpaste. Even as Beijing took extreme steps to solve the problem, such as executing Zheng Xiaoyu, the former head of the State Food and Drug Administration, for accepting $85,000 in bribes from drug companies, it aggressively pushed back against the global concern over its exports. The Chinese embassy in Washington declared that it was "unacceptable for some to launch groundless smear attacks on China" over food and drug safety problems.

A year later, that foreign criticism of China's food safety problems did not seem so groundless. Now, Chinese consumers are asking why the government can't seem to get control of a problem like toxic foods, or even a specific contaminant like melamine that has now become painfully common. "Everyone has asked why this country that can send an astronaut into space and have the most successful Olympic Games cannot provide safe milk to its own children," said Dali Yang, director of the Center for East Asian Studies at the University of Chicago.

While Yang acknowledged that ethical failures in the Chinese dairy industry led to the current crisis, the ultimate blame still falls on the government. "Fundamentally it is an issue of government responsibility. In a society you can hope everyone acts with good intentions, but you cannot trust them to always do that," he said. "The greatest irony is that with all the international criticism in 2007, they knew there were problems. They did some spot checks, but the bureaucratic system didn't pick this up as a significant issue."

It is the spotty nature of the enforcement mechanism that is causing the biggest headaches. The discovery in 2007 of melamine in Chinese-made wheat gluten that was used in pet food was a signal that it had permeated other links of the food chain, said Marion Nestle, a public health professor at New York University and author of the recent book "Pet Food Politics: The Chihuahua in the Coal Mine." Once melamine showed up in pet food supplies, Nestle said, it was likely that it would appear in animal feed and eventually human food. "You can't separate the food supplies of animals, pets and people," she said. "That's an enormous warning sign that if something wasn't done immediately to clean up the food safety problem, this would leak into the human food supply."

While some quick action was taken after last year's pet food scandals, the response was narrowly focused on the exposed cases. The country's top watchdog revoked the business licenses for two companies that produced adulterated wheat gluten blamed for the death of thousands of pets in North America and another that shipped the diethylene glycol used in cough medicine that killed more than 100 Panamanians. "While China's State Council announced new rules for stricter controls on food producers and tougher punishments for violators, poor oversight allowed producers to adulterate dairy products and animal feed with melamine until the latest scandal broke in September of 2008. And that means that after the livestock feed recall, the list of tainted products is likely to grow. If animals are fed this stuff, then they have it in their meat, said Nestle.

While Beijing had announced expanded testing procedures for the dairy industry, cracked down on melamine producers and begun investigating animal feed, it has yet to announce similar measures to test meat and eggs.

If there is one upside to the latest product scandal, said Yang, it's that companies learn the risk of selling harmful products. Not only could their businesses be destroyed, but they can face harsh criminal punishments. This takes more time. There are still a lot of problems, but grudgingly progress is being made as different stakeholders are learning the hard way. If those lessons don't sink in, then expect a Chinese Product Safety Scandal in the coming year.

Also in November, the government in Kenya...one of many countries around the world...had banned importation of eggs and related products from China, as reported in the Daily Nation. This followed an earlier ban on milk and other related products from the country by the Kenya Bureau of Standards after the detection of traces of melamine. Managing director Kioko Mang'eli said the ban affects products from territories near China and would take affect immediately. "The related egg products would include noodles, mayonnaise, animal feed and animal feed input."

He said that strict surveillance on all food and food stuff from China and related countries would also continue. "This exercise will be in force until the affected products are proved to be free from the contaminate," the MD said.

Samples of the Chinese milk impounded in Dar es Salaam and sent to South Africa in October of 2008 for tests have been found to be contaminated with the killer chemical, melamine, The Citizen publication had revealed. A confidential report seen by this publication indicated that the chemical was found in three of the nine samples of Tanzania Food and Drug Authority (TFDA) provided during the investigation.

The authority had seized 34 tons in its crackdown on milk imports following the Chinese scare, but the sample tested and found to contain melamine, was taken from seven tons, which a single trade had imported. The news confirmed the fears that Tanzania might have narrowly escaped disaster, with traders having imported contaminated milk from China, where baby milk laced with melamine caused the deaths of many children and infected 94,000 other people across several continents.

About 70 percent of the milk and milk products consumed in Tanzania are imported. With a population of more than 4 million, Dar es Salaam needs at least a million litres of milk a day, but the local processors are able to supply less than 60,000 litres a day. The Citizen independently established that the TFDA planned to destroy the 7 tons of contaminated Chinese milk that was impounded. A total of 34 tons of imported powdered milk was seized from several traders after the board banned imports of Chinese milk.

Senegal, Liberia, Benin, Burkina Faso, Burundi, the Democratic Republic of Congo, Gabon, Ivory Coast, and Togo also slapped bans on Chinese milk imports after investigations in China found in milk traces of Melamine, a chemical used to make plastics. The Chinese milk scandal involved milk and infant formula, and other food materials and components which had been adulterated and this scandal had affected countries on all of the continents. It has also been employed as a non-protein nitrogen, appearing in soy meat, corn gluten meal and cottonseed meal used in cattle feed. Melamine is known to cause renal and urinary problems in humans and animals when it reacts with cyanuric acid inside the body, sometimes present in drinking water and in animal feed, so its use in food production is universally banned.

The *TimesOnLine* Web site reported that products from the dairy company whose tainted formula killed at least four babies are back on the shelves in China just as the United States issued a ban on Chinese food imports in case of similar contamination.

Such a broad ban by the Food and Drug Administration on goods from an entire country rather than from a new rogue manufacturer is unusual and reflects the level of concern over how widespread the problem is in China.

Importers to the United States must now certify that food products are free of dairy or of the industrial chemical melamine that has been found in a vast array of Chinese products...from baby powder to milk powder to creamy confectionery. Failing that, the goods will be stopped at the border.

The FDA orders said: "The problem of melamine contamination is not limited to infant formula products. Chinese government sources indicate contamination of milk components, especially dried milk powder, which are used in a variety of finished foods." These are believed to spread throughout the food chain in China.

The *New York Times* reported a bit late but better than ever, that the Food and Drug Administration had discovered this toxic chemical in infant formula the latter part of November raising the possibility that the problem was more extensive in the United States than previously thought. But the F.D.A. officials insisted that the levels of melamine were so low that they did not pose a health threat.

"There's no cause for concern or no risk from these levels," said Judy Leon, an agency spokeswoman. Ms. Leon said the contamination was most likely the result of food contact with something like a can liner, or from some other manufacturing problems, but not from deliberate adulteration. She declined to name the company that made the tainted infant formula.

Ms. Leon said the agency had tested 87 samples and had completed all but 10 of the tests. Of those, only one contained traces of melamine. The F.D.A. allows anything below 250 parts per billion of melamine in infant formula, and the sample contained less than that, she said. She also stated that the other products containing trace elements of melamine were also below allowable levels. One must question why there are any acceptable traces of melamine at all?

The *NewsInferno.com* on December 3rd reported more melamine deaths. The China's Health Ministry reported six babies had died after ingesting melamine tainted milk powder and the count was growing and that 294,000 infants, not just 50,000, fell ill with urinary disturbances, including kidney stones, as a result of the tainting. The International Herald Tribune said the Health Ministry's statement was reported by the official Chinese news agency-Xinhua-which cited ministry and provincial health department experts.

According to the AP, the Ministry neither provided additional information nor clarified if the three originally reported deaths were included or excluded in the current figures. The BBC reported that more than 850 children are still being treated in hospitals, with no less than 150 children suffering from serious, kidney-related illnesses.

The AP pointed out that this recent tainted scandal is China's worst yet, causing a sharp decline in Chinese dairy exports. The scandal led to widespread, international recalls and prompted authorities in China to implement an overhaul of that country's dairy industry, said the AP. The overhaul revealed that melamine tainting was much more widespread than originally realized, and melamine was also discovered in animal feed following an earlier discovery that the toxic, industrial chemical was showing up in eggs, the AP said.

Again, it is worth noting that melamine is an industrial chemical used in the production of fire retardants, fertilizers, and plastics. Because of its high nitrogen levels, it can create the false appearance of high protein levels in food and is known to have been added to diluted milk to falsely raise its protein levels. In sufficient quantities, ingesting melamine can cause kidney problems, including kidney stones and kidney failure, and in the case of at least six children, death.

The *European Union (EU)* in the first part of December 2008, extended restrictions on Chinese food imports after high levels of the toxic chemical melamine were found in soya products. After banning Chinese milk products in September, the 27-nation bloc had finally decided to prohibit imports of Chinese food containing soya that was destined for infants or small children. Imports of all other feed and food products containing soya from China would have to be tested and only products containing less than 2.5 milligrams of melamine per kilogramme would be allowed into the EU. Under the decisions, shipments of Chinese-made baking powder into the EU would also have to be tested after high levels of melamine were found.

Senator Voices Concern Over Lead-Tainted Dental Imports

United States Senator Sherrod Brown urged the U.S. Food and Drug Administration (FDA) to protect American consumers from lead-contained dental imports. The Ohio Democrat published a letter he wrote to FDA Commissioner Andrew C. Von Eschenbach in a press release, in which he urged the FDA to protect consumers from dangerous dental product imports.

"As reports of tainted implants increase, it is essential that FDA take action to ensure the safety of these dental products," Brown wrote to von Eschenbach. The (Centers for Disease Control and Prevention) "CDC determined that lead levels under 200 parts per million are safe. However, some of the dental implants tested by Ohio labs...indicate higher levels of lead than that ceiling," wrote Brown.

The letter discussed, in part, Brown's concerns about reports that consumers may be implanted with dangerous, lead-contaminated products and noted one of his constituents, a 73-year-old who received faulty dental implants imported from China and containing high amounts of lead. That story was picked up by WKYC said the Senator who also discussed another individual who suffered from lead poisoning linked to a tainted crown and noted that some recently tested dental implants were found to contain lead in parts per million exceeding CDC and American Dental Association standards.

Brown also presented a number of questions to von Eschenbach regarding current and international dental product and lab standards, estimated and annual volume amounts for China-produced dental implants, tracking and inspection mechanisms, and risks posed by lead-contaminated implants, to name some. Brown indicated that his office would be following up with the FDA within weeks. Whatever has come of this, remains to be seen.

In November of 2008, WKYC.com reported that investigator Tom Meyer ordered testing at a Cleveland lab on crowns ordered from China. Test results indicated that two of three crowns tested contained "dangerous" lead levels, said WJYC. Brown told WKYC that if the FDA did not respond to this problem soon, he planned on introducing legislations to ensure consumer safety from lead-tainted dental products. According to WKYC, Brown told Meyer that, "I am just tired of U.S. companies outsourcing work to China without being held responsible."

In children and fetuses lead exposure can cause brain and nervous system damage, behavioral and learning problems, slowed growth, hearing problems, headaches, mental and physical retardation, and behavioral and other health problems. Lead is also known to cause cancer and reproductive harm and, in adults, lead can damage the nervous system. Once poisoned by lead, no organ system is immune.

Unfortunately, lead poisoning is difficult to recognize because it manifests with subtle symptoms and there are no definitive indicators that point to lead contamination. For instance, children with lead poisoning may experience irritability, sleeplessness or excess lethargy, poor appetite, headaches, abdominal pain with or without vomiting...and generally without diarrhea...constipation, and changes in activity level. When faced with peculiar symptoms that do not match any one particular disease, lead poisoning should be considered.

Walgreens Recalls Chocolate Tainted with Toxin... Melamine Found in Chinese Seafood Imports

By the first week in December, 2008 the 4-oz chocolate bar came with a gift teddy bear and had been sold at Walgreen since late September. The Food and Drug Administration found melamine, that same nasty toxic chemical, in some samples of the chocolate, according to a news release from Walgreens. The drug store had stopped selling the 'Dressy Teddy Bear,' and customers were told to return the item to Walgreens for a full refund. Walgreens had not received any reports of illness.

Just 173 of the teddy bears with chocolate were sold, but the recall raises questions of how many other products may be tainted. The announcement from Walgreens did not specify where the chocolate was made or why the

FDA tested the candy. In November, the FDA announced that all food imports with milk-based ingredients from China would not be allowed in the United States until the shipments are checked for safety.

Melamine has been found in dozens of products exported globally from China and now, it seems, experts are worried that seafood raised on Chinese fish farms might also be tainted with the industrial chemical, said MarketWatchNews, citing a Los Angeles Times report. Among other foods, as reported by NewsInferno.com, that have made headlines in recent months, a variety of milk teas and coffees, cocoas, yogurts, candies, cookies, biscuits, cheeses, eggs and crackers, have all been found to be tainted with melamine, prompting international recalls. Now, scientists and consumer advocates are worried that China-raised seafood has joined the ever-expanding list of dangerous foods produced in that country.

Reports issued by the Chinese government confirm that the original figures stating that 50,000 children were sickened by melamine-contaminated formula has been updated to state that the figure was actually closer to 300,000 instances of children and babies becoming sick with melamine-related illnesses, such as urinary and kidney ailments, reported SuperMarketNews.

Reports also revealed that melamine is "routinely" added to fish feed in the Chinese aquaculture industry for the same reasons as it was added to dairy products, to falsify protein levels, according to the SuperMarketNews report. As with other contaminants affecting seafood, melamine remains in the fish that have ingested the melamine-tainted feed. MarketWatchNews said that according to the LA Times report, recent studies conducted by the U.S. Food and Drug Administration's (FDA) Animal Drugs Research Center found disturbing levels of melamine in certain fish. The report stated that the FDA's Animal Drugs Research Center found that trout, tilapia, and catfish which were raised on melamine-tainted feed contained concentrations of the toxic chemical of up to a whopping 200 parts per million (ppm), which is over 80 times the maximum "tolerable" level the FDA has set for safe human consumption, said MarketWatch.

MarketWatch also noted that while some United States fish importers do conduct voluntary melamine tests, there is no FDA requirement in place for such testing. Meanwhile, the FDA, in its own laboratory findings regarding a similar finding of melamine in catfish in 2007, said" "Because animals may eat food contaminated with melamine residues, there is a need for analytical methods to determine melamine residues that may be present in animal tissues," Melamine is not approved by the U.S. FDA for use in food or animal feed.

— 22 —

Detroit: Another Example of Why Capitalism is Failing

As we summarize what is wrong with the import of food and other products, we most certainly must examine what is wrong with our own manufacturing of goods in this country. It must also be noted that both the House Speaker and the Senate Majority Leader did finally come together appropriately when they took on the three Detroit automaker CEO's and their less than prepared visit to Congress back in November, 2008 to ask for a tax-payer loan.

As Gary Ater of the *American Chronicle* had reported on November 24th, it did appear that after the poorly thought-out debacle of the "rush to judgment" approval on the $700 billion dollar financial bail-out program, Congress finally decided to first qualify any new requests for taxpayer money. It was a bit comforting to hear Speaker Pelosi telling the Detroit CEO's that they had to "Show us your plans before we 'show you the money'!"

It really did take a lot of gall for the three top U.S. auto executives to come to Washington, in three separate corporate jets, while asking for a loan handout from the American taxpayers. They apparently thought that because the U.S. financial community got their "Bail-out" with little or no restriction, they might just as well also 'go for it'.

Eugene Robinson of the *Washington Post* made a good comment when he said that they should have all just "piled into a tricked-out Chevy Malibu and taken turns at the wheel" in getting to Washington. He also stated that based on Detroit's poor management and planning, plus the failed visit, all three of the executives should at least start the "inevitable cost-cutting by firing all of their current public relations consultants."

And it appeared pretty obvious that the American auto manufacturers would eventually receive some kind of federal support from the government, and they did...at least two of the companies did as Ford turned it down. Obviously, neither Bush nor Obama would want to be known as the "president that lost the American auto industry."

If you recall, back a number of years ago, when Lee Iacocca came to Congress with his "tin cup" out, asking for help to save Chrysler Motors, at least he had a plan and he pledged to take a personal pay cut to just: "One dollar a day, as Chrysler's Chief Executive, until the loan was repaid." Well, not one of the current "Big Three" executives had even given the hint of such a gesture for taking a personal pay cut. However, upon their return to Detroit, the executives did announce that they were cutting their auto production levels and that more employees would soon be gone. The executives came back the following month and received about $18 billion.

But, there is a much larger problem afoot than Detroit! The current issues with Detroit's auto industry need to be dealt with, but Detroit's problem is just one example of a very large American economic "mistake", and that issue is what has really been bothering the American people.

The one key issue that is still driving all of us crazy is having to continue to hear the conservative right-wing talkers, pushing their out-dated and failed "Free Market" concept. And they continue to do all of this, without taking the time to clearly understand what "Free Market" truly means to this country. Basically, if they would just look around for themselves and see how all of their past "free market" efforts in running this country have not worked, maybe they'd wake up. Detroit's automakers have brought a big part of their current problems on themselves because they chose to be a part of the "Free Market" concept. But, based on what has happened with tainted products and the auto industry, it is possible that the current conservative philosophy of free-market governing just won't work in a democratic republic. It never has...it may never will!

Going back into our American history and probably well accepted by most economists and historians that the strongest period of economic success that the average American has ever seen was from the 1940's through the 1970's. During those years, America was the world's strongest manufacturer, the world's largest creditor nation (now the largest debtor nation), the average American's income had regularly increased annually and a family could live and grow on one, single family income. And at 35%, the U.S. also had its largest percentage of its citizens being members of an organized union.

Today, union membership is at less than 10% of the population and the U.S. has lost many of its previous manufacturing jobs to overseas factories and lower cost foreign competition. Most American don't understand that one reason that the U.S. was so successful for so long is that the United States, from its very inception, has never functioned as a "free market nation."

As any good economist knows, a nation's government must function in such a way that is good for both the country's citizens and its industries. America was never before, and until the 1980's, it had never even pretended to operate as a "free market nation." It was instead, a loosely regulated "*fair* market nation."

Ronald Reagan's famous line while he was running for U.S. president was "The nine most frightening words in the English language are: 'I'm from the government, and I'm here to help.'"

And after the conservatives in the late 1970's had finally convinced the public that "all government was bad," and "government was the problem," the Republicans, then in control, began massive government de-regulation and opened up America as a "free market" nation, which then, eventually became a virtual, "free market, free-for-all."

Other countries also saw the wonderful: "export to the U.S." opportunities and they have since taken major advantages of that change when the U.S. went from "fair" to "free". Here is a U.S./Detroit, automobile example of the differences today between a normal "duty" regulated country and the current "Free Market" United States.

Today, if America wants to sell its cars in China, China places a 20% tariff on all imported U.S. manufactured autos. However, when China, Korea, Japan or any other foreign country wants to sell their cars in the U.S., they are only required to pay a token ~3% U.S. import tariff.

Going back throughout U.S. history, the U.S. government did manage its imports and our markets as most modern countries do today, in order to protect their internal industries. When there are such differences between U.S. and foreign worker's pay scales, benefits and working conditions, changes and adjustments in the import regulations and controls must then be in order to level-out today's "global" market playing field.

As the U.S. was the world's largest consumer market, by opening up the U.S. as a "free" market, this has allowed countries like China, India, Japan and South Korea to have the vast economic export growth that they have experienced over the past 30 years.

The on-going, open U.S. markets has allowed any country with a large, low-cost work force, to grow its products cheaper, and through its labor, service or manufacturing base by providing America everything from consumer goods to satellite-connected information services. These formally

American jobs could not have been so easily exported to offshore countries, "if" the U.S. had installed the proper import-export regulations.

When Wal-Mart Corporation was just starting to become American's largest retailer, you may recall that Wal-Mart's founder Sam Walton...whom I had met many years ago when he invited me to Bentonville and offered me a job as his marketing director...used to make it a big deal that his customers could always "buy American-made products at Wal-Mart." Today, I would challenge anyone to find large quantities of "American Made" products at any Wal-Mart store.

By the way, the thought of living in an area that had disastrous tornadoes and twisters, and seeing all sorts of warnings on the TV the eve of my interview, I chose not to accept his offer. But I found Mr. Walton to be one of the most endearing and tremendous persons I had ever met. His word was gold and he made his company successful because of his love for America.

Yet, with today's Wal-Mart promise of always providing the best quality and the lowest prices to their customers, no one can blame Wal-Mart for using the current global "free market" U.S. system of offering "low-cost imports" to their best advantage. But is this the best idea for the overall economy especially when thousands of items have been recalled from the shelves?

In the world's largest population countries of China and India, they have laws that prevent companies like Wal-Mart and other large, foreign, chain-like stores from building in their countries. And why do these countries put restrictions on big stores like Wal-Mart?

Today, if anyone drives through many small American towns, they will find themselves driving through the town's abandoned "Main Street" with many of its stores closed and boarded up. On the other hand, as these same visitors are leaving these small American towns, they will probably also pass a Wal-Mart or a large shopping mall just outside of town with a parking lot full of cars. Wal-Mart's and giant malls have caused the shutting down of many "Main Street" small businesses in hundreds of small towns across America.

China, India and even South Korea and Japan have put strong restrictions on corporations such as Wal-Mart for not approving their building of big-box stores in their countries. In India, over 95% of all businesses today are owned by single families or single proprietors and there are no franchise stores in every small town or city, as there are in America and Europe.

These growing, newly industrialized countries have decided that it's better to protect their citizens and their small businesses and to only, slowly allow any large outside corporate businesses to build there, and then only in specific areas. This approach causes the least negative effect on the local people and their day-to-day small business activity.

In the past, America had also used an import duty approach with fair import tariffs and restrictions on cheap imports that might interfere with the U.S. manufacturers of similar local American industries. The American Republican conservative's change to the "free market" approach is just one of the reasons that America's major businesses in the manufacturing of: shoes, textiles, radios, stereos and TVs, steel, lumber, aluminum and now automobile manufacturing have actually, or virtually disappeared.

Yes, Detroit as an example, over the past years has made some mistakes by being late in building the cars that people really want, and they have been paying for that mistake as far back as the 1960's. However, back in 2000, the Bush Administration did encourage Detroit, with tax Incentives, to continue building their gas-guzzlers and SUV's. But that's just a small part of their problem. Today, foreign auto manufacturers have factories all over the United States.

And does the U.S. auto industry also have their factories in these other countries? In a few cases yes, but nothing like what the foreign manufacturers have here in the U.S. today…keeping in mind that America is by far, the largest available market for automobiles in the world.

And the foreign auto manufacturers don't actually "fully manufacture" their cars in these U.S. factories. Most of the foreign auto factories, now within the U.S., manufacture all or most of the components for their cars in other countries, or in their parent country. The parts are then shipped to the U.S. just for the car's assembly in the U.S.

Unfortunately, many of the American made automobiles also have thousands of their components made outside the U.S. because they cost much less than American made parts. And with the low U.S. import duties, these minor extra import costs to the American manufacturers are also not a major issue. The point here is that today, there is anything but a fair playing field for doing business in the U.S. in the current global economy.

However, one issue has become very clear, but has continued to be ignored. "For any 'Free Market' approach to work, as the GOP keeps claiming, it will only function as it should when the playing field is level." And a level playing field is impossible, when the differences between any nation's workers wages, benefits and working conditions are so far "out-of-line" as they are today. The U.S. government is currently not properly dealing with those differences, as they did in the past, for protecting America's workers and its industries.

All one has to do to see the effect of this lack of "responsible regulation" is to look back at the results of the last 50 years in the United States. With its open, free market and its lack of international import control, it has become an excellent template for "what not to do" in running a nation. Perhaps with the 2008 elections, American citizens may see that the "Free" approach just hasn't worked and it's time for a major change, in both our political and fiscal management.

By the time the Obama administration took charge the global financial crisis was bringing out the worst in the trade relationship between the United States and China. Many publications, including the Washington Post and the China News, in February 2009, reported that after three years of largely friendly talks about economic issues, both the U.S. and China blamed each other for the world's problems.

First it was Secretary Geithner accusing China of "Manipulation" its currency, vowing in written testimony submitted for his confirmation hearing that the U.S. would act "aggressively" to remedy the situation. The U.S. Trade Representative's office, in a harshly worded and wide-ranging complaint to the World Trade Organization, alleged that China uses cash grants, cheap loans and other subsidies to illegally aid its exporters.

China, for its part, has bashed the "Buy America" program embedded in the first stimulus package, calling it "poison to the solution" of the global economic crisis. At the World Economic Forum meeting in Davos the latter part of January, Chinese Premier Wen Jiabao, without naming the United States explicitly, blamed the financial crisis on unsupervised capitalism. The crisis has pushed the China-U.S. relationship to a flash point. From this point on it will either become more stable or more confrontational.

Both the United States and China, the world's number one and number three largest economies, have railed about the dangers of economic protectionism., but so far both have been guilty, according to the other, of practicing it. In the United States, industry groups are pushing for more action against China, saying it is trying to export its way out of the crisis by dumping cheap products abroad. Since the economic crisis began in America the latter part of 2006, China has been making a number of small but significant changes to its trade policy.

Some experts have said that by taking an aggressive stance on China in terms of economic issues may be dangerous. China is the biggest overseas hold of U.S. Treasury securities, having invested more than $1 trillion into government bonds and mortgage debt. The Chinese government has never officially made any threats about these holdings. However, academics who are often used to convey the prevailing feeling among the country's leaders hinted in the past that the government would not hesitate to use what state media have called the "nuclear option" of liquidating its dollar holdings if Washington imposes trade sanctions related to the debate over the yuan or other alleged problems.

There's already some evidence that China is starting to reduce its holdings of U.S. debt as it tries to diversify its portfolio to mitigate the harm a falling dollar may have on its coffers. Trade researcher with the Chinese Commerce Ministry's research arm Mei Xinyu said that Geithner's remarks on the yuan may have been a test. The comments were later tempered by the Obama administration saying it hadn't made any formal decision on the issue and Obama discussed the remarks with Chinese President Hu Jintao in a telephone call shortly after taking office.

"They may have wanted to use this to try to test China's reaction. If China acted weak, then the U.S. would probably be on China step after step. But China didn't," Mei said.

So now that the U.S. and China have been dealt with cards that could very well tell them to hold 'em or fold 'em, they both have to make some heavy decisions and fix the problems that have been hurting both nations for the past number of years. Let's see who antes up first!

— 23 —

Summarizing What We Learned From Our Mistakes… Consumers Need Better Oversight of Food Imports… 'Made in China'… is it Time for This Label to Leave America?

Cookies. Candy. Instant coffee. Pretzels. Ice Cream. Yogurt. Crackers and biscuits. Eggs and products containing powdered eggs. Cake. Powdered and condensed milk and products containing them. Livestock and fish feed. Soy milk. Pie. What gluten. Cereal. Tea.

Chances are good that you have consumed one of these products recently, or will in the coming days and weeks. If any of them are from China…and no, you may not be able to tell by looking at the label…then you may want to sit up and pay attention!

As reported in SFGate.com on November 30th, 2008 those foods of Chinese origin have been found by authorities in the United States, Canada, Australia, or parts of Asia to contain an industrial chemical called melamine that is used to make plastic. In recent months the Chinese government has admitted that adding melamine to food…which raises protein levels, making poor-quality products look more nutritious…is common practice in China.

We now know how many deaths had been caused by melamine and how many Chinese consumers were sent to the hospital…at least 54,000 at this writing, perhaps up to 200,000. The trail of trouble always begins with corrupt food processors, under-funded or unethical government inspectors, and profit-driven food exporters in China. It ends in U.S. grocery stores and kitchen cupboards. In the middle are the global food companies, which often source ingredients from China but do not disclose their origin to consumers. It is time they did.

More than 4 billion pounds of food and food ingredients enter the United States from China every year. An unknown amount of additional food is imported from other countries that use Chinese ingredients but do not disclose them.

Under the Bush administration, the Food and Drug Administration, which was charged with safeguarding the health of our nation's 300 million eaters, has seen its budget decline in real terms and its staffing levels fall far behind its workload. Let's see what the Obama administration can salvage and fix as the health and welfare of the citizens of this country rest on the precautions that the government takes in making sure that the food we eat is safe from contamination.

From 2003 to 2006, the number of food safety inspections conducted by the agency dropped by 47 percent. It inspects only 1 percent of most imported food; in 2008 its own Science Board declared that the agency could "no longer fulfill its mission without substantial and sustained additional appropriations." The FDA also lacks the regulatory authority required to protect food safety. In most cases, it can only issue guidance documents to companies found to have distributed contaminated food. This is only slightly more forceful than crossing its fingers.

The agency has also shown a disturbing hesitance to stand up to corrupt trading partners: Its initial response to the Chinese melamine scandal was not to enforce a zero-tolerance policy for the contaminant, but to set a limit for acceptable levels of melamine in food, despite scientific uncertainty about its health effects. Months later, the agency finally issued an import ban on Chinese dairy products, but other products of concern continue to be unloaded in our ports.

The FDA's apathy is dangerous, given China's track record. Last year, hundreds of U.S. pets were sickened from consuming melamine-tainted pet food from China; this year, Chinese regulators appear to have ignored warnings about melamine in milk the same month that the United States imported nearly 300,000 pounds of Chinese milk proteins. The Chinese livestock, poultry and fish-farming industries now admit they have covered up routine melamine use in feed, risking the safety of all of these animal products. Without strong government oversight of food safety, U.S. consumers are left holding the grocery bag, wondering whether it could contain things that might harm them or their families.

We should not have to rely on Chinese babies sickened by tainted milk to sound a warning bell, nor should we need advanced training in food science and international trade before venturing into a supermarket. We need a strong, well-funded and full staffed food inspection force and comprehensive food labeling.

U.S. consumers deserve to know that the Chinese food safety system meets U.S. standards before food is imported from China. The FDA recently announced it will send inspectors to China, but in far fewer numbers than are adequate: Only eight staff members will be on hand to inspect the estimated 19,000 food establishments licensed to export to the United States. If they can't do it right to begin with, why do it at all? This will prove to be worthless.

Congress and the Obama administration should increase that workforce so that staff can inspect all Chinese food exporters at least once a year. They should also press China to allow unannounced inspections, not just those carried out in the company of Chinese officials. Until a stronger FDA oversight system is in place in China, we must reduce risk by banning imports of the most suspect products, maintaining bans on high-risk products such as poultry, and increasing inspections at U.S. ports.

Congress should also close the loopholes on country-of-origin labeling and require companies to label the origin of processed food and food ingredients, not just raw food. Consumers need better oversight of food imports. Food safety must be a first priority under the new administration. This is one area where individuals should not...and cannot...go it alone.

Thanks to Mark Schlosberg, California director, and Elanor Starmer, research analyst, with Food and Water Watch, a national nonprofit working to ensure clean water and safe food.

In December of 2008, Family Security Matters had an article on 'Made in China'...Is it time for this label to leave American! It was a wake up call and I certainly agree with its content.

Over the last few years, Americans have seen a decline in service and quality. We shouldn't be surprised! We voice our opinions in all things commercial by our purchasing patterns and as a nation, we demanded lower prices: enter the Wal-Mart effect. But the old adage "you get what you pay for" is as true today as when the phrase was first coined. "Cheaply made" goes beyond the reality of early obsolescence; consumers should worry about health risks resulting from companies cutting corners through unsafe manufacturing practices, overproduction which strains safety check capacity, poor sanitation, or substituting inexpensive industrial chemicals for human safe ones to increase profit.

With the current economy all but the wealthiest will be more price sensitive, but there remains an expectation of corporate responsibility... whether manufacturing or importing products. Infant formula in the U.S. are the latest products to cause concern; probably the result of faulty manufacturing. We discussed the toy debacle of 2007 where millions of toys were recalled during the Christmas holidays…most made in China…Can this happen again? Yes!

At this writing, many stores are on the verge of going bankrupt including Lane Bryant, Starbucks, Ann Klein, Sears, K-Mart, Gap and many others. What the hell…they probably didn't carry enough products from China so they became overpriced. Now try to shop at any major retailer and avoid buying a product "made in China!" Good luck! That's just the tip of the iceberg. If you think the vast expanse of full shelves sporting: Made in China, Pakistan, Mexico, India" or quite frankly any place other than the USA is daunting, try finding a product without a Chinese component or ingredient. By the way, the stores that are going to file for bankruptcy or did so mentioned above, did not crawl to the government for a bailout as the car companies did or the banks. They will re-organize and try to come back the way a capitalist company has done so in the past and not rely on the government for a "loan" that will never be repaid.

Product labeling laws do not require companies to state where all the components or ingredients come from. I realize that it is difficult but if this were possible, it should be law. If you think the Chinese have a corner on just the electronics, consumer and toy market, think again. Many of the foods in your kitchen and medications in the local hospital have ingredients from China or other developing nations. In the process they are cornering the market, by pushing niche U.S. and allied countries' companies out of business. And with it, more American jobs are lost. In December 2008 alone, about 585,000 jobs were lost in the U.S. Millions more followed in 2009.

As if dwindling U.S. market share (translation loss of jobs, and income) isn't bad enough, over the last few years, Americans have seen a dramatic increase in the risks to their health and safety from imported products. We all remember the 2007 Christmas debacle when the term "Made in China" sent toys back to the return aisle at most department stores faster than kids can race to see what's under the tree. While the threat of lead paint was worrisome to most parents, when it came to medications, "Made in China" has far more deadly implications. So far, the FDA estimated 149 deaths attributable to tainted heparin with component origins in China. The label "Made in China" is more a warning than a place of product origin in terms of threat to health.

Before being falsely accused of xenophobia, realize that this story you are reading is all about protecting people, ours and hopefully by extension those who live in the country of origin from whence we get our products. One would only hope, perhaps on the heels of articles in ASIS International, TIME, FamilySecurityMatters.org, and other places that labels with the words "Made in China" may start raising serious concerns among consumers and policymakers. After reading this, maybe you too will make a concerted effort to boycott products "made in China."

Let's look at the facts! More than 40% of all product recalls in the U.S. and 79% of toys involved products from China. Note the range of products involved…from tires and toys to food and toothpaste. These are everyday products that if tampered with or produced with substandard parts, unsanitary procedures or cheap chemicals not designed for human consumption but illegally substituted for more expensive human safe ingredients…all common business practices in China and other nations trying to develop industries… can be harmful.

While most recalls are from China, in April 2007, the New York Health Department issued warnings about cosmetics, especially eye makeup, imported from Pakistan which had lead levels ranging from 4-47%...significantly above U.S. safety levels. As an FYI, lead is added to paint to make colors brighter and is especially toxic to youngsters whose brains are still developing. Lead can damage nerve cells and cause cognitive/behavioral problems.

Here's a snapshot of when certain products started being recalled, and the type of industries China has a strangle hold on that you might want to take into consideration when you make up your shopping list:

- April 2007 – A & A Global Industries recalled 4 million "Groovy Grabber" and other Chinese made children's bracelets that contained high levels of lead in the colorings.

- May 2007 – wheat flour laced with melamine – a toxic chemical used in manufacturing and sterilization but NOT intended for human consumption and capable of causing a variety of adverse health effects (people/animals) found its way into approximately 100 brands of pet foods and resulting in thousands of animals sickened and several pet deaths reported. Moreover, certain animal feeds… food given to livestock…were contaminated. Melamine was added to make wheat and rice products appear to be more protein-rich and substituted for more expensive food additives.

- Also, over the last few years, several brands of toothpaste imported from China contained diethylene glycol-a chemical used in antifreeze. Some estimate there were over 50,000 boxes of toothpaste were recalled. Diethylene glycol can cause kidney failure, respiratory failure, abdominal pain, nausea, headaches, liver toxicity and coma…it was the same chemical that caused the death of 100 people in Panama when they ingested cough syrup from a Chinese company that mislabeled the medication as having a harmless sweetener instead of disclosing that this cheaper and toxic additive was present. Chemicals in antifreeze are often noted for their sweet taste; something reported by street people who ingest such products as alcohol alternatives or suicide attempts.

- June 2007 – the National Highway Transportation Safety Administration recalled 450,000 tires from China
- Also during 2007 – Chinese food products were recalled because they appeared grossly decayed. Other products, such as mushrooms, were recalled due to tainting with pesticides long since banned in the U.S. Seafood was recalled that had been laced with antibiotics and antifungal medications to treat fish farm raised in severely polluted waters (sewage, garbage). Such medications include nitrofuran, fluoroquinolones, chloramphenical and malachite green…all potentially toxic or capable of causing adverse health effects as well as promote antibiotic resistance…a global problem.

In addition to toys, certain herbal teas may have high lead levels from the method of drying the leaves, which involves driving trucks over them: the exhaust dries the leaves. The trucks are fueled by leaded gasoline. Too bad we can't use the tea in our cars. I wonder how many MPG they would get?

The cocktail garnish "Rimmer Brand Mojito Cocktail Garnish" was recalled after testing positive for salmonella bacteria. Veggie Booty Snack Mix was also tainted with salmonella and resulted in 100 people, mostly children, being affected. Salmonella, one of the more common food poisonings, can cause significant gastrointestinal symptoms such as nausea, vomiting and abdominal pain. In severe cases, bloody diarrhea and kidney failure can result.

In Chicago two people became seriously ill…one requiring hospitalization…after eating fish that was labeled monkfish but instead was probably puffer fish, containing the potentially deadly toxin tetrodotoxin. The Food and Drug Administration (FDA) asserted that beginning in September 2006, a total of almost 300 22-lb boxes from China that were mislabeled as monkfish, when in fact they contained puffer fish. Tetrodotoxin is a neurotoxin that can cause ascending paralysis, respiratory arrest and death within 24 hours. The toxin is not destroyed by cooking or freezing.

- Christmas 2007 – Toys 'R Us recalled baby bibs that were tainted with lead. Soon thereafter, Wal-Mart stopped the sale of similar baby bibs which contained 9,700 parts per million (PPM), which is 16 times the legal limit for lead in paint. Disney bibs also had high lead paint levels. Fisher Price recalled almost 900,000 toys (over 80 different objects) with high lead paint levels.

Mattel, one of the world's leading toy manufacturers, announced their third product recall (over 770,000 toys) during the summer over concerns of high lead levels in 2007. The first recall involved over 400,000 die-cast cars. August 2007: Mattel's second recall included 1.5 million Chinese-made toys, again for high lead levels in the paint. This recall would have cut second quarter operating income by almost 50%. China produces 80% of the world's toys.

- January through October 2008 – In case toxic toys, hazardous heparin and deadly dinner isn't enough to turn you off from Chinese products, the latest example of Beijing's total disregard for people other then the ruling class should leave no doubt about the kind of people we are dealing with, the threat they pose to our nation…whether from a security, commercial, industrial or political perspective.

Probably starting before 2008, but continuing to date, milk products…especially baby food and infant formula…were diluted with melamine, which in this case acted as a masking agent to hide the dilution of protein. So far, over 50,000 young children in China have developed kidney stones from this toxic chemical and several have died as we discussed before. The extent of this latest wave of Chinese greed over human safety has spread to at least 11 countries, and involved tainting baby formula, coffee creamer, instant milk coffee and milk tea products, as well as chocolate products including Cadbury and other brands. Tainted products were sold during Halloween, as some were not pulled from the shelves in time.

- As of October 2008 – the government reported its FDA Import Refusals: a total of 153 "refusals" (i.e. products ranging from medical devices and pharmaceutical ingredients to food products and other consumer items) were refused entry from China into the United States because they were mislabeled; had poor manufacturing practices; were putrid or filthy; or contaminated with harmful chemicals, antifungal or antibiotic additives. China (153), India (115), Mexico (84) had the most products among the over 70 nations represented on the FDA Refusal list. Seafood, vegetables and other foods, as well as cosmetics, vitamins and pharmaceuticals intended for U.S. consumption were the leading products.

FDA testing revealed that Mead Johnson baby formula "Enfamil" contained traces of Cyanuric acid and Nestlé's Good Start had small amounts of melamine. While both were considered non-toxic exposures, and the result of manufacturing errors, not intentional tampering; time will tell how extensive or if a health effect will result.

However, tainted or substandard products imported from China is not a new phenomenon, but the recent events have occurred in such magnitude and involve such a wide variety of industries as to raise serious questions concerning regulatory oversight, security, economics, public safety and supply chain vulnerability. Are these intentional acts of greed? Or are they the natural evolution and growing pains of nations without strong infrastructures trying to emerge from being third world, underdeveloped countries to economic powers and players in the industrialized world?

China has few safety controls on food and drugs. Yet, against this backdrop, China has increased its food exports to U.S. by over 20% in 2008 alone and has become the leading supplier of many food ingredients that become part of virtually every edible category. Outdated pesticides, unsafe chemicals like lead or kerosene, or some of which are look-alike or taste-alike for safer ingredients (melamine, glycols), bacteria and poor sanitation are associated with ingredients from developing nations such as China or Pakistan.

Many U.S. companies are involved in China, such that the commercial interest of the United States has become dependent upon allowing imports to enter our borders as quickly as possible. Yet, supply chain partners may not have the government infrastructure, regulatory capacity or desire to scrutinize products when commerce is the imperative. Herein lies the complexity of the problem and a convergence point/challenge for the security professional. Cheap imports have become critical to corporate profits at a time when globalization has placed enormous pressure upon national and company economic survival.

Consider the prices of pharmaceutical ingredients. A U.S. company in September 2007 was able to purchase a kilogram of erythromycin base antibiotic for $65 from China; in 1995 a kilogram would have cost $110 if purchased from a U.S. company. It is this magnitude of cost reduction, including labor that is 1/5 to 1/10 that of domestic workers, that makes trade with China and other developing nations so attractive. Moreover, unfettered by regulatory enforcement, costs can be kept down as well. Yet, the risks to domestic companies relying upon foreign components may alter the equation as concerns about toxicity, human health (and animal health) emerge.

Heparin is a good example. Heparin is derived from pigs. Surprise! Nearly half the world's pigs are in China. A significant portion of the journey from pig to medication involved in heparin production involves Chinese companies; many are substandard or cut corners. The result...people die from a medication designed to save their lives.

China now supplies over 30% of the world's Vitamin A, along with B-12 and many health food supplements as well as 80% of the world's ascorbic acid

(Vitamin C) which is used as a preservative and enriching agent in literally thousands of foods. In the spring of 2007, lead-contaminated multivitamins were found in U.S. health food stores and Vitamin A contaminated with bacteria ended up in European baby food. It has been suggested that China sells ingredients at ultra low products in order to capture the global market. Recent events and economic indicators do not dispute this assertion.

As of March 2009, the U.S. has had a $232 billion trade deficit with China…a reality that sets the stage for competing demands among policymakers and regulators. Of concern, China is aggressively attempting to change U.S. policy and regulations to allow importation of Chinese poultry… and with it, the risk of avian influenza and other pathogens.

On September 11th, 2007, the U.S. Consumer Product Safety Commission hosted the second Sino-U.S. CPS Summit. Former President Bush created a panel to study whether the U.S. needed more stringent safeguards for imported food and consumer products. The resulting Interagency Working Group on import safety came out with their report in November 2007 with recommendations to the White House outlining strategies…many of which rested upon cooperation and memoranda of agreements with Chinese regulatory agencies. How lucky do you feel? No too lucky? Here is my take on this…

Why America is on the short end of the stick with Beijing, enamored by the growth spurt of Shanghai, or gaga over the ridiculously expensive Olympic extravaganza when the regime is built on blood and repression is beyond belief, unless you own a company benefiting from the enormous cost imbalance that China Offers. Are we so naïve to think Burger King and Wendy's will somehow transform a power hungry, oppressive government into a pro-West open society? Are we deluding ourselves to soothe the conscience and rationalize corporate decision favoring profit over people?

The medical device industry is increasingly being exported; the products of course then get imported from companies which benefit from the fact the U.S. is still the leading buyer of medical technologies. The typical product can be built in India, China, the Dominican Republic or other places at a fraction for what it can be produced in the U.S. China of course, offers the biggest bang for the buck. Or are we taking the foot in the door approach; exposing people in developing nations to better jobs, Western culture and connectivity with the world community may set the stage for greater human rights?

Consider Google…a valuable source of information worldwide, and defender of free speech; even they made concessions to Beijing before commercializing in China. Remember, this isn't an indictment, merely a cautionary tale.

Chinese officials...business, government and regulatory cannot claim innocence or error.

China set out upon a corporate strategy to under-price and thus eliminate the competition. Think Wal-Mart in the U.S. Perhaps, after all this time, China and Wal-Mart are finally joined at the hip.

As our dependence upon Chinese and other nations' exports increase, questions about supply chain integrity, quality, regulatory oversight, inspections and product safety will persist. It is wishful thinking to think this trend, this threat will stop, barring action, not year old memoranda of agreement or government sponsored talk festivals.

In 2006 there were over 13 million food imports with less than a thousand food inspectors; FDA only looked at 1% of shipments and rarely examined food ingredients like the Chinese product wheat gluten associated with melamine contamination. As the years followed, the food imports increased and the FDA still looks at 1% of shipments with less than a thousand food inspectors. Once ingredients are incorporated into processed foods (as of now, nations of origin of ingredients do not have to appear on labels), it is difficult to check whether unsafe contaminants are in the products. The likelihood of people getting unsafe is increasing. These numbers are not about to shrink any time soon unless we demand that our government inspects more, allows less into the nation, creates a tariff system that protects U.S. industry and holds Beijing accountable; without which their products can sit on docks in the Far East.

Given only a tiny fraction of all consumables are inspected, and a significant proportion of ingredients/components are imported from numerous countries, many of which are developing nations...greater attention is needed to protect the supply line and ultimately U.S. consumers. The trillion dollar bailout will likely limit the expansion of agents to protect us...whether against terrorism or food threats.

Let us not forget that for the moment the tainted products are largely born from greed.

But the intentional tampering of food and other consumables is neither difficult nor unheard of. Terrorist groups repeatedly have shown interest in exploiting weaknesses in the nation's food and agriculture industry. As recent events have shown, the U.S. and its consumers are highly vulnerable to supply chain risks. While current recalls and tainted products were presumably the result of profiteering, poor sanitation or manufacturing practices, they could have just as easily resulted from intentional tampering. In 1984, a cult in Dallas, Oregon intentionally used salmonella, sickening over 700 members of the community. It is clear an effective response requires an increased level of coordination among agencies, corporations and different levels of government...domestic and foreign.

While much of the security world is focused on personal and facility safety, executive protection, local threats, even WMD (weapons of mass destruction), the impact of a nation (China) that is both the largest monthly net buyer of U.S. securities and a leading exporter of ingredients, components and products purchased domestically...we will become, as one writer opined, victims of "weapons of mass production?"

Outsourcing, efficiencies in manufacturing, profit optimization and just-in-time inventory are business strategies that minimize costs; these also can stretch or expose supply chains. Beyond normal vulnerabilities such as natural disasters (hurricanes, earth quakes) terrorism, political instability or product fraud can impact supply chains and corporate health. Consistently, financial executives identify supply chain risk as having the greatest potential to disrupt their revenue drivers.

Compromising the quality of the end product...Mattel Toys being a good example...can undermine consumer confidence, impact profitability and damage credibility with investors, which ultimately can drive up cost of capital or jeopardize market share. While recent tainted product events and recalls were not intended to harm U.S. consumers, so the FDA says, they could just as easily been intentional acts of industrial sabotage or terrorism... biological or chemical.

In the interest of public safety, Congress and the new administration need to do a better job. I am listing some recommendations if anyone is listening:

First – change the insane policy of allowing the very industries that are supposed to be regulated by various and sundry government agencies here and in the originating nations, that allows them to examine themselves or set policy on how they should be regulated. There needs to be a clear separation between regulated and regulator. Having the pharmaceutical companies call the shots at FDA, or the meat packing industry tell USDA how increasing food safety measures or inspections imposes a burden on their industry sounds a lot like asking the 6-year-old with chocolate on his face who robbed the cookie jar and oh, by the way little fella, would you start an investigation for the culprit?

Second – our elected should initiate legislation that mandates listing the countries of origin that our products' components or ingredients originate from. The three card Monte game that U.S. corporation...domestic and foreign ownership...play by coming as close to the letter of the packaging laws in terms of how many nanoseconds off the docks a product needs a whiff of U.S. air, or what % of ingredients make it allowable to be called a U.S. product must be re-examined.

Third – this is a difficult economic environment; profit and cost will trump many other considerations. This is a bad time to ask the American consumer to pay more dollars for a better product. But should this be a zero sum game? Choosing quality/safety or cost especially when health is at stake is wrong. It is immoral to use toxicants when safe chemicals are available. We can do a better job with stronger trade policies, stricter control over imports, sanctions over nations that do not implement effective oversight are just the first realm. Holding U.S. industries accountable for their U.S. and foreign supply chain partners may be the answer of companies that cannot or will not follow good manufacturing practices across their production process.

Fourth – government investment in new cost cutting, product enhancing technologies or processes, monetary support for start up or niche companies… from food growers and ingredient producers to electronics and other consumer goods manufacturers will be an important driver towards rebuilding small businesses, which have always been the backbone of our nation and catalyst for the next industrial revolution.

Fifth – addressing our trade imbalance is critical. There remains a significant disadvantage facing U.S. industries trying to enter foreign markets compared with foreign industries trying to enter U.S. markets. Who have our government officials been working for? It is NOT wrong to remember Congress and the Administration are supposed to protect the U.S.; protectionist policies are not bad; they are responsible. Counterpoint arguments that our industries will be blocked out if we try to reduce the disadvantage that we face worldwide are lame; how much more disadvantaged can we be on the one hand while we give away the store on the other? The new administration must re-evaluate our import/export policies, courageously, strategically and tactically using tariff policies that level the playing field. Our safety and the preservation of U.S. jobs may rest in the balance.

There are few issues more fundamental to domestic security than safe products, good jobs and fostering industries reflective of the values that created America. The clock is ticking; what labels will be on our future Christmas, Hanukkah and Holiday presents? What will they be in 2009 and then in 2010, which products will be the next threats to our health and from where will they be imported from? And when will our elected officials remember to protect the interests of the U.S.?

In December 2008, Hong Kong finally set maximum standards for melamine in food of 2.5 ppm and in infant products of 1 ppm. Hong Kong has also launched a vigorous melamine surveillance and testing program on a variety of food products, and posts the government laboratory test results on an official website. In additional to government testing, major retailers' contract with certified private labs to test samples from every production lot of virtually all products containing Chinese milk, feed, or eggs. The discovery of melamine in eggs has resulted in a 90 percent reduction in imports from China, and led to a surge in demand for U.S. eggs.

The HK government launched three major initiatives as a result of the melamine outbreak: (1) HKG's quick establishment of a maximum melamine concentration in food by setting regulatory standards of melamine in food, and amending Harmful Substances in Food Regulations; (2) HKG to amend law to protect food safety by directing mandatory food recall when necessary; (3) HKG's implementation of a vigorous food surveillance program on food against melamine contamination and will have a "hold and test" policy.

New Figures Reveal China's Economic Decline

The *BBC News* first reported in the beginning of December 2008 that China's dairy exports have all but ground to a halt following the scandal earlier this year when milk was tainted with the industrial chemical melamine. Data reported in the country's state media suggested that dairy exports fell 92% year-on-year in October of that year.

Meanwhile, China's Ministry of Health had revised the number of infants who died after drinking tainted products by stating that as many as six infants died and up to 294,000 suffered from urinary tract ailments including kidney stones. More than 850 children are still being treated in hospitals; at least 150 of them are said to be seriously ill.

In the first part of 2008, an average of 12,000 tons of dairy products was exported each month. In October, after the scandal broke, that fell to just over 1000 tons. In November, the Food and Drug Administration in the United States imposed an import alert which made it hard for Chinese firms to export their products to the U.S. The businesses involved were hoping that a meeting between Chinese leaders and the U.S. treasury secretary in Beijing, part of a regular economic dialogue, would produce an easing of restrictions imposed on them.

The three figures that describe imports and exports, PPI (producer's price of industrial products) and the latest GDP released by the Chinese regime on December 10th, 2008 showed a trend of slowdown. Experts think that the Chinese economy has met with its greatest challenge as international consumers have grown increasingly suspicious of Chinese-made products and the world has been experiencing a global financial crisis.

The main Bureau of China's Customs said that exports fell 2.2 percent in November for the first time in seven years, while it grew 19.2 percent in the previous month. Imports dropped 17.9 percent in November, after increasing 15.6 percent in October.

From the second half of 2007, the growth of exports has been steadily slipping.

According to analysts, inferior quality and products that have been made with toxic chemicals are responsible for the slowdown. The products imported to China are mainly used to be processed for exports. With waning consuming, confidence and export numbers continuing to fall, experts are not optimistic of China's future production of export goods.

As China's economy faces unprecedented challenges, Mr. Huang, a provincial government official in Guangdong Province, said that enterprises in Guangdong haven't faced greater difficulties since the 1990's and said that next year is a critical year. "A factory with 100,000 employees can suddenly collapse. That was impossible before. The situation is serious," said Huang.

Recently there was news that over 50,000 businesses went bankrupt in Guangdong.

Huang believed that the real situation might be even worse. The fact remains that in China, unemployment causes social problems.

Sichuan Province has a higher number of migrant workers. As of November 18th, 280,000 migrant workers had retuned home because enterprises throughout the region had closed, according to China's official *Xinhuan News Agency*. Experts believe that if the economy continues to worsen, there could be even bigger trouble for China. They say that unemployment will not only cause people to lose confidence in the economy but also cause a series of social problems. Compared with developed nations, such as the U.S. and some European countries, China does not have an established social security system or unemployment insurance. As the unemployment number continues to grow, increasing social unrest may threaten the Chinese Communist Regime.

By the end of 2008, *the FederalTimes.com* reported that the FDA was finally beginning to change its approach to food safety inspections. Hoping to shore up sagging public confidence, the FDA had abandoned the use of random inspections to ensure food safety in favor of inspections targeted at high-risk production sites.

Under the new approach, the agency started to focus its attention on farms with poor safety records, importers with lower quality standards, and other at-risk food suppliers. FDA also struggled with its own image in 2008 because of its sluggish response to a salmonella outbreak. It took months to find the source…peppers grown in Mexico…and several more weeks to find the farm that grew the peppers. The new approach was the first step toward modernizing the inspection process, said Dr. David Acheson, FDA's associate commissioner for foods.

"We're trying to make better use of the data we've got. Do we need more data?

Probably," Acheson said in an interview in December. "But it shouldn't be: 'Well, we don't have enough data, so we'll just do random inspections.'"

But critics said the agency didn't have enough data to know which farmers and distributors were high risk. The problem was particularly acute for imported food, they claimed, because less than 1 percent of imported food is tested.

"How do they determine risks when they're doing so little testing?" asked Patty Lovera, assistant director of Food and Water Watch, a nonprofit consumer advocate. "Only a fraction of the food ever sees a lab."

Americans eat about 40 percent more imported food today than in 1995; the food is produced by more than 189,000 facilities. The growing volume of imports means FDA has little choice but to conduct risk-based inspections: It costs, on average, $16,700 to inspect a foreign facility, so the cost of inspecting each facility once…$3.2 billion…exceeds FDA's annual budget. Instead of spending billions trying to save banks that are not FDIC regulated, they should take the money and pour it into testing imports.

The agency is trying to cut down those costs by opening field offices overseas. The first one, in China, opened in November 2008; FDA planned to open two offices in India in December, but Acheson said the attacks in Mumbai would delay those openings. The foreign offices would lower the cost per inspection, but they will still tax the agency's resources, according to a Government Accountability Office report released earlier in the year. "The establishment of an FDA field office in China will likely require a long-term commitment of agency resources," GAO wrote. "The overall resource need could be significant."

And the small number of offices-FDA currently plans to open less than a dozen-means the agency is still able to inspect only a small percentage of foreign food facilities. "What will it take to inspect a higher proportion of imports?" Lovera asked. "That's where the cracks show. The agency is completely outgunned when it comes to imports."

Critics, including GAO, said that the food protection plan also didn't have enough benchmarks. There are fewer outbreaks of food-borne illness today than a decade ago, but that doesn't necessarily mean FDA is doing a better job at inspections. "There's not a lot of assessment as to whether they're being effective," said David Plunkett, a senior staff attorney at the Center for Science in the Public Interest. "There are no benchmarks."

Acheson said identifying the highest-risk producers, and inspecting them more frequently, would be one benchmark for measuring the plan's effectiveness. FDA would also improve food safety by working more closely with the private sector...but will not turn over inspections to private companies, he said. "We're not in the business of contracting out FDA inspections," he said.

Instead, the agency wants to take advantage of the private inspection data that many companies already collect. Major food retailers, for example, require their produce suppliers to meet certain standards, and they inspect those suppliers regularly. Acheson said FDA could use that information to shape its high-risk list.

FDA is working on a pilot program with several major shrimp producers. The companies will send FDA information about how they certify suppliers; Acheson said the agency would periodically send its own inspectors to "look over their shoulders."

The agency also wants to improve its computer systems to better analyze complaints about food products, Acheson said. "We're trying to pick up the more subtle signals around consumer complaints that are harder to mine," Acheson said. "Say we get complaints about a canned product...If you mine the data, and the cans all come from one manufacturer, maybe the canning process at that firm is not up to snuff."

Consumers generally make those complaints to their state health agencies, which send information to the federal Centers for Disease Control and Prevention in Atlanta. FDA intends to ask Congress for a big investment in food safety. It received a $150 million supplement at the end of 2008. Acheson said he'd like a similar amount added to FDA's budget for the next few years.

We hope that in the new administration, there will be an exception for additional funds for the FDA and to set up satellite offices in countries that export food to this country. With all the bailout monies being given to banks and auto companies, more importantly would be the funding to protect our people from getting sick from salmonella, kidney stones or other types of food poisoning. So far, we have not been a part of any bailout money given by the last administration or the new bailout monies proposed by Obama and his team.

I, for one, feel that unless we are able to get a handle on ALL of the food imported into this country, we will continue to have a problem that will affect all of us, more so than if the banks lost money or the auto companies filed for bankruptcy, got rid of the unions, and started all over again. What is more important than the safety of our own people? And like a plague, this can grow to horrendous proportions.

Trials Begin in China's Tainted Milk Scandal... China Issues Death Sentences

The *Washington Post* reported in the latter part of 2008, just a few days before the New Year that the first criminal trials of suspects implicated in China's tainted milk scandal had begun. In the meanwhile, milk producers handed out cash payments to victims and the government tried to stem public anger over the incident.

The scandal, which resulted in the deaths of six infants and illnesses to nearly 294,000 other children this summer and fall, forced Chinese government officials to offer financial aid to victim's families and allow for public debate, a rare move for the regime. China's Ministry of Health estimated at that time that 861 children under three years of age were still in the hospital as of that date.

China's Dairy Industry Association said that 22 dairy producers were making a one-time cash payment to families of victims and established a fund to cover medical bills for future health problems. Lawyers told the Associated Press that most children who suffered relatively minor injuries, such as kidney stones, would receive about $290. Sicker children would get roughly $4,380. In the U.S., these amounts would be chicken-feed.

Four of the nine defendants in a trial that started on December 29th faced the death penalty if convicted. The trials of another six men implicated in the scheme also started about the same time. All were charged with poisoning customers by using melamine, a legal but inexpensive protein booster, to increase profits. (Death penalties are common in cases where defendants are accused of bringing 'shame' to the government. Case in point: Zheng Xiaoyu, the former head of China's food and drug agency who was executed in 2007 after he was accused of taking $800,000 in bribes in exchange for approving fake medicines.)

The bad baby formula and Chinese dairy exports set off panic from Asia to Europe. The same melamine toxin in the tainted milk scandal was also linked to the deaths and illnesses of thousands of pets in the United States in 2007. (The two Chinese producers of the food were quickly shut down. Fish that were given potentially contaminated feed were found safe for human consumption.)

The chief suspect in the tainted milk case was 40-year old Zhang Yujun, who sold tainted mixture to milk producers between November 2007 and August 2008, at a cost of about $180,000. Other high-profile officials were caught up in the scandal as well.

China's chief quality supervisor resigned in September after reports surfaced that his office allowed the dairy company behind the tainted powdered milk, Sanlu Group, to be exempt from safety inspections. (He had been tasked a year earlier to upgrade food standards, boost safety checks and make sure that inspected food was properly labeled.) Tian Wenhua was facing 15 years to life in prison, if convicted.

Bloomberg reported on January 22ⁿᵈ 2009 that China had sentenced two men to death and imposed life in prison on Sanlu Group Company's former head for their involvement in the tainted-milk scandal, the Xinhua news agency said.

Sanlu's former chairwoman Tian Wenhua was sentenced to life in prison by the Shijiazhuang Intermediate People's Court. Zhang Yujun, who made and sold melamine-laced protein powder, and Geng Jinping, who produced and marketed toxic food, were sentenced to death, Xinhua said.

Between the deaths of six babies, and the fact that 294,000 suffered kidney ailments and urinary problems after drinking infant formula tainted with melamine, Sanlu and 21 other companies were found to have sold dairy products containing the toxic chemical, which was added to raw milk to make its protein content appear higher.

"China pays great attention to food safety and product quality," Foreign Ministry spokeswoman Jiang Yu said at a press briefing. "In the Sanlu case, China is strictly handling the case according to the law," she said, adding the country has strengthened its rules and regulations after the scandal. Nine others were sentenced as well.

Gao Junjie was given a suspended death sentence for his role in the scandal, Xinhua said, without providing more details on what he did. Two others were jailed for life, and six, including three former Sanlu executives, were jailed for between five and 15 years. The court had previously said it would sentence 21 people implicated but later said that nine others would be sentenced at other courts, the agency added, without saying when that would take place.

Countries and regions including the U.S., the Philippines and the EU restricted or banned imports of Chinese food containing milk or milk powder as more dairy products were found to contain melamine. China's exports of dairy produce plunged 92 percent in October 2008 compared with a year earlier, the China Daily newspaper reported. In an attempt to restore consumer confidence in Chinese dairy products in the wake of the scandal first exposed in September, the government set limits for melamine content in dairy food and banned products that don't meet the standard.

Sanlu, which filed for bankruptcy in December, was fined about 50 million yuan ($7.3 million) on January 22nd 2009 by the court over its role in supplying contaminated baby formula. Tian was fined more than 20 million yuan, according to the court ruling, the state media added. Apart from the 21 defendants, 39 others have so far been arrested for their alleged involvement in the scandal, Xinhua said.

Twenty-two Chinese dairy companies, including Sanlu, China Mengniu Dairy Co., and Inner Mongolia Yili Industrial Group Co. are now being sued by families whose children either died or were sickened after drinking melamine-tainted milk formula. Lawyers for 213 families filed the suit by post to the Supreme People's Court on January 16th, according to a statement from Gong Meng, a Beijing-based, non-profit group made up of lawyers and legal experts. The Guangzhou Intermediate People's Court refused to accept a lawsuit from parents in southern Guangdong province filed on October 8th against Sanlu and the China Dairy Industry Association demanding 900,000 yuan in compensation, according to Xinhua. The dairy companies set up a compensation fund offering 200,000 yuan to families whose children died after drinking the contaminated formula, Chinese media reports said.

Sanlu filed for bankruptcy in the latter part of 2008 after halting its business in September when the scandal broke. The company had 1.1 billion yuan of debt, including 902 million yuan it borrowed to pay the medical fees of children sickened after consuming its formula.

China GDP Growth Cools to Slowest Pace in 7 Years… The Global Recession Slams China

China has had a run for many years, least 15 to 18 but who's counting. I started Global Communications many years ago when the thought of working with Chinese manufacturers would be a great opportunity to make money and to save money for both contract assembly manufacturers and original manufacturers. . I worked with at least 35 to 40 offshore manufacturers in China, Hong Kong and Taiwan and helped them understand how it was to deal with American companies; how to package products using 1 ½ inch foam on all six sides in boxes that weighed no more than 30 pounds so the people in the warehouses can lift them without straining their back and cause injury.

I went though so many manufacturers because, after awhile, they started to get sloppy.

They started to build an inventory of printed circuit boards that sat in their warehouses in extreme heat, even though they were blister-packed, and when they arrived at the warehouses of my customers, they were 'sweating' because of the heat,…they built up moisture from condensation …and the components were not able to adhere to these bare boards.

If I only ordered 5,000 to 10,000 pieces of one part number, the manufacturer would take it upon themselves and built 50,000, enough for at least six months. But when they arrived at the warehouses of my customers and were tested, they failed. I had to switch from one manufacturer to another. If it was not one mistake, it was another. The people in the facilities in China and Honk Kong became lazy, and did not test all of the boards. The same thing occurred with transformers, valves, wire harness and cable assemblies and many other electrical products. I then started to lose customers.

From making millions of dollars, my percentage of customers dwindled because they lost trust in my judgment of choosing the proper manufacturers. Instead of wasting time and going through the same complaints each and every month, I decided that after so many years, I had had enough. I didn't want to go through this anymore…being on the phone all day long with my customers, and then being on the phone with the manufacturers all night long as they were about 15 hours ahead of us. If it was 5 pm in California, it was 8 am in China. No matter how much I complained, it was the same crap….these companies would try to cut corners and save money while at the same time, ship lousy product.

I knew that this would also occur in other markets, including food, toys, medicine, clothing and whatever else the companies in China would produce for this country, I knew that sooner or later, all of this would catch up with them. And guess what! It finally did!

Now they are paying the price for the arrogance and bad business decisions they made, the same ones we may have made when we thought we could trust them as our partners. Like any company that feels they can control you, they took advantage of the situation and we got hurt. We taught them what capitalism is all about and they thought they were better than we were. They listened but they did not learn. They knew that we were using them, and lo and behold…it was our turn to be used. And they learned from us, not only how to make money, but how to cheat and become the same kinds of business people we had become.

But when lives were involved such as the children who died, or the people who wound up with kidney stones, or our beloved pets that died, it was because our offshore partners got greedy. We finally stood up to them. But as fate has it, we all are paying the piper. The tables have turned…we all seem to be losing what we built up for years. We believed that our partners in

China could be trusted. But they could not be. We allowed them to cheat us and try to get away with murder and they did. Until it hit home! It was time to call it a day!

On January 19th 2009 Bloomberg reported that China's economy may have expanded at the slowest pace in seven years in the fourth quarter as exports collapsed, adding to pressure for more stimulus measures and undermining growth across Asia. Didn't 'our newly found Asian partners' realize that we know how the game is played and if you try to put a knife in our backs, we will turn and suck the blood out of you? Well, it's happening!

Gross domestic product in China grew 6.8 percent from a year earlier, according to the median estimate of 12 economists surveyed by Bloomberg News, down from 9 percent in the previous three months. Premier Wen Jiabao has pledged more measure after unveiling a 4 trillion yuan ($585 billion) package in November and the central bank may add to five interest-rate cuts since September. Plummeting Chinese demand for parts and materials for exports is reverberating across Asia, driving Taiwan and South Korea close to recessions and worsening Japan's economic slump.

If you think America has it tough folks, this 'ain't nuthin' like the Asian economies will feel once they realize that the gravy train is not pulling out of the depot as readily as it did for so many years. Having been in the forefront of partnering with Chinese manufacturers way before it became the lifestyle of our nation...I had learned a very important lesson. At the beginning, you make lots of money. But as time goes on and the laws change, your partners may decide not to change themselves and the products lose their quality. Every time you make a change with our Asian partners, you should expect that they may not conform to the changes and try to get around them as best they could. They hope that you don't catch them...but eventually you do. The counterfeit products emerge, the tainted products become known, and you suddenly realize that your trust has gone up in smoke. You have lost the edge and you see everything go awry.

When toys were being recalled because of excessive lead in the paint; pet food was killing our pets; toxins were found in fish and meat, vegetable and other products; and eventually melamine was found in powdered milk, the American and European nations put their feet down. They have had enough! Toy's R 'Us, Wal-Mart and other major chains started to have problems. No one wanted products made in China and even though the costs were much lower, they were afraid of developing health problems.

"China's era of hyper-growth is coming to a sudden, very disruptive end," said Kevin Lai, an economist with the Daiwa Institute of Research in Hong Kong. "China's imports are slumping dramatically and the rest of Asia relies on it very significantly."

Lei expected the key one-year lending rate to decline to 4.50 percent from 5.31 percent by the middle of the year. He also stated that he could see reduced reserve requirements for banks. After vaulting past Germany to become the world's third biggest economy in 2007, China may, in 2009 face its first drop in shipments since at least 1990.

The slowdown from the last three months in 2008 would be the sharpest since quarterly data began in 1994. The pace compares with 13 percent growth in 2007. Easing inflation would give room for more rate reductions. Consumer-price inflation may have cooled to 1.6 percent in December from a 12-year high of 8.7 percent in February, 2008, a second survey showed. Producer prices fell 0.1 percent, the first drop since 2002, economists estimated. Besides the export slowdown, slumps in stocks and property undermined consumer confidence and growth.

"Exports are not going to recover any time soon and the property market is struggling," said Ben Simpfendorfer, an economist with Royal Bank of Scotland in Hong Kong. "More easing is needed because demand won't return in a hurry."

Exports will decline 6 percent in 2009, down from a 17.2 percent gain in 2008, Fitch Ratings said January 16th. The central bank has helped exporters by halting the yuan's gains against the dollar over the past six months.

Among the biggest losers from China's waning demand are Taiwan, which shipped almost 36 percent of its exports to China in 2007; South Korea, which sent 25 percent; and Japan, which shipped 19 percent, according to UBS AG. Goldman Sachs Group Inc. forecasted the South Korean economy will contract this year, its first recession since the 1997-1998 Asian financial crisis. Taiwan probably slipped into a recession in the fourth quarter, its government said.

China's imports from Taiwan fell 44.3 percent in December 2008. Shipments from Korea declined 30 percent and those from Japan dropped by 15.4 percent. Exports were 2.8 percent lower, the biggest decline in almost a decade. At home, as many as 4 million migrant workers lost their jobs last year in China as factories closed and that figure is likely to jump another 5 million in 2009, Credit Suisse AG estimated.

Social Stability "is clearly an issue," James McCormack, the Hong Kong-based head of Asian sovereign ratings for Fitch, said January 16th. "There is a question of how easy it is to redeploy millions of tens of millions of unemployed factory workers to infrastructure construction products that may be located elsewhere in the country."

The CSI 300 Index of stocks had fallen 62 percent since the beginning of 2008. House prices across 70 cities in HK dropped for the first time on record in December and construction will contract 30 percent this year, according to an estimate by Hong Kong-based Macquarie Securities property analyst Eva Lee.

China Vanke Co., Hong Kong's biggest real-estate developer, said that the housing market was "in recession" as sales and profits fell. The economy may grow 6 percent this year, the least since 1990, according to Fitch. Still, there were signs that a revival is possible. Bank lending and money supply jumped more than economists estimated in December as money flowed into infrastructure projects. The nations arsenal for fighting the global recession spans a world-record $1.95 trillion of currency reserves and state control of the biggest banks.

Finally, *Business Week* stated on January 22nd that the Chinese economy's growth rate tumbled in the fourth quarter, and things will get a lot worse before they get better. By the standards of just about any other country, the latest growth figures in China would be a cause for jubilation. The country clocked 6.8% year-on-year growth for the fourth quarter of 2008 and 9% for the year.

But those figures mask an underlying picture that is anything but rosy for an economy that is just starting to feel the full impact of the global meltdown. In fact, the economy registered virtually no growth over the third quarter, and as David Cui, China economist at Merrill Lynch said, "This situation is quite dire. I don't expect us to come out of this any time soon because the global demand situation is so bad."

Cui isn't the only bearish one. David Wong, vice-president of the Chinese Manufacturers Association of Hong Kong, said its members are bracing for a difficult year. "This is unprecedented among our manufacturers," he said. "This is the worst that anyone can remember." Qu Hongbing, China economist at HSBC said that China could see growth dipping as low as 6%, dangerously short of 8%, widely regarded as the level needed to generate enough jobs to absorb new entrants into the workforce. "Export contraction will only be deeper when global demand continues to shrink, so we'll see more job losses. Consumers will become more cautious. And if this continues, there is a real risk of a downward spiral."

Things could have been even worse. The $586 billion fiscal stimulus package unveiled by Beijing should help restore growth in the second half as big-ticket infrastructure projects get under way. But that recovery won't provide a lot of comfort for China's neighbors and the rest of the world, as the rebound will have limited benefit beyond China's borders. "China can save itself but it cannot save the rest of the region," said Dong Tao, chief economist for Asia at Credit Suisse (CS).

Indeed, about 70% of China's imports from its neighbors are components used as inputs for export-oriented industries. As a result, the global slowdown is creating a double whammy for Taiwan, South Korea and Southeast Asia. On top of falling exports to the rest of the world, shipments to China have collapsed too. Take Korea, for which China is the biggest export market. Korean exports to China plunged 32.9% in November 2008 year-on-year and 32.3% in December, while overall exports fell about 19%. China is the biggest export market for Japan and Taiwan as well.

Some are hoping that Beijing will be able to make up for the slack in exports by encouraging its own consumers to open their wallets. But domestic rather than foreign suppliers will get the new business. For example, the government's 13% subsidy to rural buyers of household appliances will stimulate sales of low-end televisions and refrigerators that largely include components from domestic suppliers and hence will do little to boost the demand for Asian rivals like Samsung and Toshiba.

Even Chinese companies that do manage to make up for lost overseas sales by selling domestically and will see their margins squeezed more than ever. "Everybody will be trying, but the local market isn't going to double in size overnight," says Tony Huang, CEO of Shanghai Sigma Metals, which produces secondary aluminum alloys from recycled materials. The company, which operates the world's largest smelter for such alloys, has seen its exports plunge. "It's going to be a brutal fight for the domestic market," he said. That means lower profits and a reluctance to expand capacity, prompting a serious slowdown in private fixed-asset investment for non-state-linked companies that still rely primarily on retained earnings to finance their expansion.

Pump-priming by China may restore headline gross domestic product growth by year-end, but that is largely an inward-looking policy that attempts to wean China from its dependence on exports. By merely substituting government spending to replace foreign demand, China can buy additional growth for a couple more years. That, however does not address the underlying need to make consumption and private investment the principal engines of growth. "The natural tendency is to build another airport," said Huang Yashang, and economist at Massachusetts Institute of Technology. "But the issue is to channel entrepreneurial activity to help the Chinese people as a whole."

Another big part of the puzzle is the property market, where volumes have plunged as buyers wait on the sidelines in anticipation of lower prices. Housing is hugely important to the economy, accounting for 25% of fixed investment, and is a principal form of wealth holding for the Chinese, whose only other choices are bank deposits (which offer a negative real return) and the shaky market.

Sales have slowed further in recent months, which in turn have led cash-strapped developers to slash prices in a downward spiral of falling prices and sales. In essence, the overseas engines of global growth are collapsing which represents a major short-term threat to U.S. investors, U.S. companies and the U.S. economy as a whole.

The debt crisis that first appeared in the U.S. subprime mortgage market...then precipitated a Wall Street meltdown...and has now driven the American economy into its sharpest decline since the Great Depression...has now spread to the entire world.

As reported by Martin Weiss in his article on *"The Looming Collapse of Japan and the BRICS Nations"* this crisis is driving the economies of Western Europe and Japan into an unprecedented tailspin. It threatens the economic...and potentially political...stability of Russia, China and several emerging market nations. And it's setting the stage for a global depression of epic dimensions. Here are some of the most vulnerable major economies...

Russia is smashed by oil price collapse. Never in modern history has the success or failure of a major emerging economy been so dependent on one single commodity. And never before has that commodity fallen so far and so fast as Russian crude oil.

Russia does have other resource and revenue sources. But in just the last six months of 2008, Urals crude, Russia's primary export blend, has plunged from a high of nearly $141 per barrel to a low of a meager $32.34...a 77 percent crash that's pounded Russian stocks like a sledgehammer and sliced through the Russian economy like a serrated sickle.

The big dilemma: To balance its federal budget, Russia must get a minimum of $70 per barrel for its crude oil. But at $32 and change, it's getting less than HALF that amount. The entire country is losing money hand over fist. No wonder Russia's stock market has plunged 72% forcing 25 separate stock exchange shutdowns.

Transneft, the Russian oil transporter, is down from $2,025 in January 2008 to a recent low of $270. Gazprom, the natural gas monopoly has lost more than two-thirds of its market capitalization since May. Meanwhile, Lukoil fell from a May peak of $113 to a recent low of $32.

Russia's oil-driven real estate bubble is also collapsing. That's why Russian construction and real estate giant Sistema-Hals lost more than 94% of its value last year alone...why PIK Group, another major construction giant, collapsed by 96%...and why the entire RCP Shares Index of Russian developers has sunk 92% since its record high in June 2007. Ford, Renault and Volkswagen are halting production at Russian assembly lines. Unemployment is likely to surge to 10% and beyond. Massive amounts of foreign capital are fleeing the country.

In a desperate attempt to stem the tide, the Russian government has devalued the ruble 11 times since November 2008, and thrown a quarter of its foreign currency reserves at the raging debt crisis. But it's still not enough. Russia's primary source of revenues...energy exports...is in shambles; and unless crude oil prices could somehow DOUBLE in a big hurry, Russia's economic and financial decline cannot end.

Standard & Poor's has cut Russia's long-term debt rating for the first time in nine years, citing dangerous outflows and a "rapid depletion" of currency reserves. And more downgrades are in the offing. Even a major debt default is not unthinkable.

The biggest danger would be political upheaval and social unrest. Even before this crisis, Russia's middle class earned less than $500 per month. Now, with the devastating plunge in oil revenues already in place, those numbers are falling to even lower levels. For a nation with a cost of living that rivals that of the U.S., Western Europe and Japan, the last thing the Russian people needed was a depression. Yet, that's exactly what they're getting.

It should be noted that you would have expected signs of greater prosperity in the past few years in Russia. But instead, you would be surprised to see how little average citizens had benefited from the recent years of rapid economic growth. They may have more access to a wider variety of goods that were scarce during the Soviet era, but most professionals-such as teachers, doctors, nurses and government employees-are still living on the edge of poverty.

Equally surprising is the popular disgust and disdain for the government. Public opinion surveys and press reports may indicate broad support for the Kremlin's foreign policy, and they seem to be accurate. But support for domestic policies is another matter entirely. It is possible that any major disappointment with respect to pocket issues could lead to major political changes, the outcome of which is largely unpredictable.

Turning to the other large Asian country, China is far more vulnerable than expected.

China's extraordinary expansion of the past decade fueled booms in global trade, commodities and emerging markets. It was a major growth engine that turbo-charged Australia, Brazil, Southeast Asia and even Japan.

Now, however, that engine is grinding to a screeching halt. Indeed, when historians look back to major pivot points of this global economic crisis, they will undoubtedly point to the abrupt end of China's boom.

Many of us assumed that because China's economy was growing so quickly...at a breakneck pace of 10% or more per year...it could easily afford to slow down by a few percentage points and still be in far better shape than most other economies. But now you may seriously question that theory for the reason that more often than not, companies, industries and entire nations that enjoy the biggest booms are also vulnerable to some of the biggest busts.

Instead of a mere slowdown, as many still seem to expect, China's economy could suffer a wholesale collapse.

Exports, which still represent two-fifths of the Chinese economy, are already sinking fast And the domestic economy, much of which depends directly or indirectly on the revenues flowing from exports, is also beginning to sink. Warning signs are everywhere: Stocks, down 60% just in 2008 alone; imports, down 17.9% in November alone; foreign investments to China, off 36.5% in 2008.

In response, the government has slashed interest rates and pledged a $582 billion stimulus package. But that's mere pocket change compared to China's trillions in vulnerable exports. Moreover, it has done little to help millions to small-and medium-sized businesses which are already shutting down and laying off millions.

If you think about it, our own bailout in the U.S. to the banks was supposed to help secure mortgages and help the small businesses as well…but instead, the bailout did not start to do that. Instead, the banks needed more money and the U.S. government gave it to them without any responsible documented data as to how the money was to be used.

A big problem is the fact that 45% of the Chinese government bailout is earmarked for the cement and housing industry. Meanwhile, cash-flow problems are sweeping through the entire economy, downing airlines, manufacturers and property companies. Airlines like China Southern and China Eastern, for example, have been losing money hand over fist. China's auto sales are plunging. Its shipbuilding industry is in a tailspin. And its real estate market is collapsing.

Next, expect surging unemployment…mass reverse migrations from urban centers to the countryside…spreading popular unrest…and a major challenge to authority. Chinese leaders have already admitted that an economic downturn would test their ability to govern. Now, that downturn is here… and the ultimate test, on the near horizon.

Meanwhile, India, also heavily dependent on foreign demand for its goods, is suffering its worst export slump in recent memory. Overseas shipments plunged 12.1% in October 2008 and another 9.9% in November, forcing companies like Tata Motors, India's biggest truck maker, and Hyundai Motor to cut output, fire workers and shut down factories.

Brazil, which was growing at a record pace until the third quarter, has suddenly frozen in its tracks. Much of the foreign money it counted on has vanished, leaving acute capital shortages in its wake. Auto sales have gone dead, leaving biggest-ever inventories of unsold cars. Credit, abundantly available just a few months ago, is now gone as of 2009.

Japan has been slammed by its worst recession since World War II…with stock prices plunging to new 18-year lows…industrial output suffering the largest monthly drop since records were kept…Toyota reporting its first loss in 70 years…layoff victims filling tent parks…and worse.

Everywhere from Argentina and Mexico to Australia, New Zealand and even the once-rich Middle East, the worldwide debt crisis, the bust in commodities and the sharp slowdown in global trade are transforming massive booms into instant recessions.

It's happening fast and it's accelerating. Government rescue programs aren't nearly enough to turn the tide. And it's another key reason we all must approach 2009 with great caution and don't expect much in 2010. We may be looking at changes in government regulations, tax regimes, the impact of competing products and their pricing, product demand and supply constraints, exchange rate and interest rate and the economic developments in countries that may affect each and every country. All in all, whatever we do, we must do with caution and not by the seat of our pants. We did this with the bank bailouts and those for the auto industries. None of those will work for the people as it is the people who need the lift more than anyone else.

Who Should Pay the Costs of Unsafe Imports…? What is the Importance of Good U.S. - China Relations?

The *Mercury News*, in their opinion page on January 26th, 2009, written by Ken Bamberger, an assistant professor of law the University of California-Berkley raised a good question: "Who should pay costs of unsafe imports?" Well…if the government, under President Obama's plan is to bailout banks and bailout the auto industry, why not bailout people who were injured in many ways by the tainted products that affected their lives?

As bargain-basement shopping sputtered into 2009, U.S. consumers have become painfully aware that rock-bottom prices paid for goods produced overseas may not reflect their full cost. Between lead-laced toys, melamine-spiked baby formula and poisoned pharmaceuticals, the costs of globalized production have never been higher. While labels may bear the names of venerable U.S. companies, when production is outsourced abroad, consumer safety may pay the price.

Calls for better regulation abound, yet solutions that focus on increasing government resources and coordination with foreign authorities…while important…either do too little, cost too much or work too slowly to solve the problem comprehensively.

Regulators simply do not have the necessary tools to prevent unsafe imports from finding their way into the hands of consumers. Many threats, such as those involving tainted pharmaceuticals, resist identification through inspection. And as we can't test every product for every risk, it is difficult to predict the next threat that will arise, let alone catch it when it does.

Certainly, these same problems exist for American-made products, but our regulatory system can often address them with specific rules and production processes that put a metaphorical regulator...and in some cases an actual government inspector...on the factory floor. Supervising production works well enough in the United States, but is extremely difficult abroad, where the American government has no formal authority, and it is virtually impossible for American officials to monitor production effectively.

Current Washington initiatives to address the problem of dangerous imports focus on increasing inspections of both products entering the United States and production processes abroad. For example, the Food and Drug Administration in early January 2009 opened its first office in Beijing. This is a fine idea, but how will the eight employees working at the FDA's China facility inspect even a meaningful fraction of the $321 billion worth of goods imported from that country each year? Clearly, a strategy of government monitoring and inspection could only be made effective with a staggering increase in funding.

There is, however, a solution available right now! Where U.S. regulators expect a threat to consumer protection from foreign goods and services (because, for example, foreign regulatory structures are ineffective), they should increase the penalties for dangerous products levied on domestic companies involved in the importation and sale of the goods.

For example, if we are worried about Chinese-made toys, the American companies that import those toys should face additional liability. This would be over and above the sanctions imposed in the case of American-made toys, the production of which is itself subject to regulation. These companies are within the reach of American law and will respond to the threat of liability.

Such restraints will encourage U.S. companies to regulate the foreign activity from which they benefit. You can be sure that American manufacturers will worry more about the dangers created by their foreign supply chains if they are held accountable for threats to consumer safety.

From the perspective of American consumers, this proposal has the advantage of ensuring appropriate levels of safety, while also encouraging healthy competition among domestic and foreign producers and suppliers. Foreign products will compete against American-made goods based on price and quality (as they should) rather than by cutting corners on safety.

If their bottom line is affected, companies will check to see how their toys, medicines, pet food and other products are made and whether they are safe. American importers and sellers have no trouble fine-tuning their products to the precise demands of the American consumer. There is no reason to think they are any less able to make sure that the products won't injure us or our children.

On January 26th, it was reported in *"Seeking Alpha"* that our new president committed a serious gaffe in his first week of office by allowing his nominee for Treasury Secretary to say the Obama Administration "believes that China is manipulating its currency."

What makes it so unnerving for investors is talk of unfair currency exchange rates and is seen as a protectionist measure, the threat of which would be enormously damaging to the global economy at this time. That protectionist measures during the Great Depression seriously worsened the situation is economic dogma.

Chinese officials reacted somewhat angrily to the charge, saying that Beijing "has never used so-called currency manipulation to gain benefits in its international trade," in a statement released by China's commerce ministry. "Directing unsubstantiated criticism at China on the exchange-rate issue will only help U.S. protectionism and will not help towards a real solution to the issue," the statement went on to say.

What makes the timing even worse is that China has become the biggest foreign holder of U.S. debt, second only to the U.S. government itself in overall holdings. The latest figures from the Treasure Department show that for the three months to November 2008, China increased its purchases by 16.1% to $681.9 billion and by 48.6% for the year 'til then. Japan, the second largest foreign holder of U.S. debt, increased its holding by just 1.28% in the three months to November but decreased its holdings by 2.1% for the year, the only foreign holder among the top ten to do so. Given that the Treasury will have to issue some $2 trillion to $3 trillion in new debt in the next couple of years and that for better or worse we will depend on China (and other nations) to keep stepping up its purchases, antagonizing a strategic rival such as China seems to be an especially dangerously policy.

Traders in New York reacted nervously to the news, sending oil and gold up sharply as they sold Treasuries on the concern China might slow its purchases of U.S. debt. Actually, the threat of swift changes in U.S./China exchange rates either way would be enormously de-stabilizing at this time because it would cause tremendous distortions for currencies, equity markets and commodities.

If China were to sharply reduce its financing of U.S. debt a sudden appreciation of the yuan would occur. U.S. interest rates on Treasuries and private credit instruments would rise and the dollar would rapidly fall against the higher-yielding euro, pound, Australian and New Zealand dollars while the yen plummeted against everything. The Fed would likely have to step in and make up the difference, forcing it to print even more dollars than it already has been in order to monetize a debt which is expected to be $1.2 trillion in fiscal 2009 before the stimulus plan is accounted for. Oil, gold and other commodities would skyrocket as the dollar plunged and equity markets would rise abnormally on the asset inflation.

Upward pressure on China's currency would further damage its already-weakened export sector and the country's (to say nothing of the world's) economic growth. Chinese imports would not increase much if the yuan appreciated; Chinese citizens tend to be savers because little exists in the way of health benefits or social programs, and China ranks just 131st globally in per capita GDP with an estimated $6100 of yearly income (2008 figures).

If China were to suddenly increase its purchases of U.S. debt the yuan would depreciate, which would sharply accelerate its out-sized surplus, fuel protectionist sentiments and possibly start a trade war in the middle of the worst economic crisis since the Great Depression, crashing fragile equity markets the world over in the process. The dollar would likely accelerate sharply against the higher-yielders, possibly to the point of bankrupting economies like Britain which has large amounts of external debt financed in dollars. The yen would gain against everything. Oil and gold would crash and production of oil would be sharply curtailed.

It will be very important to closely observe any further comments from Washington and Beijing. As mentioned, heightened tensions between the U.S. and China will have serious ramification for global markets. Above all else, investors hate uncertainty, so it would seem that it would be best at this time if the new administration did everything in its power to maintain a semblance of calm. To paraphrase Mario Puzo from his book, THE GODFATHER, "keep your strategic friends close, but keep your strategic rivals closer."

Stated in the *New York Times* on January 27th, the Food and Drug Administration had been justly pilloried for grievous flaws in its regulation of foods and drugs. Now Congressional investigators, and some of the agency's own scientists, are charging that the FDA. has failed to adequately regulate medical devices.

The Government Accountability Office recently reported that the FDA has failed...for decades...to subject some of the riskiest devices to a rigorous review mandated by Congress. A group of FDA scientists complained to the Obama transition team...and before that to Congress and to the agency's commissioner...that during the Bush years, managers in charge of medical device reviews had corrupted and distorted the process in ways that put the public at risk.

Under a 1976 law, the FDA is required to divide medical devices into three classes and to impose different levels of scrutiny. The riskiest Class III devices...such as implantable pacemakers and replacement heart valves... require the most stringent review, usually including clinical evidence that they are safe and effective.

Unfortunately, the law left a gaping loophole. Certain types of Class III devices already on the market, and later devices deemed substantially equivalent to them, could be approved for sale with the less stringent review... until the FDA required them to pass a more rigorous test of put them into a lower class.

The agency made so little progress in closing the loophole that Congress in 1990 ordered it to quickly decide which classes the grandfathered devices should be in and to schedule rigorous reviews for those remaining in Class III. Although the agency has done that for most of the remaining devices, the G.A.O. found that it has still not completed the task. In a recent five-year period, the FDA used the less stringent procedures to clear 228 Class III devices including certain types of metal hip joints and implanted blood access devices.

The Obama administration will have to send a clear signal to the bureaucracy that the days of neglect are over. Officials will also have to make clear that the Bush administration's practice of distorting science and weakening regulation to favor industry also is over.

We are pleased to hear that FDA scientists have been raising the alarms. As Gardiner Harris reported in The Times, internal documents show that front-line scientists believe their managers have become too lenient with industry and, in one case, improperly forced them to alter reviews of a breast imaging device after Christopher Shays, a former Republican congressman from Connecticut, intervened on behalf of the manufacturer.

The G.A.O. has urged the FDA to make final decisions on all grandfathered Class III devices. That would be a good start...provided the reviews are honest and uncoerced...but not sufficient. The next FDA commissioner should ensure that past decisions on medical devices were properly made. Given its sorry performance in so many areas important to public health and safety, the agency is ready for a major overhaul.

— 24 —

On a Personal Note...

Personally speaking, I have been cautious in business and in my own personal life. I had to cut back in business expenditures as the sales started to decrease around 2005. Companies were running out of money to start new projects and the amount of products they ordered were much less. I saw the writing on the wall and realized that if I did not act accordingly, I would have been stuck with more debt than I needed to be. And I also felt that perhaps it was not the best time to purchase a new home because it was not the best time to sell a home. If positions in companies were being terminated because of fewer projects and less sales, people would lose their income, they would not be able to pay for their mortgages, and their homes would go into a "short sale" or owned by the bank. In essence, this is what started to happen in 2006.

We look at life and wonder how all of this began. It was erupting for years but no one paid any mind to it. We never thought it would happen, but it did. We kept on spending and raising the cost of living as fast as we chose to...the homes were way out of reach and it was getting to a point where no one was able to afford a home, a car, a vacation, clothes or even to live a normal life. We put ourselves in this predicament because of greed and now we are paying for it dearly. This is what happens when we allow money to rule us.

The China export syndrome started because it was a good way to get similar items for less and we bought into it. We then realized that our own manufacturing was going down the tubes but we didn't care...we were making money hand over fist and the hell with those who didn't jump on the bandwagon. The oil prices jumped because of greed. Wal-Mart decided to shuck Sam Walton's famous words "All merchandise is American-made" and spent over 22 billion dollars importing everything from China. Food, clothing, toys, tires, wall board, pet food, powdered milk, medicine, components and more all came from China.

Then it happened! We realized that China was either out to kill us with tainted products or just did not care what they sold to us. It came back to haunt us and we allowed all this to happen without checking the imports that came to these shores. The FDA only checked from 1% to 5% depending on the particular dock the goods landed on, the most critical one being the Long Beach Dock in southern California. And out of the 5% they found that 40% was tainted and improper, too dangerous for sale.

It is time to re-group...to go back to what we were after World War II and build our nation as it was meant to be. Yes, we can deal with China and Russia and the Middle East and all of the other countries who wish to import and export goods and services. But we need to set the tone...more regulations...to preserve the safety of our people first and foremost. The new administration needs to keep tight controls on ALL products coming into our country, and at the same time, we must make sure that the products we ship out to other countries are just as safe.

Lastly, if a company like General Motors or Chrysler is falling because of lack of sales, too much inventory, too many hidden costs because of paying off retired workers for their continued health insurance and excessive retired pay, that is their problem, not ours. Let them file for Chapter 11 and start all over again and don't come to the government in your big jets hoping to get a bailout. If and when my company is failing, I would not go to the government for a bailout...and if I did, they would tell me to get lost. I for one may never buy another GM, Chrysler or Ford car if I am happier with a Toyota that has a better lifespan and has fewer problems than a Chevrolet or a Dodge. Look what happened to Oldsmobile and Plymouth...they have run its course and now are gone. The same thing may happen to many other makes and models...if they do not give us the same kind of lasting ability as a Honda, a Toyota or a Nissan. We have done nothing to compete with the foreign auto makers but try to tell Americans to buy an American-made vehicle.

By the way...I love America and right now I am fighting to bring back that "Yankee Ingenuity" we once had. I would like to see our own shops rise again and this country redevelop itself as it did in the forties and fifties when we did not import so many goods from foreign soil. I don't want to see our major corporations and auto industry or even our banking institutions go out of business because of the errors in judgment by their management. I would like to see big bonuses given out to those who deserve them, not because the government gave that money to you to rebuild your company and you feel that you deserve it.

Unless U.S. industry increases its domestic production and stimulates exports, which will significantly lower the trade deficit, it's doubtful a sustained recovery will occur. The solution to the economic crisis we are facing today needs more than a stimulus plan. It needs a true recovery plan and that plan will be a slow and painful process.

At this point, all we know for sure about the proposed American Recovery and Reinvestment Plan is that the national deficit will increase by a one or two trillion dollars. There is no analysis that proves that it can work. Eyes and minds, which should observe the failures in a global economic system and its needs for renovation, have been closed. Installing new rooms in a failing structure is not productive.

Returning to the same conditions leads to the same ultimate failures. The future of President Obama's recovery plan is predictable...some short term benefits and no ultimate recovery. It might relieve the pain but the patient will perish.

One of the solutions that will work is to give Americans what they want...a better product....more competitively priced...a safer product...and most of all...the trust in the American company that wants us to believe in them. The safety of my family, my friends and my neighbors come first...and in order for us to buy any product...whether it comes from this country or from China, it better be a good product or we may never wish to buy another one again.

It is time to reflect on ourselves and then to rebuild a nation that we once believed to be the greatest nation in the world. And we can do it, just like our grandparents and parents did it before us. And if the government wants to bailout anyone, it has to be the nation's people...their businesses, their lives, and their trust in their government. We still live in the greatest nation in the world and we can make anything happen...if we try hard enough!

Note: This book is based on a collection of news stories about the economy, both in the United States and abroad. The information gathered from these articles does not reflect any individual interest as they change over time based on the economic nature happenings and real-life situations.